More Time for Politics

By the same author

The Regeneration of Britain
Speeches
Arguments for Socialism
Arguments for Democracy
Parliament, People and Power
The Sizewell Syndrome
Fighting Back: Speaking Out for Socialism in the Eighties
A Future for Socialism
Common Sense (*with Andrew Hood*)
Free Radical

Years of Hope: Diaries 1940–1962
Out of the Wilderness: Diaries 1963–1967
Office Without Power: Diaries 1968–1972
Against the Tide: Diaries 1973–1976
Conflicts of Interest: Diaries 1977–1980
The End of an Era: Diaries 1980–1990
The Benn Diaries: Single Volume Edition 1940–1990
Free at Last! Diaries 1991–2001
Dare to be a Daniel

TONY BENN

More Time for Politics

Diaries 2001–2007

Selected and edited by Ruth Winstone

HUTCHINSON
London

Published by Hutchinson 2007

2 4 6 8 10 9 7 5 3 1

Copyright © Tony Benn 2007

First published in Great Britain in 2007 by
Hutchinson
Random House, 20 Vauxhall Bridge Road,
London SW1V 2SA

www.rbooks.co.uk

Addresses for companies within The Random House Group Limited can
be found at: www.randomhouse.co.uk/offices.htm

The Random House Group Limited Reg. No. 954009

A CIP catalogue record for this book is available from the British Library

ISBN 9780091920562

The Random House Group Limited makes every effort to ensure that the
papers used in its books are made from trees that have been legally
sourced from well-managed and credibly certified forests. Our paper
procurement policy can be found at: www.rbooks.co.uk/environment

Typeset by SX Composing DTP, Rayleigh, Essex
Printed and bound in Great Britain by
CPI Mackays, Chatham, ME5 8TD

Contents

Illustrations

Tam Dalyell, 2004 (© *Topham/PA*)
John McDonnell, 2007 (© *Getty Images*)
Walter Wolfgang, Labour Party Conference, Brighton, 2005 (© *Toby Melville/Reuters/Corbis*)
Brian Haw (*Alisdair MacDonald*)
Meeting Saddam Hussein, 2003

Second section

With David Gentleman (John Rees in background)
Lindsey German of 'Stop the War'
George Galloway
Ken Livingstone
Stop the War rally, Trafalgar Square, November 2001
Rally in Hyde Park, March 2003
Tony Benn in the Left Field, Glastonbury
'An Audience with Tony Benn' (*Richard Baker*)
'Blair's War', Trafalgar Square (*Kyoka Takamura Thompson*)
Tony Benn at anti-war rally in New York
Tony Blair's 'Blood Price'
Peace doves for Vanunu
The Benns at Christmas
Concorde's last flight, October 2003 (© *Getty Images*)
With David Davis at the Royal Festival Hall debate
With Rory Bremner at Hatchards
Stephen, Hilary, Melissa and Joshua Benn with their father
With Hilary
With Joshua
Melissa Benn (*Nobuhiko-Ono*)
Caroline Benn's plaque
Ruth Winstone (*Ray Wells*)
With Natasha Kaplinsky
David and June Benn (*Frances Nestor*)
Benjamin Zephaniah and Jemma Redgrave at Tony Benn's 80th birthday
With Saffron Burrows (*Andy Gotts*)
Benn family at Stangate

Cartoons

p. 2   Dinosaurs © Peter Brookes (*The Times*, 12 May 2001)
p. 50   Tony Benn and Edward Heath © John Springs (*Daily Telegraph*, 13 May 2001)
p. 66   Tony Benn © Gary (*Sunday Times*, 21 July 2002)
p. 174   *New York Daily News*, 21 March 2004
p. 332   Tony Benn and Ann Widdecombe (© *The Oldie*, August 2006)

Foreword

Before my wife Caroline died in 2000, she suggested that when I left the House of Commons it should be 'to devote more time to politics'. The following year, I did indeed retire to do that.

This book continues my published diaries, which in totality extend from 1940, when I was fifteen, to 2007 the year when I reached eighty-two, a span of sixty-seven years.

For around fifty of these years I served as an MP, for eleven as a Cabinet Minister and for the majority of these years as an elected member of Labour's National Executive Committee which I joined in 1959. The full unedited diaries now amount to around fifteen million words and the published diaries, though they have had to be sharply cut, kept as faithful as possible to the original.

The editing of this mass of material has been undertaken by Ruth Winstone who started work in 1985. Ruth's integrity, judgement and political understanding are outstanding and she is my closest, most trusted and dearest friend to whom I am deeply indebted and for whose help I am profoundly grateful. I am also most indebted to my publishers Hutchinson and particularly to Tony Whittome, Emma Mitchell and James Nightingale; to Roger Field for legal advice; and to Alison McPherson whose transcription of my diary tapes is, as ever, impeccable. All errors are my own.

Leaving the House of Commons in May 2001 and especially leaving my Chesterfield constituency opened up a gap in my life that I wondered if I could fill but Michael Martin, the House of Commons' Speaker, kindly gave me the Freedom of the House and a permanent pass that allows me to use the Library, the Tea Room – and even sit in the Peers Gallery to listen to debates without the humiliation of being a Lord.

I have come to realise that old age has advantages and imposes new duties.

The old have a lot of experience and, if they enjoy reasonably good health as I do, should have no further personal ambition, but they do have a clear responsibility to encourage other people, especially the young, whose knowledge and intelligence are often seriously underestimated by those in power. From the young they have a great deal to learn.

Politically the last six years have been intensely interesting as New Labour completed its second and entered its third term: full credit must go to New Labour for the decision to increase public investment in education, health and international aid, for the Good Friday Agreement bringing peace to Northern Ireland and its realisation that world poverty and the challenge of climate change must be addressed seriously by the United Nations and all its members.

However the decision to follow President Bush, invade Afghanistan and Iraq, threaten Iran and give support to Israel in its occupation of Palestinian territories and its war against the Lebanon will necessarily remain as the principal legacy of the then Prime Minister, who took Britain into wars that were illegal, immoral and unwinnable and in my view involved the commission of serious war crimes.

One of the reasons why this occurred was that the Prime Minister, from the very beginning, made it clear that he was determined to take all the important political decisions himself, consulting a tight circle of his own advisers, excluding the Cabinet, Parliament, the Labour Party and its annual Conference from any significant role other than to be loyal spectators and campaigners for whatever he decided to do.

In this way he was able to launch upon a programme of privatisation, leave pensioners without the link with earnings introduced by the previous Labour government, impose huge debts upon university and college students, oppose the restitution of trade union rights enshrined in the International Labour Organisation convention, to which Britain is a signatory, and erode civil liberties in ways that even the judiciary resisted. Such erosions have been justified by the 'war on terror' which was used to attack Iraq and Afghanistan to such disastrous effect.

After sixty-five years in the Labour party I was never a supporter of New Labour, which we were told was a new political party, but I worked hard to secure the defeat of the Conservatives in the elections of 1997, 2001 and 2005 and like many others I have been disappointed and worried by a dangerous cynicism about parliamentary government; a cynicism strengthened by the suspicion that Britain was being managed and not represented and that voters could never be sure that they were being told the truth.

This cynicism has developed because New Labour was founded by those who had come to the conclusion that the only way to win an election was to embrace the neo-liberal economic values of Mrs Thatcher – who described New Labour as her greatest achievement.

The British Establishment could hardly believe its luck when a so-called Labour government was prepared to follow Conservative policies and call for loyalty from its own members to carry them through.

That establishment also received basic assistance from the media proprietors, who were able to snipe at and mock ministers personally while remaining confident that no progressive initiatives would be launched to satisfy the aspirations of Labour's core support, and for this reason Tony Blair had a better press than any previous Labour leader had ever enjoyed.

Yet despite all this, some very important political campaigns outside Parliament did begin and develop: the anti-War Movement, student fees, pensions, transport and health issues; to the point when it could truthfully be said that for the first time in history the public was to the left of a Labour Government.

This volume I hope throws some light on these themes as well as the challenges and pleasures of old age, friendships and family.

Tony Benn
July 2007

Editor's Note

This year is the 20th since Tony Benn's diaries were first published. The passage of time and change of circumstances have made their mark on the character of the diaries. My approach to editing has also changed significantly, and the cumulative effect has been to produce this volume – *More Time for Politics* – which is dramatically different from *Out of the Wilderness*, which appeared in 1987.

I have come firmly to the view that it is the small details of a life and the pace of social change, from which none of us is immune, which enrich a political Diary: the juxtaposition of the great and newsworthy events with the minutiae of domestic life, personal tastes, transport, health and technology. This volume I hope achieves that balance.

Also, as an editor I do believe that the words – hand-written, typed or dictated – contain the essence of the diarist's character and therefore the editing process is an inevitable diminution of the original work. Even the errors (perhaps especially the errors) of a diarist are revealing; and I am immensely indebted to Alison McPherson for her faithful and accurate transcription from audio cassettes, down to the most personal of anecdotes. For corrections of names and additional research, tedious but essential, I thank my friend, Laura Rohde.

This diary is perhaps the most candid of the ten volumes and exposes the diarist's personality with all its strengths and weaknesses – which has made the task of editing it all the more enjoyable.

Ruth Winstone
August 2007
www.i-research-and-edit.co.uk
ruthwinstone@hotmail.com

Biographical Notes

Descriptions are relevant to the opening years of this volume of Diaries

Family

IMMEDIATE FAMILY – see Family Tree (p. xvi)

BENN, David	Brother, b. 1928
BENN, June	Wife of David Benn, d. 2006
BENN, Piers	Son of David and June Benn
DE CAMP, Graydon	Brother of Caroline Benn
DE CAMP, Sherri	Wife of Graydon De Camp
MITCHELL, Nance	Sister of Caroline Benn, d. 2006
NESTOR, Frances	Daughter of David and June Benn
NESTOR, Michael	Husband of Frances Nestor
NESTOR, Michael	(Little Michael) Son of Frances and Michael Nestor

Friends and colleagues

BAILEY, Roy	Retired professor; folk singer
BANKS, Tony	MP for West Ham, d. 2006
BLAKER, Lord	Former Conservative MP, Peter Blaker
BURROWS, Saffron	Actress, political activist
BUTLER, David	Political historian
CAMPBELL, Barbara	Helped care for Caroline during her terminal illness
CARTER, Peter	Architect, close friend of Caroline and the family
CHITTY, Clyde	Professor of education, campaigner for comprehensive schools; close friend of Caroline and the family
CORBYN, Jeremy	MP for Islington North

CORSTON, Jean   Chairman of Parliamentary Labour Party;
                        MP for Bristol East
CRYER, Ann   MP for Keighley and Ilkley
CRYER, John   MP for Hornchurch; defeated 2005
FENN, Jessica   Helped in TB's office
GERMAN, Lindsey   Member of the Socialist Workers' Party and
                        of Respect; leading campaigner of the Stop
                        the War Movement

GIBSON, Ralph   Best man to Tony Benn; High Court judge
GIBSON, Ann   Wife of Ralph Gibson
JAY, Mary   Widow of Douglas Jay, Labour minister
KAPLINSKY, Natasha   BBC television presenter
LANEY, Jen   Member of the House of Commons Library
                        staff
McINTOSH, Maureen
  (Mrs Mac)   Looked after the Benns' house for many years
MAHON, Alice   MP for Halifax; retired 2005
MILIBAND, David   Minister for Education and Skills; Secretary
                        of State for the Environment and Rural
                        Affairs
MILIBAND, Edward   Minister for the Cabinet Office
MILIBAND, Marion   Socialist writer, mother of David and Edward,
                        widow of Ralph Miliband
MITCHELL, Emma   Publicity Director, Hutchinson (Random
                        House)
MOBERLY, Patricia   Chairman of St Thomas's and Guy's NHS
                        Foundation Trust
MOBERLY, Richard   Retired Anglican priest, married to Patricia
                        Moberly
MULLIN, Chris   MP for Sunderland South; Minister in
                        Departments of Environment, International
                        Development and Foreign Office
MURRAY, Andrew   Chair of the Stop the War Movement
O'CONNOR, Celia   Member of the House of Commons Library
                        staff
POWELL, David   Socialist writer
REES, John   Member of the Socialist Workers' Party and
                        of Respect; leading member of the Stop the
                        War Movement
SHALLICE, Jane   Former deputy head, Holland Park School
SIMPSON, Alan   MP for Nottingham South
SKINNER, Dennis   MP for Bolsover
WHITTOME, Tony   Editorial Director, Hutchinson (Random
                        House)

WILLSMER, Basil — Long-time family friend; Essex builder
WINSTONE, Ruth — Editor of the Benn Diaries since 1985

Political figures
AMOS, Baroness — Secretary of State for International Development; leader of House of Lords
ANNAN, Kofi — Secretary General of the UN
BLAIR, Tony — Prime Minister 1997–2007, MP for Sedgefield
BLUNKETT, David — Education Secretary, Home Secretary and Secretary of State for Work and Pensions
BROWN, Gordon — Chancellor of the Exchequer 1997–2007, MP for Dunfermline East 1983–2005 and for Kirkcaldy and Cowdenbeath since 2005
CAMERON, David — Leader of the Conservative Party since 2006
CAMPBELL, Alastair — Prime Minister's Official Spokesman 1997–2003
CLARKE, Charles — Chairman of the Labour Party, Education Secretary, Home Secretary
COOK, Robin — Foreign Secretary, Leader of the House d. 2005
DAVIS, David — Conservative MP, ran for leadership of the Conservative Party 2006; Shadow Home Secretary
DUNCAN SMITH, Iain — Leader of the Conservative Party 2001–3
HAGUE, William — Leader of the Conservative Party 1997–2001
HAYES, Billy — General Secretary, Communication Workers' Union
HEATH, Edward — Prime Minister 1970–4, d. 2005
HOWARD, Michael — Leader of the Conservative Party 2003–5
JONES, Jack — Former General Secretary, TGWU
MAJOR, John — Conservative Prime Minister 1990–7
MANDELSON, Peter — Former Labour MP, Cabinet Minister and EU Commissioner
MILBURN, Alan — Secretary of State for Health
REID, John — Secretary of State for Scotland, Northern Ireland, Health, Defence, Home Secretary
SHORT, Clare — Secretary of State for International Development
STRAW, Jack — Home Secretary; Foreign Secretary; Leader of the House 1997–2007
THATCHER, Baroness — Prime Minister 1979–90
TODD, Ron — Former General Secretary, TGWU, d. 2005
WOODLEY, Tony — General Secretary, TGWU

Benn Family

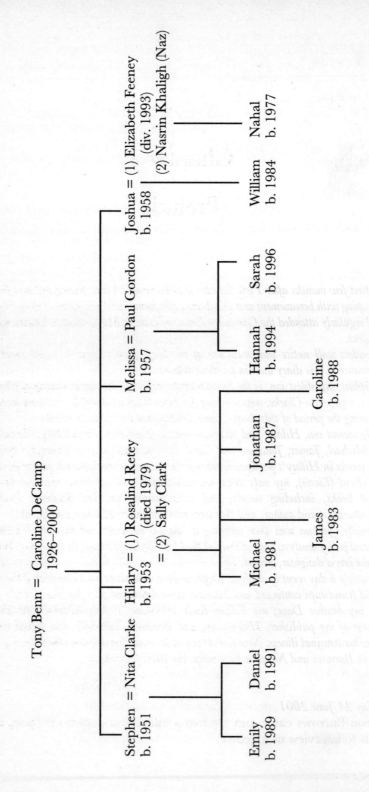

Chapter 1

Prelude

The first few months after I left the House of Commons I was feeling my way forward, still coping with bereavement and the absence of a formal parliamentary routine. However, I still regularly attended the Campaign Group of Labour MPs, which re-elected me as its President.

Readers will notice that members of my large family begin to make more of an appearance in this diary than in previous volumes.

Stephen, my oldest son, is the parliamentary officer of the Royal Society of Chemistry and his wife, Nita Clarke, was working for Tony Blair as one of his advisers at Number 10 during the period of this diary. Their children are Emily and Daniel.

My second son, Hilary, had just been made a junior minister in 2001. He and Sally have Michael, James, Jonathan and Caroline, at various stages of school and university. Sally works in Hilary's parliamentary office and teaches special-needs pupils part-time.

Melissa (Lissie), my only daughter, is a writer and journalist who has published several books, including novels, and is a campaigner. Her husband Paul is a psychotherapist and author, and they have two daughters, Hannah and Sarah.

Finally, Joshua was then working as an IT manager and his wife Nasrin as a financial policy analyst, both of them at the Housing Corporation; he has a son, William, and she has a daughter, Nahal.

Scarcely a day went by without telephone calls and visits from members of the family.

Old friendships continued and I became more dependent on a few close friends, among them my brother Dave; my Editor Ruth Winstone; Emma Mitchell, the Publicity Director of my publisher, Hutchinson; and Barbara Campbell, who helped Caroline during her terminal illness. New friends were also made, among them the left-wing actress Saffron Burrows and Natasha Kaplinsky, the BBC presenter.

Sunday 24 June 2001
Saffron Burrows came and we had a talk about *Harpers & Queen*, which wants to interview us together.

Wednesday 27 June

I had a terribly bad cough. I'm very, very tired.

The trade-union leaders had a meal with Blair, and his press office issued a statement saying there was absolutely no question of any change in his policy that the public services should be partly financed by the private sector; it was non-negotiable. He never says that when he talks to industrialists.

I can see why the public don't know what happens in the House of Commons. I don't. I rang the editor of Hansard and said I'm suffering from SHD – Severe Hansard Deficiency – so he agreed to send me the daily edition, so that I can just catch up with House business. There is an absolute press blackout on Parliament, and yet MPs do nothing to assert their role.

They really have got to do something, if they want to be taken seriously by their constituents and by the public. They leave all the cross-examination of ministers to the media, and just tamely go along with everything.

Sunday 1 July

Environmentalists and anti-globalisers clashed in Austria, where there was a meeting of the EU Summit. David Trimble has resigned as Chief Minister in Northern Ireland, to bring pressure to bear on the IRA to decommission their weapons.

Monday 2 July
Walked over the river to St Thomas's Hospital to go to the Outpatients Department for an interview with a consultant, about my supposed prostate problems. They made me empty my bladder, which wasn't full, to measure the pressure; the registrar said: you have benign prostatic hypostasy – I've never heard if it – but, he said, benign is good! He said, you haven't got cancer of the prostate, 'though you mustn't quote me'. Then the consultant came in and told me that two-thirds of men of my age have problems of this kind, and it's really up to me whether I want an operation. 'We can operate, but we're not pressing it.' I don't want one. Then they gave me some drugs.

Tuesday 17 July
Turned on the radio in the car, and heard the result of the Tory leadership contest: Kenneth Clarke came top with fifty-nine, Iain Duncan Smith second with fifty-four, and Portillo last on fifty-three. Portillo is now out of the contest, and he promptly gave an interview saying he was going to withdraw from frontline politics, not be in the Shadow Cabinet. He was interested in the arts and business and he loved Kensington. Well, so much for his local constituents, if he feels that if he's not Shadow Chancellor he has got to be a local businessman!

Sunday 22 July
Came home; I was very lonely. There will be lots more days like this – no Parliament. I decided to cook myself a pizza. I accidentally left the gas on. Having switched it off after cooking the pizza, I left the knob in a half-position. I wasn't feeling very well, so I had a sleep for about half an hour in my basement office, and when I went upstairs there was a strong smell of gas. I went into the kitchen and I was a bit nervous that I might be overcome immediately, but I opened the window, turned on the fan, turned off the gas and shut the door. I left one or two other doors and windows open, but I could have died, either by gassing myself or blowing myself up.

Thursday 26 July
Oh, one thing I must mention! Today, Roy Hattersley wrote an article about Charles Clarke, who's been appointed Chairman of the Labour Party by Blair. He pointed out that the position is not Blair's to bestow, that the Chairman of the Party used to be elected, and that during the 1980s Tony Benn used to make long speeches at the National Executive about how power was moving from the Party to the parliamentary leadership. Hattersley wrote, 'At the time Neil [Kinnock] and I thought that Tony ought to have a long rest in a dark room, but now I realise how prescient he was.' To get an endorsement from Hattersley is amusing, because it sort

of legitimises me, and discontent is beginning to move in a much bigger way than Blair realises.

I'm beginning to wonder whether Blair hasn't decided to break with the Labour Party, and I wonder whether I'll write that in my *Morning Star* column for this week. Has he decided to leave the Party? He's broken with the unions on privatisation, he's announced that he'll take no notice of the Conference decision. Is this the moment when he makes the break?

Monday 27 August
I had a talk to Nita about life at Number 10. Nita is now one of Blair's advisers. Nita said *delivery* is everything now. We don't want a lot of new policies, we want just to deliver the goods. I said I thought Blair's was a presidential style of government. She replied, 'Oh, it's not presidential at all! He has MPs in to Number 10 all the time.' Well, there's a difference between a chairman of a company whose door is always open and real consultation. She said, 'There's never been a bigger difference between the parties. We are for public services. The Tories were for tax cuts.' I said I felt that Ken Clarke would have been happy in the Labour Party. 'Oh no, he was a complete failure!' I obviously pressed the wrong button.

Tuesday 4 September
There are mass redundancies in the electronics industry – Marconi, Hewlett-Packard, Compaq – all over the world. I've never wanted to believe there was a slump coming because, although socialists are supposed to welcome the collapse of capitalism, I know perfectly well it ends up with right-wing politics, and indeed already the argument over the asylum-seekers is getting more and more bitter. David Blunkett is complaining to the French that they're setting up another refugee camp near the Channel Tunnel and Eurostar. We are recruiting teachers from Eastern Europe to fill in the gap in our schools. So here we are, on the one hand keeping out asylum-seekers, then welcoming in teachers whom we've stolen from countries that need them more than we do. It is becoming like a jungle. I am getting discouraged.

There's a new Education White Paper out today, which calls for more religious schools. Religious schools, at a time when all that is going on in Northern Ireland is absolutely mad!

Tuesday 11 September
Hilary rang from Indonesia. I wrote my column for the *Morning Star* on the security services. Went and did a bit of shopping and had lunch.

Turned on TV to watch the Trades Union Congress conference, where Tony Blair was to speak, and then there was a newsflash on BBC 1. I turned over and I heard this incredible news that a hijacked plane had crashed into the World Trade Center in New York, setting fire to it. Eighteen minutes later another plane, which was shown on television, crashed into the second tower and burst into flames. The two towers then collapsed onto the street, creating rubble over the whole of that part of Manhattan. Then we were told that the Pentagon had been hit by another hijacked plane, that there was a car bomb outside the State Department, that the White House and the Pentagon had been evacuated, that another plane had crashed in Pittsburgh and it was thought it might be on its way to attack Camp David in Maryland.

Bush, who was in Florida, came onto the television. Blair didn't make his TUC speech. He said in the circumstances he should return to London.

I was asked to do a few broadcasts for local radio about it and then I went off for the monthly Labour Action for Peace meeting in the centre of London. There were a lot of old comrades – Beryl Huffinley, Walter Wolfgang, Nicholas Russell, who's the youngest, Jim Addington, and so on. The incredible thing was, although they all knew what had happened, they spent about an hour discussing who'd got the leaflets for the forthcoming conference, who was doing the collection, was the pamphlet ready, had the room been booked. My mobile phone kept ringing, but I couldn't hear anything because the meeting was in a basement, so I said to them, 'Look, I've got to go, but don't you think we ought to have a word about this attack?' So we did have a bit of a discussion. I rushed home and found many messages asking for my comments.

When I was at home I rang Stephen, who was due to go to America at the weekend, and obviously can't now. I rang Josh, and Lissie, who was terribly upset. I rang Nance, Caroline's sister, in Cincinnati, who said she hoped this wasn't a Third World War.

Channel 4 News had good coverage, with General Sir Michael Rose saying cruise missiles were not the answer. They had Paul Rogers, the peace activist from Bradford University, very sensible, and they had James Rubin who used to be in the State Department, taking the tough American line.

I began preparing some notes, because I'm doing *Any Questions?* on Friday and I would think the whole programme will be about that.

There is going to be the usual response to terrorism – we'll bomb them, we'll never let them beat us, and so on – but in the end there has to be some re-examination of unsolved world problems. The fact that this attack could be launched is so important. This was a brilliant coordination of low-tech weapons. It shows that smart weapons don't help you; we need some smart politicians. When you're dealing with suicide bombers, threatening to kill them doesn't help. It shows Star Wars is no defence, that the anti-terrorism legislation is irrelevant.

And who was responsible? Was it Bin Laden? Well, he was the man trained and armed by America to get the Russians out of Afghanistan. Was it a sort of Timothy McVeigh, the American who did the Oklahoma bombing? Will there be retaliation? I'm sure there will be. Should Britain support the US? I'm sure Blair will.

There is total chaos in the global market. Shares are collapsing – the lowest for four years.

What we need is cool heads, no retaliation, an urgent UN meeting and a bit of a dialogue, and to begin thinking about how to plan the recovery of the world economy. And Parliament should be recalled.

Those are the thoughts I have in my mind as I dictate this. I'm going to bed at about a quarter to one. I've got to be up early in the morning. But it is an extraordinary day – a major bombing attack on the United States. It's like the Blitz! I've seen American planes on television bombing Hanoi and bombing Baghdad and bombing Belgrade, but I never thought I'd see New York being bombed. I think this is going to have a profound effect on the thinking of people about politics and peace.

Chapter 2

War

Thursday 13 September 2001
I had a phone call that I've been taken off the panel of *Any Questions?* tomorrow night. They've got a completely new line-up, and I can understand they felt they had to have a minister on, so Peter Hain was chosen.

I don't think I've quite taken on board this completely new world that has been created. The United States is going to go all out, possibly with NATO, to invade Afghanistan, try and kill Bin Laden, maybe attack Pakistan as well. New York is paralysed. The American Express building collapsed today, and other buildings are likely to follow. The anger in America is phenomenal, and Felicity Arbuthnot rang and said she'd been tuning in to American stations and there were people saying 'Nuke them', 'Capture the oil and let them rot'. I'm very frightened. Everybody is frightened. It's no good going round attacking Blair and Bush personally; you've simply got to say things that are constructive, and if you do that, maybe people will listen.

Harpers & Queen, with the interview that I did with Saffron Burrows, is published today. I must say, it looks nice. I can't complain.

A minor bit of news, Iain Duncan Smith has overwhelmingly beaten Ken Clarke for the leadership of the Tory Party.

The House of Commons is a terrorist target, but I don't think we're quite at a stage where London is going to be attacked, though you simply can't rule it out. Nothing can be ruled out.

It's a completely different world. Everything's changed. Fears have increased, hope has diminished. I'm trying to get it straight myself, but I am frightened, and if London were attacked, who knows which members of the family might be affected. On the whole, people have come up in the street and said, 'I heard you, and I agree with you as a voice of sanity', and all the rest of it. I wish I could speak in the House but I've got access to far more people without Parliament. Now I can go straight to audiences in large numbers.

Friday 14 September
To the House of Commons. I sat in the Gallery and watched Blair make his statement, which was really a sort of *Daily Mail* editorial. I didn't think there was any depth or historical understanding about it.

George Galloway said every time you bomb the Arab world, you recruit more suicide bombers, and said Muslim blood doesn't count in the same way that Western blood counts, which is a vivid way of putting it.

Saturday 15 September
President Bush has said that America is at war and it's going to be long and painful and hard, and so on, and it depressed me very much indeed. I think keeping my spirits up at the moment is the most important thing, but there is a role as a moderate. One of my children said, 'For the first time in your life, Dad, you're a moderate!'

Sunday 16 September
Blair has taken up the theme that we are at war. He's just a little puppet really, he feels he has to do it, though he doesn't. Apparently the Pakistanis have agreed to cooperate with America, presumably because if they didn't they would be punished. The Afghans have warned that if anyone attacks them, they will respond. The Pakistanis may ask the Americans to pay for debt relief or control of Kashmir, I don't know, and that would upset the Indians. What is needed now are some constructive ideas. I've been hammering away about the United Nations.

Tuesday 18 September
On the radio I heard Tony Blair had warned the Afghanistan government, the Taliban, that if they didn't give up Osama Bin Laden they would face the consequences. The man has absolutely no capacity to deliver on his promise. He's just the voice of President Bush.

Saturday 22 September
There was a story in *The Guardian* this morning that the plan to invade Afghanistan had actually been laid in July, therefore it wasn't quite what it appeared. Maybe whoever did the terrorist bombing knew about it, and it was retaliation against a threat. I mean, you cannot believe a word you're told in the papers at the moment. Absolutely impossible to believe anything.

Sunday 23 September
In the afternoon, Mushtaq Lasharie of Third World Solidarity came to see

me. He's a Labour councillor in Kensington, and I've met him over the years. He wanted to know how we could cooperate. I suggested that we might try and get world leaders to launch a peace appeal, inviting the governments of the world to agree to convene a General Assembly of the United Nations to discuss world problems within the Charter of the UN. He was quite taken with this. Later in the day I wrote my *Morning Star* column, in effect launching the idea.

David Blunkett is talking about compulsory identity cards with your fingerprint or your eye recorded, to avoid forgery, and it may require amendment of the human-rights legislation we've just so boldly introduced. So we are slipping into a police state, but that's not an issue worth opposing at this moment.

Monday 24 September
I sat down to draft my letter to world leaders. I rang Ted Heath. He answered the phone himself. I said, 'Ted, Tony Benn, I'll tell you what I rang about. I was thinking of an appeal to world leaders, world statesmen, to convene a special session of the UN General Assembly.'

'Oh,' he said, 'I haven't made any comment about the crisis.'

I said, 'I know, but I wondered whether you thought I was right? I don't like to move on these things without your help, because you helped me on my visit to Saddam Hussein and on Kosovo.'

'Well, quite right.'

'Look, I'm putting together a list of world statesmen. Do you mind if I put your name on it?'

'Right,' he said. So I can mention his name even if he doesn't respond, but it's certainly worth doing.

This afternoon, about half-past four, I had a phone call from Tacy Shore, who said that her dad, Peter Shore, had died at 3.30 this afternoon at St Thomas's Hospital. I've known Peter for fifty years, one of my closest friends. He had a heart attack in the House of Lords last summer, has been in intensive care in St Thomas's ever since and has not been able to speak. Tacy said, 'Don't ring Mum up. She'll be too distressed.' Very sad. I'm very fond of Peter. He was a man of great ability and integrity and commitment and passion, and never really had the opportunity he should have had.

I spoke to David Triesman, the new General Secretary of the Labour Party. 'I just rang for one thing. I'd like very much to speak on the debate on international affairs at the Conference, with two points in mind. I would like to thank the Party for all they have done for me personally, and also to mention my appeal to world leaders for a special meeting of the UN General Assembly.' So maybe that will do the trick.

Tuesday 25 September
Blair has told the Taliban that he'll destroy them if they don't hand over

the terrorists. He hasn't got enough weapons to do any damage to anybody, but he speaks as if he were an imperial president. Incredible man!

Wednesday 26 September
I was picked up at six o'clock to do a two-hour, one-to-one live interview for the TV station Al Jazeera, which is based in Doha and has an audience of seventy million people. I was put under pressure about having supported the state of Israel years ago. A Palestinian woman asked me afterwards, 'Why? Why should a religion have our land? It's always been our land.' It's a difficult argument to answer when you get back to it.

I had a message from an organisation called Friendship Across Frontiers, saying they were expecting an American bombing attack on Baghdad this weekend.

Tam Dalyell rang with the same message, so I rang him back. He had rung Number 10 and said, 'I want to convey my anxiety about this to the Prime Minister. Will you give him the message?' 'Well, I may' a woman replied. Tam said he absolutely lost his temper, and he pulled his rank. He said, 'I'm the Father of the House. If I tell you that I want something to go to the Prime Minister, I don't want that sort of reply. I want an absolute guarantee that it will.' So apparently she got frightened and capitulated.

It's now about twenty-five to twelve and I must go to bed.

Monday 1 October, Labour Party Conference, Brighton
I rang Ted Heath again. 'Who is it?'

'Tony Benn. Ted, you got my letter? What advice can you give me? What should I say at the Conference today?'

'Oh, I don't know. I can't advise you.'

'Well, what do you think?'

He said, 'I think Blair should pipe down! He's pretending he's the leader of the whole world. It annoys the Europeans and the Americans; he should pipe down!' He was very candid, and actually just about got it right, so I found that quite amusing.

Tuesday 2 October
I got up at 5.45, couldn't sleep, was thinking about my speech to Conference, had a bath and shaved, had breakfast and drafted a few points and timed them, and it came to two and a half minutes.

I walked over to the Conference with Hilary. Absolutely pelting with rain! It just poured down. My trousers were so wet the water was dripping on my shoes for minutes afterwards, and my legs were sodden, and my socks were sodden – awful! Hilary was in the same position.

I went into the Conference early and sat down, picked the best seat. Nita came by and patted me, so I had a feeling I might be called. Dennis Skinner came and sat next to me – it was sweet of him – and he said, 'Oh yes, your name was mentioned at the Executive on Sunday. People said I'm sure Tony Benn will want to speak.'

We had long, fraternal greetings from the head of the European Labour MEPs, then we had a speech by Jack Straw, then Clare Short.

Then Andy Gilchrist moved the Fire Brigade's resolution calling for no excessive response in retaliation to the New York attack, a very good resolution. Dennis said to me the Executive are accepting it, so it was a resolution of caution.

When I was called, I must say the Conference gave me a tremendous reception when I stood up, and I was a bit overwhelmed.

I began by saying this was probably my last Conference, and I wanted to thank the Party for all they've done for me. I went through Labour's achievements, to great cheers.

A Labour government signed the Charter of the United Nations in 1945; and I gave three examples of Labour leaders working for peace. When Truman suggested that he might drop an atom bomb in Korea, Clem Attlee went straight to Washington and stopped it. In 1956, when we were told that Nasser was another Hitler, Hugh Gaitskell campaigned against the war. And later Harold Wilson had the courage to refuse to send British troops to Vietnam, which Lyndon Johnson wanted him to do. And I said that now we face this atrocity and the terrorism, we must work within the United Nations. The nations of the world looked to the United Nations to give a state for Palestine, to lift the suffering from the Iraqi people, to deal with the exploitation of workers by multinational companies. And no military action must take place unless it's been authorised by the Security Council.

Finally I said that when I came back from the war and I heard the preamble of the Charter of the United Nations, I was very moved by it. This is what it said: 'We the peoples of the United Nations determine to save succeeding generations from the scourge of war, which twice in our lifetime has caused untold sorrow to mankind.' I said, 'That was the pledge given by that generation to this generation, and we must renew that pledge if our children and grandchildren are to live in peace. Comrades, thank you very much!' I found it difficult to fight back the tears, but I went back to my seat and there was a marvellous reception.

Walked back to the flat, had several cups of tea, watched Blair's speech. It was a powerful speech, and the Conference cheered him to the echo on every point he made, but it was the speech of a king. It wasn't the speech of a leader of a democratic party: what we had to do, how globalisation was good, how we'd intervene anywhere in the world, we'd work with the new Afghanistan government to relieve poverty – it's quite untrue, we haven't the resources to do it. I mean, it did confirm what Ted Heath had advised yesterday: that Blair should pipe down. He spoke as if he was President and Bush was Vice-President! We've got no military resources to do it all.

I walked over to the Tribune rally. I'm using the opportunity to be a bit historical, so I said the Prime Minister's speech was an imperial speech. It was a royal speech. I'm not saying he isn't a good king, but he's certainly a king, and it reminded me of what Julius Caesar must have said when he came to tell us to adopt the Roman currency, the penny; I said of course the Roman soldiers had to withdraw because there was trouble in Palestine in 410 AD.

Of course, Blair's speech has echoed round the whole Conference, been reported all over the world, this Churchillian figure warning the Taliban to give up Bin Laden or surrender power in only a few days. It's absolutely pathetic! We haven't got enough armed forces in Britain to recapture the Isle of Wight. It made no reference to anybody else, no reference to Jack Straw, no reference to Gordon Brown, no reference to Geoff Hoon, no reference to any other country, except a warm defence of the United States.

Saturday 6 October

Blair has moved from London to Moscow to Islamabad, he's now in Delhi. Everywhere he goes he threatens more military action. He really does behave as if he was running the whole Anglo-American special relationship, and I can't think it pleases them enormously in Washington, but maybe they are quite happy to have him do it. I just do not know.

Sunday 7 October

I spent most of the day working on the first of a series of lectures for the London School of Economics, where I am visiting professor. I really have put a lot of effort and research into it. In the course of the afternoon I heard that the Americans, with British military support, have bombed Afghanistan. Bush said this is not just a war against Bin Laden, against the Taliban, but against any country that harbours terrorists, and there are sixty of them where Bin Laden is supposed to have an organisation. Bin Laden had pre-recorded a message saying this is an attack upon Islam. Blair, looking a bit sweaty, with Straw and Hoon and Prescott beside him, announced that we were taking part. So we've launched into a war without any declaration of war, without any parliamentary authority for war, outside the United Nations, a war that is supposed to be directed simply at the Taliban in Afghanistan. It could have very serious consequences, could lead to the overthrow of the Pakistani, Saudi and Egyptian governments. It could of course lead to – perhaps that would have happened anyway – retaliation terrorist attacks in Britain and America, and it is a war that could spread. There are no clear war aims, and even if Bin Laden is arrested, he can hardly be given a judicial trial in America.

There was a good programme by John Simpson on Afghanistan, the unbelievable suffering they've gone through – tribal wars, poverty, intervention by the British, by the Russians, now by the Americans – the utter cynicism of big power politics. It just makes you utterly depressed, because it could go on for ten years. Blair has just done everything he's been told to do, indeed has tried to edge himself ahead. Parliament has been recalled for tomorrow – at least they've done that.

Some people will be killed, and suffer, and there are four million refugees, many of whom will die of starvation in the winter, despite the promise of humanitarian aid.

Monday 8 October
I drove to the Commons, got a cab to the London School of Economics and met writer and lecturer Richard Heffernan. We went and had a meal in Pret a Manger in the Aldwych. It was simply pelting with rain. Somehow, simple things such as going out, finding a restaurant, sitting on a stool, having a sandwich, drinking a cup of tea are a bit too much for me now! I don't know how to describe it. I'm feeling physically very old, and like a visitor in a new country.

My dear brother Dave turned up. It was sweet of him! There were fifty students there, British, Americans, Danes, Swedes, Norwegians, Spaniards and Germans. I was very nervous about it. I spoke for nearly an hour, and I encouraged questions and discussion. But what's so funny about a class like that is it's not a meeting of people who want to hear *you* particularly; there is no applause, no criticism. It's a rather mechanical relationship, and I have to think my way through that.

I got a cab back to the House of Commons. Parliament has been recalled and Tam Dalyell and Alan Simpson both asked my advice about what they should say in the House, and I said to Tam, I think you should ask, 'Is this in line with the UN Charter? Have you had legal advice?' and to Alan that he should concentrate on the UN. I don't really miss being in the House. It's strange – there are armed policemen with sub-machine guns. I find that weird.

This *is* a crusade. I mean, that stupid word that was used by Bush has really registered, and Bin Laden said this is an attack on the Muslim world. So we shall see. I think it's going to end in tears, but I'm often wrong in my judgements about wars that I don't support.

Wednesday 10 October
Latish start this morning, a troubled night as usual, but not getting any cramp.

I had a lovely letter, from Mary Robinson, the former President of the Republic of Ireland, who is now the High Commissioner for Human Rights in Geneva:

Thank you for your letter concerning your initiative to seek support for a convening of the special session of the General Assembly to discuss the most pressing problems facing the world. I appreciate very much the deep and genuine concern that lies behind this appeal, particularly at this very worrying time. However, as the United Nations High Commissioner for Human Rights, I'm afraid I'm not in a position to issue a public appeal to a body of which I'm a senior office holder. On a more positive note, the General Assembly of the United Nations is currently in session and I share the hope that the tragedy of 11 September and its continuing consequences will serve to focus the collective mind of the international community on how to ensure that the causes of conflict are addressed and eliminated.

With warm personal regards, yours sincerely,

Mary

Well, that was nice. I've never met her, but it was a very nice letter. I can't use her now as a supporter, for the reasons she gave.

Sunday 14 October
Up at 6.15, picked up at 7.30, went to the BBC to do *Breakfast with Frost*, with Anne Robinson, whom I've never met before, who does this silly programme *The Weakest Link*, which just bullies people. Then others on the programme later on were Michael Howard, Steve Marshall, recently Chief Executive of Railtrack (it's gone bankrupt, and he told me that he thought it was a great mistake to privatise the railways), and Yvonne Ridley, the *Daily Express* correspondent who was held by the Taliban for about a week and happily released, who said the Taliban were so charming and gentlemanly and kind to her (except for the clerics, she meant).

Tuesday 16 October
The Americans have now bombed a Red Cross depot near Kabul. Pictures are coming in on the Al Jazeera network of children who've been injured by the Americans, orphans going into Pakistan, looking absolutely dejected, desolate.

Wednesday 17 October
Turned on the seven o'clock news. Hilary was on – his first appearance as a minister, with a difficult brief, because the aid agencies have called for a pause in the bombing of Afghanistan to get the food in, and Clare Short and Blair have turned it down. Poor Hilary had to defend them, but he was very competent. He said the aid is coming in anyway, and obviously we all hope for the best.

Saturday 20 October
Oh, the Americans have sent troops into Afghanistan, and it's being presented as if it was a huge military triumph. Here's this pitifully poor

country being savaged by the richest country in the world, which then speaks as if this was a tremendous military achievement! It's utterly revolting.

In my heart of hearts I believe Bush and Blair acted illegally and, if I am right, they have committed war crimes. I think I shall say that, but I've got to be careful I don't overdo it, wait till public opinion shifts.

Sunday 21 October

The pressure on the anti-war MPs is growing. Apparently Paul Marsden had three-quarters of an hour being bullied by the Chief Whip, Hilary Armstrong. Then Adam Ingram, the Armed Forces Minister, said those who opposed the war were appeasers. They're getting a little bit worried, otherwise it wouldn't happen. Also, Bush announced today that he'd ordered the assassination of Bin Laden, so that ends the possibility of a trial.

Tuesday 23 October

I went over to the House. I went to have my hair cut in John Simon's, and who should come in but Paul Marsden, who is the hero of the moment. He wanted to have a word with me at some stage, so I said, well, we'll have a talk about it later. They did a nice job.

Then I walked over to Central Hall, Westminster – for the meeting to commemorate the H-block hunger-striker, Bobby Sands, and others, and of course the whole thing was just top news because of the fact that Gerry Adams was speaking. I didn't really know what I could say until the arms-decommissioning breakthrough occurred, announced in Belfast by Gerry Adams and Martin McGuinness, so I made a brief speech, about seven minutes, because it was Gerry Adams's occasion, and then I sat down.

Gerry, when he got up to speak, began by giving me a presentation of a beautiful metal plaque, which has been cast in Northern Ireland, celebrating the hunger-strike martyrs of 1981. At the bottom, after all their names, was a quote from Bobby Sands, who said, 'Our revenge is the laughter of our children', which is lovely. Then Gerry made the most moving speech, describing in detail the prison conditions, how the British authorities tried to criminalise the IRA, how they tried to break them, how they denied them things they needed, and how he'd heard from Mandela the same thing happened in South Africa. Then he talked about the future and the hope. But immensely sensitive – his capacity to communicate is almost unparalleled.

I walked down with him, though he had three heavies with him, whom I thought might be British police, but of course they were Sinn Fein bodyguards.

Wednesday 24 October

Then I went to the Commons because I wanted to hear Hilary at the

Despatch Box answering International Development questions. I had a talk
with Chris Mullin in the Tea Room. Chris said, of course don't forget there
were people dying of hunger in Afghanistan before the war, as if somehow
the war had made it better, and of course the truth is nobody was interested
in Afghanistan before the war. Labour MPs are quite incredible about the
war!

To the inaugural meeting of Labour Against the War. Alan Simpson was
in the chair. He's really coming into his own – absolutely rightly, as he
should. Paul Marsden spoke and said he'd had 300 emails after the row,
after people had read his account in the papers of the interview with the
Chief Whip. Bob Marshall-Andrews spoke on the question of an
International Court of Justice. The main desire of the meeting was to
connect the Labour Party with the anti-war campaign, because it was said
by Alan Simpson, quite rightly, that he'd never known a time when not just
the Labour Party but Parliament was so completely disconnected from
public feeling. Ann Cryer was worried because of the way the Taliban treat
women. Well, George Galloway dealt with that; he said that the only time
women in Afghanistan were treated well was when the communists were
there.

Sunday 28 October
I'm getting a bit stronger now, because it's obvious that the war is going
wrong. They are not defeating the Taliban, they're nowhere near finding
Bin Laden – Afghanistan being a mountainous country twice the size of
France – and the whole thing is really beginning to grind to a halt.
Yesterday they bombed a village held by the Northern Alliance, they're
bombing Red Cross depots, mosques, churches, schools, villages. But
what's it achieving? Nothing! Pakistanis are volunteering to go into
Afghanistan to fight for the Taliban. Bush is getting desperate.

Monday 29 October
I had a long sleep, felt much better, caught the Tube to the LSE, and gave
my lecture on the subject of Europe. I got a very blank response considering
most of them are from the continent; there were hardly any questions.
Richard Heffernan said to me afterwards, 'You must realise the whole
academic establishment takes Europe now for granted, and therefore
there's no question of whether you should or shouldn't be in. It's studied,
but not criticised, rather like communism was in Russia.' I thought it was a
shrewd comment.

Tuesday 30 October
I got up fairly early this morning. I had a very busy day. The builder came
to look at my boiler which has been backing up hot water into the top floor,
so there's condensation and there's water all over the floor. Then the guy

from Bosch came, a German called Frank, and fixed the washing machine.

Blair made his speech on the war today at the Welsh Assembly. It went down like a pancake on a wet pavement.

I did resolve I've got to leave my house. There's damp everywhere, the place is falling apart and I don't want to spend a lot of money on it. If I did, it wouldn't in any way increase the value of the house, and I'd like to go to a three-bedroom flat, one bedroom as a spare room, one bedroom as an office, and then a nice, decent-sized bedroom and a living room, a kitchen, a bathroom – that's all I need.

Friday 2 November
The builders – that is to say, Derek and his mate, Graham – came and fixed the leak in the bathroom on the top floor, and they also found that the temperature regulator in the boiler had gone wrong, so replaced that.

Had lunch; the news came through that David Trimble had been defeated for the job of First Minister in the Northern Ireland Assembly. Although all the Sinn Fein people voted for him and all the SDLP people voted for him, two of his own members didn't, and of course Paisley didn't, so he fell short by one vote. It's becoming obvious that the street fighting or violence in Northern Ireland is because people are poor. The racial problems in Bradford are because people are poor. The conflict in the world is between rich and poor. And now that individualism and globalisation have removed any sense of collective responsibility for anyone else, when things go wrong everyone rallies round their own tribe or religion or village or town and fights off anyone else. I could see the whole thing breaking up, as Yugoslavia broke up. Globalisation and the ethics of globalisation, which are non-ethics, have probably been destroyed by war.

I happened to see a television programme, when I was having my meal in the evening, about the Maya culture in Mexico. I had absolutely no idea that the temples they built were bigger than the pyramids; 1,500 years ago there was the most tremendously civilised society in Latin America, which simply disappeared, went under the jungle, and it does make you wonder whether ours might not do the same. There's no absolute law to say that our civilisation will survive for ever.

Friday 9 November
Bitterly cold overnight. I woke up several times because my feet were so cold, and there has been a sudden change of temperature, Britain having had the warmest October since 1659.

To Westminster Abbey, and handed in a little cross for my brother who died on operations in 1944 with a poppy on it saying 'For Michael Benn, DFC, Love from Anthony and David' to the RAF Air Crew section. I didn't put Bomber Command because somehow it was just too gruesome.

It was very moving. I stood there with my head uncovered for a moment and thought of Mike.

Saturday 10 November

Bin Laden is alleged to have given an interview in which he said he had nuclear and chemical weapons, and he wouldn't use them unless the Americans did. It has been reported that Richard Perle has suggested that when they have finished with Afghanistan, the US might move on to Iraq, Iran, North Korea, Syria and other states considered a threat to the US, and doesn't care whether the coalition sticks together. The US is just going to impose its will.

That's no doubt how the Roman Empire grew, the Chinese Empire grew, the Ottoman Empire grew. You feel very weak up against it, but that's the best way to see it, as an absolutely naked exercise of American global power.

Sunday 11 November

Blunkett is introducing some new legislation that will allow him to arrest and hold without trial people who are on suspicion – i.e. internment without trial, in effect. He gets very angry if anyone criticises him. I think it's all just using the crisis as an excuse for repressing civil liberties. Human-rights lawyers are planning to appeal against it under the Human Rights Act. You do just have to fight.

Otherwise, not much news that I can think of. The war goes on, winter is almost upon us, some people are no doubt starving and freezing already.

Tuesday 13 November

Jeremy Corbyn put it clearly that we've sacrificed our civil liberties, we've sacrificed the United Nations, which is now seen as a sort of inflated Oxfam, which the Americans entirely ignore. We should be demanding no resumption of the bombing of Afghanistan; secondly, no attack on Iraq or other countries; and thirdly, that humanitarian aid be given absolutely massive priority, and that the United Nations should be restored to its proper role.

Sunday 18 November

To Hyde Park, where a huge crowd was gathering. It was the biggest demonstration I can remember for many, many years. Among those who spoke later in Trafalgar Square were John Pilger, Bianca Jagger, Tariq Ali, Yvonne Ridley, New York trade unionist Michael Letwin, Tennessee-born Dr Jonathan Farley, Jeremy Corbyn, Paul Marsden, Alan Simpson, George Galloway; then there was Germaine Greer, who turned up but was a bit late, the journalist George Monbiot, John Haylett (Editor of the *Morning Star*), Louise Christian, Paul Mackney, Bernard Reagan, David Nellist, Mike Mansfield and a whole range of others.

I was terribly tired by the time I got there, could hardly walk up the steps, my feet were killing me. After I spoke, my phone rang and it was Saffron Burrows, who had been in Trafalgar Square, so we had a cup of tea.

Monday 19 November
Apparently Bush does not need British troops sent into Afghanistan, but Blair is still trying to send 6,000 troops there. Bush, having bombed Afghanistan, just wants to get out, and Blair's got this funny imperial idea that British troops would restore order; Cherie Blair made a speech about conditions for women under the Taliban. Well, the Taliban have all been beaten now, they don't exist any more. The whole thing is so odious.

Wednesday 21 November
It's the anniversary of Caroline's death this week, and I must say, I'm finding it very painful. Not only do I miss her terribly, but also I'm still riddled with guilt, the things I should have done with her that I didn't. I know it's too late, I can't do anything about it now, but it is a terrible burden, and the guilt extends to my dad when he was old. I think Caroline would have been pleased at the way I'm tackling being on my own. I've got lots of people supporting me, lots and lots and lots.

Thursday 22 November
Doris Heffer rang, and Jane Shallice rang to remember Caroline. I did appreciate that.
I went shopping and came home and had a cry. I just sobbed on the couch for a bit, and then I decided to work in the office all afternoon.
Josh arrived first for the evening family gathering. He went and bought pizzas and we had them at home, and we talked about Mum. Then at six minutes past ten, which is the exact moment she died, we all went into the front room, where I'd lit a candle, and we stood in front of the picture of her, and we hugged each other and took photographs. They are a lovely family, and I thanked them all for being so super.

Wednesday 28 November
I saw Gordon Brown today by chance, just before I had lunch, and he said, 'Oh, how are you, Tony?' So I said, 'I'm sorry I missed your statement in the Commons yesterday, but I was in Bristol getting an honorary degree.' 'Ah, very well deserved!' So he was obviously trying to be friendly. He was going into the Tea Room, and I've never seen Gordon Brown in the Tea Room before, and I think this must be a build-up for his election as Leader of the Party – he probably forgot I wasn't an MP. It made me laugh a bit!

Thursday 29 November

To the Mayfair International Hotel for the Foreign Press Association Awards.

I had been asked to go and refused, because I'd have to wear a black tie. Then they rang back and said, we didn't mean to tell you this, but actually you're due to get an award, and you can come dressed in what you like! So I did put on a dinner jacket. I had been put at a table with David Yelland, the Editor of *The Sun*, but thank God he didn't appear, and I shifted round so I wouldn't be next to him if he had.

After the dinner, Clare Short made a speech. Given my reservations about Clare, it was a good speech. She said we've reached a point in history where justice has got to be achieved internationally, just as it was once done nationally by struggles. The historical perspective was quite good, and it wasn't offensive in any way. She came up to me beforehand and said how marvellous Hilary was in the Department, how his gestures are so like mine and she couldn't believe it wasn't me. I said, well, he loves it there, it's such a marvellous job, he is so pleased to work with you. She kept patting my cheek, a thing I don't terribly like.

Then the awards were made: Journalist of Year, News Story of the Year, and all that, and then Bernard Ingham announced that Media Personality of the Year was me, and the prize was given by Virgin Atlantic, presented by the Head of Corporate Communications. I had thought a little bit, so I said if I might take up what Clare has said, technology has grown to the point where we could meet the needs of the world if we planned and distributed our resources fairly, or we could blow up the human race, and journalists had a critical part to play in that.

Saturday 1 December

Got a taxi to the Albert Hall for the Bootleg Beatles. Stephen had got tickets for the whole family, bless his old heart. He's so efficient! It was a fabulous performance, and it has been a huge success. I hadn't heard of them until quite recently. I don't know how many people you can get in the Albert Hall – there must have been 10,000, I should think. It was just so good, so well done, and the audience stood up and cheered and waved their hands – a lot of middle-aged people; I was probably one of the oldest people there. There were also a lot of young people, who seemed to enjoy it just as much. They did it in four different phases: the early Beatles, Sergeant Pepper's Band, and on right through to the end. A screen came down and showed clips of film from the Sixties, the Seventies and the Eighties. There was a clip of me talking about pirate radio, which was a bit of a surprise!

Stephen had arranged for us to go afterwards to the stage door. We all met the cast, we all shook hands with them, they gave their autographs – it was lovely.

Just before I go to bed – there's been a huge suicide bomb in Jerusalem,

130 people injured or killed, and this violence goes on and on and on, on both sides, and the argument that the other side only understands force is what the Americans are saying about al-Qaeda, what the Islamic Jihad say about the Israelis, and at some stage you do really have to think of some other way of solving problems. As Rosa Luxemburg said, the choice is between socialism and barbarism.

Of course the peace movement has been somewhat overtaken by the fact that the Americans appear to have won an outright victory in Afghanistan by bombing the Taliban and supporting the Northern Alliance, and some interim government's being worked out in Bonn. Whether it really will mean anything, I'm not sure.

Wednesday 5 December
It has been reported that Paul Marsden was physically assaulted in the Strangers' Bar in the Commons and has written to the Prime Minister about it and released a statement.

Alice Mahon has just come back from a NATO Parliamentary Assembly in America, where she said the Americans were totally on a hype about the war – 'We've won the war! It's all over. We don't want NATO involved in this anti-terrorist thing. Europe can send some troops in to police Afghanistan.' And then a vague hint that this was just stage one, and although they didn't say so obviously, Iraq was hinted at, and apparently Jack Straw in the House this afternoon warned Saddam. So it looks as if the British Government will go along with it, if the Americans do decide to attack Iraq.

But the really big news in the Middle East, of course, is that Sharon has announced that Arafat was the head of a terrorist state, and that justified anything the Israelis did, and of course by doing that and agreeing with that, Bush has buried the peace process completely.

Friday 7 December
Susie Burrows, Saffron's mother, rang me up. She told me that Saffron and she went to America for a week, visited a bar in New York, and there was Clinton, so Susie went up and spoke to him, and introduced Saffron. Clinton was so taken by Saffron he invited them to a concert of Irish music, and afterwards to dinner, Susie on one side and Saffron on the other, and four or five other people, a couple of German journalists and security people. Saffron said, 'I talked to Clinton all evening about you. He knew about you.' So of course when Clinton comes to the LSE to give his lecture, if I get a chance of seeing him, I won't say, 'I believe you know Tony Blair' as a way of introduction. I'll say, 'I believe you've met my friend Saffron Burrows, the actress.' It did make me laugh!

Tuesday 11 December
I had lunch with Saffron at the Adjournment restaurant in the Commons. At the next tables were a Catholic priest and John Hayes, the Tory MP and Richard Shepherd, another Tory MP, having a meal with Edward Pearce, the journalist.

Saffron was very sweet. She said she has decided to get a flat of her own. She's got a new friend, Fiona Shaw, a distinguished actress. She said, 'I need a little space now to develop a bit, you know. I understood it all.

Thursday 13 December
I set off for the LSE because Clinton was giving his lecture, went up to the cafeteria and had a cup of tea, but I couldn't get down again because all the staircases were blocked. So I was diverted out to another entrance, and then when I got back into Houghton Street to get in, there was a huge queue! Well, I wasn't prepared to queue because I'd already been through the doors, so I slipped round the side, knocking over a huge Christmas tree, and was scooped up by Liz Philipson, who is now a lecturer at the LSE herself.

We looked over the gallery to see who was in the audience: Greg Dyke was there, Will Hutton, Professor Fred Halliday. The academic establishment in a way, the LSE international establishment.

Clinton was half an hour late. He had a bad cold, and he was introduced by the sociologist Anthony Giddens, who talked about the Third Way. Then Lord Desai, who is the Professor of Global Governance, got up and said something. Clinton was a bit red-faced. He is a charming man. I suppose everybody knows that. He's only five years older than my eldest son, Stephen. I mean, he's young enough to be my son. He was four and a half when I got elected to Parliament. He began by talking about Prime Minister Blair and about Giddens and the Third Way; how we're moving to a stage in life where there was no conflict between capital and labour, and Christians and Muslims; we all did better by helping each other, which was quite a sensible argument. But to say there's no conflict is incredible.

It wasn't at all like Blair's speeches. Blair is bombastic and looks from side to side through his teleprompter. Clinton had a few notes, which he looked down at, so the thing was very natural – good communication, modest, thoughtful and very persuasive, for those hearing it for the first time.

He talked about the new world information technology, about terrorism and how it never has succeeded, it's got to be crushed; so he took the traditional view on that. He didn't mention the United Nations once. He didn't actually mention globalisation, except that the standard of living for everybody was rising. He did say there are people who die of poverty in the world, people who hadn't got hospitals, hadn't got anything. So he touched on the anti-globalisation argument. As I say, it was persuasive and charming.

What I realise is that if you are going to win an argument with him, because of such fundamental differences, it has to be won at that level, before that audience, as well as at big demonstrations where you shout about American policy.

When I was sitting up in the gallery, somebody came up and said, 'If you do want to shake him by the hand, come down immediately afterwards.' So as soon as he finished, I jumped up, went downstairs and waited, saw him going out another way and up in the lift. They were all very kind to me. They ushered me up in a lift. Chelsea was there. There were lots and lots of people there, and Desai and Giddens were trying to usher him into the dinner, to which I had not been invited.

Finally I was introduced to him and I said, 'Oh, I'm so pleased to meet you. I was fifty years in Parliament and am now a visiting professor here. I met LBJ and Nixon, and I'm very pleased to meet you, and it was a thoughtful lecture you gave.'

Then I said, 'As you referred to Gandhi,' which he had done in the lecture, 'I met Gandhi in 1931.' Clinton did look a bit surprised at that! I said, 'My dad took me to see him when I was very young. When Gandhi was in London, somebody asked him, "What do you think of civilisation in Britain?" and Gandhi said, "I think it would be a very good idea!"' – at which he laughed.

'And of course,' I said finally, 'you know my friend Saffron Burrows.' His face absolutely lit up, and he said, 'Oh, Saffron and her mother told me all about you in America last week!' Of course I had discovered earlier today, when I rang Saffron, that she had had a phone call from Clinton, who hoped he'd see her when he was in London.

So when I got home, I rang Saffron. Apparently Clinton wanted to have dinner with her tomorrow night and to introduce her to Chelsea, because I suppose Bill Clinton feels that Saffron and Chelsea would get on very well together. It was most entertaining.

Sunday 22 December
It was icy cold. I came home, and I decided I would try and put a new electric bar in the fire in my bedroom, because one of them had gone bust. I got my screwdriver and spanner and oil to release everything. It took me three-quarters of an hour to do, but I did it, and now that heater will give off quite a lot of heat and make the room quite a lot warmer, and I sure need it.

This will be the second Christmas without Caroline.

Wednesday 26 December
In the afternoon, I went to Ravenscourt Park for the Boxing Day tea with the Gibsons.

The thing that really made the afternoon momentous was that I had a word with Ralph Gibson. I said, 'What do you think of Lord Woolf, the Lord Chief Justice, who this morning said that dangerous people might have to be detained, without committing an offence, in order to protect the public?' So Ralph said, 'Well, we're living in new times. There are new dangers now, and we've got to face them in a new way.'

I must admit, it was just like being hit on the head with a hammer. I said, 'Well, Ralph, I feel as if the Rock of Gibraltar had melted, as if the sun hadn't risen in the morning, as if everything had gone wrong.' I thought we believed in jury trials and presumption of innocence, and so on, and here was a retired High Court judge, a very senior man whom I've known for fifty-five years, a member of the Labour Party years ago, actually saying that he thought all the legal safeguards we'd ever had had been outdated by one attack on New York in September, terrible as it was. It just knocked me for six!

Christopher Gibson, his son, agreed with me, and said, 'Oh, Dad, come on!' And then Ralph said, 'I think David Blunkett's right about one thing, opposing forced marriages and female circumcision.' Well, I dare say that's the case; I'm not in favour of either, but that wasn't really the issue.

Later Christopher said, 'I no longer believe that morality enters into any calculations by ministers in any government in reaching their decisions, and it's all the focus groups and the spin doctors and the public opinion polls.' I said, 'I agree with you; I'd go further. I no longer feel that I am required to believe what I'm told by ministers.' Well, Ralph was shocked by that.

But when I thought about it all afterwards, it confirmed what I'd been thinking in terms of the loss of democracy in Britain and worldwide, and the insistence of a new empire superpower to do what it liked. I just felt we were in the process of going through a new Dark Age, and what do you do in a Dark Age? That's the important question. You can bemoan it, but what do you actually do?

So anyway, that was our talk, and when I got home I watched *Kind Hearts and Coronets*.

Bin Laden has produced a new video, which of course is described in one news bulletin as a video nasty and terrorist propaganda, but actually he said that New York was attacked because of the Americans' support for Israel and acts against Afghanistan. Revenge, revenge, revenge. The more you think about it, the more you realise that is really the name of the game now. If you've got the power to do it, you do it. If the Americans have got the power to bomb and destroy Afghanistan, they do it. If the al-Qaeda network has got the power to bomb New York, they do it.

All these hopes that I had after the Second World War, which was such a shattering experience, that things will get better are being erased. I feel now that we are going in the opposite direction at breakneck speed. How do you deal with it? Certainly you don't make any progress by attacking people – that's a waste of time. What is required is calm, consistent analysis and support. But my God, somehow I never thought that Boxing Day 2001, which was meant to be a family party, would be such a shattering experience.

Sunday 30 December
Left home about twenty-past ten to drive to Stansgate. I was listening to cassettes in the car, and I began crying, and I sobbed and sobbed all the way to Stansgate. It was freezing cold there, and I sat in the bedroom and sobbed. It just comes back to you all of a sudden, and I wondered where Caroline was. Had she disappeared into thin air? What does death mean? Is it a complete and absolute end?

Thursday 3 January 2002
By the end of this month, more people will have died in Afghanistan of starvation and cold than were killed in the World Trade Center.

Sunday 6 January
I went up to Melissa's, picked up her daughters Hannah and Sarah and Melissa, and we went to see *Harry Potter*, the rave film which made its author, J. K. Rowling, the second-richest woman, after the Queen, in Britain. When she wrote the book she lived in a council house and had to go to the library to find a place to write. It is an amazing achievement, and it's a fantastic film. I couldn't hear any of the dialogue, I didn't follow the story and I dozed off a couple of times. Then at the end, Robbie Coltrane, who was playing the part of one of the wizards, gave Harry Potter an album and, as he opened the album, his real mother and father were seen in a moving picture with the little Harry Potter. I burst into tears. Lissie was very sympathetic, and Sarah said to me going back in the car, 'When you die, Dan-Dan, you will be in my heart, and now there is a part of you in my heart already', which for a five-year-old is very sweet.

Monday 7 January
The really sad news today is that little baby Jennifer, the two-week-old daughter of Gordon Brown, the Chancellor of the Exchequer, and his wife Sarah, died. She was terribly premature, two pounds when she was born, and she had a brain haemorrhage. I shall write a little note to him.

Thursday 10 January
Got a cab to the Albery Theatre in St Martin's Lane, where Lissie and I were met by Saffron Burrows, who had arranged tickets for *Private Lives*. It's a smashing play, I had seen it after the war.

I couldn't hear it all, but I put on little loudspeaker earphones, which helped. We were taken backstage and had dinner afterwards with Saffron

and Mike Figgis; Alan Rickman, who played the part of Elliot, and his
partner Rima Horton, who's an economics lecturer and Lindsay Duncan,
who played the part of Amanda. We stayed and talked and talked, and
Melissa took photographs. The whole evening cost about 400 quid, but it
was really enjoyable, and Melissa just shone. She said to me later, 'Dad, not
many people would be proud to take a seventy-six-year-old father out for
the evening.'

Friday 11 January
John Nichols came to see me – a nice lad, now the Political Editor of *The
Nation* in New York.

I told him that I'd liked meeting Clinton. 'Oh,' he said, 'Clinton's an
interesting guy! I've interviewed him ten or eleven times, and he's very
thoughtful.' It confirmed my analysis of the man, which was pleasing,
because I thought I'd possibly been taken in by his charm.

He went on to say that in America at the moment it is absolutely
impossible to discuss the war, other than to take the Bush line; the
Democrats have completely shut up about the war, apart from giving
support; the media didn't cover it at all, other than the official line; and
there's a lot of people listening to the BBC because the coverage was better,
from an American point of view.

Tuesday 15 January
The Government announced today the private management of some
hospitals, and Alan Milburn said we're giving the NHS freedom, we're
taking our hands off it, which is just privatisation on a huge scale.

All these prisoners captured in Afghanistan have been taken to the
American naval base in Guantanamo Bay in Cuba, with white hoods over
their heads and shackled in chains. Some of them are British. They say
British officials will be allowed to interview them, but exactly what right the
Americans have to enter Afghanistan, arrest people who are defending
their own country, take them back to another country and then try them
on some charge, I don't know.

The prisoners are being held in wire cages and are obviously going to be
tortured to get information out of them. Ministers just say they're guilty,
long before there's any sort of a trial. There's no possibility of a fair trial for
any of them. It's a terrible situation.

Friday 18 January
I had tea with Dr William Brown, the Master of Darwin College, who is an
expert in industrial relations. He's the Montague Burton Professor of
Industrial Relations. He's been a member of ACAS, he advises the Fire
Brigades Union and he's an old Labour man. He said, 'I was on the local
committee as a young socialist that picked Merlyn Rees to fight Leeds after

Gaitskell had died.' The staff of Darwin were all very decent left-wingers, no question about that. That's no doubt why they asked me.

We walked over to the lecture hall. There were 500 people there, and they opened up another hall with a video link with 200 there. Several hundred couldn't get in.

Anyway, the lecture was well received, and it inclines me to believe that this is the kind of talk I could do for the Clive Conway agency, starting on Saturday. It was political but human, and humorous. It did go down very well. After the lecture there was a reception, and a man came up to me and said, 'I haven't seen you since 1943 in Gwelo in Rhodesia.' He was training as a pilot at the same time as me. Amazing! I did feel among friends. We had a Burns supper, with a piper, and I had some vegetarian haggis.

Caught the 10.31 train to London. One guy came in with a cigarette and said to me, 'Do you mind my smoking?' Well, I showed him my pipe, and so we had a puff together. I think these no-smoking rules are beginning to break down, because of course no one ever comes round to collect tickets.

Wednesday 23 January, Glasgow
I couldn't sleep and I got up about six. I realised that I had lost my Coronation pencil, the one I bought in 1937 with all the monarchs of England along its length. I use it in my lectures as a prop and tell jokes using it. So I got a cab to the Royal Concert Hall, where I had been lecturing the night before, and had a word with the stage manager. They'd already cleared the stage from last night and he went through the rubbish, but I'm afraid I've lost it, and I'm really sad about that.

Saturday 26 January
I did a little work in the office, and then at a quarter to two I got a taxi to Waterloo to go to Guildford for the first of my public talks, 'An Audience with Tony Benn', for Clive Conway. Got to the Yvonne Arnaud Theatre early and, when I was ready, went into the theatre, before it started, and sat and talked to a few people; and then I got on the platform, as if it had suddenly occurred to me I might make a speech. I was inordinately worried about it; I am not usually worried about making speeches, but this was a serious lecture. It was basically the same one I gave in Cambridge last week. I spoke for forty-five minutes, and it went down all right.

Then there was a brief break, and then we went back, and for another three-quarters of an hour we had questions and answers. There was an easy chair, and I had my thermos and a mug, and I had my pipe. The questions were good. I was very relieved.

Thursday 31 January
The crisis at Enron (the American energy company) has really blown up.

John Wakeham, who was Energy Minister in a Conservative government and then got on the board of Enron and was on its Audit Committee, has resigned as Chairman of the Press Complaints Commission in the UK. He may have to go to Washington to give evidence. The whole thing just stinks to high heaven! Some documents have been shredded, and the thing is as corrupt as you can make it.

Other news is that the head of PostCom, which is the regulatory body of the Post Office, has recommended that the Post Office monopoly be abolished over a period of years; beginning with big-business deliveries, then smaller business deliveries, and finally being open to anybody. They are destroying a monopoly that goes back to 1666 when the Royal Mail was set up, and the legacy of Rowland Hill, the Secretary of the Post Office, who in 1840 introduced the Penny Post, which was the equivalent of the Internet in the nineteenth century. Just destroyed! It is an utter disgrace, and as a former Postmaster General I'm totally shocked by it.

I sent a cheque to my grandson William, because he's trying to get a 'vinyl' – that is to say, a gramophone record – cut for his music. I signed it D. Dan, General Director, Music Demonstration Corporation!

Had a bit of a migraine.

Saturday 2 February
Stephen Byers, the Transport Secretary, went to the Labour Party Conference in Cardiff and attacked the trade-union leaders who opposed privatisation as wreckers – 'We will not allow the wreckers to ruin modernisation.' The parallel, and this has been building up for a long time, is with Bush and Blair – you're either with us or against us – and both of them are a form of dictatorship.

The article I wrote for the *Daily Mail* on the privatisation of the Post Office, which was delicately worded but made the case for public service very strongly, was accepted. They are giving it a big spread tomorrow in *The Mail on Sunday*, so that will do a bit of good.

Tuesday 5 February
At eleven o'clock the Iranian Ambassador, Morteza Sarmadi, came to the house. I had asked the Iranian Embassy if they would send me particulars about him: he's forty-seven years old, trained as an engineer, worked in the Iranian Foreign Office in charge of public relations, dealing with negotiations with Iraq. He's been posted to Afghanistan, Kosovo, Tajikistan, New York – a very experienced guy.

As a courtesy, I stood outside the front door and, exactly at eleven o'clock, this sleek car with the number plate '1PER' drew up. We talked about the whole situation, about the US insistence that 'you are either for us or against us', and what a terrible mistake Bush was making, treating the

Muslim world as enemies. He said in Saudi Arabia all the young people want to get the Americans out.

Sarmadi described with great feeling the suffering of the Palestinians, citing one example of a Palestinian family who lived in Jerusalem, went on holiday and, when they came back, found their flat had been taken over and given to an Argentine Jew.

He didn't like Saddam Hussein at all, but Saddam was being strengthened by what was happening. I asked him whether he thought the Americans were going to attack Iran, after the State of the Union speech by Bush referring to the 'evil axis' – Iran, Iraq and North Korea. He said the speech was slowing down reform in Iran, where of course the Democrats are beginning to erode the dominant power of the Islamic revolution. He was very sensible.

He said, 'The Taliban have caused us terrible problems. We've had two and a half million Afghan refugees from Afghanistan.' He stayed for an hour and twenty minutes. I thanked him again for coming, and I took him out as his car pulled up at exactly the right moment.

When I was in the bedroom there was a funny fishy smell, which usually means an electrical fire. I pulled out the plug from the fire under the mantelpiece, and it was absolutely burning and black. I'll have to have the electricians in.

Wednesday 6 February
To the House of Commons, and two Labour Members came and sat next to me. We were talking about Chris Mullin. One said, 'I simply do not understand Chris Mullin. He was so radical, and now he's simply fallen in love with Blair.' The other said, 'He goes to Blair and comes back with an absolutely minor amendment to the Terrorism Bill – there'll be a review in ten years' time – and he tries to sell it to us as a concession.' They were both very scornful.

Thursday 7 February
At 12.30 the BBC World Service rang me up about the new citizenship oath that people have to take. Blunkett has produced wording printed on top of the Union Jack, in which every immigrant has to swear allegiance to the Queen and the United Kingdom. It is utterly outrageous, and I said so!

The Government has forced through the public/private partnership for the London Tube. Figures were shown to indicate that it would be better to use the public/private partnership because the Government allocates a 6 per cent increase in efficiency to any private company, so obviously that makes them much cheaper. I thought Byers came out on telly as a really slippery guy.

Blair has gone to Africa. Last year, our arms supply to Africa multiplied fourfold, and when questioned in the House yesterday, he had to admit that arms are being supplied to both sides in the Congo civil war. He said, 'Don't forget there are jobs are stake'!

Saturday 9 February
The Iranian Ambassador who came to see me the other day has been downgraded to the rank of Chargé d'Affaires as a tit-for-tat because the Iranian Government would not accept the latest British nominee for Ambassador to Tehran on the grounds that he was a spy and Jewish.

Wednesday 13 February
Had a terrible problem with my electricity supply. London Electricity came to cut me off, saying I'd transferred to npower. I said I hadn't. I rang npower, but they didn't know anything about it. I rang London Electricity; they gave me a reference number. I rang npower again; they said it was a mistake. I rang London Electricity back, and they said this happens two or three times a day in London. What an outrage it is! Anyway – the lights went off too later in the day. I don't know why, but all the lights in the area went off.

Sunday 17 February
William, who's been up in the Lake District, was attacked by a group of ten thugs, who punched him in the face. He just took a great kick at one of them, who kicked him in the side, and they all ran off. It's very frightening! His face is all bruised. They know who did it.

Thursday 21 February
There was a ton of mail today. I dealt with it, and then I went to Canary Wharf for lunch with Sir Victor Blank, Chairman of the *Daily Mirror*. I've never been there before, and I felt as if I was visiting a foreign country. I allowed an hour and a half, but on the Central Line and the Jubilee Line it took about half an hour, so I went to have a cup of tea in a restaurant. I lit my pipe and sat in the open air before going to the Four Seasons Hotel. There was a range of guests: Alan Milburn, the Secretary of State for Health; the Israeli Ambassador; Baron Paul of Marylebone, who's Indian and a steel owner in Wales; Mary Nightingale from ITN; Amanda Platell, who used to be Hague's spin doctor; Matt Seaton from *The Guardian*; and Michael Winner, with whom I had a talk. I think it was silly to talk to him, because he'll write it all up in his gossip column.

David Seymour, the political editor of *The Mirror*, was there. I had quite a talk to him, but my hearing is a bit of a problem on these occasions now. I do find it difficult to hear, but I picked up enough to keep the conversation going. Seymour was talking about the development of politics, and I told him what I was engaged in doing. Seymour said Piers Morgan was not interested in politics, and that of course is a bit of a problem if you are the

Editor of what is thought of as the main Labour paper, other than the broadsheets.

The City is like a sort of ghetto. It isn't human at all. It celebrates media and financial power, and I felt uneasy there. But at any rate I had a nice meal.

I came back, then got in my car to go to a broadcast for a Pakistani digital channel broadcasting to seventy-two countries.

Friday 22 February
On Monday, Steve's giving a lecture at the Royal Society with the President of the Society, then he's going next week to America for a week, for the American Chemical Society.

Monday 25 February
To the LSE, for Kofi Annan's lecture. I got there early, sat in the senior common room, and then Anthony Giddens arrived and we had lunch. I insisted on paying for his lunch today because he gave me lunch last time. I described broadly the outline of my theory, that democracy is being crushed. He said, 'Well, when did it ever work?'

Then we talked a bit afterwards in the chairman's dining room. He said, 'Where are all the intellectuals in politics? I mean, for example, there has been nobody since Anthony Crosland.' I said, 'I don't know really, but the attitude to intellectuals is that they're a bit remote.' So I told him a little bit about my own political background. He didn't know anything about it at all. And I said, 'When did you first take an interest in politics?' He said, 'I'm a sociologist. I've written books on sociology, got into trouble in South Africa for writing a book in which the word capitalism was mentioned in the title, which is not allowed.'

He said, 'Maybe I've helped to lever Labour back to power.' I said, 'You speak as if you're an election agent. You're much more than that.'

'Well, the Third Way was just a way of describing how we were approaching it.'

Kofi Annan is a distinguished man, in his sixties (thirteen years younger than me, so he's sixty-four now), tall, slim, Ghanaian, with a career largely in administration. He talked about development and poverty, but he made absolutely no reference to the idea that there was a conflict of interest that lay at the heart of African poverty.

I wanted to ask a question, and when I was called I said, 'Secretary General, you spoke of the post-imperial period, but the greatest empire the world has ever known is now rearming heavily, talking about total-spectrum dominance of space, land, sea and information, and announcing that it intends to use force to change the regimes in countries it doesn't like. How does that fit in?' There was a huge burst of applause from the audience. I didn't mention America by name, and I didn't mention Iraq by name.

When he came to reply, he said, 'Well, I don't speak for the American Government, I speak for the United Nations, and of course Iraq is required by Security Council resolution to disarm, but I'm not in favour of using force. If it is decided by the Security Council to use force, then that will be my problem.' So he gave a specific answer in public. Very interesting, and one can quote that now.

Mary Jay, the widow of Douglas Jay, was at the lecture and I drove her back home. She told me that Blair wanted to nominate Mandelson to be President of the Convention on the Future of Europe, the job that was given to the old French President Giscard d'Estaing, and Jack Straw apparently vetoed it.

Tuesday 26 February
Stephen Byers, having misled people on the *Jonathan Dimbleby* programme on Sunday about his role in respect of Jo Moore and Martin Sixsmith (who'd both been sacked as press officers from his department), made a statement in the House saying that if he'd accidentally misled the House, he regretted it; and he's now fully back in place.

Wednesday 27 February
Dennis Skinner reported back to the Campaign Group on the NEC meeting. He said Iraq was the big question coming up. I described my meeting with Kofi Annan and the Iranian Ambassador. Alan Simpson said the Iraqi Ambassador had been to see him, and they were hoping they might get some help from the Russians and from the IPU (Inter-Parliamentary Union). Diane Abbott said Bush will not go to the United Nations, and we must demand the recall of Parliament if there's any question of bombing Iraq.

Friday 1 March
Caught the train to Kemble, where I was met by a man called Nick Wilson. He drove me to the Sundial Theatre in Cirencester, for my next lecture. About 300 people, absolutely packed, were there. Also, Elinor Goodman was there, with a Channel 4 news team. My talk is changing and developing a bit, and I'm more candid about my own opinions. There were a lot of good questions. I sat on the stage during the interval and chatted to people, smoked my pipe and had a thermos – I didn't have much time to drink tea. Afterwards a number of people came up, one of whom was the husband of Diana Gould. Diana Gould was the woman who really put Thatcher under pressure at the time of the Falklands by asking her a series of questions on TV about the *Belgrano*.

Mandelson has again been cleared of wrongdoing by an investigation. What job is going to be big enough for him now? And he really is such a nonentity!

Saturday 2 March

We got to Trafalgar Square, and there were 20,000 people there. I was almost the last speaker. I was sitting there, freezing to death on the plinth, on a little cushion I'd brought. All the points had been made, so I said, 'We say "not in our name", but it is in our name. We are responsible. The Government is doing it in our name.' Jim Mortimer had said we must get the trade unions to pass resolutions. Tariq Ali said we must get onto the streets. I said we should follow the advice of Gandhi and offer non-violent resistance. Gandhi got the British Empire out of India, and we've got to adopt the same techniques to get the American Empire out of the Middle East. It was a terribly radical thing to say.

Monday 4 March

I watched a programme about Victoria Beckham, who's married to David Beckham, the football player – an hour and a half. She's a talented singer and dancer, but she is a celebrity, and she was saying how much she liked being famous. It told you so much about the society we live in at the moment, and the wholly evanescent nature of fame, because if she broke a leg or they divorced, it would all be over in a week. But there you are: that is life in Britain 2002.

Wednesday 6 March

I went to the Campaign Group, where there was some informal discussion as to whether Gordon Brown shouldn't now replace Tony Blair as Prime Minister. I had been saying at least Gordon wouldn't go to war, because he wouldn't want to spend the money. The general feeling is that Gordon would be better. Of course I've never believed in personality politics and I don't want to be the first one to say Blair should go, but that idea is now spreading a bit, and that probably is the best way of bringing pressure to bear on Blair.

A woman rang me the other day and said, 'Tony, I've got a real problem. I find when I make my tea it goes cold very quickly. What should I do?' I said, 'Well, if you go to a camping shop, you can get a thermos mug.' 'Oh, that's marvellous!' she said and rang off.

Sunday 10 March

Drove up to Highgate Cemetery to commemorate Marx's death on 14 March 1883. I noticed that communists are all old; when I say old, I mean sixties to seventies. It was quite an international gathering. The Cuban Ambassador and Minister were there, and laid a wreath on the grave. Ken Gill, whom I admire, took me up to the Cuban Ambassador and said, 'Would it be possible for Tony to come to Cuba?' The ambassador said, 'Any time!'

Some white flowers were laid by a young man from the Chinese

Embassy. I stood in front of a huge bust of Marx, granite, on top of a granite block – it's a massive thing! – and I spoke for about twelve minutes.

A Los Angeles newspaper has listed seven countries which the United States might target for nuclear weapons, including China and Russia. Stark staring bonkers! It is going to make it very difficult for Blair to carry through support for an attack on Iraq, but that there is an attack on Iraq being planned is now beyond any doubt whatever.

Tuesday 12 March

I just couldn't get round to answering letters, I don't know why. I had lunch, and then I wrote my *Morning Star* column, in effect drawing attention to what was happening in Iraq, and saying that just as Eden lost his job at the time of Suez, this could happen again. It was the boldest I've ever been.

Cheney has gone to the Middle East, where I believe King Abdullah II of Jordan has said it would be a catastrophe to attack Iraq. Apparently, just about a hundred MPs signed an Early Day Motion, seventy-five of them Labour MPs, so there will be a bit of a problem if Blair does go ahead with this. People just drift into assenting by default to things that should never, ever happen, and I felt there are no safeguards nowadays against abuse of power. Governments can do what they like.

There was an interesting message from a Democrat senator, listing all the things that had been repealed by the Patriot Act. Apparently, there are 2,000 people in America who have been detained without trial.

Wednesday 13 March

I bought a standard pensioner ticket to Truro, but I thought I'd upgrade to first class because I wanted to have a smoke, and it was a bit quieter. The ticket collector – the train manager, as they call them now – wouldn't accept a penny. He said, 'My father is such an admirer of yours.'

So anyway, it was really warm. It was four and a half hours down to the beautiful West Country – I felt very nostalgic, because of course I was the Member for Bristol for thirty-three years.

Got to Truro. The Bishop of Truro, Bill Ind, a man of sixty, maybe sixty-five now, drove me to the Bishop's house, Lis Escop, overlooking the water some mile or two from Truro. He'd been a parish priest, he was a socialist who had worked with the Labour Party. I met his wife, Frances, and we had a cup of tea together. They were charming.

To the cathedral, and there was John Ollis, whom I used to know in the Bristol group in 1960, and his daughter Kate. There were about a thousand people in the cathedral, mainly older people, and I gave a lecture and had questions – couldn't hear any of them, but fortunately the Bishop put me right.

The last question was 'If Jesus was still alive, would he be a member of the Labour Party?' I replied, 'Who am I to suggest here in this cathedral and in the presence of two bishops that Jesus is not still alive?'

In my talk I had referred to Swampy, the eco-warrior, and someone came up afterwards and said, 'I'm a friend of Swampy's!'

Thursday 14 March

I got up at seven. I heard on the news that the United Nations Security Council had voted for a Palestinian state, the first time the Americans have not vetoed it. They obviously went along with it because they want to keep the Middle East quiet while they plan their war against Iraq.

Wednesday 20 March

Spoke to Stephen tonight, and would you believe it, someone from the Royal Society of Chemistry came into Stephen's office in Burlington House and said, 'Bill Clinton is shopping in Jermyn Street', so Stephen rushed over to two black cars and lots of security people and went up to Clinton and said, 'You met my father, Tony Benn, the other day.' 'Oh, I remember him very well,' said Clinton. 'I am a great admirer of his and I've heard all about him from Saffron Burrows.' He held Stephen's hand throughout the whole conversation. An amusing story.

Thursday 21 March

To St Martin-in-the-Fields for Peter Shore's memorial service.

Michael Foot, Barbara Castle, Iain Duncan Smith for the Opposition; there were masses of peers, and people I hadn't seen for a very long time.

About half-past ten, Liz, Peter's widow, arrived. There were four addresses: Jack Straw first because he'd been Peter's PPS; then me; and Gwyneth Dunwoody, whom the audience applauded; and Crispin (Biffy) Shore, who spoke at the end. It was very moving. I broke down, as I always do at memorials.

It was a really lovely event. Peter was a man of great intellectual power, great commitment, and passionately hostile to the European Union. He joined the Bruges Group, which was of course Thatcher's great instrument. I took a different view, and although we were close friends, during the period of the deputy leadership he was hostile, and it did have some impact on our friendship. My children all knew the Shores, up until the late Seventies, I guess.

Friday 22 March

Mrs Thatcher, who's had one stroke already, has been told she may never speak again. I was asked to comment on *Newsnight* and Channel 4 News and I refused, because I didn't feel this was the moment to say anything nasty, as she would be lying in bed at home watching the telly, and I just thought that was unkind.

Wednesday 27 March

Latish start; I don't get up very early. The newspapers had an account of a meeting held in Lambeth in support of Commander Paddick, who is tremendously popular there, but got hammered by the tabloids, (a) because he was gay, (b) because a former lover of his reported that he'd smoked cannabis, and (c) because he put on his website that he found the idea of anarchism interesting.

Anyway, 400 people turned up – my editor was among them as she lives in Lambeth – and apparently he got a terrific reception. A standing ovation. So if you want good policing, have somebody closer to the people.

Sunday 31 March

At 5.15 a.m. I woke up and my left wrist was hurting, and it began to come up my arm, and then I felt something in the middle of my chest and I actually thought I was having a stroke or a heart attack. It gave me a bit of a fright.

I realise that in old age you are loved, but you're also controlled, you're marginalised, and you're weaker. I mentioned that to Lissie, and she said, 'Oh, that's just the position women are in all the time!' which I thought was very shrewd.

Thursday 4 April

At 4.30 Maureen Cleave came to interview me for *Saga Magazine,* as I was seventy-seven yesterday. I looked her up on the Internet, and she was the person who interviewed John Lennon of the Beatles, who said, 'We're more popular than Jesus Christ', which caused a tremendous row. She said he was misunderstood. What he was saying was that we live in such a crazy world that people like the Beatles are seen to be more popular than Jesus. But at any rate, she knew them well.

Saturday 6 April, North Devon

Up about 7.30, had breakfast in the Commodore Hotel in Instow and then Ruth Winstone drove me to Bideford Town Hall for the Manor Court Ceremony. I must say, it was a fascinating occasion.

The Manor Court goes back many hundreds of years. Originally, the manor was owned privately, by a landowner who used to make the laws, and it acted as a court, but also heard petitions. In 1881 the town council bought the manor, and so they had the responsibility of administering the manor as well as the local authority. The 'steward' of the manor is the Town Clerk of Bideford. The current Mayor of Bideford is Annie Brenton, the first woman Labour mayor.

The whole ceremony was quite extraordinary. The Mayor had her robes and three-cornered hat, her husband had robes, the councillors had robes and the Beadle had a robe and a three-cornered hat and carried the mace.

There was a man called the Tythingman, whose job it was to collect the tithes for the church. It was absolutely medieval in character! The town council is now elected and the local Liberal Democrat MP, John Burnett, was there, and the town mayors of Barnstable, Northam and Torrington.

The Reverend Peter Knock and the town councillors were all there dressed in various outfits.

I should add that the Manor Court began, of course, with a minute's silence for the death of the Queen Mother. The whole thing was a local reproduction of the medieval Parliament.

The 'jury' then left the court to consider the Townspeople's petitions, and while they were away I had to make my speech. I spoke for about twelve minutes, and I said I particularly want a discussion. That wasn't exactly what normally happens, but the questions were good. I should add that after my speech, the jurors came back and reported on the petitions, such as the need to have more trees, the problem of cars reversing out of the supermarket car park, and all sorts of parochial but important matters. I enjoyed it very much. There are only two or three Labour councillors in Bideford; it's entirely Liberal Democrat – i.e., West Country Conservative!

Monday 8 April
To the lying in state of the Queen Mum in the Houses of Parliament. I went with Josh, who had seen Churchill's coffin (when he thought he was going to the Lyons steak house) and wanted to see this. The Royal Company of Archers were standing guard – these men, in their fifties or sixties, in Scottish dress, with feathers in their caps, leaning on their bows, with three arrows in their belts. Some people had been queuing for five hours! There were children there, and baby buggies, and people in wheelchairs.

The establishment desperately wants to keep the monarchy going, and the death of the Queen Mother has given them a huge opportunity. By creating this great event, people want to come, and they come in the spirit of festival; people are sad she's gone because she'd been there for a long time, but there's no genuine grief of any kind; it's curiosity. The Houses of Parliament love it because they so much prefer being a museum than a debating chamber.

Monday 15 April
Secretary of State Colin Powell is in Israel; all he does is step up the criticism of Arafat and says he must stop the violence. But Arafat has no policemen, no power; he's sitting in a little room without light or heat. It's ludicrous. It just indicates Bush's total commitment to the Israeli cause and his bitter hostility to the Muslims and the Arabs and the Palestinians and everybody else. It's terribly serious.

Tuesday 16 April

To Durham and the Blackhall Working Men's Club, where there were about 200 people for the unfurling of the new banner of Blackhall Colliery, which closed in 1987. I was thrilled, because on the banner are Keir Hardie at the top, A. J. Cook, the leader of the miners in the 1926 General Strike, Nye Bevan and myself, the only one who isn't a miner, and the only one they've ever included on a banner before he died – they normally wait in case the guy sells out, and they told me, 'We didn't think you would!'

The Merton Colliery Band played, then I made a speech and answered a few questions, and then unfurled the banner. It was beautiful. On the back is Tommy Hepburn, whom I commemorated on a postage stamp when I was Postmaster General. It was very moving actually, and I sat in the Working Men's Club just looking at all these people. And I felt lonely. I wished Caroline was there, because we've done so many of these things together.

Sunday 21 April

I woke up at six. I didn't have a good night because of anxiety about the lecture this evening at the Old Vic Theatre, but I got up slowly, read the papers and spent the day just gradually preparing. I lay down for a little rest after lunch, got to the Old Vic about twenty to five; I was in Lilian Baylis's dressing room. There was a photo call, lots of photographers – *The Times*, *Daily Express* were there – and it was so hot, I took off my jacket and was in my braces and a red tie, almost open-necked. The informality of it is nice.

The whole family turned up, and friends and David Davis (the Chairman of the Tory Party), Jane Asher – the last time I met her was in Canada in about 1967 – David Gentleman. During the interval I sat with my legs dangling over the stage, signing books and sipping tea, and then we had the questions and answers, and that went on till about half-past nine; I got questions about Enoch Powell, about Iraq.

Then at the end, I went up to the bar for the party where I was able to announce that David Davis and I were going to do a joint meeting at the Royal Festival Hall.

I wore my little hearing aids – I bought them direct-mail for £37 – they look absurd, but they did allow me to hear the questions. I must go and have proper ones done.

Wednesday 24 April

Campaign Group at six o'clock. They're now talking about 'post-New Labour'. John Edmonds took up the betrayal by the Government of employment rights vis-à-vis Europe. He said that the Social Chapter had been set aside because Mandelson had reached a private deal with the CBI that under no circumstances would it be extended or even applied. He gave a number of examples in Britain: that we're committed to so many days public holidays in Europe, but in Britain the holidays include Bank Holidays and public holidays, so they are taken off the entitlement to paid holidays; parental leave only applied if the baby had been born after the date that the Social Chapter came in, so that excluded a lot of people; part-timers were being held back because in Britain they said they could find no comparisons where most of the work is part-time; on information rights – the rights of workers to know what's going on in their companies – Britain had imposed a six-year delay. He talked about Blair's relations with Berlusconi. It was an extremely strong and clear speech.

Then Alan Simpson asked, 'Do the TUC support health privatisation?' and Edmonds said, 'No, the trade unions are against privatisation; and private healthcare anyway gives you far less security, because they don't have Accident & Emergency or intensive-care units at all.' I asked him whether he thought the Stability Pact (enforcing financial controls on EU countries) was forcing Gordon Brown to do all the privatisation, and he said he didn't really think that was the case, it was more of a cock-up. Of course, Edmonds is very pro-Europe.

Thursday 25 April
Jean Corston phoned and we had a bit of a political talk. She confirmed that Peter Mandelson is completely out, Number 10 has nothing to do with him, and he's more trouble than he's worth.

Then I had a phone call about a man who's been living in makeshift accommodation in Parliament Square for nearly a year, with placards against aggression towards Iraq, and Westminster Council are evicting him tomorrow. Brian Haw is his name; he's fifty-four, he's a Christian, he went to Belfast to talk to the Catholics and Protestants, and he went to Cambodia, he went through the Berlin Wall, he went to Russia, just preaching peace. I went to Westminster and had a nice talk to him. I used my mobile phone to enable him to do a broadcast.

In the afternoon I had a bit of a rest, and I was terribly depressed. I thought of Caroline. Where is she? Her body, which I loved and knew so well, was taken away and burned, and she's not there, and all the things I should have done for her, all the time I should have given to her, I didn't give. I think she was happy, but I'll never ever see her again till the day I die, and after that, who knows? Death is such a final thing. It hits you sometimes, and it's hit me today in a terrible way.

Friday 26 April
I had a lovely handwritten letter from Cherie Blair today replying to mine about a possible honour for Mary Wilson. She assured me she was certainly on the case.

To Marion Miliband's house; I'm very fond of her. It was an interesting dinner because her son, Edward, who works in the Treasury, was there. He must be about thirty now. He used to work in my office, as a schoolboy years ago.

The Brazilian Ambassador and his wife were there. He had been one of Ralph Miliband's pupils, and quite radical. He was describing how the Americans had ousted Bustani, Director General of the Organisation for the Prohibition of Chemical Weapons, and how they tried to stop a man called Blix from an inspection of Iraq, and described the absolute brutality of American power. He said it was remarkable that Chávez had won in Venezuela, but he had been a bit of a populist and alienated the middle class, and he'd have to be a bit more careful in the future.

Edward talked a bit. He said the Third Way is finished; nobody's interested in the Third Way any more. Anthony Giddens just hovers round trying to put an ideological cloak around whatever is being discussed; his latest plan apparently is regional government, this is the next really big thing for New Labour. But when I asked Edward if he'd like to become a Member of Parliament, he was sufficiently ambivalent to make me think he would. I like Edward very much, and he's always affectionate and respectful, which is quite uncalled for, but welcome.

Sunday 28 April

Blair has made a pledge that he would cut street crime by the middle of September, which is a complete illusion. He comments on everything – on the Damilola Taylor trial, on Beckham's foot – he just can't resist it.

He has come out with a ludicrous plan that parents who can't control their children will have their Child Benefit cut. Meanwhile, Blunkett is sticking to his argument about swamping by immigrants; he's trying to deal with Le Pen by copying him.

Tuesday 30 April

A Channel 4 TV crew were coming this morning to do an obituary of Barbara Castle, because apparently she's had pneumonia. Then they rang and said could I do Jim Callaghan at the same time? When Gary Gibbon of Channel 4 arrived, he asked if I could do Denis Healey as well, so I sat there and did all three, and then I said I've got one more. He said, 'What do you mean?' I said, 'I'd like to do my own obituary.' So he said, 'Right, go ahead! Look in the camera.' So I looked at the camera and all I said was: 'As this is the last opportunity I'll have, I'd like to express my thanks to my parents and my two brothers for all the support when I was young; to Caroline, who was an inspiration to me over fifty years; and to my children and grandchildren; and to all the people who've supported me and encouraged me, and I hope I've encouraged them in return. I hope I haven't given offence, but I've just said what I thought, and that's what politics is about.' He said, 'Oh, that's marvellous', so I said, 'Well, I shall check it on transmission!'

Friday 3 May
Barbara Castle died today. Her death is a great loss to the movement. People feel that she was the conscience of the Party, speaking with passion and conviction, a figure who's survived from the old left of the Thirties right through to 2002.

Monday 6 May
To Euston Station for a meeting in Liverpool. I was at the station by half-past six, so I caught an early train, I bought a second-class pensioner return for thirty-two quid, and a first-class return would have been 258 quid – an unbelievable difference. The ticket collector and I talked, and he said, 'Come and have a puff in my cabin', so I followed him to the end of the train and smoked my pipe in his little compartment.

When I was at Liverpool Lime Street waiting to come back, a man came up to me. I asked him, 'What do you do?' 'Oh, I drive the newspapers to Smith's newsagents on the station,' he said. 'I've just bought a CD of Chomsky's speeches – what a brilliant man!' Only in Liverpool would you get an ordinary guy tell you he'd been listening to Chomsky! It is an amazing place.

Had a big lunch, because I hadn't eaten anything all day, and felt much better.

Wednesday 8 May
A suicide bombing in Israel yesterday killed sixteen, and Ariel Sharon has immediately broken off his talks with Bush and rushed home, and there will be massive military action now by the Israelis. But that totally fails to deal with suicide bombings. Bush has added Cuba to the axis of evil, so the thing is now mad imperialism, which may or may not secure military success, but will lead to a trail of disaster, because even now it is admitted that the British troops in Afghanistan have utterly failed to uncover any al-Qaeda or Taliban centres, or to locate Osama Bin Laden. All this talk about humanitarian aid, and 'this time we mustn't let the Afghans down' and all that rubbish, is just proving to be completely false.

Thursday 9 May
I went to Charing Cross Hospital for a hearing test, and it was a difficult journey because that's where I used to drive Caroline for four years, backwards and forwards along that road, and I dreaded it. A nice young woman in her mid-twenties, I should think, tested my ears. They haven't changed since they were last tested. She gave me a new set of hearing aids, which are programmable, and every time I go near the Health Service, I think how wonderful it is.

Tuesday 14 May
I went to Labour Action for Peace, of which I'm President. Jeremy
Corbyn's just off to Palestine and Israel, hoping to see Mordechai Vanunu.
He saw the Israeli Ambassador here, who was unhelpful and unfriendly
and complained about all these people who write letters to him.

I spoke to Tam Dalyell, who had just been up at Barlinnie prison in
Scotland, where a man is serving a life sentence for the Lockerbie bombing,
and Tam is absolutely persuaded he is innocent. Tam went to see Gaddafi
with an IPU delegation. He says Gaddafi's just paying two billion dollars
compensation to the families of the dead because he wants to be readmitted
to the international trading community and get the American sanctions
lifted. Tam is a shrewd guy and he thinks the whole thing was set up.

Thursday 16 May
Stephen Byers seems to have told a press lunch at the House of Commons
that there might be legislation in the Queen's Speech preparing for a
referendum on the European constitution, and this has been hotly denied
by Number 10, no doubt as a result of pressure from Gordon Brown at
Number 11. Philip Gould has been putting out comments that a
referendum can be won, but I'm not so sure. The victory of the right in the
Netherlands, in Denmark, in parts of Germany, Heider in Austria, the
extraordinary result for Le Pen in France, will, I think, stimulate the worst
type of nationalism; but it might well have an impact on the outcome of a
referendum, and if Blair is in the middle of a war with Iraq at the moment
the referendum comes, I think there will be a big change. The Third Way
social democracy, which destroyed Jospin and brought Berlusconi into
power in Italy, and could undermine Schröder in Germany, looks to me as
if it's not electorally attractive any more.

Friday 17 May
The train was delayed by an hour, and I was terribly worried I wouldn't get
to Cornwall in time. I was told it was a lightning strike at Liskeard, so I
asked the ticket collector, 'What was that about?' 'Oh,' he said, 'that was an
act of God Almighty.' How words change their meaning! A lightning strike
means a lightning strike, but I just assumed it meant unofficial industrial
action.

Saturday 18 May
Quite a day! Woke up at 6.30, and left for the Burford Festival at about ten
to eight. Got there in an hour and fifteen minutes. A beautiful morning,
driving through lovely rolling countryside – it couldn't have been nicer. I
had my thermos of course, and a Mars Bar, and various necessary bits of
equipment. Parked in the car park; by then it had got so overcast I took my
coat.

It was raining for the whole length of the Festival, and I got totally soaked. I was called on at the end to give a presentation, but before that we had Lindis Percy, a formidable woman who had been in prison twelve times, very knowledgeable about all the Star Wars developments and utterly committed to stopping them. Bruce Kent was there, who's a sweetie – I'm fond of him.

I drove back, and there was tons of traffic coming out of Oxford and out of London, but little going in, and I was going at about eighty-five miles an hour, when all of a sudden there was a terrible banging in the engine, and smoke coming out of the bonnet, so I put on my hazard lights and pulled over to the hard shoulder – a difficult thing to do on the motorway – and stopped.

I rang the AA, who located where I was, and within about three or four minutes a fire engine arrived with five firemen. They opened the hood and threw buckets of water in. Then two policemen arrived in a car, and I talked to them. Then, about three-quarters of an hour later, the AA man turned up and he said, 'You've either got to have a new car or a new engine.' So then they had to get the truck to drive me home.

It was funny, because I said to one of the firemen, 'It must be awful having to deal with all these dead bodies in the big motorway smashes' and he said, 'Well, I'd rather do that than sit in the House of Commons all night.' I thought that's an interesting parallel – dead bodies on the motorway compared to boring MPs.

Got home and Melissa picked me up, and drove me to the Lyttelton Theatre on the South Bank, to see *PowerBook* by Jeanette Winterson – it's really the story of a lesbian love affair taking place on the Internet. Fiona Shaw is the lead figure, the psychotherapist, and she falls in love with a married woman played by Saffron Burrows. It's quite explicit sexually. Afterwards I felt ought to go to the reception just to congratulate Saffron, and she was sweet, gave me several big hugs and spoke to Fiona, and I had a quick word with Deborah Warner, the producer.

Tuesday 21 May
I realised I was going to lose my lovely old Ford Fiesta – J708 YPU – and I was overcome with sadness. I've had that car for eleven years and it was second-hand when I bought it. I thought, why do I care about an old car? It's only a bit of metal; and then I realised that in that car I'd driven Caroline to the hospital, we'd driven to Stansgate, we'd done so much together, and that I was losing a link with a vehicle that she knew as well as I did, and I'd never see it again. It's a write-off, I should think. It made me realise that I could never leave this house. I've left the Commons, left Chesterfield, I've lost Caroline, and I do depend on looking round and seeing things, and imagining her sitting in bed every morning when I took her breakfast. It's not the property, it's the memory associated with it that's so valuable.

Wednesday 29 May
At half-past eleven, Chris Mullin collected me by car from Durham and took me to Sunderland. I hadn't been there for some time, and he drove me round the area where all the new big office blocks are, which I must say was quite impressive; you think of Sunderland as a rundown ship-building town, with the pits closed and everything, and here was some sign of what you might call capitalist development.

Then he took me to council house estates. Some were made up of quite decent post-war housing, and then as we got to a certain point the houses were all boarded up. There's a lot of crime, a lot of vandalism, and people who'd bought from the council under the Thatcher right-to-buy scheme are now living in between five or six boarded-up houses. It's really quite dangerous to be there, Chris said. This blight is spreading, and Sunderland has actually got more council houses than it needs. What's really required is massive refurbishing and reconstruction, but that would involve public money, and the Treasury won't let them have it.

Chris is passionately against smoking, so I smoked in his garden, and when I came into the house I put the pipe in my pocket. Went to the loo, and when I came out the jacket was burning, fortunately not onto Chris's carpet. He doused it with water. Sarah (his elder daughter who is twelve) and Emma (who's six, I think) are sweet little girls, absolutely beautiful.

At some stage in the day, Chris said he had a message from David Miliband that he had been made an Education Minister in the government reshuffle, so he wouldn't be able to come tonight to my talk in South Shields.

I rang Hilary, and he said he'd been moved himself from the Department for International Development to the Home Office, to look after prisons and legal matters, under David Blunkett. It is a big promotion for him; there are hazards to it, because Blunkett is the most authoritarian Home Secretary we've had in my lifetime, so Hilary's got to be careful. But it's a great thing to have been elected in '99, made a minister in 2001, promoted in 2002.

Thursday 30 May
I spoke to Hilary tonight, who is very excited. He was terribly proud that this morning in *The Times*, which divided ministers into Blairites, Brownites and Independents, he was in the independent category. That was a good sign.

Friday 31 May
The Guardian this morning published a poll of its readers, who had nominated the 'greatest Britons' of the last fifty years. John Lennon came top, Barbara Castle came ninth and, believe it or not, I came equal twelfth,

ahead of Churchill and Ted Heath and the Queen herself, who were equal thirteenth. It's a quite extraordinary turn-up for the book.

Reflecting on the Jubilee celebrations this year, I concluded that the middle class, or rather the economic and political establishments in Britain and Europe and America, are more confident than they've ever been. The European Union is able to prevent any future government from taking radical measures. The Americans are able to enforce their will through their enormous military power. The IMF (International Monetary Fund) and the World Trade Organisation enforce capitalist or market forces all over the world, and although there is resistance, I can't say it looks as if it's going to produce any immediate effect.

Tuesday 11 June
I went to get my new car to drive to the Commons, and found that the back window had been broken into and the radio stolen. When I bought it ten days ago, I was shown the 'safety device' that enables you to remove the front of the radio and disable it. But someone had gone in – at least they weren't able to drive it away.

I went today to pick up the Hansard for yesterday, in which Hilary answered Home Office Parliamentary Questions for the first time. The lad is now well launched as a young minister, highly regarded and respected.

Wednesday 12 June
Four Iraqis came to see me by appointment this morning– all members of the Iraqi Communist Party. I hadn't shaved; I was in an awful mess.

They told me there were four problems facing the Iraqi people: one was Saddam and his brutality; secondly, the long-term effect of the 1980s war with Iran; thirdly, the impact of the sanctions; and fourthly, the risk of another major military attack on Iraq from America. All sanctions should be lifted now, because that was the best way of creating circumstances in which Saddam could be replaced. They said the Iraqi Communist Party was against terrorists, but the US was so arrogant they wouldn't listen to what anybody else said. The United States were not interested in democracy, but in putting their own candidate into Baghdad.

I asked, 'If the sanctions are removed and there's no war, how are you going to change Iraq?' They said, 'Well, we have progressive forces supporting us.' I asked about Kurdistan. They said that the Kurds would suffer terribly if there was a war. Up until September 11, Saddam was reluctantly accepted by the Americans to avoid destabilising the area, but now he's not, and there'd be terrible bloodshed for the Kurds if there's a war, and the Shi'ites would certainly suffer as well. They said the United States doesn't want a united Iraq.

They were amusing and friendly, and cultivated, and I agreed really with everything they said. They warned me not to make it look as if I sympathised with Saddam, by opposing the sanctions. I said, 'I don't, any more than you do.' The Americans were interested in the Iraqi Communist Party as a source of information, but under no circumstances did the Americans want a progressive Iraq under a democratic leader.

Thursday 13 June
The car was returned from the garage with a new radio and the window repaired, and the bill was £478. I hope that doesn't happen every week.

Friday 14 June
Had a lovely talk to Stephen, and he told me that he'd been invited by the European Commission to chair a meeting on European Union science policy. On the panel, I think, are going to be some European prime ministers – a most staggering invitation! So we had a good talk about that, and he seemed very pleased about it.

Wednesday 19 June
I wrote to Cherie Blair today, because yesterday she had said something about understanding young Palestinians who were suicide bombers, without endorsing suicide bombing. Of course she's been criticised, so I wrote her a little note saying, 'Thank you for what you said. It had to be said. Don't let the media get you down. Love, Tony.' I think she needs a bit of support.

Friday 21 June
I woke up early and switched on the television, and the England/Brazil game had just begun, and I heard a huge roar and Michael Owen scored. Then, because I found it a bit unsettling, I turned the volume down and just kept an eye on the score, so I missed the two goals that put Brazil in the lead, but David Seaman, the English goalkeeper, apparently missed a shot he should have caught, and so England was beaten. England's out of the Cup. I must say, although I'm not in any way a football fan, I was hoping we'd do well. It's better than war, and you can't win everything, but they'll all be coming home tonight, all very depressed.

Tuesday 25 June
To Westminster, and I walked over to Parliament Square to have a talk to Brian Haw, who has been sitting for over a year opposite the House of Commons with placards opposing the war in Afghanistan, an attack on Iraq, war, and so on. Westminster Council is trying to evict him on the grounds he's blocking the highway. Next to him there's another stall in favour of hunting.

CNN and ABC have filmed him there, he's been all over Arab television and is described as 'the good man of Westminster'. He's very tanned and brown, and he's a thoughtful, serious guy.

Thursday 27 June

WorldCom, one of the biggest corporations in the world, forged and published fraudulent profit figures, and has now gone bust, like Enron. Although the whole thing is presented as if it were just an accounting error, it is actually the very nature of capitalism, and that is something to think about. Whether it will produce a serious recession or not, I don't know. George Soros was on television saying this could all be put right; he attributed it just to the fact that the boom got out of control, and this was a necessary correction. But a lot of people's pensions will be affected, and for them it's not just a little accounting error, it's their livelihood. So I think it will produce quite a number of interesting effects in terms of general perceptions of globalisation and privatisation.

Sunday 30 June

Train to Castle Cary station in Somerset, where I was met by a lad from the Workers' Beer Company. Now, I'd heard about the Workers' Beer Company, it's a good socialist group, and it's got a sister company called Clause 4.

I was taken by him to meet Mike Eavis, who runs the Glastonbury Festival. It's been going apparently since 1970, and it's so successful they've had to put a steel fence round it to prevent people breaking in. God knows what it cost to hold the Festival, but everyone who goes pays £98, that's a lot of money!

The Festival area is twice the size of Bath, with only a couple of policemen. They've got stewards, they've got medical facilities, they've got shops selling all sorts of things, and it's all set up for three or four days every year and then taken down again – absolutely amazing! I found it thrilling. There were lots of young people, but quite a number of older people as well. It wasn't just teenagers by any means. I'd say the average age was twenty-five, thirty, and there were quite a few people of fifty, sixty.

I was taken to the Workers' Beer Tent, and had a cup of tea and talked to them. Then they took me to the Mandela Bar, which is a huge place, and because all the people there are volunteers, they trust them to take the cash. Instead of giving vouchers for a beer and so on, to prevent fraud, they just rely on everybody.

Monday 1 July

Dinner with friends at the House of Commons. We sat on the Terrace, and who should come along but David Blunkett, with four friends, all with guide dogs, and I had a chat to him and introduced him to all my guests. I said, 'I hope you're looking after my son', and he said, 'I hope he'll keep me on the straight and narrow', and I said, 'That's exactly what I told him to do!'

Tuesday 2 July

The bombing yesterday by the Americans of an Afghan wedding party, where dozens and dozens of quite innocent people were killed, has just been brushed aside by Geoff Hoon and by the Americans: 'In a war against terrorists, innocent people get killed.' I think the gap between Bush and Blair is bound to widen, because Blair can't maintain his present position.

Sunday 7 July

The reports now in the papers suggest that not only are the Americans planning to invade Iraq from Kuwait, from Turkey and from Jordan, with a quarter of a million troops, but also Britain is apparently ready to make 20,000 troops available. I find it terribly depressing.

The Vice-President of Afghanistan has been assassinated. The world is in a state of turmoil. Terribly, terribly depressing.

Monday 8 July

Half a million people are starving to death in Angola, and of course the news is about preparing for the war against Iraq. There's no sense of proportion that the saving of life is what matters. It's about the boosting of American and British military power.

Thursday 11 July

In the afternoon I was so tired I caught a taxi to the University of London, for the Marxism 2002 debate with Paul Foot. Paul spoke first. He's affectionate and friendly. He loved Caroline. Paul asked me to go and have a meal afterwards; I was frightfully tired, but I did go. He and his partner, Claire have an eight-year-old daughter called Kate and a son by a previous marriage called Tom. John Rees and Lindsey German from the Socialist Workers' Party were there. Piers Corbyn, Jeremy's brother, who is a weather expert, told me he was sceptical about global warming, and promised to send me his analysis. I was told to be wary about environmentalists because they're the ones pushing nuclear power, which I thought was interesting. I don't normally go out socially, and I haven't got a lot of friends, but I enjoyed it very much, and I was dropped home, absolutely exhausted, and went to bed.

Tuesday 16 July

Oh no, no, I mustn't forget the really big news today that Derek Simpson, the left-wing candidate, has unexpectedly defeated Kenneth Jackson, as General Secretary of the union Amicus (the union of manufacturing, finance, science and engineering workers). Jackson and Barry Reamsbottom have both refused to accept their defeat by left candidates.

I've never met Derek Simpson, but I'm absolutely delighted.

Wednesday 17 July
I went to the House of Commons, had a haircut, talked to Alice Mahon on the Terrace, and she told me that Scott Ritter, the former weapons inspector in Iraq, had said that the Americans planned in October to bomb for sixty days and then send a quarter of a million troops in with 35,000 British troops.

Sunday 21 July
I was taken up to do *Breakfast with Frost* (actually with Peter Sissons), and when I got there, who should I see but Derek Simpson, the newly elected General Secretary of Amicus. He reminded me so much of Harry Perkins in the film *A Very British Coup*. He was interviewed by Sissons, and he was modest, and reassuring. He said he was a member of the Labour Party and wanted Labour to succeed, and so on.

Then I went on, and Peter Sissons had a little clip of me at Glastonbury, and at the meeting yesterday, talking to protestors, and speaking to the miners in 1985. The line, of course, they're all taking now is: are we back to the bad old days?

So I turned it round and said, 'We can't go back to the old days, because that would mean Thatcherism', and it threw him completely. 'I believe in the public services. After all, the BBC is a public service,' I said. 'The Director General gets very well paid, and quite properly so.' He couldn't cope with that. I was quite pleased with it.

Tuesday 23 July
To Salisbury station, from where I walked to Ted Heath's house, which is just by the cathedral. As I arrived somebody was leaving who'd obviously had lunch with Ted. A policeman opened the gate and I rang the bell, and who should be ambling towards me, but Ted himself.

He was wearing a check shirt outside his trousers, a pair of slacks, socks, but no shoes because his feet are so swollen, and he took me inside. His secretary, Patsy, brought me a cup of tea, and I had a really lovely talk to him for about an hour and ten minutes. I had rung up and told him I'd be a bit early, and did he want to have a snooze after lunch? He said, 'I don't have a snooze when I have distinguished guests to see me', which was nice of him.

It is the most beautiful house. I don't know if it belongs to the cathedral or to him, but it's got a huge garden, perfectly kept, and the house itself is beautifully decorated, full of models of *Morning Cloud* and other boats, and his bust, and signed photographs of him with Clinton and Nixon and the Queen, etc.

He said he had sixteen policemen guarding him. Presumably that would be eight on and eight off at any one time.

I made a note immediately afterwards of what we talked about, but it's a bit higgledy-piggledy. I'll just report it as I noted it down.

Talking about Iain Duncan Smith, I said I presumed he was moving towards a caring Conservatism of the old kind, and Ted said, 'No one will believe him any more because of the fact that he's trying to change his image.'

So I compared it to Neil Kinnock, and he said, 'Yes, yes' because Neil began as a leftie and then ended up trying to persuade everybody that he was a responsible moderate, and seemed to give up so much that he held dear that nobody now believed what he said. 'Exactly,' said Ted.

Then I put to him at some stage that if he had not called the election in March 1974, but had settled with the miners and then appealed to everybody to help him with inflation, he might have won, and he agreed with that.

I asked him about John Major, and he said, 'Oh, he's left politics now and is making millions of pounds abroad.'

He said that, as far as Iraq was concerned, George W. Bush was avenging his brother (he meant his father), George Bush, who had of course failed to carry the war against Iraq to its conclusion in 1991.

He did say, 'You can't go round the world any more without the risk of getting shot!'

So I said, 'Well, apart from Spencer Perceval, we've never had any prime ministerial assassinations, whereas American presidents seem to be assassinated quite frequently.'

'Oh,' he said, 'not frequently enough as far as the present one is concerned!'

He went on, 'The House of Commons is completely dead. They do nothing. What about your chaps?' (This was in respect of the impending war.)

So I said, 'Well, I think a lot of Labour people are very doubtful about it, but you know how loyal they are to the Party. I understand that half the Conservative Party is not keen on it, but of course once the war begins, they'll be loyal to the troops.' He was really trying to see what I could do to get the House of Commons to stop the war.

I asked him whether he'd speak out himself, at least about the need for respecting the UN Charter. He said, 'Not once it begins.'

'Well,' I said, 'I appreciate that, but what about you and Jimmy Carter and Gorbachev and Mandela and Boutros Boutros-Ghali issuing a statement?' So he seemed to take it on board.

He said, as far as Israel is concerned, they will lose in the end, and of course he's right, because Israel cannot maintain itself against the Arab world.

I asked him whether it was true that when he was in Germany before the war, he went to one of the Nuremberg rallies and Hitler actually brushed against his shoulder on his way to the rostrum. He said, yes.

He told me that he used to keep a full diary, and had kept everything since he was thirteen. So I said, 'What's going to happen to them? Churchill College would be the obvious place, because Mrs Thatcher's papers are there.'

He said Thatcher wasn't very well, and confirmed that Blair is a Thatcherite. I asked him about the Cabinet, and he said, 'Blair's Cabinets last about twenty minutes.'

'How long did yours last?'

'Oh, two and a half hours every week!'

So I said, 'You weren't in Mrs Thatcher's Cabinet, of course, but what did Mrs Thatcher say when she was in your Cabinet?'

'Nothing.'

So anyway, that was it. He took me round, showed me the house. He plays the organ and the piano, showed me the music room, where they have musical evenings, and the dining room, where they have dinners. I think he's got a grudging affection for me, and I must say, I was touched that he invited me to come.

He waved at me as I walked towards the gate, which was locked, and a policeman came out and released me.

Wednesday 24 July

I heard from somebody who was at the Parliamentary Labour Party meeting this morning that Blair was absolutely non-committal on the war against Iraq, and also dismissed last Saturday's event as the 'unreconstructed left, who would keep us out of office for ever'.

I just had time to go over to the Queen Elizabeth Conference Centre, where Sir Richard Wilson, the Cabinet Secretary, was having a retirement party. I only got his invitation today, rang up to say I couldn't come, but thought it would be nice to go and see him, and it was packed with people.

Robert Galley was there, the former French minister for scientific research, who once spoke contemptuously about public consultations, and said, 'If you are draining a swamp, you don't consult the frogs', which, given the meaning of 'frog' in English, was comic.

Thursday 25 July

A West Midlands contact, Jerry Langford, rang about a family from Afghanistan who had been detained and tortured by the Taliban, and had their house burned down, escaped to Germany and then managed to get into Britain, and were due to be deported. They had been brought to London airport to go on a 7.55 plane in the morning. The children were being cared for by somebody.

So I decided to write to David Blunkett with all the relevant information. Beverley Hughes in the Home Office has been in charge of the case. Later in the day, I had a phone call from Beverley Hughes's private office, in effect saying nothing doing.

I did say to them at the Home Office, 'Well, is it right to separate the parents from the children?' And they said, 'Beverley Hughes will not allow them to go without their children', so I have a feeling the police are tonight looking for the children to arrest and take them to the airport. But it is an outrageous story. It just turns your stomach!

Friday 26 July

Oh, very funny! *The Mail on Sunday* rang about Iraq, so I told them to look at my column in the *Morning Star*. I faxed it to them; they liked it so much they asked me for another hundred words, and I think that, for the first time ever, *The Mail on Sunday* will reprint an article from a communist paper. It would be amazing.

Sunday 28 July
David Davis, who was sacked as Chairman of the Conservative Party a couple of days ago, rang to say that he hoped we could still go ahead with our debate in October at the Royal Festival Hall, 'unless', he asked, 'you want Teresa May?' (the new Chairman of the Tory Party). I said, 'No, certainly not. Indeed, I think it will probably arouse greater interest now.'

I've always teased David about being the future Leader of the Tory Party, and I think he took it seriously. I think he has a chance, because Duncan Smith isn't up to much.

Tuesday 30 July
Stephen rang from Italy. I said, 'Tell Nita that Derek Simpson has seen the Prime Minister,' so he said, 'Well, speak to her yourself.' Nita came to the phone – and I said, 'Just to let you know that Derek Simpson has seen the Prime Minister.' 'Oh, I fixed that!' she said. Simpson was of course the unexpected victor of the Amicus elections and Nita, Blair's trade-union adviser, had got Simpson's own phone number from me and arranged the meeting. Blair asked her, 'Where did you get his number from?' and Nita said, 'My father-in-law', and he gave a great laugh.

It's now about half-past nine. I have no food in the house at all. I've eaten everything! I've got no soup left, I've got only a couple of buns, I am out of tea, haven't got any tinned grapefruit, I'm running out of baked beans. No salad. I must say, I'm in a real mess.

Monday 5 August
I spent the morning writing letters, the difficult ones that require thought, and filing and everything.

Maggie O'Kane from *The Guardian* rang up, and said *The Guardian* has started a film unit and want to make a film about the Iraq attacks, and 'We would like you to go to Baghdad and interview Saddam Hussein and present the film.'

So I said, 'Well, I'm terribly busy.'

'Yes, I know, but we'd give you a lot of support.'

I looked at my diary and offered some dates in November. I think it is a good idea, though I suspect the war will have begun by then.

Tam Dalyell has demanded the recall of Parliament, and you know, when I heard that, for the first time I felt it would be nice to be in the House of Commons, where I could be participating. But I have got the freedom that I wouldn't otherwise have.

Thursday 8 August
I went into the Commons today, and I saw Michael Ancram, who I rather
think is still the Conservative spokesman on foreign affairs, so I said, 'Can
I have a word with you about Iraq?'

'Oh, by all means!' he said.

'What do you feel about it all?' I asked him.

'Well,' he said, 'I'm an Atlanticist and I think that the Government will
have to produce evidence of the possession of weapons of mass destruction
and the intent to use them. I think if that were done, there wouldn't be
much of a problem.' He also said to me, 'I'm on the Privy Councillors'
Committee looking into the security services.'

I said, 'Well, how very convenient it is to have that sort of consensus at
the top!' What are called 'Privy Councillor terms' really mean the all-party
coalition at the heart of everything, whereby you can discuss important
affairs with your opponents as Privy Councillors more easily than you can
with your own colleagues in the Party or with the public.

Saddam has made a speech saying 'We'll defend Iraq', described of
course by the BBC as 'defiant', whereas when Bush says he's going to attack
Saddam, that's described as an 'address to the nation'. The way propaganda works is so subtle, but it isn't making an impact on public opinion,
and I imagine Blair's a little worried.

Sunday 11 August
Fifty-four years ago today, in Oxford, I proposed to Caroline, and that was
in my mind all day.

Tom and Margaret Vallins arrived from Chesterfield. They had brought
my miners' bench in the back of the car. Because of the fear that it might
be stolen from my front garden, we brought it in the house and put it in the
front room. The plaque on it says 'Tony Benn, the Miners' Friend', which
is a lovely thing to have.

We had a good old talk about my time as MP in Chesterfield. They said
that there's nothing happening in the Labour Club at all, and the Labour
Party office hadn't been touched since the 2001 election. Looking back on
it now, the whole of the Chesterfield era seems a thousand years away. I do
realise that a curtain has dropped. It's a completely new and different world
now.

Wednesday 14 August, Edinburgh
Went to visit the new Scottish Parliament building.

My old friend Ann Henderson took me to the construction site. It's going
to cost about £260 million and has been much criticised, but the
architecture is fantastic.

They gave me a hard hat and wellington boots and a yellow jacket and
a pass, and we went into the building itself, clambering up scaffolding and

ladders, and I was absolutely exhausted. I mean, this is how you realise you've reached the end of your physical limitations, but it was enjoyable.

Thursday 15 August
I heard on the phone that James, my grandson, Hilary's second son, had got two A-level A grades and a B, and therefore is okay for Jesus College, Oxford.

I spoke to the woman who's working with Maggie O'Kane on this film that they want to call 'Benn in Baghdad' and I pulled out of it. If there's a war, I'll be engaged in campaigns against it, and I can't be just making a television programme – it's absolutely wrong. And also, I doubt if Saddam would give me an interview, because if I arrive with a television crew, he's not going to tell me where he is, in case the Americans find him and assassinate him. So it just won't work, but it was a nice idea.

Tuesday 20 August
This story of the murder of Holly Wells and Jessica Chapman is still going on. They've now charged Ian Huntley with murder, and detained him at Rampton hospital, and his partner, Maxine Carr, has been charged with perverting the course of justice. So whether we'll ever know the truth, I don't know. If he's held to be unfit to plead, we won't know what happened. It's such a horrible story, and the papers are beginning now to talk about the return of capital punishment. Lissie's girls are very distressed.

Thursday 22–Saturday 31 August, Stansgate
Hilary, James and Carrie arrived on Thursday, and we sat up and talked until 2.20 in the morning. Just sat and talked. We are a great family of talkers, going over all the members of the family and what they were doing – it was great fun.

We had a little service, to inter Caroline's ashes in the garden. Dave and June and their children Frances and Piers came over from their cottage, though big Michael and his boy, little Michael, didn't come because they thought it would be too distressing for him. Emily and Daniel played on the cello and violin, and there were flowers, and I read a poem, but I burst into tears.

Now that Caroline is safely in the little grave that we planned, I feel it's a turning point. She's at rest where she wanted to be, and the house is being done, and it is a new start for my life. It's nearly two years since she died, and I've got to make a life again.

The war hysteria is rising in America, but there's a lot of anxiety about it now. I think there's a majority against, and Blair's in real difficulty. If he doesn't support it, he should make it clear that he doesn't, give his reasons and leave it at that. But I don't think he could take that challenge; it would be too big a thing for him to do, and so he will pay a price. All this talk that

President Bush is Winston Churchill warning against the Nazis and all that, there's simply not a parallel of any kind.

There was a memorial service in Ely Cathedral for Holly and Jessica, and that story is such a sad one.

Talked to Hilary about parole policy, because one of the things that's always worried me is that a prisoner cannot get parole if he doesn't admit to his crime. An innocent person can't admit to his crime, unlike a guilty person who finds no difficulty at all in saying, 'Oh yes, I did it, I'm terribly sorry', and so on, and then gets released. So, innocent people are penalised.

Sunday 1 September
On *The World at One* today they said, 'Of course, unlike Britain where there's no debate about Iraq, there really is a lively debate in America.' It's an absolutely bloody lie! They just don't report the debate in Britain. If I'd thought about it at the time, I'd have rung up and complained. But as far as the BBC is concerned, a debate that doesn't take place between important persons isn't a debate, although actually the bottom-up movement has won the day.

Tuesday 3 September
I've got this lovely game with Melissa's children, Hannah and Sarah, in which I say the opposite of what I mean. So I'd say, 'Good evening, Paul', when I meant 'Good morning, Sarah', and she picked that up very quickly. Then if you want to say 'yes', you shake your head from side to side, and if you want to say 'no', you nod. Oh, they picked it up in a flash, had really a lot of fun with that!

Blair gave a press conference at Sedgefield at 2.30, lasting for an hour and a half, in which, not to put too fine a point upon it, he said he had the evidence and – well, he declared war on behalf of Britain in support of America. Totally riddled with error, and he was standing there smirking and smiling. You'd think he'd just done something very clever. But there's no doubt whatever that there will be a war, probably in the New Year.

Colin Powell was jeered at the Earth Summit, and Bush has called Blair over this weekend at his holiday home. The war plans are now well advanced.

Friday 6 September
The Iraq story absolutely dominates everything, particularly as Blair said that we have to pay a 'blood price' for our special relationship with America, which is a horrific, tribal, medieval thing to say.

Anyway, today I did eleven BBC broadcasts – London, Shropshire, Merseyside, Sheffield, West Midlands, York, Leeds, the Asian Network, Bristol, *The World at One* and, in the evening, *Any Questions?*

Saturday 7 September

To the Imperial War Museum, which I'd never been in before. I must say, it was extremely well organised. In the front main hall were all the aircraft and tanks and guns of various periods, and an old London bus that was used to move troops in the First World War.

I went into the 'Trench Experience', where you are in a First World War trench and there is continual firing and banging, and it was dark and muddy, and there were figures of soldiers in a corner. The horrific slaughter of innocent Germans and British in an imperial war really registered with me. That little exhibition explained the political motivation for uniting Europe against another war.

I decided also to see the Holocaust Exhibition. I was dreading going; it was what you would expect, except that it had no political context. There was no explanation as to why Hitler came to power, what the conditions in Germany were when he had come to power, why big business supported Hitler, or anything, other than this apparent independent hatred of the Jews, and not much made of the communists and the homosexuals and the trade unionists, they were just mentioned, as a sort of addendum at the end. But certainly, seeing it and seeing interviews with the Jews who survived, you can understand why the Israeli Government says, 'Never again; the Jews will stand up for themselves.' The Israelis are terribly well armed; they are taking the Palestinians' country and occupying it and crushing the Arabs and denying them anything. Sharon has now said anyway that the Oslo Accords, which have been the basis of the peace process, are dead.

Also at the exhibition there was a computer terminal on which you could type in the name of anyone killed in the war and get their particulars. I typed in Benn, and the very first name that came up was Captain Oliver Benn, my uncle. It was quite extraordinary, because there must have been a lot of Benns killed, but that was the first one, in the First World War.

Then, for the Second War, I typed in Benn, and the first name that came up was my brother, Flight Lieutenant Michael Benn. It was a bit inaccurate, because it said he had no decorations, and the cause of death was not known, and so on, but it was a way of remembering people for all time – young kids in their twenties. I think Oliver was killed at perhaps twenty-five, thirty, I don't know; Mike at twenty-two – I found it very moving.

Monday 9 September

To Kensington Town Hall for a conference organised by Third World Solidarity, which is run by Kensington and Chelsea councillor Mushtaq Lasharie and supported by the Mayor of Kensington and Chelsea, who is apparently a well-known doctor. The Tories were represented, and it was full of what one might call moderate Muslims.

The Pakistani Ambassador spoke; the Ambassador representing the

League of Arab States spoke; Afif Safieh, the Palestinian delegate to the UK; Lord Hylton, an independent peer; and so on. It was quite a weighty conference. After I spoke I went and had a cup of tea in the Mayor's office. I've never, in fifty years of living in the borough, been to the Council Chamber or to the Mayor's Office.

The TUC had passed a resolution opposing any military action not authorised by the Security Council. Bush is addressing the Security Council later this week, but he'll never get a majority. That means the TUC, and hence the Labour Party Conference, will come out against the war. It's really important, and Blair is totally isolated.

I was frightfully tired. I had a phone call: would I do BBC News 24? When I got there, Sir Crispin Tickell, who'd been the British Ambassador to the UN, was in the studio. I'd met him once or twice in my life. He was good on the question of explicit Security Council approval for war; and that Israel was in breach of UN resolutions. I thought I held my own.

Tuesday 10 September
After lunch, I watched Tony Blair at the TUC. It was a skilful performance. He made no attempt to be matey. He was as hard as nails on Iraq, and was listened to in absolute silence, and then he went on to the theme of partnership and the minimum wage and what Labour had done, and so on, and he ended up getting a standing ovation. From his point of view, he must have been absolutely delighted, and I'm sure Nita would be equally delighted. He hasn't convinced anybody on Iraq, but he made as clear as a bell what his view was.

Josh came over in the evening. Described an atheist as somebody who 'lacked invisible means of support'. He told me another joke. 'A man went to the doctor, and the doctor said, "I've got two bits of news for you, one good and one bad. The good news was you've got twenty-four hours to live, and the bad news is I forgot to tell you yesterday!"' He's always full of jokes, is Joshua.

Wednesday 11 September
The media and all the news today focused on the first anniversary of 11 September, or 9/11 as the Americans call it, and it was terribly sad. There were the widows of people killed, and the children of people who'd been killed, and so on. But what clouded it in my mind, and really destroyed its purpose, was that it was to the backdrop of the threat of another war, when even more innocent people are going to be killed. Blair and Prince Charles went to St Paul's Cathedral, and there were all the pictures and the television programmes, but behind it all was the knowledge that the anniversary was being used to create more war.

At a quarter-past two, Fiona Lloyd-Davis and Patrick Cockburn from Guardian Films came. I had originally said I might go to Iraq to interview

Saddam, then I rang them up and said I couldn't; so they wanted to come and see me, and we discussed it in the garden.

After they'd gone I thought about it, and then I rang Ted Heath and said how much I'd enjoyed tea with him, and then, 'I want your advice, Ted. I asked your advice about going to Baghdad twelve years ago, and now I've had the opportunity of going again.'

'Oh well,' he said, in a slightly doubtful way. 'With your reputation, it might make the situation worse.'

I said, 'Well, thanks very much. But the fact that you haven't said no is all I really need.'

Then I rang Tam Dalyell, who said, 'You must go! It's absolutely essential. It's the most important thing you could do.'

Thursday 12 September
I watched Bush addressing the United Nations. It was a tough, measured, quite plausible speech, in which he listed all the offences that Saddam had committed; never mentioned Israel, never mentioned the fact that the United States had supported Iraq in the past, just so selective, and of course adding a lot of new conditions, including internationally supervised elections, and so on.

It certainly makes my trip much more important, if the Iraqis let me in, but also makes it much more dangerous, because the Americans and the British Government would not want to hear an interview with Saddam.

Friday 13 September
I heard last night BBC *Question Time*, held in New York, with Geoff Hoon, the Defence Minister, Michael Moore, this brilliant American social critic and satirist and a couple of other people, and the audience was overwhelmingly against the war.

Friday 20 September
Tariq Aziz was at the United Nations yesterday, saying Iraq had no weapons of mass destruction, and of course that annoys the Americans because they're trying to get powers to go to war.

Tonight at West Point, Bush announced that American policy now includes the right to take pre-emptive strikes against nations that threaten the United States, so the Charter of the UN has been completely torn up. All you can say about it is that now there's no phoney cover of UN action for what America does. The peace movement will really build up quite rapidly, and I cannot believe the Prime Minister will be happy about pre-emptive strikes; or certainly Labour MPs won't.

Saturday 21 September
There are press reports of the new American doctrine, which is the end of

the Charter of the UN, the end of NATO, unilateralism. It is imperial domination of the world, spelled out very clearly, and we'll just have to think how to deal with that.

Sunday 22 September
The Countryside Alliance march of 400,000 people got massive BBC coverage. The Prince of Wales is reported to have said that farmers, country people, are treated worse than blacks or gays, that if hunting was banned he'd emigrate and spend his life skiing abroad. The Duke of Westminster, I believe, was there. Kate Hoey was there. Ugh! This is a march, allegedly to look after the countryside, but all about hunting. So the BBC gives massive coverage to those who want to kill foxes, but next Saturday, when it's the march against killing people, they'll treat it as 'the usual suspects'. The BBC is disgraceful!

Monday 23 September
The build-up to the war is going on at such a scale. We are now in the middle of a war fever, and according to *The Guardian*, if tomorrow the dossier shows that Saddam has weapons of mass destruction, support for the war will rise to 65 per cent. I'm not so sure. I spent the morning drafting a Point of Order for Tam, and I rang the Clerk of the House and Sir Nicolas Bevan, the Speaker's Secretary. So that is what I can do as a sort of adviser.

The Cabinet met today, and was described as being briefed by the Prime Minister – no question of the Cabinet discussing Iraq. Clare Short came out and said they were all agreed, so her opposition, which was so strong yesterday, has begun to fade, but somehow I don't have the feeling that this is credible. Pre-emptive strikes against anyone the United States doesn't like, who has weapons, is the beginning of the law of the jungle, and in a way Bush is launching globally the same process that Sharon is launching against the Palestinians, and it isn't working in Palestine, and it won't work to protect the United States.

Tuesday 24 September
Feeling a little better. I think Lemsip has dealt with a head cold.

When I went into the Commons, the security guy who examined my car, for bombs, said, 'Give 'em hell today, Tony!' And the woman who was with him said, 'We don't want a war.'

Well, two things about it: first of all, I've never known staff of the House be so political; but secondly, they seemed to think I was still a Member of Parliament!

To the Commons Gallery for the opening statements on Iraq, then Tam raised my Point of Order, absolutely as I had discussed it with him. It was really weird, sitting in the Gallery, and hearing my own Point of Order being read by the Father of the House. It was turned down, and Gerald Kaufman, predictably, made a vicious attack on Tam.

After I heard Tam, I went into the Terrace Cafeteria, and Michael Meacher came and sat next to me. I don't talk to him often, but he's always terribly friendly. He said there is practically no support in the Government for environmental concerns. His boss is Margaret Beckett, and one of the reasons he hadn't got into the Cabinet was because he was taking up the environmental cause. The truth is he's the one link between the Government and the environmental movement.

He said young women MPs loathe Blair because of the way he treats them. He told me Blair does occasionally meet junior ministers and they all talk, and then he says, 'Thank you very much, but I'd like you to think of more radical policies', and what he means by that is more ultra-Blairite policies, so Meacher thought. So I said, 'You mean, like abolishing the Health Service?' 'Yes, yes, yes!'

Some of the opinion polls on the telly suggested that even after the dossier (making a forty-five-minute claim for the launching of Weapons of Mass Destruction, WMD), most people are against military action, and I think that's encouraging. I don't think it's going to be easy for Blair. The man has got that possessed look that Eden had at the time of Suez. There's a Tube strike tonight, and there's the firemen's strike coming up, and there's the pressure from the Countryside Alliance, and the stock market's collapsing, and when the bloodshed in Iraq begins, Blair will face his first real challenge. He'll fall like Herbert Asquith. My mother used to say, 'Asquith fell from Mount Olympus with the lightness of thistle down', when he was replaced by Lloyd George in 1916 in the middle of the First World War.

Friday 27 September
Lissie and Josh arrived, and we went off in Lissie's car to Marks & Spencer, and they helped me to buy clothes. I bought two grey suits, a sports jacket, three pairs of trousers, three cardigans, twelve shirts, two belts, and the bill came to £872. I have never before in my life spent anything like that on clothes, but I must say it was overdue, because I haven't bought any clothes since Caroline last bought me a suit about five years ago. When we got back, Lissie went up to the bedroom, went through my cupboard, ruthlessly threw out old suits, old cardigans with holes in them, old shirts with frayed sleeves. It was a lovely day.

Saturday 28 September
Michael Foot rang up. He started by saying, 'I saw your piece in the *Mail* . . .' so I thought he'd rung about Caroline or about my leukaemia, but not at all. He continued, 'I think it's a disgrace that you should publish your diaries in the *Daily Mail* [because it is serialising *Free at Last! 1991–2001*], it's

the most bitterly anti-government paper.' So I was a bit taken aback. He said, 'I want to tell you personally.'

So I said, 'Fine, I know you don't approve of me, Michael, and you don't approve of diaries, and you don't approve of the *Mail*, but at least I didn't go to Australia at the expense of Rupert Murdoch!'

That shook him a bit. Boy, he was angry! I thought, bloody hell, that man joined in the witch hunt of the left, with the full support of all the right-wing papers; he was a great personal friend of Beaverbrook, so I didn't in the end take a lot of notice of it, but still, it registered.

Set off just after three in a taxi to Hyde Park. Got there, and there was a huge crowd of people, masses and masses of Muslims, some of whom had in orange on their T-shirts 'Reject Western solutions – Islamist philosophy is best', so the thing has got a religious dimension to it, which is a bit frightening. The media will of course build up the fact that this was Muslims protesting.

I was the third speaker, spoke for about three minutes, quite strongly. Did a few television and radio interviews. Got a bus back home.

World news – oh, I think the Americans, with British support, have tabled a resolution calling on Saddam to admit the inspectors within seven days, and if they don't disarm within thirty days, military action will be taken. That is quite unacceptable. I thought the UN might go along with the Americans if they were prepared to compromise, but I think what the Americans have decided to do is put the most aggressive resolution down, knowing it will be rejected, and then say, well, as you won't move, we'll do it ourselves. So war could come quite quickly.

Sunday 29 September
Watched *Breakfast with Frost*, and believe it or not, Peter Kellner, who is the chairman of a public-opinion polling company, YouGov, was commenting on the demonstration yesterday. He said it was 'Trotskyites having a day out'.

It's absolutely clear the United States do intend to go to war; it's clear they have the military weapons to destroy Iraq, and no doubt kill Saddam, the power to put a puppet in there, and to frighten everybody else into agreeing, although as a matter of fact, Russia, France and China are very doubtful about a war resolution, and are holding up the inspectors until it's been obtained. That could lead Bush to go to war without the UN.

Tuesday 1 October, Labour Party Conference, Blackpool
I went to Politico's bookshop at the Conference and I saw Cherie Blair. I touched her on the back, and she turned round and gave me an affectionate kiss, and we sort of hugged each other for a few minutes. I'm very fond of her. I said, 'How lovely to see. I enjoyed your dad's book,' that's Tony Booth's book, and, 'I hope my *Diaries* aren't embarrassing you.' She said,

'Oh, don't be ridiculous!' So I don't know whether she's read the *Daily Mail* or not, but she was so sweet.

Tony Booth was himself in Politico's, signing a few copies of his book, so I bought another copy off him.

At two o'clock the media began covering the Labour Conference. What the BBC means now by 'covering' is that they show ministerial speeches, and then the rest of the time, when anyone else is speaking, they interview ministers, or journalists interview each other, or one or two politicians, so there is no coverage of the Conference any more, other than as the media determine.

Blow me down, when BBC 2 came on the air, there was Andrew Neil, Peter Mandelson and Andrew Marr, talking for half an hour. Mandelson said, 'This is a very important speech', and so on, forecasting it all, and then Tony Blair walked on to the platform with Cherie, at about twenty to three. I could see exactly where the teleprompters, the glass panels he reads from, are. I've just got such a yearning one year to put a cushion on each of them, so that it would destroy the speech.

At any rate, Blair began with an inconsequential joke.

Then he launched into a totally unreconstructed case for the war against Iraq. In effect, it was a speech very like the speech Bush made to the UN. Bush was giving an ultimatum to the UN: 'Support me, and even if you don't, I'll go to war.' Blair was appealing to the Conference to support him, otherwise he'd do it anyway. Very over-confident. It was a managing director's speech. There was no participative sense in it at all. It was an ultimatum, in effect: do what I say, or else.

He got an appropriate ovation because he played one or two of the right notes. Labour Leaders are always able to do that. I've seen Wilson do it. I've seen Callaghan do it. They always do that. There never is the expected row.

But, as Peter Mandelson said immediately afterwards, 'This is as important as Clause 4,' because Blair had said we've got to dismantle the 1945 Welfare settlement – i.e., bring in private capital. So Mandelson explained it all, but then Mandelson probably wrote the speech, or played a large part in writing it.

Bill Clinton came in, and made, from his point of view, an absolutely brilliant speech. It was a masterpiece! He started by introducing himself: 'Clinton, B., Arkansas Constituency Labour Party', and of course people hooted with laughter.

Then he did what he'd done at the LSE. He didn't have a teleprompter; he had a few words on a bit of paper. He was thoughtful, setting out how humanity had to choose between integration and destruction, and so on. It was the sort of lecture I'm giving at the moment, dare I say it, but it was very sensitive, warm tributes to Tony Blair, violent criticism of compassionate conservatism.

He said, 'All political phrases are part-rhetoric and part-reality, and in compassionate conservatives, the "compassionate" is rhetoric and the "conservative" is reality.' Of course they loved that!

Bush, today, I might add, got a resolution from Congress, both Democrats and Republicans, both the Senate and the House, giving him authority to go to war. It hasn't been passed, but it's drafted.

Anyway, Clinton was very good. He hugged Peter Mandelson as he went by. Gave big hugs to Cherie Blair. You have to hand it to him.

Monday 7 October
Michael Benn, my eldest grandson is twenty-one, and I rang him to congratulate him. He's so mature and grown-up – well, he is a man now.

Tuesday 8 October
Up at six, picked up by cab at 7.45, met Emma Mitchell at Paddington, and caught the train to Heathrow for the British Airways flight to Aberdeen, for a book promotion – 1,200 people, the largest attendance they'd ever had.

I did some book signing, and who should come up and introduce herself but Ruth Seymour. Now, I looked her up in the diary afterwards, and I'd met Ruth in February 1979. She was a biologist, and her husband was a gerontologist. She had taken me to Dundee station, and there was something romantic about the station. Ever since, she's sent me a Christmas card, and I think I probably send her one, too. She was there, and when she said, 'I'm Ruth Seymour', I got up from the table, went round and gave her a big hug, and she gave me a big hug.

Emma was marvellous, looked after me perfectly. Indeed, at one stage she said, 'I think you ought to go to the loo now', and on another occasion I said to her, 'Do you think I should go to the loo now?' and she said, 'Yes, it might be advisable.'

Friday 11 October
George Galloway phoned me from Beirut to say that he was having dinner with Tariq Aziz and that the Iraqis were considering my request for an interview with Saddam Hussein. George said it was important, it would be broadcast worldwide, and I have a feeling it might now happen.

Saturday 12 October
I got a cab to King's Cross, Thameside – I've never been in that station before – the cab driver, who was a man of seventy, just griping about everything. People were morons, the traffic was chaos, everything was wrong! He said he had no time for politicians. I said to him after a bit, 'Well, tell me something that's going well.'

'The NHS, I think,' he said.

I said, 'Well, that's something. How do you think that happened? If you have a gripe, what do you do about it? Sitting griping doesn't get you anywhere.' At the end, I said, 'You're what people think every cab driver's like.' He gave me a funny sort of smile, was quite friendly, but I must say, it was an incredible exchange.

Sunday 13 October

I was picked up at nine o'clock by a young man of twenty-nine called Andrew Hunt, who drove me all the way to St Deiniol's Library at Hawarden, which was the home of Gladstone, to give the Gladstone Memorial Lecture. This young man was charming. He'd driven all the way down to London last night to collect me. Although it was a long and tiring journey back up, I found him such an interesting person. He'd wanted to become an Anglican minister and went for the training, then realised that pastoral work didn't interest him, and he really wanted to be what's called a 'religious' – that is to say, a Dominican monk – and write and publish and pray and think.

We discussed original sin and the resurrection, and all sorts of theological ideas. He was extremely well read, quoted Reinhold Niebuhr and Martin Buber and some theologians whom I'd never heard of. I did find him clever and engaging. He's doing a PhD on the link between science and theology.

Got to Hawarden about half-past one, and there were sandwiches and a cup of tea. A number of people there, including a tall man in a check shirt and a pair of slacks, who turned out to be Bishop Spong from the American Episcopal Church. I talked to him about Niebuhr, whom he had once met. He reminded me a little bit of the Kennedy era, or the lawyer Ramsay Clark, one of those tall, lanky, modest Americans.

Anyway, we went into this great marquee that had been erected for the Centenary Lecture of the foundation of the Library. They had pressed me and pressed me to go. I didn't reply to begin with, because I was a bit overawed by it. Three former prime ministers have given the Gladstone Memorial Lecture, two former archbishops, Habgood and Carey, and I didn't think I was up to it. But I did some work on Gladstone, and to be quite honest, I gave an amusing lecture.

I was taken back by the same guy, Andrew Hunt, to Crewe station; I was there only for three hours. At the station he had to meet the new Archbishop of Canterbury, the Rt Revd Rowan Williams, whom I saw briefly. I was so pleased to meet Williams, and I congratulated him warmly, and said how glad I was he'd got the job. He was of course an archbishop elected by the Welsh Church, so that to be appointed later as Archbishop of Canterbury, he called 'the icing on the cake'. I said, 'When will disestablishment come?' 'Well, it will,' he said, 'but it will take a bit of time.'

Gary

Monday 14 October

To the Royal Festival Hall for the debate with David Davis. Did the sound-check, had a cup of tea, was given a dressing room, and about 1,400 people turned up, I would think. Lots of family and friends and, in fairness, it went as well as I could possibly have expected. There was no hostility. There was profound disagreement between us on market forces, and so on, but David Davis played it straight, and so did I. We just spoke for fifteen minutes, or thereabouts, and then each answered questions. The trouble is I am so deaf, I couldn't hear a single question, but David did and he told me what they were and I was able to answer them. So it was all right.

Then afterwards, a little chat in the green room, and then Josh brought me home, bless his heart.

I discovered the washing machine was broken, so I opened it, found a loose wire, and I think I managed to fix it. I wouldn't rely on it being perfect, but I think I got it right.

Sunday 20 October

I had a lovely letter from Professor Sir Christopher Frayling, the Rector of the Royal College of Art, who wrote to thank me for coming to open an exhibition last week. I had put to him my idea for a suitcase that you could transform into a seat, and he wrote to say what a terrific idea my idea for a 'seatcase' was, and could I send some drawings? So I'll ring him up, and go over in a taxi and show him the various designs. It's got to meet four requirements: it's got to be small enough to be accepted on board an aeroplane; it's got to have wheels; it's got to be a backpack; and it's got to have a seat. You want to be able to zip it open as a little soft-covered briefcase, only a bit bigger than that. So I think I might take it round and show them what I have in mind, and see what they can make of it.

Monday 21 October
Went to the National Portrait Gallery by taxi for the BBC *Great Britons* series. They identified 100 great Britons, and I was ninety-seventh, the only politician chosen, apart from Blair and Thatcher, who is still alive. It was just one great big media event! They had printed little books about it and showed little video clips of the Britons in question.

I saw Andrew Neil coming in, saw Greg Dyke – I didn't speak to him; he didn't recognise me as he walked by. Had a word with Lauren Booth.

Then at the end, I met the Director of the Cabinet War Rooms museum. Josh had told me that the War Rooms were looking for a cooker similar to the one Churchill used, which is exactly like the one I have in my basement kitchen at home, which I've hardly used in fifty years. It is really a 1930s cooker. Josh thought it would be exciting to have it in the Cabinet War Rooms, with a notice: 'On loan from the Benn Archives'.

As I drove home, the car wouldn't work. The clutch had gone. To begin with, it didn't seem to have any pulling power, and by the time I got into Bayswater Road, I could hardly move; at Notting Hill Gate, it was the speed of an old man on a Zimmer frame!

Thursday 24 October
I decided to draw up a specification for the 'seatcase'. I decided to call it the chaircase, like a staircase. Or it could be called a sitcase. But I laid the specifications down, and then I took a lot of photographs of bits of luggage I've been adapting, to see how it works. I think I could make quite a nice little presentation.

Sunday 27 October
I spoke to Tam Dalyell two or three times today. He rang this morning to ask what he should do, following the statement made by Colin Powell that Bush had given the UN a few more days to agree a resolution, and if the Security Council did not agree it, Powell said, then they could assemble a coalition to wage war.

Friday 1 November
Sensational news today: this guy Paul Burrell, who was a footman to the Queen and then later became a butler to Princess Diana, was charged with having stolen a lot of stuff from Princess Diana after her death. The trial has

been going on for months. I was absolutely certain he was going to go to jail. But today the Queen intervened to say that he had told her he was keeping Diana's things for safekeeping. Apparently, he had had a three-hour audience with the Queen after the death of Diana, which the Queen later confirmed. So the court case collapsed. The prosecution withdrew the case, the jury was discharged and Burrell was free.

Now, what is astonishing about it is why, if it's true – and I'm sure it is – the Queen did not actually speak up earlier? I mean, she knew Burrell very well, he'd been her footman. She knew he'd had this interview with her, which he'd mentioned in his evidence to the defence, and the answer is of course that the trial had reached the point where Burrell was going to give evidence. It might have been that he was Princess Diana's lover, but I don't think it was that. No, I think it was that his evidence would have revealed the horrific rows between Princess Diana and Prince Charles, Diana's view that Charles wasn't fit to be King, etc., and that was something the monarchy couldn't tolerate.

Sunday 3 November
There were two films on Iraq, which I felt I had to watch. One was allegedly a profile of Saddam Hussein, and it was pure war propaganda. The other one was a John Simpson piece on *Panorama*, about Iraq, which sounded to me like propaganda. I know Saddam is a brute, I know he used chemical weapons against Halabja, and all the rest of it, but no reference to the fact the Americans have armed him, that we'd armed him, that the Americans had encouraged him to go into Kuwait.

Wednesday 6 November
Bush has won overwhelmingly in the American elections, so my forecast that the result would not be as good as he thought was completely wrong – shows how out of touch I am with American opinion, and how far September 11th still is an electoral asset for Bush.

Paul Burrell has sold his story to *The Mirror* for £300,000. There will be nothing in it that would damage Diana or the Queen.

Sunday 10 November
My supposition about why the Queen intervened in the Burrell case has been confirmed totally. She was terrified he'd give evidence that might bring out scandals affecting the Prince of Wales.

Monday 11 November
Tonight Blair made his Mansion House speech, and I must say, seeing him in a white tie, and the traditional parade of seventeenth-century soldiers, guarded by policemen with sub-machine guns and snipers, was ridiculous. He gave a grave warning about terrorist attacks when he himself is just

about to bomb Iraq and kill a lot of innocent people. I thought it was utterly disgusting.

Stephen had his conference today. He chaired a meeting of 9,000 people. He followed a prime minister and a European commissioner. The Indian Minister of Science immediately asked him to go and talk to the Indian Science Congress in Bangalore in January, and he's an adviser to the American Chemical Society.

Wednesday 13 November
To the Savoy, and got there just after midday. Emma was there, marvellous as usual. We went into this *Daily Mail*-sponsored lunch, of 500 people, not my natural audience.

The novelist Elizabeth Jane Howard was the other speaker. Caroline and I had been for a meal or went to a party of hers when Kingsley Amis was alive; she remembered it and thought it was about 1966. She made a little speech and answered questions. I was introduced by Lynda Lee Potter, who gave me the most elaborate introduction. It was so strange and over-the-top that I said, 'Thanks for supporting me, and for your kind words. It would have been appreciated if you'd given it when I needed it', but I got a strong response. I defended the fire-fighters, I defended the miners, I opposed the forthcoming war and, just as I was coming to the end of my speech, an alarm went off and somebody shouted, 'Fire alarm!' so 500 people all scampered out. I sat tight and signed some books, and then they all came back and I answered questions.

On the way home I dropped into the London Fire Brigade HQ on Albert Embankment and, being the headquarters, there was a mass of journalists there. They wanted a comment, so I said, 'I support the fire-fighters. They do a dangerous, important job. They should be paid a decent amount.'

They said, 'Well, what about inflation?'

'The employers offered them sixteen per cent and the Government stopped it. I just hope the Prime Minister, the Government, isn't trying to do to the fire-fighters what Thatcher did to the miners. I just hope that isn't the case.' In fact, I think it is the case.

Thursday 14 November
Prescott made a statement about the fire-fighters' strike, in the House of Commons; he was totally unbending, saying they were going to allow the army to use the fire appliances because the old Green Goddesses were not good enough, and if necessary they'll cross picket lines. They even hinted they might make such strikes illegal. Of course, if they do that, I think the whole trade-union movement will be up in arms, because this isn't only about the fire-fighters, it is about low-paid workers.

I got a cab to my local fire station, which is just at the bottom of Kensington Church Street. The fire-fighters there much appreciated it.

They're so disciplined, some of them called me 'Sir'. I said to them, 'Look, a strike is not the exercise of brute force by you against the public – quite the opposite. It's like an election. You're trying to win public support.' But of course the media just show fires burning; they don't talk about the fire-fighters at all.

Sunday 17 November

The Sunday Times had a lovely two-page article, 'Relative Values', about Josh and me – lovely photographs, a piece by me about Josh, a piece by Josh about me, so tender, so authentic, so real, so loving. I was so pleased, because it's the first time Josh has ever been mentioned in a public context.

Monday 18 November

Got home from a meeting to find a note in the front hall from Josh, 'Dad, I've fixed the hot water.' I had told Melissa that the hot water was off, but I didn't want to bother Josh, because I can perfectly well bath in the basement. The lad had come in and put a new element in the boiler.

The nuclear inspectors have gone back to Iraq. Big headlines about a possible terrorist attack on the London Underground, which has got everybody in a panic.

Wednesday 20 November

I went to the Campaign Group, to discuss how to handle a resolution the Government is putting down, fully supporting the UN resolution, and hoping that nobody would be able to vote against that. I suggested that what they did was to add: 'but declines to go to war against Iraq without the explicit support of the House of Commons'. Well, the Campaign Group thought about it, and they've got a meeting tomorrow to decide. Later in the day Tam rang me up, and I dictated a meticulously careful addendum, because the addendum doesn't contradict the Government motion, but if the Labour Members vote it down, then there will be an excuse for voting against the Government motion. So I think that's the best thing to do, because the Government wants to minimise the support for us, and we want to maximise our support for peace.

Friday 22 November

I went to do *Newsnight* on the fire strike. They wanted me to talk with Heseltine about the Winter of Discontent and all that. Chris Leslie, a very young MP, still in his twenties, represented the Government, in place of Gus Macdonald, the Labour Minister.

So we were a threesome, and I said, 'Who better than Michael Heseltine to defend the Government, which is continuing Tory policies.' I was courteous to him, but it made the point. Kirsty Wark was good, and *Newsnight* was really quite sympathetic to the fire-fighters, to be perfectly honest.

Sunday 24 November
Went and looked at my email, there are 368 unread emails, so I flipped through them quickly and wiped them.

Tuesday 26 November
There was a debate in the House of Commons on Iraq last night. What happened was that the Government motion just endorsed the United Nations resolution, said nothing about the future. The Tories had put down an amendment, and normally the Opposition gets its amendment called, but apparently, according to Tam who rang me this evening, the Government asked the Tories to put down an innocuous amendment to keep out any other amendments. The Liberal Democrats put one down, which endorsed the UN resolution, but declined to go to war with Bush without UN authority and the authority of Parliament, which is exactly what I wanted.

The Speaker, Michael Martin, courageously called the Liberal Democrats' amendment, but not the Opposition amendment, and of course that allowed fifty-five Liberals and various Nationalists and thirty-two Labour rebels to vote for it, and apparently, according to Tam, well over 100 people from all parts of the House abstained. Tam said Michael Martin was his hero.

The BBC has an idea for a programme every four or five weeks, in which William Hague and I would discuss, with no chairman, matters that interested us. William is quite keen on it, as am I. I rang William, and he said we could take the principles of arguments: for example, we wouldn't discuss the fire-fighters' dispute itself, but we'd discuss the role of trade unions; we wouldn't discuss the Iraq issue, we'd discuss the role of Parliament in international affairs.

Blair made a statement yesterday, I think, attacking the fire-fighters, and the bitterness reached an absolute peak. Apparently another report commissioned by the Government recommended 10,000 fire-fighters be made redundant. It's quite obvious that privatisation and cuts are what the whole modernisation agenda is all about.

Wednesday 27 November
Had a bite to eat, and then went to see Dr Amin, the minister in charge of the Iraqi interests' sections at the Jordanian Embassy. A charming man, educated in Britain, got his PhD from Durham and, like so many Iraqis, intelligent and pro-British and deeply distressed. Fiona Lloyd-Davis from Guardian Films came with me. The discussion really was about how we could firm this invitation up, and after long discussion he said, 'You won't get a final decision about the interview till you're in Baghdad.'

I'm a little bit nervous in case my visit there was made the occasion for an attempt to assassinate Saddam, – it would probably blow me up as well

– but I think it's worth doing, and I've got fairly clear in my mind what I'd want to ask. Amin was extremely friendly.

There has been a terrible massacre in Mombasa in Kenya – terrorists blew up an Israeli-owned hotel, and killed a lot of Israeli tourists, and fired missiles at an Israeli aeroplane carrying tourists home. That's sent shockwaves through the world.

Sunday 1 December

The Fire Brigades Union has suspended the strike that was due on Wednesday, and of course this is being presented as a capitulation by the union to the Government, and Blair is seen smiling, and Andrew Marr, the political correspondent, said, 'No government can be defeated. This is a test of the management of the economy', and so on. So it looks as if they may have beaten the fire-fighters, but the price they will pay for that in the long term in the Labour movement is going to be really great, I think.

Thursday 5 December

I caught the Tube to the Barbican, and walked from the underground to the Barbican Theatre, for the award of an Honorary Doctorate from London Metropolitan University.

The Vice-Chancellor, Brian Roper, gave a really radical address about how we must maintain comprehensive education, we don't want to saddle people with fees, and it was an excellent speech.

After the award of honorary degrees, there was a huge procession of people onto the platform. What they did was ask everyone to give their names, so there was no confusion. The graduates moved into the middle of the stage and shook hands with one of the academics, and then went off the other side. They got through a huge number of people in about three-quarters of an hour by that method. About 90 per cent of the students who graduated were Caribbean, about 80 per cent of the Caribbean graduates were women, and about 30 per cent of the Caribbean women were over forty. I mean, it was amazing! They all waved and cheered and hooted. One man who came on the platform went and kissed his three teachers, came and shook hands with me, then shook hands with the woman who was handing out the degrees, and went off again. Enoch Powell would have turned in his grave!

Monday 9 December

Yesterday I popped into the post a note to Cherie Blair, because she's the subject of a filthy media campaign over some flats she bought in Bristol. I also wrote a postcard to Ted Heath, because he's broken his wrist.

I went to the Royal Courts of Justice in Fleet Street because the Campaign for Nuclear Disarmament have asked whether or not the Government can go to war without UN Security Council agreement. The court decided to hear the application and to cap the expenditure of CND at £25,000. Bruce Kent was there; Jeremy Corbyn; Carol Naughton, the President of CND; Mark Thomas, the comedian. There was quite a big media presence: Sky, BBC Television, lots of photographers. It was very cold.

Later I rang William Hague, to discuss Thursday's programme.

The Cherie Blair story is blowing and blowing and blowing up. You can make anything look sleazy. Whether it was sensible to have a controversial 'lifestyle advisor', whose boyfriend is a conman, in your entourage I don't know. It may be a bit of a problem for Blair, if the press have been misled.

Tuesday 10 December
Cherie Blair made a television statement today at a charity she was visiting. She said she was the wife of a prime minister, she wasn't a superwoman; she'd make mistakes, but she wanted to protect the family, to protect Euan – and at this point, you know, her voice began breaking – 'His first term away from home, and I'm a mother', and so on. I think, from the point of view of the public as a whole, it will do a lot of good, but the cynics will find new criticisms of her, because it's said that she tried to influence a solicitor in connection with the partner of her friend, Carole Caplin, so it's all rather messy. I'm so glad I wrote to her last night.

Wednesday 11 December
I was driven to Osterley, the Sky TV headquarters, and did a half-an-hour interview covering Cherie Blair and fire-fighters and Iraq, and so on, and then half an hour answering emails in what they call the Chat Room.

I came home and had a meal. There was a nice letter from Ted Heath in response to the one I had sent him, saying, 'Very kind of you to write. My wrist is broken, so I can't sign this letter', plus a Christmas card.

This morning a Spanish warship intercepted a North Korean ship on its way to the Yemen with Scud missiles, and the reaction is shock, horror, disgust, but of course America supplies military equipment to Israel all the time. Americans supply weapons of mass destruction. The whole thing is totally hypocritical. They're building up a case for attacking North Korea, you wait and see.

Jimmy Carter got his Nobel Peace Prize yesterday, and warned America against going it alone, which is very good.

Thursday 12 December
I forgot to mention that when I went to *The Oldie* lunch, I found myself sitting next to Richard Ingrams, and apparently his great-grandfather was Queen Victoria's doctor. He told me two things: first of all, Queen Victoria insisted that a photograph of John Brown be placed in her hand when she was put into her coffin; and second, it was thought that she had been

pregnant by John Brown, and a daughter was born, who was sent off to America. I just note it; no idea whether there's any truth in it.

Went to the Commons. Had lunch with Alan Simpson, who's working on the possibility that if Blair goes to war, he will be a war criminal. He is also trying to draft something that would not be a breach of the sedition laws, to encourage soldiers who might not want to fight. I gave him a bit of advice on that.

Then Chris Mullin turned up and I had a cup of tea with him, and it was his fifty-fifth birthday. So we had quite a friendly talk. He's a bit critical of me. He said, 'I think you're too negative in your lectures. You ought to say more positive things about what the Government's doing.'

Sunday 15 December —
Went and did a lot of shopping, Coca-Colas and everything, put up the Christmas cards and then rested.

Monday 16 December
Clyde Chitty came at 11.30 for a talk. He just wanted an hour. He was so affectionate about Caroline. He talked about his new book on eugenics; that what really lies behind the opposition to comprehensive education is the concept, based on Darwinism, of the survival of the fittest; that there are some who are inherently more able than others and deserve to be treated specially, and the feeble-minded should be isolated, segregated and possibly, in the case of the fascist extreme of eugenics, exterminated. It's a powerful book.

The President has authorised the CIA to assassinate people, which is pure terrorism. There's no distinction between that and Osama Bin Laden authorising assassinations, so I think that, in a sense, al-Qaeda have won the battle, because they've persuaded the Americans to give up their civil liberties, and have also persuaded the Americans to go for terrorism. There is no moral difference between the two.

Thursday 19 December
In the evening I listened to the whole of the Dimbleby Lecture by the new Archbishop of Canterbury, Rowan Williams. I must say, it was a marvellous lecture. It was introduced, most insubstantially, by David Dimbleby, who really did less than justice to the man.

The lecture was a thoughtful analysis of where power had gone and the effect of market forces on society. Greg Dyke, Douglas Hurd, Clare Short, Jonathan Dimbleby and Bel Mooney were present; and a lot of other people. Williams put the moral case for believing that we are brothers and sisters, and have a responsibility to each other – worldwide, not just within the nation state. It was a tremendously powerful attack upon what he called the market state. It illustrated how a religious leader can be a teacher, quite unlike Carey or Fisher or any of the other archbishops, and I think probably a bit more like Archbishop William Temple, though I never heard him speak.

He was doing what I'm trying to do in my lectures – that is to say, look thoughtfully at problems, rather than relate them simply to Labour or Tory philosophy. It represents a powerful turning of the spiritual tide, in the way that the new forces from the trade unions, internationalism, and so on represent a turning of the political tide.

Tuesday 24 December

I had a postcard from Roy Jenkins, which I will read. I must say, it gave me enormous pleasure. It was from his home in Oxfordshire.

> Dear Tony,
> I've been reading the latest vol of your diaries with compelling interest. In the old cliché, I could hardly put it down. I can agree with some of your points. A happy Christmas.
> Yours ever,
> Roy

News is still of the threat of war. I picked up on the Internet that the Americans removed 8,000 pages from Saddam Hussein's report to the UN, including the names of all the companies that supplied nuclear materials to Iraq. Of course, it's open to Saddam to issue a second set to anybody, and I would have thought that, from Saddam's point of view, that was quite a sensible thing to do.

It's a really difficult period. I have quite a struggle hanging on to any optimism at all. There will be a war. We're up against what is a really evil empire. I never thought I'd say that about the United States, but it's about the Bush administration, not the United States, and living under the control of such an empire is something we've never had to contemplate in British politics before. I think the campaigns have got to emerge in the United States. Only the Americans can change the policy of the United States, and there's a mass support for peace views in America.

Friday 27 December

The United States is openly talking about fighting two wars at once – Iraq and now North Korea – God knows how it's all going to end.

Wednesday 1 January 2003

Home from Stansgate, unpacked, had a bath and a meal, and then was taken by car to the BBC World Service to comment on Tony Blair's New Year message, which is very pessimistic. They gave me five minutes.

Home, wrote my *Morning Star* article, bed at one o'clock.

Friday 3 January

From four to five-thirty, a young woman came to interview me for a magazine. She said we'd met before. She was a charming, good-looking woman, forty-one years old, had been a nurse for seventeen years, had had a partner and had set up a business; that had all ended, and she now works entirely for the Maitreya, who is a 'master and teacher' who lives in London. No one's actually seen him, but he's going to disclose himself shortly, and when he does, he'll broadcast on American, British, French, Russian and Chinese television, and the world's problems will be automatically solved.

This woman was completely taken with this idea. I asked her how it would be done.

'Well, it will be disclosed.'

'How old is he?'

'Well, he's lived for two thousand five hundred years.'

'Where does he live?'

'He comes from the Himalayas, and his masters still live in the Himalayas, and they transmit to a Scotsman, Benjamin Creme. They transmit by telepathy what they want to say, and he publishes it.' So Creme's the John the Baptist to the Maitreya.

The whole thing is just absolute nonsense.

Saturday 4 January

I'd tried to ring Roy Jenkins before Christmas, and when I rang today, Charles, his son, said he wasn't very well and couldn't come to the phone. I just wanted to thank him personally for his postcard.

Did a fifty-minute broadcast on RTÉ in Dublin with Robert Fisk, Felicity Arbuthnot and other journalists, about Iraq. The whole programme was overwhelmingly opposed to war. Archbishop Tutu has come out against the war.

Sunday 5 January

I was sitting in my office and the phone rang, and I was told Roy Jenkins had died. I'd phoned him only yesterday. It absolutely took me by surprise. Apparently, he had a heart attack in the garden, and I heard later in the day that he had had a pacemaker fitted. It is incredibly sad, you know, when your friends die. Tony Crosland died in 1976. He was not more than fifty-eight. Now Roy's gone, and it is a reminder that you're at the end of the road, and if you survive, your main function is to do obituaries of people you know.

Monday 6 January

All day at home. My visit to see the Iraqi minister in London was cancelled because he's still in Baghdad, and I think that trip to Baghdad is totally off.

Saddam, quite understandably, is now making speeches to the soldiers saying we'll beat the Americans, and so on, and the possibility of a serious talk that might avert it is, I think, out of the question.

I read *Tribune*, which had just arrived, and there was a two-page spread about who might ultimately lead the Labour Party, and guess who was named? Hilary Benn and Yvette Cooper. They are the latest recruits to the largest group of MPs, the 'ex-future prime ministers', of which I have been honorary President for some years. But at the same time, it marks him out a bit. He'd be an excellent Leader, and I have often thought that with his experience in local government, the trade-union movement, education and international development, and now home affairs, and with his great competence and ability to get on with people, and listen to people, he might very well be someone they look for in the future. But no one should build a political life around expectations of promotion, because they are usually disappointed and it diverts attention from the real job, which is representing people.

Tuesday 7 January
Blair has spoken to the British ambassadors. Hoon announced the call-up of reservists, and some ricin poison was apparently found in north London and six North Africans were arrested. The war propaganda builds and builds and builds.

I had a phone call from Carlton TV saying would I go and do a debate in Manchester on whether we should have national service. I said, 'No! You should have programmes about how to keep peace.' I'm quite frightened actually by it all.

Friday 10 January
I got out that lovely Henry Fonda, Katharine Hepburn, Jane Fonda film, *On Golden Pond*. Henry Fonda as an old man reminded me a little bit of one or two old people I know or knew. I'm just drained of energy, and I think I'm a bit demoralised. I read about the Swiss charity Dignitas in Zurich, and euthanasia, and I am totally persuaded. You turn up, you produce your birth certificate and your marriage certificate, and a note from your doctor about your illness, you arrange for your own funeral and they will, if they're satisfied, kill you. It's a gloomy thing to talk about, but I'm aware that I'm getting old and I'm tired.

Very restless night, at the moment I'm having to get up every hour and a half to have a wee, so my prostate must be in a frightful state. I didn't sleep well, had a cramp in my knee. And in a dream I went to see Clinton and Jimmy Carter and was trying to fill in an address book.

Wednesday 15 January
I had a phone call from Natasha Shallice, who is working on this series of

discussions that I'm doing with William Hague for the BBC. She rang to say that they wanted to call it 'Bill and Benn', so I put my foot down. I said, 'I'm sorry, I'm not having that; it's a serious discussion, and *Bill and Ben* is a children's programme.'

She said, 'The producer very much wants it.'

'Well, you'll just have to tell him, no,' I said. 'If he insists, I'm not doing the programme. I'm simply not doing it.'

Believe it or not, BBC Radio 2 have voted *Writings on the Wall*, which Roy Bailey and I do all over the country, the Best Live Act for its Folk Awards 2003.

Thursday 16 January

The propaganda now for war is unbelievable. Not just the news bulletins, but programmes about the First World War, the *Empire* series by Niall Ferguson, a young right-wing professor. It's quite frightening. Blair is going to see Bush, and Blix has come back and said Iraq has got to cooperate more actively. The whole thing is a nightmare! It must have been like that just before the Boer War, and the Napoleonic Wars, and the First World War. How you deal with it, I don't know. I talk quietly and calmly and analytically, and try to encourage people who *are* doing something about it.

Saturday 18 January

I got up at six, was picked up at 7.45 and taken to Television Centre, where I did the *Today* programme with Edward Stourton. Freddie Forsyth was brought in by phone. It was a good discussion. At the end, I said that Blair shouldn't go to war without Parliament's agreement, and Freddie Forsyth said, 'Who cares about Parliament? It has exported all our powers to Brussels. Who cares about Parliament?'

Wednesday 22 January

At nine o'clock Mushtaq Lasharie, of Third World Solidarity, came to see me. He thought the next enemy of the United States would be Pakistan. Pakistan was once a friend, and then an enemy because of its nuclear policy, then a friend again because of Afghanistan; but now, with a strong Muslim movement there, it would be seen as an enemy again.

I asked him about corruption. He said, 'Well, everybody's corrupt in Pakistan, in terms of money, but you mustn't let that put you off, and some of them are quite serious people.' Benazir Bhutto still had a chance, her People's Party was still popular, but it was up against the Islamist parties.

I asked him what would happen in a war in Iraq. He said, 'Well, war will cause a terrible upsurge of anger in Pakistan, but Musharraf is strong enough to control it.' Because he is a General, the army would put down any problems, either from the left or from the Muslim parties.

I asked about Saudi Arabia. 'Oh,' he said, 'all they could do there would be to have a mob, and the mob would have no leader, so it couldn't do anything, and it would be put down.'

He was pessimistic about the likely consequences. He very much wanted me to go to Pakistan, which I can't do immediately, or indeed perhaps at any time. He's a thoughtful guy.

Later I rang Denis Halliday, former UN Humantarian Coordinator in Iraq, in New York to find out exactly what had happened to Scott Ritter. Scott Ritter was set up by the FBI in a scandal and when they discovered that he was going to Baghdad this week they said to him, 'If you go to Baghdad, we'll release this.' So he said, 'Well, I'm going', so they did release it.

Went to the Tea Room and saw Chris Mullin and Jean Corston. Jean was very angry that I'd referred to Tony Blair as 'the Führer'.

'Well,' I said, 'I don't honestly think Tony Blair gives any indication he understands what we're saying.'

'Oh yes, he knows all right.'

Thursday 23 January

The Iraq war situation is far more serious today. France, Germany, China and Russia have all indicated that they're not in favour of a war. The Americans are now talking about war within weeks and not months, and Jack Straw is in Washington at the moment. He was still saying, with Powell, that it's not inevitable, but that's a view no one else takes.

I came back home in a taxi with a tall, black driver who had pictures of his two little children on the dashboard. He said that three and a half million people had been killed in the Congo war over copper.

Friday 24 January

I was just going to have a bath when the phone rang, and it was Amin, the Iraqi minister in London, who said he'd just heard from Baghdad that I *can* see Saddam Hussein, so my whole life will be transformed for the next ten days.

The first thing I did, immediately, was to ring Number 10 Downing Street and tell the duty officer I was going to see Saddam, and if the Prime Minister wished to see me, I'd make myself available at any moment. I did that to protect Hilary. Then I rang Hilary, left a message at his Leeds office.

I rang Jessica Fenn, and asked her if she could come in tomorrow, which she said she would. I'd met her in Pizza Express, and she came to see me the other day, offering to help any time I needed it.

Saturday 25 January

Jessie Fenn came. She worked today from ten till about six. Very efficient! She typed a whole series of documents for my Baghdad trip, and then tackled letters. I have great confidence in her. She is political, competent, bright, cheerful. We worked on the Baghdad trip all day.

In the afternoon, Riad al-Tahir came to see me to talk about the trip. He said that you've got to be careful, you've got to take your own water, you can't eat vegetables because they're never washed, and if they are, it's in impure water; it's difficult to be a vegetarian because everybody in Iraq eats meat, got to be careful with the cheese, and so in effect, I decided to take my own food for a week. Bananas I can buy there, I presume, but I'll take bread and butter, cheese, figs, and powdered milk and teabags and my little boilette water heater. It'll be a camping trip really, but I don't want to get ill.

We talked a little bit about George Galloway and, without being disloyal to George, Riad said he was too publicity-conscious. He said this has got to be a serious visit, which I know perfectly well.

I spent a lot of the day ringing round to register that I am going: the Archbishop of Westminster, the Chief Rabbi, the Moderator of the Church of Scotland, the Archbishop of Canterbury.

Then I rang Ted Heath, and said, 'All I want, Ted, is a word of hope from you that we can resolve this in peace.'

So he said, 'Right, I'll do it for you tomorrow.'

Sunday 26 January
George Galloway arrived with Stuart Halford at 10.30 and we talked about the trip. Clearly Tariq Aziz wants him to arrange my trip. I was afraid George might want to come himself, but he didn't, so that was a great relief, and Stuart has been many times to Baghdad, and he'll carry my bag and book the tickets and clear the visa and get everything ready.

I had a bit of a talk to George about the Labour Party. He said Gordon Brown's anger against Blair knows no limits, and he plans to be the Macmillan who replaces Eden, and that could well happen.

Then Maggie O'Kane rang again. We had a bit of a disagreement about the ownership of any film taken of my interview with Saddam.

Monday 27 January
I had two emails in my in-box, both identical, called Adult Talk. 'It's easy to get started, Just Click, and sign up free', and it was signed 'Adult taste team'.

After what happened to Scott Ritter, I thought this was possibly an example of an entrapment, so I filed the email.

I had messages from the Archbishop at Lambeth Palace, the Cardinal Archbishop of Westminster and the Moderator of the Church of Scotland about my trip, and they've all decided to issue a statement on the moral issues involved in the war.

Endless media enquiries! One of the members of the Iraqi Communist

Party rang me today. It is important that I am available to the Iraqi dissidents in Britain. He wasn't as critical as I thought he might be. I thought he might consider my visit as support for Saddam, but actually he was quite understanding.

Tuesday 28 January
Well, I got up just after six, and I did nine radio interviews today.

I popped into the Tea Room, and saw Ken Purchase, who is Robin Cook's PPS, and told him that I had put it to Walter Monckton, Eden's Minister of Defence in 1956 that he should resign over Suez, and I said, 'Someone we know very well might consider doing it now . . .'

He said, 'Well, if the UN doesn't approve the war, then it would happen.'

I said, 'It would be too late then. It's got to be absolutely clear; but I'll leave it to you.'

If Cook did go, I think it would alter the whole course of history, and I indicated that to him. He's a good lad, is Ken Purchase.

Went to Channel 4 in Horseferry Road for the annual political awards. Rory Bremner was there. I was sitting between Iain Dale and Matthew Parris. The whole thing was very cosy and made a nonsense of serious political disagreement.

I was elected, apparently by a huge majority, to be Politician of the Year, beating Blair, Duncan Smith, Charles Kennedy and Estelle Morris. I made a short speech – must have lasted about two and a half minutes – about peace, and I said it with some feeling, but I don't think I overdid it.

Talked to Chris Mullin, who thinks I shouldn't go to see Saddam: 'You'll be a tool', and so on. Chris is so right-wing now, and so loyal, and so Blairite.

Wednesday 29 January
Maggie O'Kane and Alan Rusbridger, the Editor of *The Guardian*, came. We couldn't get agreement about the film of the meeting in Iraq. *The Guardian* hasn't even reported that my visit is taking place.

Denis Halliday phoned from New York and said that he'd had a word with Tariq Aziz, and he thought Tariq might be ready to make a statement that they'd agree to the United Nations supervising elections in Iraq in the autumn. The President would become a formality; power would be in the hand of the Prime Minister, and they would negotiate oil deals with anyone they wanted to in the world, at market prices. A very important statement!

I'm much happier about the visit to Iraq now, but of course there are all sorts of hazards. If I could get the interview on Saturday, and be home on Monday, it would be marvellous, because then I'd have time to edit it before Colin Powell does his bit at the Security Council.

I heard the twelve o'clock news, and the Prime Minister was actually barracked by Labour MPs in the House of Commons. They shouted at him.

I don't remember there being anything like it in the House of Commons before. Blair said that next they're going to confront North Korea. There's no doubt there is going to be a war against Iraq. I'm not even sure they're going to try to get another UN resolution, because if they can't get it through and they're going to go ahead anyway, why be frustrated by the UN? I'd rather that if there was a war, it *didn't* have a UN resolution.

The French and Germans are standing firm, but Blair has persuaded the Spaniards, the Portuguese, the Italians, the Czechs, the Poles and the Hungarians all to support the war. Germany and France are now 'the old Europe'. It's really an amazing situation, and building up.

It's quarter-past twelve and I'm going to bed.

Thursday 30 January
I got up at six, began packing for Baghdad.

Jessica arrived and I had endless phone calls from the press.

Maggie O'Kane called to see me. She's now worried about how the film can be handled. I told her that the film would belong to Arab TV and they would negotiate its placement, so that lifts all the responsibility off my shoulders. But it means that she does not have much of a role.

I went and stopped the papers and bought some water.

Each member of the family phoned, and then Josh arrived and we drove to Heathrow. I checked in, with Stuart Halford, who's coming with me, and while I was checking in, BBC Television and ITN came and did short interviews, and also Reuters.

Jonathan Dimbleby was in the Executive Suite. He's going to Iraq to see Tariq Aziz on Sunday. When we got to the plane, they said it was delayed, and when we actually got on board, they said there was ice on the wings and it would take a long time to clear it. So I got off the plane and had a smoke.

Then they said there was ice was on every plane in the airport, they began de-icing it, and ran out of de-icing fluid because it was so rare!

At any rate, to cut a long story short, we left about nine o'clock at night, and I was terrified that we would get to Amman too late to catch the plane to Baghdad, but in fact I didn't have to worry. On the plane I had a huge meal, ate everything they gave me, and went to sleep.

Friday 31 January, Iraq
I was met in Amman by one of the officials from the Iraqi Embassy, and we were in time for the connection to Baghdad.

In the morning, as the dawn broke, it was beautiful, the light slowly coming up, red; we crossed the River Tigris and arrived in Baghdad at 7 a.m.

We were met by a number of people, including Sadoon al-Zubaydi, who was the interpreter when I saw Saddam in 1990, educated at Birmingham University, a great Shakespearean scholar, now a powerful man.

Then there was Dr Harith al-Khashali, and an Iraqi official.

They said to me, 'Would you like a government guest house, or would you rather stay in a suite in the hotel?'

So I said, 'Well, it's very kind of you. I don't want to be ungrateful, but I'm paying my own fare, and all my own expenses for my own reasons, and I would be grateful if you could put me in the hotel and then I'll pay the bill.'

So they accepted that at once. I was put in Room 526 of the Al-Rasheed Hotel, with a little sitting room next door. I made various phone calls. I phoned Josh, I phoned Nita, I phoned Melissa. I heard later from Stuart that he phoned his wife, and she had said that on the news tonight there were two news items: Tony Blair leaves to see Bush; and Tony Benn leaves to see Saddam Hussein.

They left us for three hours, to sleep, but actually I shaved, I bathed, I washed my shirt and hung it up to dry.

Ron Mackay turned up, a Scotsman who's responsible for Arab Television, which has just been set up and is handling the distribution of the film, although it will probably be made by the President's own film crew.

At twelve o'clock, Dr al-Zubaydi came with Dr al-Khashali and another Iraqi. We had an interesting talk. I went over all the questions I wanted to ask, and they commented upon them, because my purpose is only to get the best possible response. They had no idea there was any suggestion this interview would be filmed, because Saddam has not been filmed talking with anybody for over twelve years. So I was terribly frightened when I heard this, in case I had misunderstood the whole thing, but I left it anyway.

The phone kept ringing. I listened to the Voice of America, the only English radio station I could get, and it was pure propaganda.

At six o'clock I was met and taken to Tariq Aziz's home with Fawaz and al-Zubaydi and Stuart.

We sat in his sitting room, and his wife later came and brought some tea. He has eight grandchildren. He's a nice guy.

On the walls were photographs of him with all sorts of people, it was really terribly interesting to see them. There was a picture of him with President Bush, Senior. There was a picture of him with the Pope. There was a picture of him with Mrs Thatcher!

Anyway, we sat down and I went over all the questions again, and some of the comments that he made were helpful to me in guiding the way I should put the questions.

First of all he said, 'Israel will not survive. The Israelis, the Jews, will leave; they won't survive.' It was *the* most categorical statement, and of course deeply worrying to the Israelis, and would confirm the Americans in their need to destroy Iraq.

I asked about al-Qaeda. He said there was no connection between Saddam and al-Qaeda, but since the al-Qaeda was anti-American, 'our enemy's enemy is our friend', so that's got to be clear.

Then I came to the question of the lists of companies that supplied Iraq with military equipment, and he said, 'Oh yes, we'll provide those.' He said it wasn't arms equipment, but equipment that could be used for the production of weapons, and those were the pages suppressed from the dossier provided to the US, so that in itself would make it interesting.

On the question of the interrogation of scientists, I think it was Stuart who had said this to me: he thought possibly one of the anxieties would be that if the scientists were taken to Cyprus and were interrogated, the Americans might turn up with millions of dollars and try to bribe them, just as they bribed many of the Afghan warlords, literally with suitcases full of dollars.

I asked about links with the Americans in the past. When Reagan was President in 1983, Donald Rumsfeld had come as his adviser. He had given Tariq Aziz a little box of artificial sweeteners, which his company produced, because Rumsfeld was a businessman then, producing chemicals; so that's rather amusing.

He also told me something I had no idea about, that during the period before the first Gulf War of 1990–1, Iraq had subsidised and provided an aid programme all over the world through its oil revenues, and that's never mentioned.

I asked about the role of the United Nations. Tariq said, 'Saddam's very doubtful about it.'

I said, 'Well, I know you accepted Resolution 1441, but the UN ought to do a proper job', and Saddam might like to say something about that.

Then we had a long discussion about when I could see the President. I said my interview must be broadcast forty-eight hours before Powell goes to the Security Council on Wednesday. They thought it was possible I might see Saddam on Sunday, and then I might get an afternoon plane, and I'd be back in London on Monday, which would be marvellous.

I also gave Tariq the questions Jack Straw had produced, and he looked at them. I said, 'I don't want to make anything of them, but if anyone says to me, "Did you put difficult questions?", I'll say, "Yes, indeed, of course I put the questions."'

He said that Saddam had invited Blix and ElBaradei, the nuclear inspector, back for discussions.

We talked about a lot of other things. I asked about Gaddafi. Tariq hadn't any time for Gaddafi. He thought he was low-profile, more interested in Africa.

Of Mandela he had a high regard.

On communism, it had collapsed because it was bureaucratic.

Was he a socialist? Yes, Tariq was a socialist.

On Arab unity, yes, that was the objective, but he didn't know how it could come about.

On the war, if it came, they expected intensive bombing, but it would be difficult for the Americans to mount an invasion.

He asked a lot about Blair and New Labour.

He said he thought America was finished because it had no cultural identity. It was a strange thing to say. I thought that was interesting.

On the question of the UN, he said, 'Don't expect a new United Nations resolution, but if there is one, there'll be a lot of abstentions.' He thought the French might not use the veto, but they might abstain, and of course if there were a lot of abstentions, it would weaken the effect of the UN resolution if there was one; but he wasn't sure there would be one.

Then I talked about China, and he said China was so absorbed in its own development, with 11 per cent economic growth a year, it wasn't really concerned with the outside world.

He said Russia was very weak.

Then we talked about Islam and Christianity and the Jihad. Tariq Aziz said, 'Well, Islam isn't holy war.' There were some people – the extremists, if you like – who wanted martyrdom, but that wasn't really the way Islam looked at it.

Then he told me himself that he had been a poet and a writer and a painter, and he'd come into politics in 1958. In that year there was a communist demonstration, and his mother was afraid they would come and occupy the house, and she burned all his poems.

He said that the world journalists who were in Baghdad liked the Iraqis very much indeed, and that might help.

I asked about a new constitution for Iraq, and he said, 'Well, if there was, Saddam would still be obviously the Executive Commander of the Army and the Government'; but still, that's worth exploring.

It was a three-hour meeting, very friendly, lots of laughter and jokes, and philosophical and serious, and I just jotted down everything from memory when I came back.

Phoned Lissie, and told her I was okay.

Funnily enough, after I'd spoken to Lissie, I picked up the phone again and I heard a recording of my entire conversation so there's no doubt it was all being recorded. That happened when I was a minister, so it doesn't surprise me.

It's now just after eleven, which is just after eight London time, and I think I'm going to bed. I might have a bit of cheese, and am drinking water as best I can.

Saturday 1 February

Over this period, I have come to trust Stuart implicitly. He's a person who's absolutely genuine, I'm certain of that.

Anyway, we went down at about 10.30 to the coffee shop. I had a cheese sandwich, with white cheese, which I didn't much like, and there was some salad around it, which I ate, having forgotten that you shouldn't eat salad.

Al-Zubaydi joined us. Then Jon Snow joined us, which was nice, and they got on extremely well together.

Came up to my room and phoned the family, and then went off to the Ministry of Information. I met a man called Udai al-Taie, who is Director of the Foreign Press Centre. He gave me a little brochure: 'Who are the Iraqis?'

Twelve thousand years ago, Iraqis invented irrigation, allowing them to produce their own food. They invented writing. They discovered calculation and mathematics. They were the first to invent a legal structure to protect the weak, the orphaned and the widowed. Five thousand years ago, they had philosophers who wrote about everything known to the world. They used Pythagoras' theory before Pythagoras by 1,700 years. They invented constructional materials they used to build high towers in Southern Iraq. Or (Ur) is a place where supposedly mankind started. They were the first to build cities and live in them. For thousands of years, they wrote the best poetry and history known to mankind. They were famous as horse breeders and equestrians. The Iraq Museum in Baghdad contains some of the best sculptures.

'If this place is bombed,' said the leaflet, 'art lovers around the world will declare a day of mourning.'

Abraham, the father of Israel, came from Iraq. Abraham, the father of Islam, came from Iraq. Abraham, the father of Christianity, came from Iraq.

When the Mongols arrived, they threw the books in the Tigris – Baghdad had the best library in the world – and it's said that the river was black with the ink of the books, and red with the blood of the Iraqis who fought the invaders off.

Anyway, we discussed the whole question of the Iraqi attitude to the war. They feel such cultural confidence. They've had such a long history, and they feel the Americans are uncivilised, and the British are pretty uncivilised, though they much prefer the British to the Americans, so I got a feeling of the attitude of people towards the war: if it happens, it happens.

Back to the Al-Rasheed Hotel, went to the restaurant, had another cheese sandwich, and then Jon Snow appeared again. He said how much he loved the Iraqi people; their generosity is such that he went to one place in northern Iraq where British planes had bombed a village, and an old shopkeeper had lost his wife and both his children, and half his shop, and when the British journalist came to look at it, he took out some oranges for the journalist. Jon said, 'How could you ever come across generosity of that kind?'

Apparently, Blix has asked to see the President, and we discussed whether that was sensible. I said I thought it was. Indeed, I said I thought that other people from America and Britain should come to Iraq, but none of them have. They're not interested in Iraq. They're interested in the power of oil.

There are no signs of war preparations, and the security, as far as I could make out, is minimal. Nobody asks you to go through a security barrier where your bags are examined. No identity cards were asked for.

Jon said he got out of Baghdad as much as he could, and how important the media is, which of course it certainly is. He said few foreign journalists bother.

I think Jon Snow wondered whether he could interview Saddam, and we'll see how it goes; it's not impossible.

Stuart and I walked out in the back garden. The sun was bright, it was warm and there was a huge swimming pool, so we sat in chairs and had a Pepsi-Cola each brought to us. It was so unreal. It might have been in Hollywood: luxurious hotel, swimming pool, men and women swimming.

I took a picture of him, and he took a picture of me, and then the waiter took a picture of both of us. The thing was as unreal as you could imagine, but it was interesting. Part of the experience was that I hadn't done anything but concentrate on the interview. I didn't want to be out of Baghdad for a moment.

At 5.30 I came back to my room. I'm doing my diary, and then I believe this evening at 7.30, Dr Amir al-Saadi, the head of the ministry responsible for weapons of mass destruction, and for the negotiations with inspectors, is going to come, and that will be interesting.

All I've eaten in Iraq is two cheese sandwiches. I've got the bananas, and I had a few little biscuits when I was with Tariq last night, and I did pinch two rolls when I was talking to Jon Snow and his team.

So it's now – what is the time? It must be about . . . it's about twenty-past six. I've just got time to reorganise the questions. My inclination is to have a proper talk to Saddam first, so that he understands the purpose of my visit and the drift of my questions, and then they'll start filming. I don't want the filming to start from the beginning. I'm trying to bring out any information that will make the war less likely by strengthening the peace movement, and undermining the case for war, and getting it broadcast before Colin Powell talks to the Security Council on Wednesday. That's what it's about.

If I get home on Monday, I could have a press conference at London airport, to whip up more interest in the programme.

Stuart got from the Internet the BBC News online, which was quite reasonable.

Apparently Simon Hoggart asked in the paper: how did I know that, when I went to Iraq, I wouldn't meet one of Saddam Hussein's doubles?

Just after seven o'clock Dr Amir al-Saadi came. He's a chemist himself. At one stage went to Britain on a scholarship and visited some of the Royal Ordnance factories, and when he returned, he was made a lieutenant in the Iraqi Army.

He stayed for about an hour and a half. 'Before we begin,' I said to him, 'can I say a word about myself?'

'You don't have to,' he said, 'I lived in Bristol when you were the local Member of Parliament. I then went on to Battersea College of Advanced Technology, where you came to speak about the monarchy and Parliament and the constitution, and I've been a supporter ever since.' That was funny!

Anyway, I said, 'Well, thank you very much' and I described my own experience as Minister of Technology, Industry and Energy.

He told me that Hans Blix, the chief inspector, had been Director General of the International Atomic Energy Agency (IAEA) for twenty years, and when he came in 1991, on the first UNSCOM (United Nations Special Commission) inspection, the Iraqis had hidden what they were doing on nuclear energy, and Blix never forgot, and he was very angry about it. That had left him with a sort of residual resistance to what he was being told now.

Al-Saadi told me that there had been 100 per cent eradication in 1992 of their whole nuclear programme, all done under the supervision of the IAEA.

He said that when the Israelis bombed the Iraqi reactor in 1981, it was never rebuilt, and they decided to go down other routes: separation of the uranium by laser technology and isotope separation. The interesting thing about it was that, from an Israeli point of view, it justified their bombing, because they did in effect obliterate the original plan for Iraq's nuclear programme.

I asked why they wouldn't let scientists be interviewed, and he said, 'Well, candidly, because we're afraid that if people leave the country and go to Cyprus to be interviewed, there's nobody there to monitor what is said in the interview, and it might be falsely published. Also, the scientists could be bribed or blackmailed: "If you don't tell us this, we'll charge you with war crimes."'

Al-Saadi himself had refused to be interviewed and had got the blame for stopping other Iraqi scientists, but he said, 'Our view is that this is a matter of free choice by scientists, not a matter the Iraqi Government can insist upon.'

Blix and ElBaradei apparently have agreed to come to see Saddam Hussein.

I asked about Scott Ritter. Ritter was apparently one of *the* most belligerent of the inspectors under UNSCOM. Ritter subsequently said he thought all the weapons of mass destruction had been destroyed.

One of the arguments, of course, is that Iraq will not allow U-2 spy-planes to fly over Iraq for the purpose of assisting the inspectors. Al-Saadi told me that of course, right up till 1998, U-2 flights took place all the time, but from 1998 up to today the no-fly zones are being policed by British and American aircraft that are bombing Iraq; and he said that what the Iraqi Government had told the inspectors was that they couldn't guarantee the safety of the U-2s. They said, 'We would need notification of when the U-2s are coming so that we could provide some guarantees, and also because if we were defending ourselves in the no-fly zones and the U-2s came through, it would be impossible to safeguard.' He said Blix said he had no authority to deal with planes in the no-fly zone.

The notification was refused, and Iraqis said they couldn't guarantee the safety of the U-2s.

Then al-Saadi moved over to chemical weapons. He said the shell cases were in fact reported by the Iraqis in their dossier. They had been built at a time they were contemplating chemical weapons, but they were never filled with chemical weapons. Some were bombed during the first war, some were melted down for their aluminium, and some had been lost, and it was an Iraqi mistake. But he said, as a matter of fact, the chemical weapons expire quite quickly, and the shelf life of some of them is only six months.

Then we came to the naming of the companies. I had been asking all along if they would let me have a list of the companies that supplied them with materials, because that would be very relevant. I think he said yes, and, 'Well, they're also in the Scott Report', of 1992, and it would be interesting to get hold of that, but of course it would be much more interesting to get hold of the names as given by Iraq to the United States and as suppressed by the United States. He was a little nervous of that.

He said none of the companies concerned supplied weapons of mass destruction, but they did supply sophisticated equipment, including computers, and components that could be used for chemical weapons, and they also supplied dual-use equipment.

He went on to say that in dealings with the United Nations inspectors, UNMOVIC (the United Nations Monitoring, Verification and Inspection Commission), they never, ever give us a final list of what they want.

Saddam himself in 1991 ordered the destruction of all the biological weapons, and of all weaponisation of such materials. The only items that had continued were research-related.

He said they destroyed all the papers, so there was no proof whatever that they had destroyed the weapons. I found that a bit less credible, but he said the burden of proof was on the UN to demonstrate their existence.

I asked about the mobile laboratories. He said, 'There are none. There are a couple of food-testing laboratories, but there are no chemical establishments.'

Then we came to the VX used in nerve gas. Al-Saadi said the Iraqis had never had it, but samples of gas were provided for UNMOVIC, and they were sent back to America. When they tested them, the Americans said they contained ingredients of VX, but he said, 'To be absolutely sure, we supplied identical samples to laboratories in Switzerland and France, and they found no trace of VX there, and we think that the samples we gave to the United States were tampered with in Baghdad before they were sent.' He said, 'We don't fault the analysis of the American research labs, because what they got did have VX in it.'

I should add that Sadoon al-Zubaydi was at this talk, and took it all on board. He's obviously watching me closely.

So there we are – a very thrilling day, learned so much!

Sunday 2 February

Up at seven o'clock.

At 9.30, Hans von Sponeck came to see me. Von Sponeck was a UN inspector responsible for the Oil for Food Programme, who followed Denis Halliday, and then resigned. He said that what is needed now is a civic initiative, and that it must raise certain questions, but the hope is that it can include Mandela, Jimmy Carter and former prime minister of Finland, Atasari.

He said Carter would come, but not if his name is mentioned. But Mandela and Carter have made it clear they could not come and go back empty-handed. There would have to be an agenda – that is to say, they would have to go beyond Resolution 1441. There would have to be semi-permanent monitoring of Iraq. There would have to be some guarantee of good neighbourly relations, dealing with human rights, and possibly a Human Rights Commission in Baghdad. He said domestic issues would also have to be dealt with. He said Aziz has removed Israel from the list of countries where there could be some guarantee. Saddam was not prepared to have meetings on any pre-conditions or ultimatum, but anything could be raised.

Von Sponeck is a friendly guy, so courteous and polite. He said that Tariq was going to see the Pope on 14 February. He was really working like anything to try and help in any way he could, just as I am. He said the Iraqi Minister of Information had not been quite as helpful as he might.

Then I asked him about all the bits removed from the report to the UN, and he said a German had actually published the uncut document (i.e., including the bits the Americans removed), and he got the document in a leak from the Pentagon. That suggests there are some soldiers not very happy about it.

I asked him about the French, and he said, 'I do expect a French veto.' He was going today to a power station, to see what the effect would be of the bombing of that power station on water supply and water purification.

Sanctions, he said, may have cost a million and three-quarter lives, and sanctions were weapons of mass destruction.

I followed him from 11.30 to 12.15 to the Ministry of Information. The minister was in uniform.

He called me 'Your Excellency' and I said, 'I'm not an Excellency!'

He said he'd talked to Tam, and most of the conversation was about me. I explained to him why I'd come. They have followed with great care my activities over the years.

He said some of the press was hostile, but in general, it wasn't too bad, and he had said to CNN, 'If one per cent of your coverage is fair, we shall be satisfied.'

'If you don't mind my saying so, I think it would be very inadvisable – and I don't say you're doing it – to attack Bush or Blair personally, because that doesn't help. I don't do it at home,' I said.

He did agree that they needed Saddam to address the West.

I got on to the timing of the interview, and hoped that I could see Saddam today, to get home tonight. I then went over all the questions I was proposing to ask Saddam. Al-Zubaydi was there, and he heard them all.

The Minister gave his examples of betrayal of trust by people who had come. The Japanese, for example, had sent a former minister, who had been very friendly, and when he went home he attacked Iraq.

He said there was a congressman who came to Iraq and said after the meeting with Saddam, 'My visit with you has changed my perception of the situation', and when he went on to Israel he said, 'When I met Saddam, I met a monster, not a man.'

He said Rumsfeld and King Hussein had had a project for an oil pipeline to go to Aqaba, but the Iraqis had refused because Aqaba was so close to the Israeli border.

I was about three-quarters of an hour with him.

Then I had a talk to Ron Mackay of Arab TV. He showed me the Internet reports of this Columbia spacecraft, which had crashed, 20,000 feet up. No suggestion that it had anything to do with terrorism. *The Observer* had a report that there would be a massive air strike on the Iraqi presidential palaces and the republican guard, a terribly frightening account. Al-Zubaydi was doubtful about getting back tonight. He said, 'Be ready at four o'clock.'

So I rang Hilary and Joshua and Ruth, and had a bit of a kip. At 4.30 I was taken in the car to see the President. They didn't let Stuart come, which I'm sorry about.

I wondered how I'd get there; they just drove to a small villa, then I went to what was obviously a presidential palace. I waited in one room for a moment, and then I was taken into another room, and then I was taken into a third room in the palace.

Tariq Aziz was with me. There was Saddam sitting. I sat and he referred to Allah. I said, 'Well, we have free will', and he said, 'If there is a war, Satan will have done it.' It was very sort of religious and I would have liked to pursue that.

There was no camera there, and I asked him, 'Would you like to know the questions?' and he said no. He was very friendly.

I think I was put temporarily in another room. He went into the room where the cameras were, I followed in and then the filming began. I shook hands with him and sat down at a table opposite him, one camera on him and one on me, and one a free shot. Al-Zubaydi and another interpreter sitting there, and the interview began.

I must say, I should convey the feeling of entering the palace, being called 'Your Excellency' and generals saluting. It was a funny feeling, a bit like being Secretary of State again, not that I ever want to. But it was seen as a top-level meeting.

Well, I greeted him. I said, 'As-salam alaikum', and said what an honour it was to be with him. The whole interview is on film.

This is an edited text of the interview:

TONY BENN: I come for one reason only – to see whether in a talk we can explore, or you can help me to see, what the paths to peace may be. My only reason, I remember the war because I lost a brother. I never want to see another war.

SADDAM HUSSEIN: Welcome to Baghdad. You are conscious of the role that Iraqis have set out for themselves, inspired by their own culture, their civilisation and their role in human history. This role requires peace in order to prosper and progress.

BENN: Mr President, may I ask you some questions. The first is: does Iraq have any weapons of mass destruction?

SADDAM: Most Iraqi officials have been in power for over thirty-four years and have experience of dealing with the outside world. Every fair-minded person knows that when Iraqi officials say something, they are trustworthy. A few minutes ago when you asked me if I wanted to look at the questions beforehand, I told you I didn't feel the need so that we don't waste time, and I gave you the freedom to ask me any question directly so that my reply would be direct. This is an opportunity to reach the British people and the forces of peace in the world. There is only one truth and therefore I tell you, as I have said on many occasions before, that Iraq has no weapons of mass destruction whatsoever. We challenge anyone who claims that we have to bring forward any evidence and present it to public opinion.

BENN: I have another which has been raised: do you have links with al-Qaeda?

SADDAM: If we had a relationship with al-Qaeda and we believed in that relationship, we wouldn't be ashamed to admit it. Therefore I would like to tell you directly, and also through you to anyone who is interested to know, that we have no relationship with al-Qaeda.

BENN: In relation to the inspectors, there appear to be difficulties with inspectors, and I wonder whether there's anything you can tell me about these difficulties, and whether you believe they will be cleared up before Mr Hans Blix and Mr ElBaradei come back to Baghdad?

SADDAM: You are aware that every major event must encounter some difficulty. On the subject of the inspectors and the resolutions that deal with Iraq, you must have been following it, and you must have a view and a vision as to whether these resolutions have any basis in international law. Nevertheless the Security Council produced them. These resolutions – implemented or not – or the motivation behind these resolutions could lead the current situation to the path of peace or war. Therefore it's a critical situation. Let us also remember the unjust suffering of the Iraqi people.

For the last thirteen years since the blockade was imposed, you must be aware of the amount of harm that it has caused the Iraqi people, particularly children and the elderly, as a result of the shortage of food and medicine and other aspects of their life . . . Every fair-minded person knows that as far as Resolution 1441 is concerned, the Iraqis have been fulfilling their obligations under the resolution.

When Iraq objects to the conduct of those implementing the Security Council resolutions, that doesn't mean that Iraq wishes to push things to confrontation. Iraq has no interest in war. No Iraqi official or ordinary citizen has expressed a wish to go to war. The question should be directed at the other side. Are they looking for a pretext so they could justify war against Iraq? If the purpose was to make sure that Iraq is free of nuclear, chemical and biological weapons, then they can do that. These weapons do not come in small pills that you can hide in your pocket. These are weapons of mass destruction and it is easy to work out if Iraq has them or not. We have said many times before, and we say it again today, that Iraq is free of such weapons . . .

BENN: May I broaden the question out, Mr President, to the relations between Iraq and the UN, and the prospects for peace more broadly, and I wonder whether, with all its weaknesses and all the difficulties, whether you see a way in which the UN can reach that objective for the benefit of humanity?

SADDAM: The point you raised can be found in the United Nations Charter. As you know, Iraq is one of the founders and first signatories of the Charter. If we look at the representatives of two superpowers – America and Britain – and look at their conduct and their language, we would notice that they are more motivated by war than by their responsibility for peace.

BENN: There are people who believe this present conflict is about oil, and I wonder if you would say something about how you see the enormous oil reserves of Iraq being developed, first for the benefit of the people of Iraq, and secondly for the needs of mankind.

SADDAM: When we speak about oil in this part of the world – we are an integral part of the world – we have to deal with others in all aspects of life, economic as well as social, technical, scientific and other areas . . . The first factor is the role of those influential people in the decision taken by the President of the US, based on sympathy with the Zionist entity that was created at the expense of Palestine and its people and their humanity. These people force the hand of the American administration by claiming that the Arabs pose a danger to Israel, without remembering their obligation to God and how the Palestinian people were driven out of their homeland. The consecutive American administrations were led down a path of hostility against the people of this region, including our own nation, and we are part of it. Those people and others have been telling the various US administrations, especially the current one, that if you want to control the world you need to control the oil. Therefore the destruction of Iraq is a pre-requisite to controlling oil . . . It seems to me that this hostility is a trademark of the current US administration and is based on its wish to control the world and spread its hegemony.

People have the right to say that if this aggression by the American administration continues, it would lead to widespread enmity and resistance.

BENN: There are tens of millions, maybe hundreds of millions, of people in Britain and America, in Europe and worldwide, who want to see a peaceful outcome to this problem, and they are the real Americans in my opinion, the real British, the real French, the real Germans, because they think of the world in terms of their children . . . I wonder whether you could say something yourself directly through this interview to the peace movement of the world that might help to advance the cause they have in mind?

SADDAM: First of all, we admire the development of the peace movement around the world in the last few years. We pray to God to empower all those working against war and for the cause of peace and security, based on just peace for all. And through you we say to the British people that Iraqis do not hate the British people. Before 1991 Iraq and Britain had a normal relationship as well as normal relations with America . . . Tell the British people if the Iraqis are subjected to aggression or humiliation, they would fight bravely. Just as the British people did in the Second World War, and we will defend our country as they defended their country each in its own way.

After about forty minutes he got up and left because he had to go to prayers, and the whole interview, including interpretation, took about an hour and ten minutes, and then we had a final talk. He was uncomfortably friendly! He said, 'Oh, I wish you'd come more often.' Thank God the cameras were off by then.

He said, 'Come back', and so on. A lot of people will be absolutely disgusted to hear that he was so friendly, and disgusted that I was friendly to him, but for God's sake, it was to stop a war!

I was then driven back to the hotel.

When I got back to the hotel, we went on to the International Press Centre for a press conference. There must have been forty or fifty microphones balanced on the table, and I made a little statement. I described the questions and then, at the end, I said why I'd come, and I said I would ask Blair to see me.

I should add, beforehand, that al-Zubaydi introduced me. 'And now,' he said, 'I ask you to greet Tony Blair – Benn' and he said it again later. It was ludicrous. And then later he said the film belonged to me, which was equally ridiculous.

It was a tremendous scrum to get out of the press conference, because of course they all wanted to know how to get hold of the film.

I went from there to Tariq Aziz's house, and we had dinner with him, and his son who was hovering about. The Minister of Information was there, whom I'd met earlier in the day. Gosh, I can't remember who the other one was. Al-Zubaydi turned up later.

There were piles of food on large dishes, with everybody sitting round. We talked a bit. We waited for about an hour before the meal began, and told lots of jokes. They all know Britain extremely well, and it was just so friendly! Considering they're just about to have the most murderous military assault on them, it was quite astonishing!

Anyway, we got up, said our goodbyes, went to the airport, there was the plane on the tarmac. Stuart Halford, of course, had been with me for the dinner. I was the last up; I turned round and waved at al-Zubaydi and a man from Protocol, and we caught the flight to Amman.

Monday 3 February

Caught Royal Jordanian Airlines 111 from Amman to London, with Jonathan Dimbleby sitting just behind. Ron Mackay from Arab Television had all the films in a little nylon bag.

We got to London, bang on time, and when I got there the police came up and said, 'Your son, Joshua, is here.' As we moved forward, there were two of these highly armed policemen, with Sten guns on their chests and revolvers in their belts. I said, 'Why are you here?'

They said, 'Oh, we're protecting you from journalists.'

Indeed, there was a huge crowd and I did a little press conference there.

There's a tremendous battle to get hold of the film. I thought it was all settled, that BBC2 were showing it. But Arab Television rang up and said, 'No, we'd like to put it on at seven o'clock on Wednesday', and apparently they've paid more money.

I said, 'Well, you do whatever you like.' Tomorrow morning I've got to go in and record the introduction to the film.

Channel 4 News had a bit about my return home. Nothing in the BBC bulletin. Josh thought Alastair Campbell has probably warned the media to keep off it.

Tuesday 4 February
Got up about eight. I bought all the papers. David Aaronovitch had a mock interview, with a cartoon of me with my thermos, and Saddam offering me toffees. Since *The Guardian* claims to have been trying to help, I thought it was disgraceful.

I went off to the media centre, and there I saw Ron Mackay and Stuart Halford. I insisted on doing the introduction to camera. Channel 4 is playing it tonight at seven o'clock. I topped and tailed it, and then I went and did an interview with TV presenter Kristiane Backer, very attractive and charming.

When I got home there were about thirty-eight messages; all requests for interviews. I suppose, in the last couple of days, not exaggerating, I must have refused nearly 200 from all over the world.

Word is even going round that I'm making a profit out of the film. *The Sun* rang up and said, 'How much are you charging?' I said, 'I've nothing to do with it!'

So there will be a lot of knocking, but anyway, I can live with that.

A car picked me up at 5.30 and took me to Channel 4. They showed the interview, pretty well in full. It was perfectly good. Then afterwards Krishnan Guru-Murthy, the Indian presenter, just began a punch-up with me. I got angry with him. So I'm really fed up.

Number 10 issued a statement, which apparently they made before the broadcast of the interview, saying it would make no difference.

Then I went and did a webcast, telephone thing, and 10,000 people phoned in, and I sat and answered questions.

I went to CBS to do an interview for *60 Minutes*, the really big American programme, with an audience of about twenty million. They are showing it tomorrow. Their interviewer was terribly friendly. I think British interviewing is uniquely destructive.

Wednesday 5 February
I saw Nicholas Soames in the House of Commons, who said, 'Congratulations on what you're doing. There won't be a war, you know.'
'What do you mean?'

He said, 'The Arab leaders will get rid of Saddam; they'll force him to leave.'

That's an interesting viewpoint.

Waiting for a cab, who should I see but Harriet Harman, the Solicitor General, who said, 'You were brilliant with Jim Naughtie! It's time somebody said it.'

So I said, 'Well, you've suffered too.' She was referring to my broadcast on *Today* this morning, in which I clashed with Jim Naughtie who bullied me about my trip to Iraq. I said that if people are killed, Blair will be guilty of a criminal offence. She was pleased that somebody kicked Naughtie in the balls.

Came home to 120 emails, which I flipped through quickly.

What else today . . .? Oh, in Prime Minister's Questions Blair attacked me for my interview with Saddam Hussein. There *are* doubts. Josh and Lissie had said I must make it clear I'm not a supporter of Saddam Hussein, which of course I'm not, and also to finish my sentences and not get angry, and all sorts of good advice, bless their hearts.

Thursday 6 February
Got to York about 11.38. Anne Henderson was there to meet me. We went to the Railway Hotel, and had a talk and a cup of tea. While we were talking, my mobile rang and a woman said, 'This is Sir Edward Heath's secretary. Can you take a call?'

Ted came through and said, 'How can we get rid of Blair?', which I thought was very funny.

I was taken to York University, and there were 1,100 people in the auditorium. They listened very quietly. While I was on the platform, my mobile phone rang again, and I did a five-minute interview with C-SPAN in America – because they're also showing the Saddam Hussein interview this afternoon. The students peppered my answers with cheers, although they couldn't hear the questions!

Then I was taken to the Theatre Royal, for one of my lectures. I decided just to talk about Iraq, nothing else, and then we had questions, mainly – almost entirely – on Iraq. I was driven home and got back by twenty-past one, went to bed at two, exhausted.

The Colin Powell statement at the Security Council yesterday is now being analysed carefully.

Friday 7 February
Colin Powell's evidence to the Security Council has virtually been completely rubbished. Al-Saadi, the general I met in Baghdad, issued a detailed repudiation of it, and his repudiation consists of the fact that much of the evidence the Americans have now produced was submitted to the Security Council in response to Resolution 1441, by the Iraqis, and the Americans

suppressed it. Also, it turns out that the British, who'd supplied some intelligence evidence to the Americans, had actually supported their case with material drawn from an Iraqi PhD student's essay or project in 1997; they'd reproduced the spelling mistakes. So the whole thing is blown to shreds.

I got a cheque for over £2,000 from Arab Television to cover my expenses for Baghdad, and on the advice of Josh I returned the cheque. I know there's going to be a lot of questions about money, and I think that's the best thing to do. I faxed off the letter in advance, and I've sent the cheque back this evening. That's just worth noting.

The police called. I thought, God, what's that about. And they said, 'Your car has been broken into in Ladbroke Square', so I walked round, and there it was, window broken, glass all over the place. A nice woman had reported it to the police.

Sunday 9 February
Believe it or not, I found my car window had been smashed again overnight, outside my front door, less than twelve hours after it was repaired.

Tuesday 11 February
Do you know, the House of Commons adjourned tonight at 5.30! So, on the eve of war, Tam Dalyell having been unable yesterday to get a debate on it, the House goes away, and on Thursday, in two days' time, the House rises for a week's holiday. I'm not exaggerating, I think the House of Commons is taking its own life while the balance of its mind is disturbed. It is incredible! But Blair's popularity has dropped now to the same level as that for Iain Duncan Smith. Blairites will disappear once they realise Blair can't win the election for them – we'll see.

Wednesday 12 February
I heard that the Party meeting this morning was apparently told by one Cabinet Minister, 'You've just got to get out there and make the case for war. Many more people will die if we don't have a war.' An incredible argument, but still, that was what he said. The Parliamentary Labour Party is apparently in shell shock at the moment.

I commented yesterday that the House rose at 5.30. Tomorrow it goes on holiday till Monday week. It's the House of Commons absolutely abandoning its function, and if anyone tries to do anything about it, like Tam Dalyell, a senior MP, Father of the House, he is nearly suspended from the House for raising a Point of Order about the misleading statement the Prime Minister made. I mean, I do see Parliament totally differently now from when I was there. I think of MPs as local councillors, just doing a good job, not terribly interested in politics or anything outside Parliament, and more out of touch with public opinion than I can even recall.

Friday 14 February

I got a taxi later to the Greater London Authority headquarters for Ken Livingstone's reception for the mayors of European cities. It was an absolutely beautiful evening! The new building was lovely.

Went up to the ninth floor. There were so many people there: Kenneth Kaunda, Jemma, Corin and Vanessa Redgrave, Alice Mahon, Afif Safieh, David Gentleman. Jesse Jackson was speaking just as I left to go to the Friends' Meeting House for 'Stop the War'. I was the first speaker. Bianca Jagger turned up, and spoke after me, Denis Halliday was there. Ben Bella, President of Algeria, was turning up later. It's absolutely obvious to me, and to everybody else, that Britain and America are totally isolated. Bush is determined to go on, judging by Colin Powell, and the French are determined not to go. If Bush goes to war now, in the light of this, Blair can't follow him because he would be totally isolated. So Blair is in acute difficulty, and although the BBC is just a war-propaganda machine for the government, the truth of the matter is, it's the worst day in the whole story for Bush and Blair; the rest of the world, basing itself on the Blix report, which repudiated some of the things Powell said last week, is asking for more time. What it means is of course Bush will go to war alone, unilaterally, and Blair will have to decide, and if he does decide to go, truthfully, that's the end of the man. I've been terribly depressed, emotionally stressed, and now tonight I'm a bit more cheerful. I really am.

Saturday 15 February

I had an absolute nightmare, woke up in a muck sweat, dreamed that I had been re-elected to Parliament. There I was in the House, couldn't leave without the Whips' permission.

I joined the protest march at the Embankment just before twelve. I started at the front, but gradually dropped back, and by the time I got to Hyde Park, I think I must have been about a mile behind. By then my feet were giving out. I had cramp in my legs. But I managed to stagger to the back of the platform, where of course there were TV interviews going on. There was Ben Bella sitting, and next to him, Joseph Rotblat, who's ninety-four, a radical scientist, a Nobel Prize-winner. I had only had about an eggcup full of tea this morning, because I was terrified I wouldn't be able to find anywhere to go to the loo. Somebody offered me a half a drop of tea, which I had.

I sat on my little stool on the back of the platform, and Bianca Jagger spoke, and the last speaker was Jesse Jackson, 'Keep Hope Alive', which is his great theme. Saw Ken Loach, Jeremy Corbyn and his former wife, Claudia, and their three boys. Mick Rix was there; Billy Hayes of the Communication Workers' Union (CWU) spoke; I spoke for three minutes about the new world organisation we were forming today. It is amazing.

There are demonstrations in 800 cities, towns and villages in sixty countries, simultaneously.

I thought I wouldn't be able to walk to Bayswater Road, to get home, but I did just manage it. I sat on my little stool in the corner, and a guy offered me a lift and picked me up with his four-year-old boy and dropped me home. He said, 'Would you like to have tea with me?' but I wasn't in a fit state.

Sunday 16 February

The *Sunday Mirror* said two million people were on the march. Just nobody could ignore it! It was on a fantastic scale. Blair made a speech in Glasgow in which he quoted a letter he'd had from a nineteen-year-old Iraqi girl, calling for war, and he said it was his moral duty to make war to liberate Iraq from this tyrant. So it's shifting all the time from weapons of mass destruction to regime change, and so on.

Friday 21 February

The Guardian had a half-page today about Holland Park School, saying Colin Hall, the new headmaster, with the help of the Kensington Tories, was trying to turn it into a selective school. I'm just glad Mum didn't live to see that, because she would have been absolutely heartbroken. They were describing it as the first of the post-comprehensive schools, which is what Blair is encouraging them to do. God, there's nothing about New Labour that I like!

Monday 24 February

Emma Mitchell picked me up at a quarter to six in a taxi, and we went to the Grosvenor House Hotel in Park Lane for the British Book Awards celebration, which has become a huge event. Patrick Moore was just ahead of me with his monocle.

A woman came up and asked, 'Would you mind if we take a photograph for *Hello*?' Well, the last thing I wanted to do was to be in *Hello* magazine, so I said, 'I'm already booked with *OK!* magazine', following this ridiculous court case by Michael Douglas and his wife Catherine Zeta-Jones.

There were about 1,500 people, there were lots of awards: the Book Industry Award, Award for Exporting, Best Sales Rep, etc. All the tables had been booked by publishers and others, and they cheered like anything; I was sitting at the Random House table with Emma; Susan Sandon, publisher of Hutchinson and Arrow; Richard Cable, who runs the division; and Gail Rebuck, the chief executive of Random House. She's married to the great Third Way guru who advises Blair, Philip Gould.

I was in for Audio Book of the Year, but I didn't get it and didn't expect to. When it came to Independent Bookshop of the Year, I was asked to say something. I spoke for about two and a half minutes, about how bookshops were universities, but you could enter without any A-levels, and about how books 'allowed you to take counsel with the dead and gather in wisdom from the ends of the Earth, and allow mankind to straighten out its difficulties'.

I referred to my visit to Baghdad and quoted from the booklet describing what happened when the Mongols arrived 745 years ago: they killed two million people, put the Caliph of Baghdad in a sack and trampled him to death with horses. They threw the books from the library into the river, and it was said that the Tigris was black with the ink of the books and red with the blood of the defenders; and I ended by saying I hoped to God the barbarians didn't do it again.

I must say, the response was phenomenal. Later Michael Moore, who wrote this book *Stupid White Men*, which has sold 600,000 copies, paid a warm tribute to me, and particularly my reference to student fees leading to everyone being up to their neck in debt. At the very end, Iain Duncan Smith, who presented the last award, said how he'd sat opposite me in the House of Commons for years, and I'd made him laugh and cry and think, and what a tragedy that I've left Parliament. I was a bit overcome. But everybody came up, all these beautiful young women who are publishers and publishers' agents and publicity people, and so on. I was taken up to meet Michael Moore by the head of Penguin. He and his wife come from Michigan, and live in Traverse City, where I had my honeymoon with Caroline fifty-four years ago. He couldn't have been nicer, and so I had a good talk to him.

Then Emma took me out, ordered a taxi and put me safely in it. She's so affectionate and so sweet. They're trying to build it up to be comparable to the BAFTA Awards, and therefore there was a lot of publicity, and there were batteries of photographers everywhere taking pictures.

I saw the Marquis of Bath there. I'm glad I went in a dinner jacket, because everybody else was wearing one. It's been an extraordinary flowering of my Indian summer.

Wednesday 26 February
At half-past seven I heard the result of the vote in the House of Commons in the Iraq debate. The all-party resolution, which Chris Smith and Douglas Hogg had signed, saying the case for war was unproven, got 199 votes – staggering! All the Liberals and about 120 Labour people and one or two others. Of course the 'payroll' vote – that is to say, ministers and PPSs – all had to vote with the government, and the vote doesn't take account of abstentions.

Saturday 1 March
The world news on Iraq is really interesting today. The Iraqis say they are destroying missiles and of course Bush and Blair say it's just a gimmick. The

Arab League has voted against the war, and the Turkish Parliament is in a deadlock on the question of US troops passing through Turkey. This is a big setback for Bush and Blair.

Monday 3 March

The war has in effect begun, because the United States and Britain are bombing intensively now in the no-fly zones.

To the TUC for Jack Jones's ninetieth birthday party. I saw Ron Todd, Rodney Bickerstaffe. Bill Morris made a speech. He's just not quite up to it. Gordon Brown made a most passionate socialist speech. I thought it was a bit phoney, but certainly he knows how to play a left crowd.

Then Jack made the most marvellous speech. He didn't talk about his past at all, except casually, and he said now we've got the real problem of organising trade unions in small workplaces, getting the right to represent people who haven't got a union, dealing with trade-union legislation, linking pensions to earnings. I mean, it was the passionate speech of somebody of twenty, a left-winger of twenty, and of course it got a terrific response. I dearly love the man.

I met one of his great-grandchildren, who's seventeen – blimey!

Friday 7 March

A car was sent, to take me to the RAF Club for the Concorde Pilots' Dinner, a black-tie event.

I was asked to come by Peter Benn, who is my first cousin twice removed, a man of forty-one, very charming. I had a photograph of him as a baby, which I gave him. I thought I'd make an amusing speech. I started by talking about my dad flying in the First World War. I described my brother, Michael, and my first solo, and then went on to talk about the importance of engineering. Then I talked about Concorde. They did hoot with laughter.

Sunday 9 March

Josh has installed broadband so that I'm always on the Internet. It's an amazing development. I'm just on the fringes of understanding it, I'm a bit nervous.

Andy Reed, who was PPS to Margaret Beckett, resigned because of the impending war, and later in the day Clare Short made it clear publicly that she would resign from the Cabinet if Britain went to war without UN resolutions. So the whole thing is beginning to break up now. Blair must be in a terrible state, because the Americans do intend to go to war, and it really depends on whether the Anglo-American resolution gets the majority. If it doesn't, Bush will go to war anyway; and if it does, the French, Russians or Chinese may veto it, in which case the US would still go against the UN, and then Blair is absolutely at a critical point.

Monday 10 March
Clare Short is surviving, and predictably Alan Milburn attacked her, but Blair hasn't dared to sack her. It is the beginning of the end of Blair, of that I've no doubt. I think that is the beginning of the end, truthfully. It's quite exciting. Who would have thought it would have come in this form, at this time, but that's how history is made.

Tuesday 11 March
Donald Rumsfeld, who really is a jerk, said at a press conference that the Americans didn't need the British, that we might not fight with the Americans in Iraq. This caused absolute panic in London. Blair had to reassure people that it wasn't true, and that we would; but at the same time there's a rumour, and I'm sure there's something in it, that the Law Officers went to the Cabinet today and said they thought an invasion would be illegal. So Blair must be absolutely tortured – public opposition, a UN resolution very unlikely, legal doubts.

It is chaos for Blair, and he looks increasingly desperate.

Wednesday 12 March
I thought I'd go and hear Prime Minister's Questions, so I got into the Peers' Gallery, surrounded by all my old mates, former MPs now in the Lords. Blair is now totally obsessed, and whatever you say to him, he'll simply say, 'We've got to force Saddam to disarm', but Rumsfeld's statement has undermined Blair substantially. The reports in the papers suggest that anyway the troops haven't got the supplies they need, they're having to borrow off the Americans and they're not really a relevant military consideration at all.

The Serbian Prime Minister was assassinated today.

Thursday 13 March
Clare Short has now made a statement brushing aside her threatened resignation, which makes her look even less credible. There are rumours that Robin Cook may go.

Undoubtedly there's been some rallying to Blair from loyalists who think the demand that he should be replaced as Leader of the Party makes it a question of party loyalty and not about the war. On the other hand, Douglas Hogg is trying to build up Tory opposition to the war, and Duncan Smith was seen in Downing Street, having had an early briefing from Blair, and sounded as if he was the Prime Minister's press officer. So the whole thing is still confused, but I presume the war will come next week.

Sunday 15 March
Not much of a diary today. War imminent. Everybody knows it. Demonstrations everywhere.

Sunday 16 March

Bush and José-María Aznar of Spain, Blair and José Barosso met in the Azores, and in effect announced that they were giving up any hope of a second UN resolution, and the war will begin.

Monday 17 March

To the Commons. Went to Jean Corston's room and had a talk to her. As the Chairman of the Parliamentary Party, she can't vote against the Government and she is terribly worried about it. So I said, 'What you could do, you know, would be to put your name to the amendment and not vote, so at least people know.' I sympathise with her; she is in a difficult position, but anyway she said she was thinking about it and really wanted my advice.

Saw Glenda Jackson and thanked her for what she was doing. She always seems to me to be a cold woman, but still, I did thank her.

To the Tea Room and found that Robin Cook had resigned. There was an emergency Campaign Group meeting in Committee Room 13, where we were shown an amendment that has been produced by Chris Smith and Graham Allen, which says there's no case for war, but supports the troops and wishes them a successful and speedy conclusion, which is really quite unsatisfactory, but everybody said you've got to seek the maximum support. I think Douglas Hogg, the Tory, will probably get about fifty Tories to support. The Liberals will support. And maybe you could get more than half the Parliamentary Party.

Jack Straw made a statement in the House, in effect announcing that they had abandoned a second resolution. Oh, I might add, Clare Short persuaded the Prime Minister to say that he had confidence in her, and she's going to think about her position overnight.

Cook made his resignation statement. He said he didn't want to be associated in any way with an attack on Blair, who is a successful Leader, and hoped he would remain a successful Leader, but he then, in a clinical way, very modestly, completely unpicked the argument, said you can't go to war without international and domestic support.

After that, a thing happened I've never seen before in my life: MPs, Labour MPs, about a third of them, got up and applauded and clapped, and gave him a standing ovation in the House. So it's an indication that the House of Commons is now becoming part of the popular movement and not the parliamentary process. Normally you'd expect them to vote and reach a decision. This time, they behaved like a mass meeting. So Robin will be pleased; I've never had a lot of time for Robin, not recently anyway, but he presented the case in a devastating way.

Hilary rang me up tonight to talk about Iraq. I told him, say what you really think, that's the right thing to do. Say what you really think to people, because you're not in the Cabinet. I was touched that he should have thought of ringing me. I think that possibly will have helped him, but he said he might ring me later tonight.

Chris Mullin apparently hasn't made up his mind what to do, having made a point in the House of saying that 'Some members, including myself, would find it difficult to support a war without a second resolution.'

I think this is a remarkable period of history, and of course Bush is making a statement in about two and a half hours – I won't stay up for it – in which he's in effect going to give Saddam forty-eight hours to leave the country, which Saddam won't do, and then the war will begin.

We must expect terrorist attacks. I mean, it wouldn't surprise me at all if Big Ben wasn't blown up, or something of that kind. It is a momentous period of history. I am tempted to think I'd like to be in the House of Commons now, but I think I'm doing more good by broadcasting and at meetings and being free.

Tuesday 18 March

I paid my congestion charge by telephone and drove to the House of Commons. It seems quite an organised system.

Sat outside St Stephen's entrance waiting for Jessica, and Chris Mullin came and sat down beside me.

I said, 'What are you going to do tonight?'

He said, 'I'm voting against the regime.'

So I said, 'Which regime? Saddam or Blair?'

He said, 'I'm voting against Blair.'

That restored my confidence in Chris.

Clare Short withdrew her resignation. I never thought she'd stick to it. The argument is that she's the best person to supervise the reconstruction of Iraq, but of course that requires Iraq to be destroyed first, so she's going along with the destruction so that she can help with the reconstruction.

John Denham, the Home Office minister, has resigned, as has Lord Hunt, who was a health minister.

Blair, in his speech, in effect said, 'Back me or sack me', and tried to turn it into a vote of confidence.

Outside the House of Commons masses of people protesting, people smiling and cheering – really, it was stirring, and to see the House of Commons attracting so many people indicated a recovery of parliament. Instead of just letting it rot away with its bureaucratic, managerial language, people now think it matters, so just as world opinion is backing the UN, now people expect Parliament to deliver, and it will be interesting to see what happens.

Well, at ten o'clock there was the vote. I haven't got all the figures, they'll all be in the records, but about 140 Labour MPs revolted, which was eighteen more than last time, and a majority of backbench Labour MPs, but the Government won overwhelmingly. Then on the second vote against the Government resolution, the Government had a bigger majority. That means the war is authorised by the House of Commons.

Hilary obviously had to vote with the Government, and there you are.

Thursday 20 March

Television reports of the war

. . . About 5.30 in the morning local time in Baghdad, the air-raid sirens started, and as the aircraft artillery began firing across the night sky, I could hear tracer fire arcing up into the skies over Baghdad. Shortly afterwards there were a few heavy explosions that seemed to come from the edges of the city. I saw one large plume of black smoke.

. . . The bombs fell silent for a short while, but began after fifteen minutes or so again, at around five past six in the morning, local time. The city had been completely empty and quiet through the night, people obviously expecting that as soon as President Bush's forty-eight-hour ultimatum ran out, the bombing would begin. They weren't proven that far wrong, because it was shortly after that deadline when they fired, when the air-raid sirens had started. It's now light, there are cars and civilians out on the streets, people are still venturing out, and again, the guns have fallen silent for a short while, and it all seems to go in waves.

President Bush at 3.15

. . . More than seventy-five countries are giving crucial support, from the use of military air bases, and help with intelligence and logistics to the deployment of combat units. Every unit in this coalition has chosen to bear the burden and share the cost of serving in our common defence. To all the men and women of the United States Armed Forces now in the Middle East, the peace of a troubled world and the hopes of oppressed people now depend on me. Their trust is well placed.

The enemies you confront will come to know your skill and bravery. The people you liberate will witness the honourable and decent spirit of the American military. In this conflict, America faces an enemy who has no regard for conventions of war or rules or morality. Saddam Hussein has placed Iraqi troops and equipment in civilian areas, attempting to use innocent men, women and children as shields for his own military – a final atrocity against his people.

I want Americans and all the world to know that coalition forces will make every effort to spare innocent civilians from harm.

. . . To help the Iraqis achieve a united, stable and free country will require our sustained commitment.

We come to Iraq with respect for its citizens, for a great civilisation, full of religious faith and practice. We have no ambition in Iraq except to remove a threat and restore control of that country to its own people. I know that the families of our military are praying that all those who serve will return safely and soon. Millions of Americans are praying with you for the safety of your loved ones and for the protection of the innocent. For your sacrifice, you have the gratitude and respect of the American people, and our forces will be coming home as soon as their work is done. Our nation enters this conflict reluctantly, but our purpose is sure. The people of the United States and our friends and allies will not live at the mercy of an outlaw regime that threatens the peace with weapons of mass murder. We will meet that threat now with our army, air force, navy, coastguard and marines, so that we do not have to meet a greater one with armies of fire-fighters and police and doctors on the streets of our cities. Now the conflict has come, the only way to win it in its duration is to require decisive force, and I assure you, this will not be a campaign of half-measures. We will accept no outcome but victory. My fellow citizens, the dangers to our country and the world will be overcome. We'll pass through this time of peril. We carry on the work for peace. We will defend our freedom. We will bring freedom to others, and we will prevail on them. May God bless our country, the American defender.

That was recorded in the middle of the night on 20 March.

The whole war has begun on a really big scale, with a massive attack on Baghdad, and Tariq Aziz's home or his office has been destroyed. Looking at it quite objectively, in 1990 Saddam Hussein invaded Kuwait because he wanted the oil under his control, and he wanted power, and was immediately condemned. Today, the Americans invaded Iraq for exactly the same reasons. On September 11th, there was a tremendous attack upon the Twin Towers in New York, and that was denounced as terrorism, and today the Americans have launched a terrorist attack and tried to assassinate the Government. The French, the Germans, the Russians, the Chinese and Pakistan have denounced it, and the real cost of this war is coming home.

Monday 24 March
A lovely spring day!

The war isn't going quite as well as people expected. I thought it would be over in forty-eight hours, and I'm quite wrong. I think the Iraqi technique is almost to invite the Americans in and harass them from behind, guerrilla warfare, and put up a real battle for Baghdad, which could be as classic as the siege of Leningrad. Terribly depressing.

Wednesday 26 March
My grandson James arrived, and he took Caroline's clothes from the bedroom to the Oxfam shop just up the road. There was a huge pile of them. They'd all been carefully sorted. I didn't go with him. I couldn't have done it myself, but the time had come, and it had to be done. The one thing I did know was that she'd be so pleased to think they were being sold for famine relief, so I expect as I go by the shop I'll find her clothes in the window, and it's going to be difficult. He was marvellous about it.

We had lunch together, and watched Prime Minister's Questions on TV: not a single question critical of the war was asked. The House of Commons has consolidated itself around the war. It's simply horrific.

Thursday 27 March
To Westminster Abbey for Roy Jenkins's memorial service.

I found myself sitting in the North Lantern, with the altar on my left. It was the British establishment en masse. I cannot think of a better description. Ted Heath was there. Jim Callaghan was there. The Dean of Westminster conducted the service. There was a choir of course. Bill Rodgers read something. Nicholas Henderson, the former Ambassador to Paris, read something. Shirley Williams delivered the address, which was a perfect account of Roy's life.

I saw Chris Patten afterwards. Jennifer Jenkins was sitting not far away, I wanted to see her, but couldn't because there were so many people round her, with Charles Jenkins and Cynthia, her daughter, next to her. She looked very distinguished and a bit distressed, as you'd expect.

Denis Healey was there, Ludovic Kennedy, Simon Hughes, Harold Pinter and Antonia Fraser. I wandered out afterwards and saw a lot of other people, some of whom I recognised.

It was the memorial service of a Roman emperor, a man who had great talent, a great capacity for friendship, great charm, wildly ambitious, and who believed in maintaining the Establishment and the power of the Establishment, first in Britain and then in Europe. He split the Labour Party, which had made him what he was, and deserted it for the SDP. But he was friendly to me, liked the *Diaries*, was fond of Caroline and I knew him a long time, so I'm glad I went.

Anyway, came home by Underground; the Circle Line wasn't working, and I had to go to Earls Court. I mean really, there is a breakdown in the public transport system in London.

Friday 28 March
I went to Sky News to do the papers. It wasn't too difficult because the papers were full of propaganda. We are now told the war could last for months, having been told it would be over quickly. Then Blair saying we're working for peace, when *The Mirror* had a headline 'Our job is to kill'. Then

Blair said that two British prisoners of war had been executed, whereas *The Mirror* said that a colonel had written to one of the men's sisters to say her brother had been killed in battle, so Number 10 backtracked. Then a bit about the cost of the war, and how it was going to come out of student fees and pensions and fire-fighters' pay.

In the evening I drove off to have supper with Saffron, to Moro restaurant, which was full of people. The head waiter was very friendly to me, and Saffron said that many of the people who went there wrote for *The Guardian*, so that'll do a lot of good, or a lot of evil as the case may be.

The media keep producing the same pictures, day after day, of a tank knocking over a picture of Saddam Hussein's statue, the bombing of Baghdad, of refugees allegedly shot at by the Republican Guard. The Ministry of Defence has had to qualify what the Prime Minister said about those two British lads being executed: they *may* have been executed. Well, Blair said, at Camp David yesterday, at a press conference with Bush, that they *were* executed. How can he be believed?

Saturday 29 March
There's a pause in the war now because I think the Americans realise they can't capture Basra or Baghdad without massive reinforcements. The guerrilla warfare by the Iraqis is going well. According to the poll, 97 per cent of Spaniards are against the war, and a similar percentage of people in Jordan, and the Arab world is incensed by what is happening. Now Rumsfeld has indicated that they might go into Syria and Iran because they supplied some night-goggles to Saddam. I mean, the thing is just mad!

But it's quite obvious Blair is totally outflanked by Bush, who doesn't care about him any more. He's provided the political cover that Bush needed, and I don't think Blair has any influence.

Chapter 3

Lord Button

Before the long-awaited invasion of Iraq, the Government had published two documents, which had been prepared for some months, and on which Dr David Kelly, a senior MOD scientist and weapons expert, had been consulted. The first was published in September 2002, and made the case that Iraq could deploy weapons of mass destruction within forty-five minutes. The second was published in February 2003 and was dubbed the 'dodgy dossier', some of its findings having been taken from a PhD thesis written twelve years previously. In the next few weeks Andrew Gilligan, BBC journalist, reported misgivings about the way this dossier had been 'sexed up' to make the case for war more credible. Gilligan and a BBC colleague refused to say who the source of this information was. In June and July the Foreign Affairs Select Committee interviewed Gilligan, David Kelly and Alastair Campbell. In the fallout, two inquiries were set up by the Government, chaired by Lords Hutton and Butler, into the Gilligan affair and into the Government's presentation of the case for war.

Thursday 3 April

I was seventy-eight today. I had the usual singing phone calls, starting with Stephen, then Melissa and the girls, then Hilary, then Josh, and lots of birthday cards.

In the afternoon Hilary arrived, parked round the corner and there he was on the doorstep, with his card and a bar of chocolate wrapped up in a Home Office envelope, saying 'Home Office Special Delivery'. It was very sweet of him.

I worked on letters, and then in the evening my editor Ruth came over. She brought me a beautiful blue cashmere pullover and some socks, and she took me out for dinner. So that was my birthday.

Monday 7 April

I got a taxi to Waterloo, and caught the train to Portsmouth. Into the compartment came a lady of about sixty-five, grey hair; it turned out she worked at St Thomas's Hospital as medical secretary to a professor. She described the bureaucratic nightmare in the hospital – layer upon layer of managers who control the consultants. She said every doctor in the hospital, *everyone* in the hospital, hated Tony Blair. The professor she worked for had put in a detailed commentary on the Government's plan for the NHS, having consulted throughout the Royal College of Surgeons, and all he got back was a standard letter from Blair saying, 'Dear Professor, thank you for your letter, which I was very glad to receive.'

The Guildhall in Portsmouth holds 2,000 seats, and only 400 people turned up for my talk. It was the first time a venue hasn't been packed to the doors, and I wondered why.

The Tory candidate for Eastleigh at the last election came up to me tonight. He said he'd been to a party, last November I think, at which Lady Thatcher was present with Norman Tebbit, and he'd gone up to her and asked her what she regarded as her greatest achievement, and she replied, 'New Labour.' That says it all really.

Tuesday 8 April

Caught the train to Bristol to receive the Freedom of the City, and was met by the political activist Paul Stephenson and his wife Joyce, in a 1963 Bristol bus. On it was an HTV film unit that was filming as we drove round the city and up to the Mansion House, which I hadn't been in for years and years. Bill Martin, the Lord Mayor, made a little speech, and so did I. I talked to a mass of different people, and then we were driven down to the council chamber, where the whole council was meeting, with the sword, the mace-bearer and all the usual municipal ritual. I was very emotional and said, which I believed, that it was the greatest honour ever done to me, having represented Bristol for one-third of a century – that they should bring me back and take me back into their heart – more important than being a peer or a Cabinet minister. I talked about the nature of representative government and how important it was that we be represented and not managed. Funnily enough, all the councillors of all the parties who spoke drew attention to the work I had done as a constituency member. I was a bit overwhelmed, I must admit.

I got back, with my lovely certificate, all framed, as Freeman of the City of Bristol. I'm absolutely exhausted!

Wednesday 9 April

I went to St Thomas's Hospital to have a blood test. Then I walked to the Commons. Saw Chris Mullin and I said, 'Let's have a bite to eat', so he paid for my lunch, which was sweet of him, and we had a friendly talk. He's very reserved still, but he's a member of the Parliamentary Committee and Chairman of the Home Affairs Committee, so he's an influential person.

He said he wouldn't take a job unless it was a Cabinet job, and there is a strong rumour that when the Easter recess begins, there might be a reshuffle.

I went back to the hospital about my leukaemia to see Dr Carr, who has taken over from Professor Tom Pearson. He didn't keep me waiting any time at all. I got there a bit early. He had the result of the blood test, and he filled in the form and said, 'There's absolutely no change in eighteen months. You're going to live for twenty years more, if this remains as it is.' So that was good news.

Then we had a talk about bureaucracy in the hospital, and he gave one example. 'In order to be a foundation hospital,' which is obviously what Alan Milburn, the Health Secretary, wants St Thomas's to be, 'you have to say there will be no more than four hours' wait in the Accident and Emergency Department. I had a very seriously ill patient, who needed intensive care. I tried to get the patient into intensive care, but was told that we had a woman there who should have been admitted in a routine way, but all the wards were busy, so we put her in the intensive care unit even though it wasn't necessary. So,' he said, 'my patient, who did need it, couldn't get in.' It was a good example of the problem of having all these management consultants with their four-hour targets. I mean, if ten people get stabbed one night, or a plane crashes, how could you possibly stick to a four-hour maximum wait?

Baghdad is almost occupied. It's generally thought that Saddam Hussein's regime has completely collapsed, and there are pictures on the television of people waving, but the real problem is there is mass looting and revenge killing, and of course the army is not equipped to deal with the law and order or policing. So I think it's going to get a lot worse.

Thursday 10 April

Concorde is to be taken out of service.

News from Baghdad: chaos and looting; indeed, all over Iraq there is a total breakdown of law and order. A little girl of six was shot in the head by a marine. A man who came on the balcony to see what was happening was shot by an American sniper. A Shi'ite cleric, who was a great friend of Tony Blair and had gone back to the south, was murdered by one of his rivals. Blair did a broadcast, of all things, to the Iraqi people, saying: we want you to govern yourself. It won't be by the British or the Americans; it'll be for you – totally hypocritical! I don't suppose it'll win any support in Iraq whatsoever.

Tuesday 15 April

The Americans have brought together an interim authority under retired General Jay Garner, who is apparently pro-Israel. General Tommy Franks is in charge of the military. There's no United Nations presence. The

WHAT FUTURE FOR
HUMANITY?

Listening to and learning
from Presidents Chavez (*left*),
Carter (*above*), Gorbachev
(*below left*) and (*below right*)
UN leader Kofi Annan
(with his wife Nane)

My son Stephen (*left*) meets an informal President Clinton and I meet an informal Archbishop Tutu (*below*)

Two grand old men of Labour: former Prime Minister Jim Callaghan (*above*) and former TGWU leader, Jack Jones (*right*)

MY MATES

'Pensioners' leader
Rodney Bickerstaffe
(*right*); Hiroshima Day
with Jeremy Corbyn
(*below*)

(*Above*) Roy Bailey
with two of our
friends, and (*left*)
Billy Bragg with
one of his blokes

(*Above*) The conspirators

(*Right*) Photo opportunity in Baghdad

Victims of war: David Kelly
(*above*) and the people of
New York

Guardian of the Blair legacy,
Alastair Campbell (*right*)

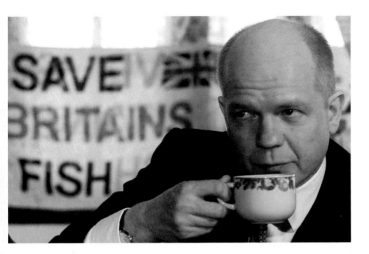

(*Left*) William Hague,
first to fall

(*Above*) The Quiet Man,
Iain Duncan Smith

(*Above right*) Howard's End

(*Right*) David Cameron,
'Blue Labour'

Brown makes a point (*left*); Straw as Foreign Secretary (*below*), with Jeremy Greenstock looking worried

(*Above*)
'United Kingdom?'
(left to right) Martin McGuinness, Ian Paisley, Alex Salmond

Blunkett's final goodbye

THE AWKWARD SQUAD

A great Father of the House, Tam Dalyell
(*above*); John McDonnell and Michael
Meacher (*top right*); Walter Wolfgang silenced
at Conference (*right*); Brian Haw, the tenant
of Parliament Square (*below*)

'Do you have Weapons of Mass Destruction?' 'No!'

Shi'ites are objecting. I think the problems of post-war Iraq are going to be much more difficult, much, much more difficult, but still, we'll see. Many of my predictions of disaster in the past have turned out to be quite wrong.

Sunday 20 April, Stansgate
Doubts about the war are rising because they just haven't found any weapons of mass destruction, and that was the basis on which they decided the 'material breach' had occurred. So the Government's moral position is impossible, but of course they're building up what they want and it doesn't make any difference what people say.

We had an Easter-egg hunt.

Had a meal, and then the family watched an awful video called *Shriek* [*sic*], and I dozed off again. I went to bed about half-past midnight.

Monday 21 April
It was a lovely, lovely holiday. It just did me such a lot of good. I told all the children how much I'd appreciated it. They were so kind, and so thoughtful of their old dad. Melissa reminds me so much of Caroline, just unbelievable . . . she's a good mum, she's thoughtful, and jolly.

Tuesday 22 April
I got a parking ticket for £100 for leaving my car outside my home on a bank holiday, so I decided to write to the town clerk.

There are four pages of the *Daily Telegraph*, claiming that their correspondent in Iraq had come across a file about George Galloway in the Iraqi Foreign Office in which, to put it plainly, it was alleged that he had asked for £375,000 in oil-sales rights. George denied it hotly, and said that he would sue the *Daily Telegraph*. Of course the Government is thrilled by the discrediting of, or attempt to discredit, Galloway.

Thursday 24 April
A young lad called Jacob came to do some work experience. He is the son of Tracey Sanders-Wood, who is the partner of Johnny Moberly, who is Patricia Moberly's son. We began tackling videos, of which there are now about a couple of hundred to be dated and indexed.

Jean Corston telephoned. I asked her about George Galloway, and she said well, quite apart from the current allegations, there have been complaints from other MPs whom he criticises. His constituency is disappearing in Glasgow under boundary changes and he's announced that he will stand as an Independent in another constituency.

Jon Snow telephoned. He wanted to know what I thought about the situation in Iraq. He said that Isabel Hilton, who's been in Baghdad for Channel 4, has come back today, and the situation there is awful. I was quite touched that he thought of ringing me because he's a very good lad.

Saturday 26 April

Took part in the *Today* programme with a constitutional monarchist from the Iraqi National Congress about the capture, or surrender, of Tariq Aziz. I haven't been on the *Today* programme since I had the flaming row with Jim Naughtie early in February, and I thought perhaps they'd never ask me again. I said to John Humphrys that I thought I'd been banned, and he joked, 'No, no, we decided to ban Jim Naughtie!' So he was friendly, but it was really annoying to have to talk about Tariq Aziz with this guy; the idea that a king could take over in Iraq is just so ludicrous.

Monday 5 May

From five to seven, John Nichols, who works for *The Nation* magazine and is an American Quaker, and his wife Mary Bottari, turned up. She is an expert on globalisation. John said he had met President Bush, and what a charming man he is personally; anyone who meets him is completely charmed by him – informal, casual, always gives people nicknames, and I wonder what nickname he gave Tony Blair. I think it is important to realise that individuals don't rise to the top for nothing; they've got something.

Mary said something that staggered me, but I now understand what she said. She said the most progressive president in her lifetime was President Nixon, and gave a whole list of progressive legislation that he had passed, which I'd completely forgotten about, and compared it to the ghastly right-wing agenda under Bush.

John said that CNN announced at one stage in one of their television programmes about the war in Iraq, 'We are now going to show something that may cause great distress, but we have a responsibility as a broadcasting organisation to let the facts be known.' Then they cut to footage not of Iraqi children dying or anything of that kind. What they showed was an anti-war demonstration. That tells you something about how the balance of broadcasting has changed in America.

I had an invitation from Gerhard Schröder, the German Chancellor, to go to Berlin to celebrate the 140th anniversary of the foundation of the German Social Democratic Party, but I'm doing *Any Questions?*, so I couldn't go. The letters keep on coming in. I can cope, with one or possibly one and a half days a week from Jessie, which is not too bad.

Tuesday 6 May

George Galloway was suspended from the Labour Party by the General Secretary today – quite incredible really, I think he should raise it with the Speaker as a breach of privilege, that some outside body can alter your status in the House of Commons. That's the nature of the Labour Party – no free speech in Blair's Labour Party. The fact that Galloway, who spoke against the war, would be bringing the party into disrepute when Blair, who took us into the war, wasn't bringing it into disrepute is quite extraordinary.

Wednesday 7 May

I went to a meeting with Gerry Adams and Martin McGuinness at the House of Commons. They were explaining that the British Government had absolutely gone along with David Trimble, who, they believed, would not accept the restoration of the Northern Ireland institutions, for fear of being defeated by more right-wing members of the Unionist Party. They both spoke about the peace process, and also the democratic aspects. I intervened and said I was interested in both of these, and it seemed to me outrageous that the Prime Minister should prevent the people of Northern Ireland from voting. He laid great emphasis on democracy in Iraq, and this should be seen, not as denying Sinn Fein their rights, so much as the people of Northern Ireland their rights. I did say to Gerry Adams and Martin privately before the meeting that I thought they might almost say to Blair, well, we're breaking off with you and we're just going to engage in a campaign for an election, which would greatly strengthen their own position.

Just before the meeting with the Irish, I saw Roy Hattersley. Roy came up to me, very friendly; I think the reason for it was that he wrote an absolutely foul review of my *Diaries*, said he strongly recommended people not to buy the book, and then when I saw him a couple of days later, at the Caroline Benn Memorial Lecture, I paid a warm tribute to him.

We talked for quite a while about Blair, because some time ago I'd said to Roy that I thought Blair was very ideological, and he said, 'No, no, he has no ideology. Whatever works, works.' We talked about that a little bit, and then we talked about all the people who had become Blairites, what the reason for it was. Roy said it was absolute opportunism, nothing in it other than opportunism, which was a bit more cynical than I might have been.

Then he talked about David Blunkett, and Blunkett's famous speech as our education spokesman that under Labour there will be no selection – 'Watch my lips, no selection.' And of course there was selection! Hattersley heard later that Blunkett had said, 'Oh, what a fool Roy is! Doesn't he realise I am a politician?' That was devastating.

Thursday 8 May

Brushed my teeth, forgot to put the dentures in and went to Bristol for the ceremony of making two more people Freedom of the City! I was so embarrassed, but still, you just have to live with that.

The two people who got the Freedom of the City were Sir Jack Hayward and Bishop Barry Rogerson. Sir Jack is a very wealthy man. I think he owns Barbados or the Port of Barbados, and he was the one who personally underwrote the rescue and return of the *Great Britain* from the Falkland Islands. It's a huge enterprise and paid to have it all restored, and he also opened the Empire and Commonwealth Museum in Brunel's old railway station. He was a nice old boy. I didn't know much about him. I've heard his name. He owns Wolverhampton Wanderers. He was nice to me, and his wife was there. I think he leads a modest life.

Then the other freeman was Bishop Rogerson, a passionate supporter of the ordination of women; he ordained the first women in the Church of England in Bristol Cathedral. He referred in his speech to the need for women bishops in the Church of England. I had to say thank you at the lunch, so although I was handicapped by my dentures not being in, so that there was a great gap in my teeth, I got up and said a few appropriate words.

Saturday 10 May
Stephen sent me all the photographs from our Stansgate weekend, and a photocopy of a quite astonishing letter from Tony Blair to my grand-daughter, Emily.

Dear Emily,
Your Mum [Nita] has told me about all the hard work you've been doing at school making the case for using military action to disarm Saddam's regime of its weapons of mass destruction. I hear you are a natural politician. It obviously runs in the family.
[And in his own hand] Thank you. It must have been a hard sell.
Yours ever,
Tony Blair

Well, I didn't know how to respond, so I photocopied the Prime Minister's notepaper, and I wrote:

Dear Emily,
I've just heard from Tony Blair, who is one of our bright new MPs and friend of your mother's, of your interest in politics. It's really good news to know that when I retire you'll be able to take over straight away to save Gordon Brown the heavy burden that might otherwise fall on his unwilling shoulders. I also told the Queen of your plans to stand in a by-election quite soon, and she was absolutely delighted to hear this and looks forward to seeing you at Windsor Castle to discuss the composition of your Government. I naturally hope you might be able to appoint Tony Blair himself to some ministerial position as he would, I'm sure, be helpful to you when you're here at Number 10.
Yours,
Tony Benn

I put an envelope with the Prime Minister's imprint on the outside (which I copied from the letter).

Monday 12 May

Turned on the radio and heard that Clare Short had resigned as International Secretary.

I went to the House of Commons, to the Members' Lobby, where Ted Heath had his bust unveiled. I had my little tiny video camera and I filmed it. Tony Banks introduced it briefly, and the Speaker said something, wearing a lounge suit (unusual for a Speaker even at that time of the morning); and then Ted made a speech, mainly about the need to revitalise Parliament. Things that I've been saying for years are now part of the conventional wisdom.

Then to the Speaker's House for drinks. I said to Ted, in a jocular way, 'Ted, you're lucky to have your bust made after you knocked the head off Mrs Thatcher's statue!' and he laughed.

While this was all going on, Clare Short was making her statement, which I watched later on television. It was an attack on the Government over Iraq, over the advice that the Law Officers had given, which we hadn't been properly informed of, over the presidential system of government, over spin, over control freakery, over authoritarianism, over everything; and as I left I saw Chris Mullin and Jean Corston talking. They said that it had made quite a powerful impact, the speech. They asked me what I thought of Clare, and I said, 'I'm afraid I have no time for her whatsoever. That isn't to say her speech won't be effective.'

In the evening I went to the Speaker's dinner for Ted. I found myself next to Mary Martin and I said, 'Oh, what a pleasure!' because she's such a nice woman. She said, 'Well, I arranged it', which was sweet of her, because it gave me the principal position on the hostess's right.

Trimble wasn't there at the start, because the Northern Ireland debate was taking place, and a bill was being pushed through all its stages in a single day, to re-create the legislative assembly in Stormont, even though there are going to be no elections. Michael Martin made a lovely generous speech, paid tribute to his secretary who had organised the dinner, who was leaving because she was having a baby, and everybody clapped.

Ted spoke after Michael, and he gave an interesting speech. He talked about his youth, how he campaigned in the election of 1931 when he was fifteen; how he went to Spain at the time of the civil war, and tried to go back later, but they wouldn't let him in because his position was known; how he'd been to Germany, how he's an anti-fascist. He talked about Churchill offering him a job, saying, 'No remuneration, but you would not go unthanked' – a nice quote. Then he described his own time as Chief Whip at the time of Suez. 'I told Eden he'd made a mistake, I had to do that on behalf of the Party,' and of course Eden was replaced, 'and then we sounded the Cabinet out, and I had the job of going to see Rab Butler, who expected to be Leader and wasn't, and it was obviously a very shattering experience.'

He's an attractive old boy; and Clare Short's resignation, judging from the news that I heard at midnight, has been very powerful, although a lot of people have contempt for her for not resigning when she should have done, but she has done it in style. That will be the big story tomorrow.

Tuesday 13 May

I had a late lie-in this morning because I didn't get to bed till late, but the phone rang and it was Hilary. 'The Prime Minister wants to offer me the job as Minister of State at the Department for International Development, which would mean of course that I would be responsible for the Department in the House of Commons' (as Valerie Amos, the Secretary, is in the Lords).

I just laughed out loud and danced around the office – I was so proud! He's been in Parliament for less than four years, and he's been a minister for less than two years, and he's now a Minister of State! He'll be the only one available to answer questions in the Commons, because there's no other minister.

Anyway, the headlines today are all about Clare Short; after she made her devastating critique and explanation yesterday, she gave an interview to *The Times* and *The Guardian* saying that Blair should resign and pave the way for a successor – i.e., meaning Gordon Brown, because she's supposed to be a Brownite.

This is a crack, it's the first serious crack in the Government since Blair became Prime Minister, and today Iain Duncan Smith made a most watery speech about how a Conservative government would see that everyone advanced together, no one would live in poverty – it was just crap! There wasn't a word of substance in it or a word of explanation about the way in which power works in the world.

Wednesday 14 May

I paid my congestion charge by phone, and then I went into the House. The news is entirely dominated by the al-Qaeda bombing, the suicide bombing, in Riyadh, which has killed Americans and British.

Friday 16 May

I bought a digital radio – quite expensive, and then of course I couldn't make it work! Came back – I really wasted today. Worked on my speech on Palestine for tomorrow.

Saturday 17 May

Walked to Trafalgar Square for the Palestine demo.

When I was called, it was about a quarter-past four, and as I began to speak it began to rain. As I was walking back, the heavens broke, and by the time I got to my car, I was absolutely soaking wet. I sat in the car – I was very tired – and drove home. I was going to have a hot bath, but I was too tired.

The terrorist attack in Casablanca is on a huge scale, and now there are threats of terrorist attacks all over Africa, and of course once there is a terrorist attack, it has an enormously adverse effect on the local economy. I don't quite know what the Americans can do. Far from having defeated terrorism by attacking and occupying Iraq, the US has had no impact at all.

Sunday 18 May
Suicide bombing in Israel. Sharon has cancelled his visit to see President Bush, and is trying in effect to terminate the Middle East Road Map before it starts.

The media just treats every Palestinian as a terrorist and all Israeli killings as police actions, even though Israel occupies territory that doesn't belong to it. The whole media coverage is so biased against the Palestinians.

Jessica turned up today. She's such a bright, cheerful girl, and of course having an audience, whose response you can watch while you're dictating, is like seeing the reviews before a book is published.

Monday 19 May
Valéry Giscard d'Estaing, the former President of France, who is chairing the great forum on the new European Constitution, came to Number 10 today, and the Government is determined not to give us a referendum on it. The *Daily Mail* wants it, *The Times* wants it, *The Sun* wants it, and the Tories want it. Andrew Marr was candid as he stood outside Number 10 Downing Street. He said the Government don't want it because they think they'd lose it. But the fundamentally undemocratic nature of Blair is coming out bit by bit.

Thursday 22 May
Just after lunch I finished reading *1984,* because I'm doing an interview about George Orwell tomorrow. I must say, it is a terrifying book. When it first came out fifty years ago, you know, you read it and said, oh, that's Hitler's Germany, that's Stalin's Russia; it had nothing to do with us. But now, after the Iraq war and with Bush and Blair in power, the whole thing looks so different and more relevant here. History is abolished in Britain. Discussion and diversity of opinion are banned, and you've got to be on-message. All enemies are demonised, and anyone like George Galloway, who takes a different view, is denounced as a traitor. Language has been adjusted. What used to be a hydrogen bomb is now a deterrent. What used to be the Ministry of War is the Ministry of Defence. What used to be accidental death is friendly fire. What used to be human beings is collateral damage. War equals peace, and terrorism has no meaning. Civil liberties are eroded, what with the Patriot Act in America, and Blunkett trying to

abolish trials here and holding people without trial. Lies are told all the time. There are Big Brothers, and the Big Brothers are Bush and Blair. What came out of it was that it's the power of information, not weapons, that controls everybody. The political class have seized control of the information – that's the Government and the media, and so on – and the proles or the working class just take it all, are expected to be kept quiet, while the people at the top run everything. It's a prophetic book, but a deeply depressing one.

Animal Farm I read quickly. That's another deeply pessimistic book: all revolutions are bound to fail.

So, with those gloomy thoughts, I'm going to bed.

Friday 23 May
Well, I got up early, and the BBC arrived at eleven o'clock to do this *1984* interview. They wanted me to talk about Room 101, where Winston Smith, the protagonist of *1984*, was tortured, but I said I didn't want to; I wanted to talk about the lies, the abolition of history, the demonisation of the enemy, the use of fear, the corruption of language; and they let me do that.

Monday 26 May
To Hereford by train and then car for the Hay-on-Wye Literature Festival. The most interesting part of the day was the dinner, at which the comedy scriptwriter Laurence Marks was present, with his wife Brigitte. He told me that he had helped Jack Straw to make one of his speeches amusing, and it was such a success that Number 10 asked if he would help Tony Blair. Of course it's not uncommon, but to get it from Laurence Marks himself was fascinating.

Wednesday 28 May
While I was sitting in the bedroom this morning, I had a phone call from LBC saying that Donald Rumsfeld had announced that nuclear weapons may not be found in Iraq, and they wanted me to do an interview. I did about a seven- or eight-minute interview, in the course of which I said that Rumsfeld had lied. They said, 'What about the Prime Minister?' and I said, 'He did too,' and gave some examples. Afterwards they said to me, 'You're not covered by parliamentary procedure. Will they bring a libel action against you?' I said, 'Well, I said what I believed', but I did think about it afterwards. I should have said, 'I don't feel under any obligation to believe anything that I'm told.' I thought later in the day it might be in the *Evening Standard*, but it wasn't – I'm not important!

At ten past five a BBC crew arrived for the programme *Heaven on Earth*, which is a semi-religious programme on Sundays. Natasha Kaplinsky, who presents the BBC *Breakfast* programme, did the interview – she is very professional and exceptionally beautiful, and of course she'd had to do all the research on me. We sat in the garden; it took about a couple of hours. She had to rush off, because she has to be up again at three o'clock tomorrow morning.

After she'd gone I took my big shopping trolley out because I had no food.

Thursday 29 May
A nice guy from Middle East Broadcasting came to do an interview. He had a little £400 camera from Dixons and said, 'I can edit it on my laptop, and I can send it via my mobile phone to Dubai.' He could carry in one hand all the equipment necessary to film, edit and transmit a complete interview across the world. I find that staggering!

Then I did Radio Sheffield, Radio Derby, Radio Scotland, Radio Bristol, Radio Birmingham, BBC Radio Wales, BBC Belfast and BBC Manchester, about Donald Rumsfeld's statement of yesterday and Blair in Iraq, with photo opportunities of him picking up babies, saying that the war had been the defining moment of the century, implying that this will set the pattern for future combat. Absolutely disgraceful!

Friday 30 May
While I was in the basement there was a knock at the door, and there was Natasha Kaplinsky, who'd come round with a box of chocolates, which was really sweet of her. She couldn't stop because she had someone in the car.

Watched the seven o'clock news, and I must say there were some sensational news stories: 2,400 people have been sacked by a company by text message. The workforce haven't received their pay, and there is no redundancy money. For the first time Channel 4 actually interviewed a trade-union leader about it, followed by a lawyer.

Then the chief executive of HSBC's subsidiary in America, Household International, was paid £35 million by the directors, and it was upheld by institutional shareholders at the shareholders' meeting, against the votes of individual shareholders.

Another news item was that a British soldier in Iraq had sent photographs to be developed in a photo shop in Birmingham, and the guy who developed these was so shocked at seeing an Iraqi soldier gagged and bound, and hanging in a net from a hook in a forklift truck, that he reported it to the police.

Sunday 1 June
Jack Straw was on the *Frost Programme* about the weapons of mass destruction. All the newspapers today are talking about lies, lies, lies. Sixty-two per cent of the people in a YouGov poll did not believe that Iraq had weapons of mass destruction. So there is this strange transformation of

opinion: before the war, there was a lot against the war; when the war began, those who were against the war were criticised; and now it's all coming back the other way again. It's so strange. You have to hold your nerve.

I went to see Ralph Gibson. I got there at half-past two, and he was lying on his back with his mouth open, breathing very lightly, on a drip, and his hands quivering. I didn't wake him. I thought it would be quite wrong, but he did really look on his last legs. A few minutes later his children arrived, and so I stayed for about an hour and talked to them, but I got the feeling he was really, really ill.

Tuesday 3 June

I caught the Tube to Lincoln's Inn for my cousin Peter Pain's memorial meeting in the Lincoln's Inn chapel. The Lord Chancellor was there, and Cherie Blair, Bill Wedderburn, my brother Dave and June. There were genuinely warm tributes paid to Peter. He did become a High Court judge, having been a communist during the war; the judge who paid a tribute to him said he was in the Labour Party, but he was in the Communist Party at one stage. Came back on the Tube, terribly tired and feeling simply lousy.

Wednesday 4 June

Blair defended himself without compromise of any kind in the House on the question of truth. John Reid, the Leader of the House, had said that rogue elements in the security services had tried to attack the Government, which I think is a silly thing for him to have said, because security services know all about everybody and they would be quite ready to bring out scandal on anyone. So I think Blair wasn't pleased about that. He just batted a straight bat and there was a vote against holding an inquiry. Labour MPs have got to think about whether, if they bring down the Prime Minister, it will affect their prospects of being re-elected. I can understand that.

Friday 6 June

I went to Oxford this morning. Met by my grandson James, went to the Apollo Theatre to drop my bag and then, though it was pelting with rain, I decided I'd walk round all the sentimental sites. I found the place where I proposed to Caroline. When I proposed to her, there were three benches in front of the church, facing towards the middle of Oxford but there was a gap in the middle, and that probably was the bench I had bought, which they never replaced. So I sat on one of the benches for a moment and thought of her and was a bit tearful – fifty-five years ago.

I walked to the Apollo Theatre. I was feeling absolutely lousy. My legs were simply giving way under me. It was painful to stand. The bottom of my feet hurt. Utterly exhausted. I went to my dressing room. I made a cup of tea and lay down, and I didn't go out before the show or during the interval, though I did go out at the end. But 700 people turned up and it went down well. James and his friend Joe were there. I'm glad I could sit; if I'd had to stand to speak, I couldn't have done it.

Saturday 7 June

I phoned Ann Gibson. Ralph wants to come home to die. I said to Ann, well, you've got to think of yourself; because if he did come home and then was suddenly in great pain or there was some crisis, she wouldn't be able to cope. I didn't put it quite like that, but she's eighty-five now, she's an old lady, and it's a big responsibility.

Monday 9 June

Today Gordon Brown made his statement about the euro. Of the five conditions, two weren't met, two might possibly be met, one was met. He committed himself to membership of the euro in principle, and everybody's happy. What is at stake here is the simple single question of democracy, because when they talk about modernising the European Union, what they mean is using commercial discipline to destroy all those progressive policies that have ever been voted in by people using the ballot box. I mean it really couldn't be clearer.

The top item of news – that's ahead of the joint press conference of Brown and Blair about the euro – is that Manchester United is prepared to sell Beckham for £30 million; and a man who was hanged fifty years ago has had his conviction quashed by the Court of Appeal (which is the case against the death penalty).

Wednesday 11 June

I went into the Commons, got a good seat, to watch Hilary, his first time taking questions as Minister of State at the Department for International Development. Up in the Gallery was Lady Amos, the Secretary of State, who gave me a friendly smile.

Hilary dealt with all the questions so well. I had congratulations from everybody. Stayed for Prime Minister's Questions afterwards, but Duncan Smith just rambles on – 'Will the Prime Minister admit that he's lied to the House?', 'Will he agree that everything he said is untrue?' It doesn't work, and Blair just knocks him back all the time. Then a couple of loyal backbenchers asked questions, so I left before the end because it was so boring.

There is a joint Select Committee considering a draft bill on corruption, so I went up and sat in the public seats. It was very interesting. Lord Slynn, who's a High Court judge, was in the chair. Paul Stinchcombe, the Labour MP, was there; I recognised him. Dale Campbell-Savours, who's now a peer, was there, came up and had a word. Janet Whitaker came up, I haven't seen her for thirty or forty years. She must be in her late sixties, a handsome woman, very supportive of Hilary, which is pleasing.

Saturday 14 June
I had a bit of a snooze, and then I worked on Samuel Pepys, because I've been asked to do a broadcast on Pepys's diary. I've never read Pepys properly, so I got hold of *The Shorter Pepys* and, I must say, I do find it extremely interesting. He had high responsibilities, and yet his diary is very personal, about what the weather was like, how his health was, what books he read, what plays he went to see, and it does make the seventeenth century real. He lived through a momentous period, starting his diary just before the Restoration of Charles II. It only lasted for ten years, but even so, it was a million and a quarter words in ten years, which is astonishing, writing in code. I'm getting an understanding of the man, and I hope I can do a decent job.

Tuesday 17 June
I went to the press conference organised by John McDonnell in support of Brian Haw, this man who's been in Parliament Square for two years. There's an attempt by Graham Allen and other MPs to add an amendment to the Anti-Social Behaviour Bill, making this type of protest illegal. A number of people spoke: an Iraqi woman, one of the Greenham Common Women, and Selma James was there, the widow of C.L.R. James, the Trinidadian socialist. They have a loudspeaker which you can hear across the road in Parliament.

Later I happened to see Graham Allen, so I said, 'I'm a bit shocked that you're trying to get Brian Haw and the women protestors off Parliament Square.'

'Well,' he said – he was magisterial about it – 'he's done it for two years. He should be given an award and left at that. And anyway, who do they represent?'

So I said, 'They're in favour of peace.'

'Oh, I know, I know, but that's not the way. They don't represent anybody.'

I said, 'Look, Graham, all progressive movements begin outside the House of Commons. They all cause trouble, and this idea that because their loudspeaker makes it difficult for MPs to work in their offices really isn't a reason for making it illegal. You're very progressive on the development of parliamentary democracy,' which he is, 'but you can't exclude the role of people outside.'

'Oh, but who do the protestors represent?'

'Well,' I said, 'the twelve apostles didn't represent anybody, but they started the Christian Church.'

Friday 20 June

Hilary rang up to say that Michael, his eldest, had got a first-class honours degree in Leeds, so I rang immediately. He's so laid-back about it!

I had a doze after lunch, and then in the afternoon who should turn up for an hour and a half but Saffron. She was on her way between one engagement and another in Hammersmith, so we sat in the garden for an hour and a half. She's making a film with Brad Pitt on the Trojan War. She's got the possibility of doing something in New Zealand in the New Year. She seemed more relaxed.

Monday 23 June

A comedian dressed as Osama Bin Laden broke into Windsor Castle for Prince William's twenty-first birthday party; it has been treated so seriously, you'd hardly believe it. Also the Government is about to sign an extradition agreement with America, whereby America expects the UK to hand over anybody without a court hearing in Britain. Blunkett is an impossible man. Caroline Flint, the new minister, a tough woman, was justifying it. I'm so glad Hilary is nothing to do with the Home Office now.

Tuesday 24 June

To the Commons, where I heard the last half-hour of the meeting of the Royal Society of Chemistry, which Stephen had organised, with Harry Kroto, who is the President of the Royal Society, a Nobel Prize-winner.

Then walked up to the House of Lords for the annual lunch, which followed in the Cholmondeley Room. Lissie was there, and Hilary turned up. Charles Clarke made a speech. He looked a bit stressed. Melissa had to go on to Number 10 to have tea with Nita, because Melissa is working on an interesting idea for a novel and wants to know what Number 10 is like.

I saw George Galloway. He said he'd got substantial damages from the *Christian Science Monitor* newspaper, so he's doing well.

Then to Maritime House, the old National Union of Seamen head-quarters, in Clapham for the annual party in support of Cuba – old comrades galore! Ken Livingstone was there; Simon Fletcher, Mick Rix, Tony Woodley (the newly elected General Secretary of the Transport and General Workers' Union). Jennie Walsh, Pam Tatlow and Bob Crow were there. It was a gathering of the clans – quite a few hundred people, I would think.

About a quarter to eight Bob Crow introduced Ken Livingstone, who made a good speech. Then Tony Woodley began his speech with an elaborate tribute to me. I said that I'd made a great sacrifice and decided to give my raffle tickets to Tony Blair if I won, because I felt a fortnight in Cuba would be good for him, and to have a fortnight without him would be good here. By the end of my speech I had an acute pain in my chest – not in the centre of my chest, where heart attacks are; it was a sort of cramp in the left side of my chest, but still, it was very painful, so I decided to come straight home.

Wednesday 25 June

I was asked to review the papers for the *Daily Politics* show with Andrew Neil, so of course I'd bought all the papers first thing, chosen some stories, and when I got there, I found Neil had decided what was to be shown – *The Sun*, and Max Hastings in the *Express*, both papers that supported the war. 'Hunt them down' said *The Sun*, and, 'This is not a Vietnam.' I had a terrible argument with them. I said, 'Look, you asked me to review the papers. You're now asking me to comment on the review of the papers by Andrew Neil!'

'Oh, that is the way we've done the graphics.'

I said, 'Well, there you are.' Anyway, Tim Garden, Air Marshal Lord Garden who was an Assistant Chief of Defence staff, was also there. I've known him some time. He's a decent guy.

We went in, and when I said to him that I thought we had been misled on the war, Andrew Neil interrupted: 'So you say the Prime Minister's a liar, do you?'

I said, 'Look, don't personalise it. I think we were misled.'

'Oh, so it's—'

So I said, 'If you want to do all the talking, I'll sit and listen. I'm quite happy to do that.' I was really angry, but I did get my points across.

And then when I mentioned Vietnam, Neil said, 'Oh, if I had five pounds for every time Vietnam was mentioned, I wouldn't have to work.' He said, 'You talked about Vietnam in the first Gulf War.'

'Well,' I said, 'it's led to this, and anyway, why did Britain and America at one time support Saddam?' Of course he couldn't answer. Anyway, I did the best I could, but I regretted afterwards having agreed to it.

Then I walked over to the House of Commons, and at 12.30 Natasha Kaplinsky came over to lunch with me. She did actually work with Neil Kinnock for a year, 1991 to '92, before she went up to Oxford. She went into radio and then Sky TV, which she said was sexist and awful. She moved over to the BBC, and works with Dermot Murnaghan, whom she likes.

I took her down to the broom cupboard and showed her the plaque to the suffragette Emily Wilding Davidson, and we had lunch in the Adjournment restaurant. We looked at my portrait on the first floor, and then I went over to the Terrace Cafeteria to have a cup of tea. She had a peppermint tea. After that I drove her to Dickens & Jones store.

Today Alastair Campbell gave evidence to the Foreign Affairs Committee. It was such a poor interrogation. They hadn't done any homework. Sir John Stanley did quite well, and Andrew Mackinlay tried, but they hadn't prepared their questions. It was so casual and cosy, and as

Alan Simpson said, Campbell was being gored by dead sheep – the phrase that Denis Healey used against his opposite number, Geoffrey Howe, in the 1980s.

I put my head round the door of the Stop the War Coalition because they were making me Honorary President.

Tomorrow is a free day, and then I've got an absolutely killing programme! It really frightens me physically – Liverpool and Bristol, then Glastonbury. I suppose I can manage, but quite how, I do not know.

More incidents in Iraq. The British General in charge of Basra said that many Iraqis regarded the British occupation as worse than Saddam's regime. The truth is they never thought out what would happen when they occupied. All they wanted to do was defeat Saddam, and after that they planned nothing. It's an incredible story. Alastair Campbell's response yesterday, 'Are you suggesting, a grave charge against the Prime Minister, that he took Britain to war and cost the lives of British and Iraqis by telling a deliberate lie? Are you suggesting that?' Well, of course, that is exactly what is being suggested, and he counter-attacked by accusing the BBC of lying. The BBC have defended themselves quite vigorously. But it is all crumbling. I keep saying this, but it is.

Saturday 28 June
To Bristol, where I am being picked up and taken to Glastonbury by my editor. She turned up at about quarter to eleven and we went to Bristol Temple Meads station, where her twin sister Diana Martin was with her son Matthew, who's nineteen, who realised that his best chance of getting in to the Festival was with me!

We had a sticker for the car, which I had put in my diary notes, and with that everyone waved us on and we got to the Festival site about half-past one and were found a place at the car park.

Everything is done by mobile phone. There are 120,000, 140,000, 160,000 people at Glastonbury. It is an astonishing site! All these little tents, all the cars, all the motorbikes, masses of stewards, volunteers, all young, and the most elaborate, completely informal structure. And lots of stalls.

Ruth decided to go off for the day, and I don't blame her. I was taken to the Left Field, and Bianca Jagger turned up. The Left Field had been made three times as big as it was last year, but there was a concert going on next to us and the noise was unbelievable. I could hardly hear myself speak, and I wondered whether anyone could come, but there were 2,000 people in the tent. We had a lot of questions, again mainly 'What's the point of voting for the Labour Party?', it's all hopeless, what are we going to do, get rid of Blair, and so on.

Then to the Green Tent, and there was Mark Thomas, the activist and comedian, chairing it, and a huge circle of people. Somebody stamped my arm with one of these transfers that looks like a tattoo, for Save the Children. Somebody also gave me a little envelope that said, 'War on want. Screw poverty', and later I opened it and found a condom inside.

The Tory MP, Ian Liddell-Grainger, the local MP, was there. Ruth later picked me up and brought me home – she found the noise and pollution unbearable. I got home about ten o'clock, maybe a little bit later.

I was so tired, I didn't even make a cup of tea, I just dumped my stuff and went straight to bed.

Saturday 5 July

To the London Pavilion with the family for *Chitty Chitty Bang Bang*. It was my treat, of course, the meal and the tickets. I was terribly tired, and my feet are very painful now – I can't walk much. I dozed off, but it was a fantastic performance – the scenery and the car that flew were unbelievable, and the girls had a whale of a time.

There is violence in Iraq, Chechnyan violence in Russia – wherever you look, there's violence. It's terribly, terribly difficult, and easy to get frightfully depressed.

Sunday 6 July

Well, I had a lazy morning. I just sat in the bedroom in my underpants and nightgown and read all the papers.

The top of the news this evening is that the new Bishop of Reading, who's just been appointed suffragan bishop by the Bishop of Oxford, has asked permission to withdraw. He has to ask the Queen's permission, because she's already appointed him. The reason is, quite frankly, that the African members of the Lambeth Conference would have withdrawn from the Anglican communion worldwide if a gay bishop had been consecrated. They could quite happily live with war and bloodshed, but not with homosexuality, and it shows how terribly vulnerable the Church is, because these African churches have become very evangelical and fundamentalist, and for them, gay relations are just worse than killing people. It shows how weak Christian teaching, or Jesus's teaching, is.

Monday 7 July

The Foreign Affairs Committee reported today. Alastair Campbell was saved from censure by Donald Anderson, who is the chairman of the committee, a Government appointee of course and a solid Labour man, a former Foreign Office man. But the real disgrace of the report was that they accepted that Campbell could be blamed for something, when actually the Prime Minister is his boss. He's not elected, he's not a civil servant, so to blame Campbell is a diversion, which suits Blair very well indeed. Also, they never had any opportunity of assessing whether Campbell had tightened up and sharpened up the intelligence report, because the committee weren't allowed to see the original. So the whole thing is a complete fraud. Number 10 and the BBC will claim it as a victory, and the BBC governors met last night and took a strong line, much to my surprise.

Tuesday 8 July
Had lunch, and went out and got some cake for my visitors, Dr Sanjiv Shah and his colleague, Dr Joseph McGowan.

They're an interesting couple. I have met them briefly before; they send huge cheques, for £500 and £200, to all sorts of good organisations, like the Campaign for Nuclear Disarmament, the Stop the War Coalition, and they always put on the cheque 'In honour of Tony Benn'. They're based in a hospital in the Bronx, and they're both HIV Aids experts. They're both presenting papers next week in Paris, on Aids, and asked if they could come and see me. I said I couldn't offer them a meal, but suggested tea.

Sanjiv is an Indian whose family moved to Tanzania and then emigrated to England; he was educated at Leicester as a doctor, and then went to New York. Joseph was born in New York. They were very shrewd. They talked about relations between health and living standards, and Aids and the cost of drugs. New York City does provide Aids drugs free; in Africa, the cost of the drugs is astronomical. With drugs, you can now have a reasonable life.

Tony Blair appeared before the Liaison Committee (of Select Committee chairmen) this morning, and I saw little clips of it on the television. He reminds me more and more of Anthony Eden at the time of Suez, a man absolutely possessed, won't contemplate any alternative explanation. 'Oh, we know the weapons were there! The intelligence was right. We know it was right. We did the right thing. Won't budge an inch,' and the only thing you can do is to ask short factual questions.

Saturday 12 July
I heard that the CIA has now repudiated the story that Nigeria was asked to supply uranium for Iraq, and that's another nail in Blair's coffin.

Wednesday 16 July
Had a lovely anonymous letter from someone in Tring:

Dear Arsehole,
     Saw you on the *Politics Show*. It's time you buggered off and lived with Saddam Hussein, or die like your ghastly dead wife.

So at least I haven't sold out.

I went to the Campaign Group; I'm glad I did because Jack Straw came along at his own request. He said the Parliamentary Labour Party is falling apart. We're having all these rows, and what's really worrying is the attitude to the Government. The elections are coming, and we've got to have confidence in Labour. Then he went round the table for comments. It was a speech absolutely without substance. It was either a leadership bid or a pep talk.

Anyway, Alice Mahon said it's the Government v. the Party – for example foundation hospitals, fox hunting and Iraq. She said the British National Party is growing in strength, and Muslims are leaving the Party.

Bob Wareing said the Government is the worst he'd known, Blair is a liability. Take student fees, for example. He contrasted him with Attlee.

Neil Gerrard said most Labour MPs support the Government in the lobbies, but if you had a secret poll they wouldn't, and Party members are leaving.

Bob Marshall-Andrews asked, are we wrecking the PLP? He called Bush the most right-wing president in history and asked, why is Blair supporting him?

I said, 'Well, I haven't voted against the Government for the past two years', and people laughed, 'but I'm going round and having to respond to people who say "I'm tearing up my Party card" and asking them to stay. People don't want student fees. They don't want the public services privatised. People want a Labour government! Truthfully I think Blair is doing to the Labour Party from the inside what MacDonald did, and I can hardly believe our arguments are hard left. I didn't know Trotsky had such modest objectives.'

John Cryer said that we're breaking up the Welfare State, that's what the Third Way is about.

Kelvin Hopkins said it used to be socialists against social democracy, and now it's neo-conservatives against social democracy, and Blair's a neo-conservative. Andrew Adonis, at Number 10, the education adviser, was a Liberal Democrat candidate. He tried to be a Tory candidate, and now he's at Number 10.

Alan Simpson says Number 10 is tearing the Party apart, and to try and convert Europe into adopting American neo-conservatism is ridiculous.

Then Jack Straw said: thank you very much. It was interesting actually, the fact that Jack listened. But although he's Foreign Secretary, he doesn't sound much more than a rather inadequate backbencher.

Thursday 17 July
Blair is in America, meeting Bush, and addressing a joint session of Congress, and going round the world.

Friday 18 July
I got taken by car to South Africa House for the BBC World Service *Outlook* programme to celebrate Mandela's eighty-fifth birthday. We were on the clock floor, went out on the balcony, a beautiful day, overlooking Trafalgar

Square. It felt strange being in South Africa House, outside which so many protests had taken place.

The *New Statesman* today has got pages attacking Blair, including a psychological analysis of him, and of course as the *New Statesman* is owned by the MP Geoffrey Robinson, people think this is a Brownite plot to get rid of Blair.

Watched the six o'clock news, and of course *the* sensational news today is that Dr David Kelly, the expert on chemical weapons – who'd been a UN inspector, who was forced by the Ministry of Defence to say he had seen Andrew Gilligan, the BBC correspondent – was found dead two and a half miles from his home. Gilligan had denied he was the source (of the 'sexing up the dossier' story). But Kelly was forced to appear before the Foreign Affairs Committee this week and really roasted there.

Of course immediately the question is: did Kelly commit suicide or was he murdered? It's an incredible story. Blair was told on the flight from Washington to Japan, because he's doing a world trip, a lap of honour after the Iraq invasion, and he's ordered an independent inquiry.

It was a beautiful evening.

Saturday 19 July
News today of course entirely dominated by the death of David Kelly. The anxiety I'd had that he might have been murdered was disproved, because he had cut his wrists and was found in a pool of blood. Now everybody's turning on the Government. Who was responsible? Was it Geoff Hoon, who gave Kelly's name to the press and exposed him to this? Was it MI5? Was it Alastair Campbell, who wanted to show him up as the source of the allegation? Was it the BBC? Was it the Prime Minister? Even in Tokyo, where the Prime Minister is on an extraordinary world tour at this moment, a journalist asked him, 'Prime Minister, is there blood on your hands?' and he just looked blank and didn't respond. The voices are really beginning to be raised now against him. It is *the* most extraordinary crisis. I think the effect of it will be that his popularity will fall, and Labour MPs will begin thinking again. Gordon Brown may be riding high.

Sunday 20 July
Glenda Jackson has now called on the Prime Minister to resign. It is just one frightful tragedy for the family, but it is also, in a sense, the result of the Government deciding to convert the question of whether we should go to war into a libel action between Alastair Campbell and the BBC, with people trying to get witnesses on both sides. I don't think anybody comes out of it very well.

A chap called Paul Dunn and his wife Eva drove me to Tolpuddle for the annual festival. Eva is a young Portuguese woman who organises sex workers into a union, not just prostitutes but lap dancers, pole dancers and people who work in the sex industry. I have to brace myself for the idea that sex workers are organised.

I got to Tolpuddle and tons of people wanted photographs and autographs.

This evening Andrew Gilligan, the BBC correspondent, said that Kelly had been the main source and that he had interpreted what Kelly had told him correctly. Maybe that explains Kelly's death. Gilligan, in order to protect Kelly, said he wasn't his only source, but now Kelly's dead, he confirmed that he was. The whole thing is a ghastly tragedy, an unending tragedy.

Tuesday 22 July
There was a telephone call from Washington, from Democracy Now, about the Kelly case. I tried to set it in its proper historical context, that Blair was desperately trying to find retrospective justification for going to war, and that the BBC argument that the Government had hyped up the dossier to make Parliament more ready to vote for the war was what it was all about.

Wednesday 23 July
James, my grandson, arrived and worked in the office from ten to four, that's six hours, and he typed sixty letters and answered the phone. He's brilliant at it. And he is such fun. He says he loves coming to help – and the money's useful. He's got a new girlfriend called Blake, who is a medic at Cambridge.

To 1 Carlton Gardens, and there was the reception, given by *Tribune*, for Michael Foot's ninetieth birthday. Jack Straw had allowed his official residence to be made available for it. There was a little orchestra playing down below, and I went up to the first floor. I said, 'Michael, I'm Tony Benn, and I hope you'll ask me to your one hundredth birthday', so it registered with him that I was there.

Michael spoke for about ten minutes. He was sitting all the time. His head was shaking about, as it does. He highlighted his support for the war in Yugoslavia, which I thought was strange, but still, he is ninety.

Had a talk to the trade-union leaders there, Brendan Barber, the new General Secretary of the TUC, Derek Simpson of Amicus and Billy Hayes of the CWU.

The Americans have confirmed that Saddam Hussein's two sons were killed, which is being hailed as a great victory. Whatever crooks they were, they've never been tried for anything, just been killed.

There is an underlying unity in the Labour Party. Although Michael Foot disagrees with Government policy and made a few jokes about it, and Straw is strongly in favour of the war, and Peter Hain is in favour of a federal Europe and the war, and Mick Rix is on the left, there is a certain affectionate respect, which means the Labour Party still exists as a party. I felt that strongly in the past, that we were having family rows and, astonishing as it is, that is still the position. Is it so different from the old days? Frankly, when Callaghan was there during the Winter of Discontent, or when the IMF capitulation occurred in 1976, or when Wilson had a row with the unions in 1969, the hatred of the leadership was just as strong as it is now, although now it's more direct.

I'm on a fruit diet at the moment. I think I've lost about a quarter of a stone over the last few days. I'm trying to stick to fruit. All I want is my tum to be filled up, but I do yearn for my favourite pizzas, for something a bit more substantial. I love my hot-cross buns and butter and marmalade in the morning. How long I'll keep it up, I don't know.

Thursday 24 July

I had a simply hideous night. My legs were hurting like anything. I don't know whether it was cramp. I thought I might have a blood clot. I felt a pressure on my chest. I was really anxious and woke on every hour, and tried to sleep, but couldn't.

The Americans have decided to display on Iraqi television and their own television pictures of Saddam's two sons, who have been killed by American forces on a tip-off, I think. Just a few weeks ago when the Iraqis showed some dead American soldiers, it led to an outcry from Washington.

Friday 25 July

I went to the shop where there are two Indian brothers from whom I buy my tobacco, and one of them said, 'People, many people, would not buy newspapers today because of the pictures of Saddam Hussein's sons after they had been killed by the Americans.' The *Daily Mail* refused to print the pictures. He said, 'I'm not a Muslim, but I'm really, really shocked', and so am I.

Had a bite to eat. I'm ashamed to say I had a pizza because I was so hungry.

Saturday 26 July

To the Westminster and Chelsea Hospital to see Ralph Gibson. Last time I saw him I thought he was at death's door and, after that, he had a couple of strokes, but today he was sitting in his chair, his head almost completely shaved. Ann Gibson, his wife, and Mary, his daughter, were there. We had a lovely talk on the question of the Lord Chancellor, and Lord Hutton, and various other matters.

Wednesday 30 July

I watched Tony Blair's press conference before he went off on holiday, and it was like the president of a multinational corporation giving a report. He called on Michael Barber, the Head of the Delivery Unit, to show a lot of charts, and then he answered questions. I must say, the press questions were pretty awful. 'Are you thinking of resigning?' 'Don't you think that the captain of the England cricket team must have been under a lot of stress?' which was another reference to resignation, because the captain has resigned. Questions about Iraq. All he does is to say that he himself believes the evidence.

Saturday 2 August
I met Caroline, I met my darling Caroline, fifty-five years ago today in Oxford.

By extraordinary coincidence, there was a photograph in *The Guardian* of her with me canvassing in Bristol in 1950. It was attached to a comment I made on the fact that today Tony Blair exceeds Clem Attlee's record as Labour Prime Minister.

After lunch, I had an hour and half's sleep in the deckchair in the garden. It was a beautiful day!

Sunday 3 August
Had a meal, and then I watched the programme on Channel 4 about Denis Thatcher, by Carol Thatcher. It did really reveal the true nature of his relationship with Mrs Thatcher. She said there was no question of romance. He was just Victor Meldrew, which future readers of the *Diaries* will not understand, but a sort of classic, old-fashioned, stick-in-the-mud, retired, middle-class English pensioner.

There was also an article in the paper today saying how lonely Mrs Thatcher was, and I felt for her as an individual. She's not very well, she's had a couple of strokes, Denis Thatcher's gone. Her name is still in the papers because she's set the tone for British politics from about 1975, when she became Leader, until today. That thirty-year period I would like to say has ended, but of course it hasn't, because the neo-conservatives in the form of President Bush in America have taken it up and developed it. Blair has taken it up and adopted it. So we're still in the grip of that woman's ideas, and what it does show is that if you use the premiership in order to argue your philosophy, you can have a bigger influence than by being a chief executive for a period.

Monday 4 August
The news today is all about Gene Robinson, the gay bishop in the States. It is of course a fact that if the American Anglicans or the Church of England were to appoint a gay bishop, it would create a terrible crisis, and the Nigerians and African bishops would probably break away. But what a church, to accept that you can kill people, but you can't have a homosexual relationship – incredible.

Tuesday 5 August

Had a shattering cramp in the back of both thighs at 6.30, and leaped out of bed. It really hurts so much I could scream. Nothing I can do about it, but I decided to bring ice cubes up into the bedroom and keep them in a cool container and put them on my legs if it happens again.

At Number 10, a senior press officer (also called Kelly) has apologised to David Kelly's family for having described him as a fantasist, a Walter Mitty figure. It is quite incredible that Number 10 feels free to rubbish anybody who gets in their way! I mean, it's undermined the credibility of Campbell, and it'll strengthen the credibility of Kelly, whose friends will rally round. It makes Blair's appeal for restraint look contemptible.

Thursday 7 August

To BBC Television Centre to discuss with Charles Bailey the album which he has made of my speeches, set to rap. We did the interview with Jon Sopel and Natasha Kaplinsky. They illustrated it by showing a clip from my speech at the mass rally in Hyde Park in February, and I must say it is powerful. It was, from their point of view, a celebrity event, but at the same time it was an opportunity to make an argument. I compared rap with spin – spin is when you change what you believe to get power, and rap is when you reaffirm what you believe and embellish it with music to get an audience. Afterwards, Natasha asked me to go and have what she called breakfast with her – I had a cup of tea and a banana. She's very sweet.

Monday 11 August

I wrote my *Morning Star* article on Tony Blair's speech to Congress in which he said that 'There never has been a time when . . . except in the most general sense, the study of history provides so little instruction for our present day.' Dave spotted it. I got the full text from the Internet, and I argued in my piece that there's nothing to fear from Blair because he doesn't understand the movement, or socialism, or anything. He doesn't want us to study these things, because that might challenge what he says.

Then what happened? The Hutton Inquiry into the Kelly affair has opened, and some interesting things have been said. It's quite clear that Kelly did reflect the anxiety of very senior people, as he himself was the greatest expert on the Iraq arms question, and although there was an attempt by a Cabinet Office official to say that there was no anxiety about the dossier at the top, it's quite clear there was.

Tuesday 12 August

Another very hot day. After lunch I cleared my in-tray in seven hours, apart from a few inconsequential letters that are no problem. It saved me £100 that I would have had to pay somebody to come and do it, and apart from a few spelling mistakes in the letters, I was quite happy.

The thing that has come out of the Kelly business, but I don't know how long it will take for people to realise it, is the incredibly close relations between the BBC and the Government. Alastair Campbell rings up and complains all the time, puts pressure on journalists, and I think that was one of the reasons why Gilligan was happy to hit back.

Also, the extent and role of these private briefings, and who does them and why, is important. The BBC never mention that they're under pressure from the Government, and I think that needs to be brought out.

Tuesday 19 August
Alastair Campbell was at the Hutton Inquiry – absolutely no concessions whatever.

Saturday 23 August, Stansgate
Basil Willsmer, who has been our builder in Essex for years and years, came to tea, and Stephen, Hilary, Melissa and Joshua and I sat with him on the front lawn, and we did some long-term planning. The house has to be repainted, and we will have to make more space for archives.

Tuesday 26 August
The intelligence people are staying absolutely close to Campbell, and Campbell to them, and Blair has got a sound foundation to give evidence, but his role in this is extraordinary. The 'forty-five minutes' came from what's called one reliable source, which turns out to have been an Iraqi general. Well, an Iraqi general who wanted to be rid of Saddam would have realised the quickest way is to tell the Americans that Saddam has the capacity to fire off weapons of mass destruction. Saddam *was* got rid of, and I don't know what's happened to the General, but it would be interesting to know if he turns up on the top of the pile. The whole thing is so corrupt.

My grandson James turned up for about ten minutes. He was going round the corner to meet his girlfriend Blake. He wants to bring her to see me. So I went to the top of the house and looked out of the window, and I saw him with this dark-haired girl, shorter than he is. Very sweet.

Wednesday 27 August
I got up at 5.30. Was picked up by a Nigerian driver, who took me to Sky, to review the papers. I concentrated on Hutton, which is what they wanted me to do. Coming back, the same Nigerian told me he'd been in Israel a couple of times. He was one of those Christian Evangelicals who believed that God had given Israel to the Jews, and the 'Palestinians are just nomads. They've never had a home.' When I argued with him, in a friendly way, he got passionate and said, 'You've got to crush terrorists everywhere.' He sounded like Sharon or Bush. He was friendly enough. He was a boxer and

he said, 'When you're a boxer, you only punch a man when he's down' and was really quite crude about it.

Hoon is the big story today. He didn't take the rap and blame himself. He said, 'The Prime Minister decided this' – acted just like Alastair Campbell.

Thursday 28 August

Had a phone call from Baghdad from Sadoon al-Zubaydi, who had interpreted for me both in 1990 and this year with Saddam Hussein, and who in the interval had been Iraqi Ambassador in Jakarta. I asked for his address, but he said, 'Well, you can write to me at the Administration Department at the Foreign Office in Baghdad', so I wrote a cautious letter there.

Friday 29 August

Snoozed after lunch, and then awoke to the news that Alastair Campbell has resigned.

I've never seen anything like it before in terms of coverage. I mean, if the Prime Minister had resigned, it would have been no greater.

I did ITV News, Sky, News 24, Star FM, BBC Birmingham, LBC twice. Then I was taken by car to TV Centre for News 24 with Julia Langdon. Then a soundbite for the *News at Ten*. Came home, and Democracy Now! in America rang me up, and I did about quarter of an hour or more with them. I'm going to bed, because I've got to be up early tomorrow.

It has been an incredible day, and the point I've made in all these broadcasts is that Campbell is a charming, loyal, dedicated person, but nobody has ever been given such power as he was given by the Prime Minister, who'd made him effectively Deputy Prime Minister, part of the Cabinet, not accountable to Parliament. I think I established a different interpretation.

As to the rest, it was all about Campbell and his partner Fiona Millar, and how did he feel, and how did Blair feel, and so on, and that's typical media coverage.

To have sat at home and done twelve broadcasts is not a bad day's work!

Sunday 31 August

Mrs Kelly is giving evidence this week, and I must say, if she were to say she wasn't certain that her husband had committed suicide, the whole thing would explode in a way that nobody could contain.

Monday 1 September

I had a hell of a struggle defrosting the fridge, which is frozen solid.

David Kelly's widow gave evidence, very modestly and quietly, on a video link from another room at the Royal Courts of Justice. It was moving.

She said her husband had been totally devastated by the way he'd been treated by the Ministry of Defence. There was apparently a letter found in his desk offering him a knighthood, so that made even more disreputable the idea that he was just a medium-rank official who was a Walter Mitty fantasist. I think, from the human point of view, that statement by her, which was modest and presented clearly, will probably cost Geoff Hoon his job and do immense damage to the Prime Minister.

Saturday 6 September

It is quite obvious that Sharon has not given Abu Mazen enough concessions to retain the confidence of the Palestinian Authority, let alone deal with Hamas and the other people engaged in military action against Israel. The real problem, of course, is Bush. He's lost all interest in the Road Map. He just did it for a photoshoot in the desert with Abu Mazen and Sharon. Sharon won't deal with Arafat, both Bush and Sharon are trying to get Arafat out, but the thing has run absolutely into the sand. It was, as in all previous peace initiatives, just a question of trying to carry the Americans through a difficult period.

Colin Powell appears now to be much more influential in the State Department, and the neo-cons, Cheney and Wolfowitz, Rice and Rumsfeld, seem to be diminishing in power. Colin Powell is trying to get the French and Russians in, and the Germans, but I very much hope they don't give way, unless they have total control of the operation, which the Americans won't concede.

I cleared out six sacks of rubbish, old papers, old envelopes that I've collected over the years, and I must say the office is beginning to look much better.

Tuesday 9 September

Went out shopping, looking for my favourite triple-cheese pizzas, which have disappeared from the local supermarket. I go in search of them because I've eaten two of them every day for years.

There's been another suicide bombing, soldiers have been killed at a bus stop in Israel, and the Israelis are busy assassinating people they suspect as Hamas leaders. It's just awful.

Wednesday 10 September

To the Gallery to hear Prime Minister's Questions. I haven't heard it for a time, and I must say it was awful! Blair didn't answer any question properly. Duncan Smith just launched into his usual tirade – 'Isn't it time the Prime Minister admitted he's been lying to the nation for years on everything?' and so on. That doesn't help. Duncan Smith is a complete flop, and it gives Blair an opportunity to shine, when actually he's got nothing to shine about. But anyway, I went.

Then I had a cup of tea in the Tea Room. I saw Andrew Mackinlay, who was desperately keen to talk, because he's got hammered for being aggressive to David Kelly when the latter appeared at the Foreign Affairs Committee in July.

Anyway, then I went from there up to Committee Room 21 because there was an inquiry by the Procedure Committee on what to do about demonstrators in Parliament Square, notably Brian Haw, who's been camping there for two years protesting – sometimes noisily and with lots of placards – against the government. There were three witnesses giving evidence, Nicholas Soames, Jeremy Corbyn and Jenny Tonge. I listened for about an hour and a quarter. Nicholas Soames was very keen not to be anti-Haw or anti-demonstrations, but said you've got to be sensible. Corbyn was in favour of letting him carry on. Jenny Tonge was good.

Before the Committee, I was talking to Nicholas Soames, who told me a story about Churchill. He said that during the war, just before the Anzio landing, one of the cleaners from the War Office went out into Whitehall and saw in the street under a bus some papers that looked official. So she picked them up and they appeared to be important, and she took them back to the War Office. She said, 'I'm not handing them over to anybody other than a general.' Finally, after a lot of hoo-ha – I think she was there for hours – a general appeared. She explained and he saw what they were and took them from her. The Cabinet Committee that afternoon was told, and Churchill said to his staff, 'See that woman gets a Dame of the British Empire.' So anyway, it was put to the palace and the King turned it down. So, Soames said, in 1945, after the war, Churchill's Honours List included a DBE for this woman. It is a lovely and typical story!

Friday 12 September
Charles Bailey and his sister Grace picked me up and took me to HMV in Oxford Street for the launch of the rap album. Dear Josh turned up, bless his heart. I haven't been into the HMV shop for fifty years, maybe longer, and as you walk round, you see thousands and thousands and thousands of albums. It really makes a bookshop seem quite understocked!

There were about thirty photographers, all saying, 'Look here', 'Look there', 'Look here'. Australian Television was there, because apparently the album is being played in Australia. Then I did some album-signing. It was interesting – older people, younger people, black people.

Saturday 13 September
Michel Abdel-Masih, QC picked me up and took me to SOAS, the School of Oriental and African Studies for the conference on the future of Palestine. Professor Naseer Aruri, who is at the University of Massachusetts at Dartmouth, gave an account of the situation that was very penetrating,

and at the end he said he inclined to a one-nation state. I think the reasons the Palestinians are coming back to the idea is because their territories have been so cut up that it is just a little group of Bantustans, and how that could be a state, I really do not know.

Michel himself was powerful on the absolute crime of governments that resort to assassination. He said normally assassination is part of the practice of governments, who nevertheless always deny it, but in the case of Sharon, he's admitting it, and they're even talking openly about assassinating Arafat.

I did the best I could, but I didn't feel at all well.

Sunday 14 September

Taxi to see Hilary, because he's off on Tuesday, and it's a tremendously responsible mission. He's going to be staying in Basra, and then flying up to Baghdad for a day, and he'll be back on Friday morning. If anything happened to that boy, I don't know how any of the family could survive. But he's practical about it, is old Hilary.

I rang Lissie and Stephen. They're aggressively anxious about my health, which doesn't help – you can't bully an old man who's not feeling too well! But I will go and have a flu jab, and have my ears syringed and one or two other things in the course of the week, if I have time.

Monday 15 September

The Swedish voted against the euro – a brilliant result. The World Trade Organisation talks broke down because the developed countries simply wouldn't concede any more to the developing countries. So you just get the feeling, as I keep saying in the diary, that something is going on under the surface.

Friday 19 September

Well, the Liberal Democrats won Brent East. They overturned a 13,000 Labour majority, The Labour candidate, who had been supported by Ken Livingstone, was defeated, and this twenty-nine-year-old Liberal Democrat woman was elected. The Tory vote went down 2,000, the Liberal vote went up about a couple of thousand, but the Labour vote just simply collapsed. The left candidates, of which there are a number, picked up 130, 140 votes, so the Socialist Alliance and the Socialist Party and all that are really irrelevant in the situation we're in at the moment. But it's a big shock for Blair, and it'll greatly strengthen the *Party* at the Conference next week in Bournemouth, because people will realise that the leader's a loser.

Laura Rohde came along with her little baby, Lilianna, who's eight months old – absolutely enchanting!

At about eleven o'clock a woman from Eritrea came to see me. She works in a local supermarket and I have got to know her. Her husband was killed ten years ago. She's been in Britain since then, she's educated herself, but she has no right of permanent residence, as she is an asylum claimant. She asked if she could come and talk to me. When I asked about her mother and father, she just sat there sobbing. But they haven't chased her out, so I wrote to David Blunkett and Michael Portillo, the local MP whom she'd already seen and who has been helpful, and I wrote to her lawyer, and I sent a copy to her. It was really like being a constituency MP again. I spent a couple of hours on it, but I haven't really got the resources to do it.

Daniel is doing his six nights in the Trinity Boys' choir of the opera at Covent Garden. It's a phenomenal achievement!

Blair's over in Berlin seeing Schröder, the German Chancellor, and Chirac, the French President, but Berlusconi, the current President of the European Council, wasn't there, and neither was Prodi, the President of the Commission. So this is obviously an attempt to mend the fences between Blair and France and Germany.

Sunday 21 September
It is the Liberal Democrats' conference this week, with Charles Kennedy cock-a-hoop, but actually what happened at Brent East was a big Conservative defeat because the Thatcherite/Blairite policy just isn't popular any more. So there's a vacuum, and that's what the Labour Conference has to do, fill the vacuum, because you cannot have a democratic system without a serious alternative, and people want a *Labour* Government.

I went for dinner with Marion Miliband, Ralph's widow, and her son David. Also there were Leo Panitch and Colin Leys, Hilary Wainwright and a couple of others. It's very difficult with David Miliband – I have to be careful, but we did discuss a number of things. Leo asked him about Iraq. I said I was surprised the Cabinet didn't insist on meeting for longer, and we had a word about Campbell. I thought Campbell was being unfairly attacked, because he was entirely loyal to the Prime Minister, and it was the Prime Minister who gave him the powers he had. David said there wasn't that much power.

When I arrived, I gave the rap album to Leo, and he insisted on playing the major anti-Iraq war speech at Hyde Park. An intellectual audience like that might have thought it was just silly, but they didn't, they were quite impressed by it.

Tuesday 23 September
The American Government has announced that foreign investors can invest in any companies or services, hospitals, schools in Iraq, and export the profits (except in minerals and oil, which the American Government intends to hang on to). It is a vivid example of American imperialism, followed by privatisation of the assets of the conquered country.

I sorted out my Conference programme, wrote my *Morning Star* article and then I watched Bush at the United Nations. He was preceded by Kofi Annan, the Secretary General, who issued the most solemn warning against pre-emptive action. He didn't mention America or Britain, but it was obvious what he was talking about. It was exactly what I had said in 1998 about there being no provision in international law for pre-emptive action. But the real thrill watching Bush, of course, was that as the camera flashed round, there was Jack Straw and next to him Hilary, sitting with the world's leaders. Oh, I was so thrilled! I never got to the UN General Assembly. The only ambition I ever really had was to be Secretary General of the UN.

Wednesday 24 September
I drove to Lewisham for the Lewisham Pensioners' Forum. Had lunch in the Mayor's Parlour. I like Lewisham Council. It's always open to people. One of the local MPs, Jim Dowd, was there. I had a poor impression of him, and of course he was a Whip and a real Blairite.

There were 800 pensioners in the theatre, and I was the second speaker. I was feeling shaky. I wasn't even sure I'd be able to stand to do it, but I managed all right and afterwards I slipped off and came home.

The CIA have now published, or leaked, the report by 1,400 people who've been looking for weapons of mass destruction in Iraq, and have found none. Jon Snow tonight interviewed somebody about it, and he said, 'Well, of course Saddam would never admit he didn't happen to have them', but that is exactly what he did when I saw him! I nearly rang up Jon Snow and said, 'Half a minute! Saddam told me he didn't have them.' They were making out that he'd pretended he had weapons in order to prevent an attack on Iraq.

Thursday 25 September
I only heard when I got back in the evening that Hilary addressed the General Assembly of the United Nations when he was there this week, on the question of aid, and – because Britain is the President of the Security Council this month – he attended a Security Council meeting with Jack Straw, and Jack had to go off, so he chaired the Security Council. He had dinner with Kofi Annan, who asked after me, which was sweet of him.

Nick picked me up at 4.30, took me to the Swan Theatre in High Wycombe, where there were 1,000 people. It was a lovely meeting, lots of friendly people, and the local Labour Party came. They were all pensioners, and you could see immediately what was wrong. I mean, the young people who are interested in politics just don't connect with the Labour Party. I don't know whether it can be saved, because the Labour Party now is an old-age pensioners' gathering of loyal people who love the Party, but are too old to be active, and all the young people, who need to be active, are working outside. So it may be that the Labour Party is beyond recall – I don't rule it out.

Anyway, it's now just before midnight. The Hutton Inquiry today was sensational, with counsel winding up for the BBC and for the Kelly family and the Government, and the most powerful presentation was by the QC representing the Kelly family. He said they didn't want retribution but the Government have behaved improperly, the Ministry of Defence have behaved disgracefully, and he referred to the side-swipe at Gilligan and the BBC. Of course the Government lawyer defended everything that the Government had done, but if Hutton does his stuff, in about six weeks we will come out with a really stern report. So in a way, the whole Hutton thing is culminating in a good summary of the argument by the lawyers. I mean, that's all you really need is to read what they said, and it will all be in the papers tomorrow.

Saturday 27 September
I didn't get to bed very early last night, overslept a little bit. Main news is that Blair's popularity has slumped. Half the people seem to think he should resign, and a quarter of the Labour MPs who were polled and answered the question thought he should resign.

Of course there's the usual build-up – 'Leader Crisis at the Conference' – which enables Blair to triumph.

Anyway, I cancelled the papers, packed up all my stuff, and I managed to get it into one big bag and a backpack.

Sunday 28 September, Labour Party Conference, Bournemouth
A really lovely day! It couldn't have been nicer.

I went and had breakfast downstairs, and all the Campaign Group mates were there. Then I walked to the Bournemouth International Hotel for the Campaign for Labour Party Democracy fringe, which I've done for years.

I made really a few simple points. One is that democracy was very controversial, nobody in power liked democracy. Secondly, this was not the time to launch a campaign to get rid of Tony Blair. It was a complete waste of time because it would divert attention from the real issues. Thirdly, that setting up a new Socialist Party is a waste of time – look at what happened at Brent.

On my way back to the Pavilion, I saw Jack Straw. I shouted out 'Jack!' and he turned round. He had his security people with him, looking a bit startled. I said, 'Hilary greatly enjoyed being with you in New York, and chairing the Security Council.' Then later as I left the Bath Hotel with Hilary, there was Charlie Falconer, the new Lord Chancellor. He came up and gave me a big hug, both cheeks, and had a talk to Hilary. I'm not surprised everybody likes Charlie Falconer, because he's an agreeable person. What his politics are, I don't know.

Monday 29 September

Melissa had gone on her own up to the Marriott Hotel, so I went up there, in the little sort of tram system, and I sat through the meeting that Melissa was chairing. Patricia Hewitt, who's now Secretary of State for Trade and Industry and Minister for Women and Equality, was unmistakably bland. I dozed off during her speech. My hearing aids gave out, so I couldn't hear a word. But it was a big success for Melissa, and she really enjoyed it.

All I've eaten this weekend is sandwiches.

I saw Patricia Hewitt later in the day, and I said, 'By the way, do you realise that Appledore shipyard's closing? I wanted just to mention it because I know you knew I saved it in 1975.' She said, 'Well, there are no ships, no market' and so on, but I don't think they really care very much. Anyway, I made the point, as I'd undertaken to my friends in north Devon that I would do.

I watched Blair's speech to Conference on television – there's some seductive quality about him. He's a very attractive speaker, punctuated by standing ovations every five minutes. He had eight minutes' standing ovation, organised by the Party.

When I look at it, I think he decided to leave the Labour Party, to resign the leadership of the Labour Party, today. He said there's no turning back, the gentleman's not for turning, there's no alternative . . . 'I'm a car with no reverse gear,' which would disqualify him for an MOT. He justified entirely his attitude to Iraq. Indeed, he was the only delegate in Bournemouth allowed to discuss Iraq, because it's been banned from the Conference, but he was able to make a speech justifying it. He made no reference to Brent East, and I think truthfully he didn't mind the Liberal Democrats winning it, because he reckons that the worst that could happen in the next election is the Liberal Democrats do so well that there's a Labour/Liberal Democrat coalition. I thought it was Ramsay MacDonald really. Blair broke with the Party, and reaffirmed his conviction about foundation hospitals and privatisation, the use of private capital, tuition fees, and so on, and just no move from it. It was a contemptuous speech, and the Party went wild because he's been hammered and so they wanted to show their support for their Leader. I think it's an effervescent success, but it is a strategy of a clear character.

Then I walked down and found the Stop the War march – I marched right round the town once. When there was another mile to go, a nice lad, who was the Labour candidate for Bournemouth West, got me a taxi. Actually, I said to a mounted policeman, 'Will you give me a lift?' He said, 'Yes, if you can get on my horse!' Well, I couldn't, but it would have been rather a nice picture to have gone to the demo on the back of a police horse.

I realised I'd lived on sandwiches for a week, so I went to a restaurant, found a seat in the garden and ordered vegetarian soup, salmon, ice cream and a Coca-Cola, and a mug of tea. It was £20 for one meal. It is the first time I've been out consciously and deliberately to a restaurant alone for years and years. It will keep me going tomorrow.

I've been treated so well by everybody. They know I'm a critic. I have been saying everywhere: don't demand that Blair resigns, just concentrate on the main thing. I said that at the Stop the War meeting as well. People were a bit surprised. They had big banners: 'Blair must go', 'Blair, Blair, Out, Out, Out', but that's the wrong line, I think. Be constructive and positive, and set up a Labour Party again.

Wednesday 1 October
I got up at about a quarter to six to do an interview with Jim Naughtie. I discovered that Blair was going on right ahead of me, so I sat and listened to him, and it was the usual crap, I thought. Also, this morning, the foundation-hospitals policy was defeated by Conference, and of course there was an immediate attack on the trade unions by John Reid.

I went home by train, an absolutely lovely journey back. There were lots of people on the train, and we just turned it into a seminar. There was a man who'd been a major in the army, a couple of NUS people, a charming Chief News Editor of Agence France-Presse. She was very cautious, and she didn't want me to smoke my pipe, but I talked to her quite a bit.

Thursday 2 October
It was in fact an interesting Conference. New Labour's come out more violently anti-union and anti-left than for many, many years. The union leaders are good, although there's a little right-wing gang led by Richard Rosser. Constituencies are no longer on the left, because all the decent socialists have left, so it's a Blairite romp. But Blair is in deep trouble with the public as a whole.

From a personal point of view, in the 1979/80 period I was a bit of a hero, and then Kinnock was Leader and I was defeated, and I was a sort of pariah, with all these New Labour people frowning at me. Now, of course, it's quite the opposite. Everyone is friendly – Tom Sawyer, Patricia Hewitt, all sorts of people. Two cab drivers wouldn't take a fare; a shop I went to wouldn't allow me to pay for a little carton of apple juice and a Mars Bar. And one cab driver said, 'I'm so sorry about the death of your wife.' I feel very happy, personally. I suppose that's what happens when you get old. And the fact people still want to hear me is worthwhile.

Friday 3 October
The meter man arrived early this morning. He said the job he'd enjoyed best of all was working on the sewers. He said sewers were unbelievable – you could drive a car through them. He said that all the excrement turns

into black silt; you waded through the black silt. I've always thought sewers were quite romantic. It would make a marvellous programme.

Rory Bremner rang – he and his researcher want to come and have a talk about a Channel 4 special coming up on 27 November. They came about half-past two and stayed for a couple of hours. I'd given a little bit of thought to it, and I did say to him I thought that the friendly, smiling Blair wasn't quite right, because there was a tough authoritarian nature to him, which ought to be reflected. He agreed with that. He wanted to know about Eden and Suez, and the 'Pretext Committee'. I gave him a bit of stuff from the Suez War.

The Iraq Survey Group set up by the Americans, which has cost God knows how many millions of dollars, has found absolutely no weapons of mass destruction, so not only is Blair in trouble in Britain, despite his huge Conference success at Bournemouth, but Bush is in trouble in America – and not only from the Democrats. So it may be that this war will bring down Bush. I doubt it'll bring down Blair because there's no provision for it. Those who opposed the war – not that one wants to say, 'I told you so' – certainly do stand tall. I rang up, left a message for Jon Snow tonight, saying that he might consider possibly using a little extract from the Saddam Hussein interview in February, when he said, on camera, that he had no weapons of mass destruction. I don't know if Jon did, because I forgot to watch Channel 4 News.

Saturday 4 October

Blair is in Rome for the discussion of the European Union constitution, and the draft now before ministers includes an end to our veto on tax harmonisation, an end to our control of immigration and would also establish a European Union Foreign Secretary. So I mean the idea that this could slither through without a referendum is just unsupportable! It would be a theft of public rights.

Monday 6 October

Phone rang. 'Dad, it's Hilary. I've been made Secretary of State for International Development.' The lad is in the Cabinet, at forty-nine! Oh, it was just so fantastic! Lady Amos, the current Secretary of State, has been made Leader of the House of Lords. He's a safe pair of hands, and his feet are on the ground.

Lissie rang, said she burst into tears when she heard. Rang Stephen, who's not very well. Josh rang me later.

I'm tired, very excited, and I'll have to think of a new role now. You can't be an arch-critic of the Labour Cabinet when your son's in it. Alan Simpson rang me and said, 'You shouldn't be dashing round the country. You should be just helping us to understand things.' I think there's something in that. I don't think my health allows me to do much more now.

I think I have got to slow down. He said I should broadcast and make the occasional speech, and help to explain what is going on. It was sweet of him.

Wednesday 8 October
I got the train, arriving in Plymouth at five o'clock, went straight to the Pavilion Theatre. The theatre holds about 700, but only 500 tickets had been sold. I spoke for forty-three minutes, a bit long, and then answered questions, and I asked a member of the audience to come and sit next to me in case I didn't hear the questions. A blonde girl sat there, and I said to her at the end, 'You have the right to ask the last question.' So she said, 'Should you kiss on your first date?', so I leaned over and gave her a kiss and thanked her very much.

Thursday 9 October
To the Royal Spa Theatre, Leamington; got there early, so signed all the books, then went to my dressing room, and every seat was sold – 750. It was a nice theatre, good questions, and then Nick drove me home. I got to bed about two minutes to two, because I had a few things to do when I got back, including listening to my phone messages.

Friday 10 October
I decided to end my column for the *Morning Star*. I've written it for two and a half years and I'm getting a bit repetitive. Also, I just don't want to be in the position where I criticise Blair all the time. He's just put Hilary in the Cabinet, and I think there are more positive things I could do.

Saturday 11 October, Cheltenham Literary Festival
The first event was a 'Big Read' discussion on people's favourite books. In the chair was Jim Naughtie, with Robert Harris, Kate Adie, who remembered me from her Radio Bristol days, and me. I was terribly nervous, because, first of all, I haven't read many books, and secondly, I can't remember the books I have read, so I cited the Bible, *Das Kapital,* and the *Encyclopaedia Britannica.* I sort of joked and bluffed my way through.

I had a nice talk to Robert Harris. He's a great friend of Peter Mandelson's, therefore I thought he wouldn't like me and I would find it difficult to be nice to him, but as a matter of fact he was absolutely charming. He had two of his children there, a girl of about thirteen and a boy of eleven, Charlie. They were as bright as anything. The little boy put up his hand during the discussion about books to say, 'Which is the book you hate most?' His bigger sister pulled it down and wouldn't let him ask it, which I'm sorry about. So I got on with him.

I did another event for about an hour with Ion Trewin, of Weidenfeld & Nicolson, who edited Alan Clark's diaries. He asked me to read a little bit from my *Diaries* about Alan Clark, and he read what Alan Clark had said about me, and we got through it fairly quickly. There were really good questions, and extremely sympathetic. Another thousand people there, some of them the same people who had been there this morning. It was great.

When I got back to London there wasn't a single message on my answer machine. Normally there are eight or nine. I don't know what on earth happened. I thought, God, if nobody ever rings me, what will life be like?

Wednesday 15 October
Hilary's first day for answering International Development Questions in the Commons Chamber. His Parliamentary Secretary answered the first two questions and then he dealt with the rest, about Iraq and Afghanistan and India. The tributes paid to him were so elaborate! One Tory MP said, 'It's very nice to have a minister you can trust.' Then Graham Allen said, 'It's nice to know that merit is not an obstacle to promotion.' Caroline would have been just thrilled, and is thrilled, wherever she is . . .

I felt strongly today that Hilary is Mr Big now, and I'm just the father. My dad used to joke about it and say, 'I'm fed up with people coming up and telling me, "I heard your son's speech."' He said it of course entirely in a generous spirit, but I can see it now Hilary's in the Cabinet.

Thursday 16 October
Went to the BBC for the *Jeremy Vine Show*; Michael Portillo was there. Last week he lived on the income of a single mother – a bit of a gimmick – and he was interviewed about it and came across as his new soft self. A lot of people phoned in and said if Michael Portillo was Leader of the Tory Party, they would shift their allegiance from Labour to Tory, so from his point of view it was successful.

Sunday 19 October
At 12.30 I was picked up by Salma Yaqoob, a woman in her mid-thirties, a psychotherapist married to a GP; she's been working very closely with the Stop the War Coalition. She and her husband and her little one-year-old baby – she's got three children – picked me up, and we talked all the way to Birmingham. Her husband is also a faith adviser at the University of Birmingham, does sometimes take prayers at the local mosque. I didn't realise that imams and mullahs were elected, like Congregationalist ministers. I know so little about the Muslim faith, and it's so important and interesting, and I found our views on religion corresponded exactly.

Wednesday 22 October
Well, I got up at six. I took some flowers to Saffron for her thirty-first

birthday party. She's been to Mexico and to Paris and Rome, and she's been offered a film in Canada and may go to New Zealand. I didn't stay long.

Then I walked to Gray's Inn Road to give evidence for George Galloway, who is being drummed out of the Labour Party. When I got there George was standing on the steps, giving a press conference, and so the media came round and interviewed him and me. Then we went upstairs; he had three lawyers, and we went into the hearing, where there were four people comprising the National Constitutional Committee of the National Executive. I was asked to present a short document that I had prepared, and they had no questions.

There was another press conference in the street. I said that I had opposed the war, as had the Pope and Kofi Annan; that it was a war against the Charter of the UN; and that because people get killed, very strong things are said in war, and George had spoken strongly. The Prime Minister had said that those who opposed the war had blood on their hands. I reminded them of the peace tradition in the Labour Party, that Keir Hardie had opposed the First World War, so had Ramsay MacDonald, who later became the first Labour Prime Minister. George Lansbury was a pacifist. I went through the people who had been expelled from the Party at different stages: Stafford Cripps, who later became Chancellor of the Exchequer; Aneurin Bevan, who founded the Health Service, and who was expelled for supporting the Popular Front; Michael Foot; Jim Mortimer.

Thursday 23 October
I heard on the television, about three o'clock, that George had been expelled from the Party, so I did more interviews about that.

Friday 24 October
Got up at six. Concorde's last day. I'm going off in just over a couple of hours to Heathrow for the last flight.

Got to Heathrow at about 10.30 and was at the Concorde desk for a long time. John Cochrane, who was the co-pilot when I went up with the chief Concorde pilot Brian Trubshaw in 1970, was there, and I had a bit of a talk to him.

To the Concorde Lounge, and they were mainly businessmen there. There were a few people I knew. Nigel Havers, the actor, I knew, and the Duke of Kent appeared. I said, 'I remember the wedding of your mother' – that's Princess Marina – 'in 1934.' His father Prince George was killed in 1942. He is the Queen's cousin, but he looks like the Duke of Edinburgh. They all look the same, the royal family. But he was friendly. He flew on the first flight in Bahrain apparently.

We were watching the other Concordes on television screens – one took off from New York and one from Edinburgh. We were due to take off at about 2.15.

I was in the front row of the plane, next to Lord Macfarlane. The air hostesses were charming and asked us to sign their programmes. I wandered up and down the plane with my video camera. I asked one of the hostesses to take the camera into the cockpit, which she did. They wouldn't let me in while we were flying. I got a picture of the controls, showing Mach II and speed 1,350 miles an hour at 50,000 feet and a temperature of minus 53 degrees, and all that. We went supersonic briefly, and then we slowly came in. We landed at about two minutes past four back at Heathrow.

The plane was full of people, I was told, who were corporate customers – that is to say, big companies like Pfizer, who produce Viagra, were there, and Coca-Cola. One of the people from British Airways said, 'We were actually assassinated by our corporate customers, who no longer used Concorde.' It is a beautiful plane. It's quite small and normal when you're sitting in it. Having flown in it thirty-three years ago, at the very beginning, I felt that John Cochrane and I had flown over a longer span than anybody else.

We came in first, and the Concorde from Edinburgh came in second, and the Concorde from New York came in third.

We were unloaded third, and I went into a hospitality tent and there was Colin Marshall, the Chairman of British Airways, who came up. David Frost was there, of course. It was a moving day, and I made a little comment about the people who'd designed and built it – that's what I care about. Of course, typical of Britain, the people who really did the work weren't included. There were no shop stewards, there were no engineers, there were none of the people there who'd made it possible: 'It's the rich what gets the pleasure, it's the poor what gets the blame.' Nice people, very nice people today, personally, but simply living off the back of the guys who do all the work. I felt that a bit, but still, I mustn't gripe about it, because I did enjoy it very much.

Anyway, I had to go on the Heathrow Express, and caught a cab home from Paddington.

Monday 27 October
Another massive bomb in Baghdad, and they're now beginning to talk about resistance rather than terrorism. The whole situation is completely out of control. It's so obvious.

It has absolutely shaken the confidence of the people in London and Washington about their capacity to govern Iraq. So how it will develop, I don't know. The target this time has been the aid agencies, and of course if you can get rid of the Red Cross, get rid of the UN, and so on, then the Americans can't cope with the crisis, and they will be confronted with the problem of what to do. Reprisals will make it worse.

Twenty-five Tory MPs have asked for a vote of confidence in Iain Duncan Smith, which will take place tomorrow. I don't know what the outcome will be because I don't know the Tory Party very well, but it will certainly paralyse them for a matter of weeks.

Wednesday 29 October
I heard that Iain Duncan Smith had been defeated as Tory Leader by ninety votes to seventy-five. So now there'll be a Tory leadership election, and it's thought (and probably correctly) that they'll all rally round Michael Howard, because any *serious* future Tory Leader would not want to be defeated in the next election, and that's what seems likely to happen. The story was created by the media really. A couple of weeks ago Duncan Smith got a huge standing ovation at the Tory Conference. Now, he's thrown out by Tory MPs. Howard is a figure of the past. But he's a lawyer and he might be better against Blair in the House of Commons. Also, it will no longer be fashionable to support Blair any more, so that might help him.

Friday 31 October
Ralph Gibson has died at home. I didn't hear till today. An old friend, my best man, I've known him for – goodness me – nearly sixty years, a lovely guy.

Saturday 1 November
I was at home all day. I rang Ann Gibson, because I thought I might go and see her, but she said, 'I'd rather leave it till later.' She went on, 'It was a release for Ralph, and then when he'd gone, I realised that I'd lost my main support', and that is of course what death does.

Wednesday 5 November
I went to the Tea Room and had an hour with Michael Meacher – he was keen to discuss what he should do now. He said it was the best thing that ever happened to him, to be sacked, and he wondered what he should do. I said, 'Write, broadcast, perhaps you could publish a book.' He said, 'Oh, it'd take too much time.' 'Well, a pamphlet then, identifying the things that need to be done.' It took me back to the days when he was my Parliamentary Secretary in 1974. He said he had twenty-nine years on the front bench, which is a fantastic period.

Then I went to the Royal Society of Chemistry function, because this is Chemistry Week, and Stephen had organised a meeting in a little dining room at the House of Commons. I saw David Giachardi, the Chief Executive of the Royal Society of Chemistry; Harry Kroto, the Nobel Prize-winner, who's the President; and others.

There was a party in the evening to celebrate the *Daily Mirror*'s centenary, and so I turned up to that at 6.30.

As I arrived, Tony Blair was leaving. He greeted me, and I said, 'I haven't shaken you by the hand for a long time.' He said, 'Hilary is doing a brilliant job!' I replied, 'I'll tell him what you said.' That was photographed, of course.

I saw Piers Morgan, the Editor, very briefly, and then I wandered in and there was Geoffrey Goodman, who's eighty-two now, and I had a chat to him about his relations with Robert Maxwell, and he said that one-third of his pension had been stopped because of Maxwell's theft.

Coming out, Gordon Brown shouted, 'Hello, Tony' and went by, so I waved at him. I must say the thought did occur to me that the *Mirror* might be interested in a column from me; I don't know. It'd certainly earn a lot of money, and I have written for a couple of years for the *Morning Star*.

Wednesday 19 November
Had coffee with Alan Sillitoe and Ruth Fainlight, who live round the corner. Alan, of course, is a famous novelist, comes from Nottingham. Ruth is a poet, very nice.

The foundation hospitals were carried by seventeen votes. Labour MPs are just absolutely useless when it comes to defending the Party.

Saturday 22 November
Mrs Mac came in to do her last day's work before she goes off to New Zealand. She is so frail and in such pain that I persuaded her to stop and have a cup of tea, so we talked for about an hour and a quarter.

In the evening, the family had a little gathering to remember Caroline; she died three years ago today. Stephen arrived, with Emily and Daniel. Hilary turned up. Lissie came with Hannah and Sarah. Josh and Naz came and we had a bit of a talk, and went over to the Pizza Express, where Frederico, the Spanish anarchist waiter, is so friendly.

My relationship with Hilary is rather like my dad's relations with me. My dad had been a minister before the First World War, then Secretary of State for India when Gandhi was put in prison and all sorts of hideous things happened, then Secretary for Air after the war. I got into Parliament in 1950, four years after he had been dropped from the Cabinet, and he got very much to the left in his old age, criticised the Americans in the Cold War and disliked the anti-Soviet stance. I'd say to him, 'Now look, Dad, you've got to remember . . .' and so on, and I put perfectly reasonable arguments to him. It's exactly like me and Hilary. I say something to him about the Iraq war and he says, 'You've got to remember, Dad . . .' It's just natural. I have been through all that myself. I can see it all.

Sunday 23 November
Stephen rang to say that Ann Gibson had fallen and broken her hip and is in St Thomas's Hospital, having just been widowed two weeks ago. So I

stopped what I was doing and went to the hospital, went up to the Gordon Perkins Ward. I was overcome with emotion really – this woman, just lost her husband, now lying in bed – and held her hand, and we had a lovely talk for about an hour and a quarter. She said it was only a crack and it might be all right, but she was angry at what had happened. We talked about Ralph and about the children and about her granddaughter, Miranda.

The woman in the next bed in the ward shouted all the time. Apparently last night she had to be moved on a trolley to the day room. It was terribly distressing and difficult.

I came home. Saw on the television that there'd been a coup in Georgia. Edvard Shevardnadze, former Foreign Minister of the Soviet Union, who was the President of Georgia, had simply been overwhelmed in a 'velvet' revolution – no violence, nobody killed – so he's resigned.

Monday 24 November
Up at six o'clock. Caught the 8.30 to Bristol Parkway and was met by David Parker, of the company Available Light, who's making a film about Concorde. The last one ever to leave the ground is landing at Filton on Wednesday. Very moving.

Anyway, I was taken to the Rolls-Royce engine workshop, where John Wragg, a former Rolls-Royce engineer, explained how the Olympus engine was built. On the shop floor they were working on an engine for the Euro fighter. I talked to a few of the workers. John Wragg was an interesting man. He was an Establishment figure, tall, military, I think he had been in the army; and very much a Rolls-Royce official, now seventy-six. Very courteous to me, respectful; after all I was still, in his eyes, the Secretary of State for Industry, and of course everybody there knew that I had done all I could to keep Concorde going.

While I was talking to them, a woman came up who worked for the company and said that the trade unions would like to see me. So I went down to the trade-union room, where round a table there were about twenty shop stewards and officials from Amicus. They were absolutely furious that they hadn't been told I was coming, and that no arrangement had been made for me to meet them. Somehow, that was absolutely typical of Rolls-Royce. Rolls-Royce is just the crème de la crème of the British Establishment, and the workers are workers are workers. So I had a lovely talk to them, and at the end the chief shop steward said to me, 'Oh, I wish you were still in the Labour Party.' I said, 'I am!' Then I was taken to the Heritage Centre, where they had some Olympus engines. David Parker's film unit was filming everything. So that was interesting, and being a great archivist and believer in keeping things, I found it fascinating, but of course they should put the engine on public show, just as the *Great Britain* is in the old shipyard where it was built, in Bristol. I dare say that day will come, but of course Rolls-Royce is a defence establishment and has, for security reasons, to be tightly controlled.

There were few women, I might add, although a lot of women work at Rolls-Royce, and that's another Rolls-Royce characteristic. But I did enjoy it. They were all terribly friendly and affectionate.

Then I was taken to the Concorde Simulator. This was the most sophisticated piece of equipment I've ever seen in my life! It was about twenty feet high, and it had hydraulic drives round it, so that when you moved the controls, the cockpit altered to reflect it. I climbed up the ladder and went in with the pilot who is going to bring the last Concorde in. Mike Bannister, the chief Concorde test pilot, was there.

I climbed into the co-pilot's seat and looked out, and there was the air field ahead. It was so beautifully done – you felt you were just about to take off. It was immensely complicated, but basically you had the control stick and you had a rudder, and you had the throttles, and you could lift and lower the undercarriage. Les, the pilot, explained it all to me, and then he opened the throttles and we moved along, and at 160 miles an hour I rotated, I pulled the stick back and we took off, and there was a noise to give the impression that the engines were roaring; and then you climbed and the snook came up, and you saw the horizon, and then you could turn to the left and turn to the right, and dip and climb. We went up, about 3,000 feet, I think. It was absolutely riveting! I mean, it just wasn't possible to believe you weren't flying Concorde, and the controls there are absolutely identical to the ones in a Concorde. I brought it in to land. I think probably the pilot landed it. I was trying to do the right thing. Then they wanted me to do it again, because David Parker wanted to film it. It was an extraordinary experience, I must say. That is an absolutely integral part of the heritage of Rolls-Royce; while that's there, people will be able to fly Concorde.

Wednesday 26 November
To the Speaker's House for the State Opening party, and greeted the Speaker, thanked him very much for asking me and gave his wife Mary a kiss. I had agreed to meet Hilary there; it's his birthday today, and I gave him a kiss too.

Cardinal Cormac Murphy-O'Connor was there; of course the Speaker is a Catholic. I said to Cardinal Murphy-O'Connor, 'The Speaker, as you know, is the first Catholic Speaker since Thomas More, and he read the lesson at my wife's funeral and said to me afterwards that it was the first time a lay person as a Catholic had ever been allowed to take part in St Margaret's Church.' So Cardinal Murphy-O'Connor said, 'Well, we're making progress slowly.' So I said, 'Like the Labour Party! There are some socialists in the Labour Party, just as there are some Christians in the churches.' It's an old joke of mine. He laughed.

I slipped off quite quickly to go to Preston.

Thursday 27 November

I was picked up by a car and driven to Queen Mary College, for the Peter Shore Memorial Lecture. I discovered it was a tremendous affair. They had publicised it widely. Jack Profumo was there, and I had a chat with him. He was elected in a by-election in 1940, and was present in Parliament in the famous Norway debate. He was elected ten years before me, and he's ten years older than me. He looked very frail, but he was frightfully friendly, and of course, after he was disgraced, he was stripped of his Privy Councillorship, sacked as Secretary of State for War, and for the last forty years he's been at Toynbee Hall.

Then we went into the Grand Hall, and there were 650 people there. Peter Hennessy, who is Professor of Politics at Queen Mary College, was playing a leading part. He told me he'd been reading the official papers that have just been released for the 1960s and is going to write a book. Sir Michael Palliser, former Under-Permanent Secretary, I think, at the Foreign Office, was there. Mary Jay; Mary Wilson; David Stoddart, who has now left the Labour Party; Nigel Spearing, former MP; Richard Reiser and Susie Burrows; John Mills from the Euro Safeguards Committee; Michael Barnes and Anne Barnes. He left the Labour Party, joined the SDP and came back.

Liz Shore was there of course, and all the Shores, in the front row. I spoke for about thirty-five minutes on democracy, then there were good questions: Are you in favour of an attempt to indict the Prime Minister for war crimes? What about nuclear power? How might China become democratic? Alan Lee Williams asked, 'Is Britain becoming anti-American?' Of course I'm fairly experienced now at answering questions, because I get them at all the lectures.

The young people wanted me to do meetings at their universities and colleges, and wherever I go I attract large numbers of invitations, not all of which I can undertake.

We retired to a dinner in the Principal's house. Most of the people I mentioned were there. Jack Profumo didn't stay. I was between the Principal and Liz Shore, who's now moved to Cornwall and joined UKIP (UK Independence Party). Beside her was Peter Hennessy.

I was absolutely exhausted. I had stomach ache, which didn't help. I'd got to bed at three o'clock this morning and the dinner went on till quarter past eleven. I didn't get home till just before midnight. I was absolutely whacked! But it did go well.

Friday 28 November

In the Northern Ireland elections, Sinn Fein have overtaken the SDLP (Social Democratic and Labour Party), and Ian Paisley's DUP (Democratic Unionist Party) have overtaken Ian Trimble's UUP (Ulster Unionist Party). So in the end, the so-called hard men on each side will have to come to some sort of agreement.

Saturday 29 November

I cooked myself a tiny Christmas pudding, which will probably make me fat, but I must say it was very tasty with brandy butter.

Sunday 30 November

Book signing in Hatchards of Piccadilly. Afterwards Emma from Hutchinson took me to Fortnum & Masons for tea. Now, I've never been in there before. It has a reputation as the most expensive fancy-food shop. We found the tea room upstairs and it was crowded. To give you an idea of the cost, we each had a pot of tea – she had Earl Grey and I had regular – and I had a tartlet and she had a lemon sponge, and the cost came to £18.62. It was unbelievable! I looked round and wondered who they all were. There were four ladies at one table, and they were clearly friends who met at Fortnum's, no doubt every time they came to London once a month. I found it really fascinating. When I think of the cost of the day – the taxi that took us round cost £56, the tea cost £18, and then I was sent home in a taxi, which probably cost about £12, and Emma went back in a taxi that probably cost about £6, so the total cost would have been around a hundred pounds, and all I did was sign perhaps two or three hundred books. As you get older, you do see the world with new eyes, like a child. I've lived such a sheltered life.

Friday 5 December

During lunch the phone rang, and a voice said it was Number 10, the Prime Minister's Office: 'I've got a call for you.' I didn't know what it was about. On the line came Alastair Campbell, who reached me through the Number 10 office, because he'd been approached to do some of these evening lectures. I had a brief word with him and said it was fun, and I'm sure his would be a great success. I said that although we'd had some marginal differences of opinion, we've got to get Labour back in office, and it would be nice to see him at some stage.

Saturday 6 December

Watched *Lawrence of Arabia* on television, and it did remind me of the utter treachery of the British in persuading the Arabs to organise a revolt against the Ottoman Empire and promising them that the Arab countries would be free, and then doing a secret deal with France, who took over Syria while we took over Palestine.

The Commonwealth Conference is deadlocked on whether Zimbabwe should be expelled from the Commonwealth, and Hilary's there of course, absolutely at the heart of everything.

The United States have bombed a house in Afghanistan because, they said, the Taliban were there, and I think they've killed nineteen children. It's a horrible, horrible, horrible world.

Tuesday 9 December

Got up at half-past five. Had a lovely hot bath, thanks to dear old Josh who'd fixed the boiler.

Caught the Tube to Holborn, and walked over to the new Transport and General Workers' Union headquarters. Went up to Tony Woodley's office, and he was already there at 7.35. I had about an hour and twenty minutes in there. He's so warm. He said, 'You're an icon, along with Jack Jones.'

I said, 'Well, I'm really honoured that you should want to see me', and we had a talk about the role of the trade unions.

He said, 'They are actually declining, like the churches, and we've got to campaign again. People ask: what's the point of joining the trade unions?'

I talked about using the media, and raising with the BBC why they don't cover trade unionism. He asked about the euro, because he said that Derek Simpson of Amicus is worried that if we didn't join, it might damage our exports, and I went over the arguments with him.

Wednesday 10 December

I went to the Tea Room and Chris Mullin was there. I haven't talked to him for a long time. He is the minister for all of Africa, except the north. He said how awful Mugabe was, which I don't doubt. He didn't understand why Mbeki, the South African President, was so hostile to the expulsion or suspension of Mugabe from the Commonwealth. In the paper today, incidentally, it said Blair might remove Mugabe's knighthood, as if Blair was the King! But that's the mood of the moment.

I asked Chris about tuition fees, and he took an absolute loyal view, as I thought he would. He also said he would send me some information from the Foreign Office about Cairo, for the trip this weekend.

Thursday 11 December

Cleared all my phone calls, and packed for Cairo. I went and collected my Egyptian pounds from the bank and cancelled the papers.

Drafted my speech for the Conference.

In mid-December 2003 my editor Ruth Winstone and I flew to Cairo for a peace conference, which brought together speakers from all over the world and included active representatives from Iraq, Palestine, Egypt and other Middle Eastern countries.

I was invited to give the keynote address and had the opportunity for talks with Ramsay Clark, the former Attorney General under President Johnson, and Denis Halliday, who had been the UN representative in the oil-for-food programme, who both made powerful contributions.

During that week Saddam Hussein was discovered and arrested in Iraq, and 'exhibited' on television, and it was obvious that he would be tried and executed – as he later was.

During the conference the Muslim Brotherhood, who are very strong in Egypt, though banned as a political party, descended on the hall in large numbers, in a disciplined manner. Although there was no trouble, it was a bit intimidating, and it was clear they represented a serious political force in the Middle East.

Tuesday 16 December
Absolutely filthy cold; I coughed violently and I was sick. It was awful.

I had a Christmas card from Tony Blair, sent I think by Cherie, with the family sitting on a bench at Chequers.

Friday 19 December
Gaddafi has unilaterally disarmed and was welcomed by Bush and Blair on re-entering the international community. Quite why he should be able to re-enter the international community by giving up his weapons, when we're resolutely sticking to ours, I don't know.

Saturday 27 December
In 2003 I delivered 142 speeches in forty-six towns and cities, including Baghdad and Cairo. I did thirty-three press interviews, 385 broadcasts (235 radio and 150 television), to thirty foreign countries. I published a hardback, *Free Radical*, a paperback, *Free At Last!*, and I must have written sixty, seventy, eighty articles. So that's not a bad record for a man of seventy-eight.

Sunday 28 December
I'm exploring the concept of truth in politics, trying to get to the *real* reason why things happen. I mean the *real* reason why we went to war alongside America is because America is very powerful and Blair couldn't alienate Bush, because he'd pay a heavy price. Also it made Blair look strong. So we are now a colony, dependent on the United States. That's not a new idea, but if it had been presented in that way, it would be so much more believable than saying: oh, it's about democracy in Iraq, and all that.

Similarly, on the question of Foundation hospitals, if we simply said, well, we're locked into a situation where the IMF and the multinationals in Washington and the Frankfurt bank insist on privatisation, and if we didn't do it we'd be in serious trouble, then people would know where they were. But spin has got completely out of control by pretending it's about values, and there's not a word of truth in it.

Monday 29 December, Stansgate
I looked through the letters that needed to be answered, but my capacity to do nothing is almost unrivalled. I pretend I'm busy. I'm not busy at all. I've got nothing whatever to do. The family do all the washing up, lay the table and everything . . . they're an amazing family, and I'm terribly lucky.

Tuesday 30 December

Back to London, went in the evening to the Churchill Hotel, because Patricia Moberly had suggested I meet Kenneth Kaunda, the former President of Zambia. Just before dinner the High Commissioner said to Kenneth, 'You ought to get Tony to give you his rap record.' Well, I'd taken it with me just in case, so I gave it to him. They'd all heard about it.

At dinner, people asked Kenneth questions. On Mugabe, his view is exactly the one that I had been giving at the lectures: that the British went there, stole all the land, there was no democracy, and now Mugabe, who had after all been in prison for ten years himself, had tried to get the land back again. He said there was an absolute promise given at the conference where Zimbabwe's independence was agreed, that Britain would give compensation for the land that was taken, and it never happened. He said the Tories honoured it, Thatcher honoured it, Major honoured it, but it was only 'when our socialist comrade came to power, they failed to honour it'. That was a reference to Blair, and I pressed him on that. He said, 'Oh yes, that's absolutely right.' But what Kenneth fully understood was the point I make all the time, that with a record of slavery and occupation and repression, we are the worst people in the world to lecture Mugabe on how he should run things. He said, 'Anyway, Africans will find a way round the problem.'

We also talked a little bit about Saddam Hussein. Kenneth said he'd been to see Saddam in the 1980s, and how impressed he was by the schools and the hospitals and the roads, and so on. He'd been in touch with Saddam more recently, and Saddam had told him he didn't have weapons of mass destruction – exactly what he'd said to me.

He said that the Carter Foundation was helping him, and he had had a job at an American university, called 'President in Residence', and taught a bit. An interesting idea – we ought really to have him over to be a visiting professor at the School of Oriental and African Studies, or something of that kind.

I said how much I admired him, which I do, and he was very affectionate. He said, 'Tomorrow, I'm going to see Rowan Williams, the Archbishop of Canterbury, and also the Secretary of State.' So I asked, 'Which one's that?' 'I think it must be the Secretary of State for International Development.' So I said, 'Well, that's my son.'

Blair has been in Basra saying the British troops are pioneers of the twenty-first century in the war against terrorism and rogue states – utterly ridiculous! They are classic colonial soldiers, working-class kids in Britain sent to control the colonies, and this idea that a rogue state now has some status in international law throws total doubt on the man's commitment to any form of United Nations or international justice.

Tuesday 6 January 2004

Ken Livingstone has been readmitted to the Labour Party and of course Prescott is furious: they made a great mistake in expelling Ken and they now need him back. So Ken's won.

Princess Diana's inquest has opened, and Mohamed al-Fayed, whose son was killed with her, says she was murdered.

Osama Bin Laden has made a broadcast, the text of which was in the paper, in which he bitterly denounced Saddam for treacherously allying himself with the Americans during the Iran–Iraq war.

Wednesday 7 January

Michael Howard pressed Blair on whether he still stuck by what he said, that he emphatically denied playing any part in getting David Kelly's name into the public domain. It may be that that is an early warning of what the Hutton Report might say.

Friday 9 January

Oh yes, Robert Kilroy-Silk, who was once allegedly a left-wing MP, wrote a filthy article in the *Sunday Express*, attacking Arabs as suicide bombers and murderers. The BBC, to its credit, has taken his show off the air; it's been reported to the police, and Trevor Phillips of the Commission for Racial Equality commented on it. It's time he got his come-uppance. This couldn't have been a worse moment for him as a UKIP Member of the European Parliament.

Monday 12 January

To the Tricycle Theatre this evening for a show organised in support of the Salusbury Refugee Centre (which is attached to Sarah and Hannah's school). I met Zadie Smith's mother, who is a psychotherapist and writes a bit, and a lot of other people. We chatted with a few friends of Melissa's, there were readings by Meera Syal, who was in *Goodness Gracious Me* and plays Granny Kumar in *The Kumars at No. 42*. She's a talented woman. Somebody called Elizabeth Mansfield did a one-woman performance of songs and poetry.

I rang *Any Questions?* to say I would do it on 6 February as they wanted, but they did say to me, 'Of course, if the Hutton Inquiry is published by then, the Government will insist on a Labour MP', which means I'll be knocked off. So I said, 'I didn't know the Government decided who was on *Any Questions?*' 'Oh well, you must understand . . .' 'Well,' I said, 'I do, I was taken off *Any Questions?* last spring because of my attitude to the war.'

Tuesday 13 January

Harold Shipman, the doctor who's alleged to have murdered 260 people by giving them a deadly morphine injection, has hanged himself using prison bedding. That has absolutely obliterated all other news.

27 January is the key vote in the House of Commons on tuition fees, on which the Government will probably just scrape home, because of the weakness of Labour MPs. The following day the Hutton Report comes out. I feel Hutton is likely to say that the Prime Minister's answers in Parliament didn't cover all aspects of his role, but it won't be more than that, so he'll scrape by. But by the end of the month he will be a more wounded Prime Minister because of the hatred among many Labour MPs of what he's doing to them, making everything a vote of confidence, and because of the renewal of public disquiet about the Government's handling of the Iraq war, including the way Kelly was driven to suicide.

Friday 16 January

I was picked up by a Ghanaian driver and driven to the BBC. His father was a Muslim, his mother a Christian. He was a man of fifty-five, with three children. The eldest wants to be a lawyer, the second might be a scientist and the youngest a doctor. He said his father had five wives, and when he died, this man had to come to Britain and get any job he could to send money home. That tells you something!

Tuesday 20 January

In the Commons dining room there was Charles Falconer, the Lord Chancellor, in his shirt sleeves, sitting with quite a few people. So I went up to him and said, 'In fifty years I've never seen a Lord Chancellor in shirt sleeves in here.' He said lovely things about Hilary. I said, 'Well, I'm glad he's not at the Home Office now, with all the problems about prisons.' 'Oh,' he said, 'but we're going to try and tackle the problem of prisoners by having more education.' So I said, 'I suppose there'll be tuition fees imposed.' He laughed. 'That's an idea!'

Friday 23 January

The phone rang endlessly, because today David Kay, the head of the US survey team sent in by Bush to Iraq to find weapons of mass destruction, resigned and said there weren't any. It absolutely undermines the whole Blair story. Bush never cared about it. It's going to be very interesting this week.

I watched an interesting Channel 4 programme, about what Hutton won't tell you, simply going into the whole question of weapons of mass destruction. It was a devastating, 100 per cent effective destruction of the idea that the war was about weapons of mass destruction. Coming on the eve of Hutton, it really is most powerful.

The vote on tuition fees will take place at seven on Tuesday, and Blair will know by then what Hutton said because he will have an advance copy.

So it will be a pretty miserable day for him, Tuesday and then he goes to Prime Minister's Questions on Wednesday.

Saturday 24 January
ITV News came along with a landline and I did an interview on David Kay, who retired yesterday as head of the Iraq Survey Group. I went back to my Baghdad diary: I had an hour-and-a-half talk on 1 February 2003 with General Amir al-Saadi and he said exactly what David Kay said. There's no doubt whatever that coming just before the publication of the Hutton Report, it's very significant.

Also today the British Medical Association has announced that medical students will end up with a debt of £64,000 when they graduate. Well, two doctors marrying means a debt of £128,000, and a mortgage will increase it to a quarter of a million, and I think that may have an impact also upon the votes on Tuesday.

At seven o'clock there was a two-hour programme on the 1984/5 miners' strike. It began with the cultural times – with Torvill and Dean, and pop groups – and presented the strike as being led by a Marxist revolutionary Scargill against democracy. They had lots of Nottinghamshire miners. They had Neil Kinnock; Matthew Parris, who is a Tory journalist; Phil Willis, who is a Liberal Democrat; Boris Johnson; and John O'Farrell. There was no presentation of the miners' case whatever, I could hardly contain myself! It was presented as the final defeat of union militancy for ever and ever, the suggestion being that the unions ran the country, which they never have. I was so angry I could hardly sleep, but still, that is the propaganda you're up against. New Labour MPs will probably go along with its analysis.

Sunday 25 January
Colin Powell, the American Secretary of State, has said he doubts whether weapons of mass destruction will ever be found, whereas Blair says he's certain they will be. It did make we wonder whether we could argue that the Prime Minister claims he's speaking the truth, and searches are being made to find out if there is any truth in the Prime Minister, and so far no evidence has been found.

I had prepared a meal for Tommy Sheridan, who said he'd be here at half-past twelve. He actually arrived at ten to two and we sat down and had a talk. He'd just come from the founding convention to set up the Respect Party, which is a new party of the left, bringing together Muslims and the Socialist Alliance, the SWP and the Stop the War Coalition. What was nice about Tommy is that I could talk quite openly to him about it. Of course he was very supportive and friendly to me. I pointed out to him that you had to be reasonably united in opposition. He had remembered my list of the alternative socialist parties, all eleven of them!

He said Arthur Scargill had a totally closed mind; there was no discussing anything with him, that Arthur won't have anything to do with Respect. Scargill put up candidates all over Scotland against Tommy Sheridan. It was quite an incredible thing to do. The cost of that, in terms of lost deposits, must have been enormous. It just makes you wonder who paid it.

Tommy said, 'The Labour Party in Scotland is a shell.' I think the Labour Party in England is a shell too, because Blair had degutted it completely.

I put to him that my object wasn't to cram socialism down everybody's throats, but to develop policies that honestly looked after old people and young people and sick people and unemployed people, that worked for peace and justice and democracy. For me, socialism was useful, but it wasn't ideological lecturing. He agreed with that.

Secondly, I said to him, 'I wonder how many people realise that if we did even the modest things we want – link pensions to earnings, abolish tuition fees, bring the railways into public service, and build a foreign policy on the UN and ask the Americans to go – we would then be seen as a rogue state.'

He said, oh well, he'd been in Venezuela, so he understood that, and that's why it's got to be a global movement we're building.

I took a picture of him with my little Polaroid camera, sitting in Keir Hardie's chair, and when he'd gone, I blew it up on my colour photocopier and sent a copy to his mother Alice, who had sent me a bottle of champagne and a card. I know Alice well.

Tuesday 27 January
Nick Brown, who was one of the leaders of the revolt against tuition fees, has given in to the Government, and also Barbara Roche. Why did Brown do it?

Went over to Channel 4 for an interview, where I saw Mark Seddon. The Labour Party Executive has today decided to expel the RMT (Rail, Maritime and Transport Union) because the Scottish branches are supporting Tommy Sheridan. Now, that is a very serious thing. The other unions might think it was worth following the RMT, and I think there is a possibility that the Labour Party will die if that happens.

I didn't do Channel 4 News, but I appeared on ITV News from the same studio. While I was there I heard the result of the vote. The Government won by 316 to 311, a majority of five. This was because Nick Brown had defected, and one or two other people had abstained, but I just felt as sick as a dog. I felt the sniff of treachery and treason was in the House. What they've done is to destroy the credibility of everything they say. If the Manifesto doesn't mean anything, how do you know all these concessions that were made mean anything? They don't. They'll say anything to get what they want!

In the course of being in the House today, I saw Jenny Tonge, who's been sacked as Liberal Democrat spokesman for international development, because she said she understood suicide bombers' motives.

I also saw Chris Mullin, who was talking about how he enjoys his work in Africa. Then he said, 'Forgive me, I've got to go. I've got a little bit of governing to do.' So I smiled and he went off. A couple of minutes later I left the Tea Room and he was talking to Andy McSmith, the journalist.

Although Blair won by five votes, the Further Education Bill will go on throughout the whole of the year, and the Lords may create difficulties. By God, to expel the RMT, to defy the UN Charter, and to break up the Welfare State by introducing market criteria for education, that is the end of all the Labour Party used to stand for. So I'm a bit depressed tonight, but I suppose I'll recover.

A couple of footnotes since I dictated that. I forgot to mention I saw Ian Paisley in the corridor at the House of Commons, just outside the Library. He came up and he was so friendly. He looked so old. He's only seventy-seven. He just couldn't have been nicer! He said, 'How are you?' I said, 'I'm fine. And you?' He said, 'I've given up the European Parliament.' I said, 'Well, you can't be on the Assembly – not that it's meeting – in Parliament and the EU.' And I said, 'I often talk about you, about the time you voted against abortion, you and the Pope together.' Then I told him the story about Stephen in Belfast, being driven round by one of his firmest supporters, cursing Sinn Fein and then at the end saying, 'Well, I'll say this for Gerry Adams – he's stuck to his guns!' He nearly killed himself with laughter.

So that was friendly. I like Ian Paisley actually. He's a genuine representative. I said to him, and he agreed, 'I'm waiting for the two real men to meet and talk', because you get Trimble and Hume, you know, they're always worried about the guys behind them, but when the real people . . . He said, 'Oh, we're making progress.' I thought that was a good sign.

At 11.20 p.m. my phone rang and it was James. He was outside the front door on his way home, and he popped in and asked me to lend him a quid to get a bus home, so I gave him ten quid to go in a taxi, but I think he'll probably go on the bus anyway. It's nice, you know, when a grandson and a grandfather have really close relations. Michael's more laid-back. Jonathan's very sweet. William I get on with very well. They're all lovely, and it's just important that grandfathers are supportive.

Wednesday 28 January
The press absolutely full today of Blair's narrow victory on fees, a majority of five. A lot of people abstaining gave him his majority. One Tory, Robert Jackson, voted with the Government, and a couple of Tories abstained. So it was very tight, and people are beginning to say you can't go on doing this.

But today was really Hutton day. As soon as Prime Minister's Questions were over, I listened to Hutton delivering a summary of his report, from 12.30 to 1.55. I didn't quite know what to expect: I thought he might produce a balance, but quite the opposite. He spent the first half denouncing Gilligan and the BBC for having allowed a broadcast containing a gross allegation against the Government's integrity, doing nothing about it. Then he came to the Government, and how the Government handled it very wisely. He criticised Kelly for seeing Gilligan. He said the Prime Minister played it perfectly. There was nothing underhand or duplicitous or shameful about the way Kelly's name got into the public domain. He made no reference to the fact that a press officer at Number 10 had described Kelly as a Walter Mitty. He ended up with a warm tribute to Kelly.

The more I reflected on it, the more I realised it was 100 per cent whitewash. When Hutton was appointed, I thought the Chief Justice of Northern Ireland would be so used to skulduggery that he would be experienced at dealing with it. So that was it, the beginning and end of it, and of course Blair was cock-a-hoop. There was a statement in the House of Commons by Blair. Howard made a show of defending himself, but he's compromised, first of all by saying that Blair lied about naming Kelly, and secondly because the Tories were in favour of the war anyway. Blair just destroyed him really, and Kennedy was brushed aside.

But on further reflection, I thought, if there had never been a war, David Kelly would still have been in the Ministry of Defence. So he was a victim of the war, like everyone who has been killed. Secondly, if you're a journalist, and somebody from the security services comes and says to you what the Government is putting out is false, that's a big story, and you can't blame Gilligan for that. To attack Richard Sambrook and Greg Dyke at the BBC and the governors, the way Hutton did, was utterly disgraceful.

The other thing was criticising Kelly for talking to journalists. Now Kelly's a member of the Baha'i Faith, and he obviously thought the war was immoral, and he was a whistle-blower of the best tradition. Then to acquit the Government of everything, after all that was said – this was a major attack on the BBC by the Government. Hutton was not allowed to consider the issues that really mattered. Anyway, the real lie wasn't about whether there were weapons. The real lie was that we were never told that we went to war because the Prime Minister decided long ago to follow Bush wherever he wanted to go. That was the untruth, and that wasn't even considered or referred to by the BBC, or considered by Hutton.

Journalists feel that this is an attack on journalism. They are put in a position where the Government can condemn them for saying something that, frankly, was a perfectly reasonable thing to say, in view of what one of them had been told by Kelly. So maybe Hutton won't have such a good press. We'll just have to see.

Blair must be over the moon. Gavyn Davies, the Chairman of the BBC, a friend of Gordon Brown's, immediately resigned, which was an amusing consequence.

Friday 30 January
Andrew Gilligan resigned. I suppose in a way it was inevitable after Gavyn Davies and Greg Dyke. So the whole story is boiling.

I looked up Hutton, and discovered that he's a real Establishment figure. I think that might be a reason why Blair asked him to do it.

Sunday 1 February
Greg Dyke has said that Alastair Campbell bullied him all the time, so the truth is coming out in an interesting way. Also, Jonathan Dimbleby had an extended programme about the Hutton Report and, to cut a long story short, in a poll at the end, of the 42,000 people who had telephoned in, 91 per cent thought that Hutton was a whitewash. I think that Blair is going to pay a terrible price for this, because once you alienate journalists, they won't find anything good in what you do.

I caught a train down to East Croydon and was met by Stephen and Nita and Emily and Daniel, after a bit of a hiccup because I'd forgotten to take my mobile phone and I couldn't get in touch with them, but at any rate they arrived. They took me to the Fairfield Hall for the Holocaust Memorial Concert. They had asked me to introduce it. I was a bit nervous, but I had prepared a few thoughts. I came onto the stage from the side, spoke for nine and a half minutes (they'd asked for ten) and then went and sat with Stephen and Nita. Heard the first part of the concert, saw Emily and Daniel playing, and then Nita dropped me at the station for a train to Victoria.

There was a South African sitting opposite me. He was very scruffy, he hadn't shaved properly and I thought he might be a South African tourist. But he was a doctor, and his speciality was invasive radiology. He told me that, in fighting cancer, you can send a fibre-optic camera to identify the cancer, and then you can, via electronic means, close the arteries that feed the cancer cells, kill them, and then allow the capillaries to grow and replace the blood supply when the cancer is dead. It was absolutely fascinating.

Tuesday 3 February
Blair appeared before the Liaison Committee (of all the Select Committee chairmen) and announced an investigation into the intelligence on Iraq, under Lord Butler, the former Cabinet Secretary. I can see what the strategy is. Hutton blamed everything on the BBC, and the Chairman and Director General resigned. This inquiry will blame the intelligence services, and Blair will spring free from it all, a man vindicated on every front. But

he will not allow the committee to discuss *why* he went to war. Menzies Campbell, the Liberal Democrat spokesman, has not gone on the committee, and he can now criticise the committee from the outside. But what a shambles!

Also, it interests me that the media have not invited John Rees or Lindsey German or Alan Simpson, or anybody who opposed the war, to appear in the press at the very moment when what we said about the war has turned out to be right. I'm in a slightly special position. It's interesting to see how this works. It doesn't mean that the Stop the War people haven't been influential, but their influence has to be denied to prevent people thinking that if you go on the streets it'll make any difference. That's the political process at work. It's like pushing on one end of a piece of string, and the other end of the piece of the string moves, allegedly on its own, under its own steam, ignoring the pressure, but it is the pressure that does it. Anyway, I don't think Blair can go to war again; that's one advantage.

Saturday 7 February
Mrs Mac came in this morning. She's back from New Zealand, where she had a lovely time. Showed me pictures of her son and grandson and his wife and two little daughters, and she brought me a lovely woolly hat, a scarf and bedsocks.

The news is getting worse and worse and worse for Blair. Fifty-one per cent think he should now resign. The war's gone wrong for him in an absolutely horrific way. The attempt to blame it all on the intelligence is not going to work.

Tuesday 10 February
I had a phone call, or indeed I phoned Birnberg, Peirce and Partners, who told me about two Turks who were charged under the 2000 Terrorism Act because they were members of the DHKC (the Turkish Revolutionary People's Liberation Front) which is a Marxist organisation. The Terrorism Act is really quite terrifying. The organisation of which they were members was quite legal until a particular date, so they couldn't have been charged up to the date when it became illegal, and then they became terrorists. The decision was taken, not by what they did, but by what Blunkett decided. They are appearing before a court with a jury, and I sent a letter to be put before the court. Under new terrorism legislation, they wouldn't even have a jury, and they would never know the evidence against them. The defence lawyer as well as the prosecution would be appointed by the Government and the judge would be specially vetted, and they could be put away for years. There hasn't, to the best of my knowledge, been a single terrorist act in Britain since the incident outside the Libyan Embassy years ago. So Blunkett is using Bush's war to take away our civil liberties. The man is an absolute threat to civil liberties and democracy, and of course the Cabinet

goes along with it. The Turks could both serve between five and eight years.

I don't know, I never thought it would come to us, but I remember that after the French Revolution, the British Government suspended habeas corpus, and this new 'war against terror' is whipping up all the same sort of feeling, this Cold War-like sentiment. One of the reasons why the Turkish Marxists were treated as terrorists was because they spoke about a world revolution. When you get to the point where a Marxist who believes in a world revolution – which is a perfectly permissible thing to believe in, particularly when you're dealing with dictatorships – becomes a terrorist, then the Cold War propaganda against the left and the anti-terrorist propaganda come together to make it possible to arrest and imprison almost anybody they like.

Wednesday 11 February

The Chinese cockle-pickers who died in Morecombe Bay, in an incoming tide, had apparently paid £20,000 to be smuggled into Britain, and were earning a pound for every thousand cockles they picked. The gang masters got a hundred pounds. One tragic guy had rung all the way home to his wife in China on his mobile phone, stuck in the mud, 'I think I'm going to die. The water's up to my neck. There's nothing I can do about it.' Oh God, talk about the exploitation of capitalism!

Monday 16 February

Picked up at 7.45 and taken to the BBC for *Start the Week*. Sue McGregor was chairing and it just was such fun. It began with Archbishop Tutu describing truth and reconciliation, talking in that way he does. He's a lovely guy, so funny. I said, 'What should I call you? I suppose it'll have to be Archbishop. I can't call you Desmond!' In *The Independent* he suggested that Blair and Bush should apologise for the war, and it gave me an opportunity to talk about morality in politics – not being successful and profitable, but being right. Then Sue McGregor said, 'We never thought of you as having any Christian origins, so I'm a bit surprised.'

Tutu was an absolute charmer. I got a photograph with him afterwards, and I said, 'I must be photographed with you, because I met Gandhi as a child, and Mandela, and yourself, and those are the three people who've inspired me most in my life.'

Wednesday 18 February

I caught a cab to the Athenaeum for lunch with Rudolph Weisweiller, who's eighty-one now and was a contemporary of mine at Oxford during the war. I was told one smashing story about Rowan Williams's visit to the Pope recently: they went to the Vatican and the Pope read a homily, welcoming him and so on, pointing out the importance of the apostolic succession. The Archbishop of Canterbury kissed the Pope's ring, and the

Pope kissed his ring, and then when they left, the Pope turned to one of his cardinals, saying, 'Who were those guys?' I must say, it's terribly funny.

Saturday 21 February

Caught the Tube to Bloomsbury Baptist Church for the Annual General Meeting of Labour Action for Peace. There were about twenty-five people. We discussed resolutions about peace and the arms trade and Israel, and people moved amendments, but I must say, democracy is so slow. For example, one amendment was 'This Annual General Meeting condemns the war against terrorism because you cannot make war on a noun.' Well, it was a rather silly way of putting it. Then somebody said – I think I said this – 'If you can't make war on a noun, how do you make war on poverty?' So that discussion went on for ages! Then there was another debate about whether you should have to have a referendum before you went to war, which is a ludicrous idea. But you couldn't but like them, and they're very warm to me. I'd forgotten to take food, so they forced sandwiches and buns on me.

Monday 23 February

I spoke to Hilary, he and Sally went to Chequers for dinner on Saturday, the only Cabinet minister there. Actors Richard Wilson and Patrick Stewart were there. It was a purely social gathering, and they were taken round. Hilary enjoyed it.

The Government is now going to have compulsory drug-testing of students at school. That's an outrage. Whether people will stand up for civil liberties, I don't know. If you keep people in a state of fear all the time, they'll go along with all these things. Bremner had a funny skit last night about a 'bearded man who terrorises Britain'. It turned out to be Blunkett, of course.

Wednesday 25 February

I was driven to the studio for the recording of my 'Benn and Hague' slot, about the BBC. We talked a bit beforehand, and he told me one interesting thing. I can't say I was surprised. He told me that when he was Leader of the Opposition, MI5 regularly reported to him. Gaitskell, when he became Leader of the Labour Party, asked MI5 to vet everybody, and that's probably the normal procedure, but the idea that the Executive, through the security services, can bug and vet elected Members of Parliament is so horrific I just don't know how to come to terms with it.

I was asked by Lindsey German to be President of the Stop the War Coalition, which I've agreed to do, so long as it didn't involve me in Respect, which is a political party.

Thursday 26 February

Well, this was a remarkable day. On the *Today* programme, this morning, Clare Short said that when she was in the Cabinet she saw a transcript of something Kofi Annan had said, and she implied that the Government had bugged Kofi Annan when they were trying to get a majority on the second resolution for the war with Iraq.

Jeremy Vine rang and asked me if I'd do an interview on the citizenship ceremonies, which have been launched by Blunkett and the Prince of Wales, under which people take British citizenship, in the presence of the Union Jack, sing the national anthem and pledge an oath of allegiance to the Queen. It was revolting! I said, 'Well, I'm a citizen of the world.' I quoted Tom Paine, 'My country is the world. My religion is to do good.' It was ridiculous to take an oath of allegiance. Although we had to do it as MPs, my allegiance was to my constituents and my conscience. The interview was only forty seconds long, and I don't think it was quite what they wanted, and I'm sure there was a scream of protest later.

I did several more broadcasts – eight in a day. That is the beauty of retirement!

I watched 'Benn and Hague', and they had completely removed what I said at the very beginning, which was that you can't discuss the BBC without discussing Hutton. I said his report was sloppy and that it was unsafe and unsatisfactory, and he tried to frighten the BBC. They cut all that out. So that's what Hutton's done to the BBC. I'm going to take it up. I'm going to raise it with the producers, and if necessary write to the Acting Director General, Mark Byford, and release a letter to the press, depending on what he says in response. The cuts were not a problem of time; they had plenty of time.

Friday 27 February

I worked in pyjamas till about noon.

The Clare Short thing is *the* big story, and later in the day the *Evening Standard* had evidence that the Australians knew that we had bugged Hans Blix all the time that he was in Iraq. It's terribly embarrassing, and Blair would love to get beyond Iraq, but he can't. Blunkett even hinted today that they're contemplating a charge against Clare Short under the Official Secrets Act, which will make her a martyr. I've no time for Clare Short, but she certainly helped to keep the thing alive.

Saturday 28 February

For the last couple of nights I've had pains in my leg, which have made me get up and jump about. I was told years ago in Bristol by a doctor that if you smoke, your legs go wrong. So I just note that, in case it happens again.

To Camden Centre for the Stop the War Annual General Meeting and my speech wasn't a rabble-rousing speech. It was about how you turned the movement into politically effective action, winning support in Britain, in Parliament, and about the role of the United Nations. Of course, the left doesn't like the United Nations; takes the same view of the United Nations that it takes of Parliament: the whole thing's a fraud. On the other hand, I argued that you take the hot air of a movement and convert it into orderly movement and a steam engine. It's an old argument of mine. George Galloway made a powerful speech, and Jeremy Corbyn made a brilliant speech. I must say, Jeremy is so thoughtful and experienced and clear. John Rees made a classic socialist speech about the international class struggle. It made me feel a bit stick-in-the mud.

Sunday 29 February
The papers today are full of this business about the Attorney General's advice on the war. It seems that his first advice in December 2002 was that it would require a second resolution to make the war legal. Then the army pressed him, because they didn't want to send soldiers to Iraq without being sure of the legal position, and asked, 'Well, if there isn't a second resolution, what do we do?' It would appear – I'm only guessing, but I think it's possible – that Blair even tried to lean on the Attorney General to say, oh no, you could go to war legally on the basis of Resolutions 678, 687 and 1441. This is what led Elizabeth Wilmshurst, who is a Foreign Office deputy legal adviser, to resign in protest after thirty years there.

It can only be resolved by publishing the evidence, i.e., the Attorney General's advice. Peter Hain said of it, 'Oh, there's a lot of confusion.' Well, there's only confusion because they won't publish anything! It's a big issue, because it touches on trust.

Tuesday 2 March
I got a cab to Heathrow for a flight to Amsterdam for the Random House (my publishers) sales conference. Dame Stella Rimington, the former head of MI5, was on the plane also on her way there. I thought she looked very grey. Anyway, when we got to the airport, there was a car to take us into Amsterdam, so I talked to her on the journey. She raised the question of Clare Short, which I didn't, because I thought it was for her to raise it. I said I thought it was strange the Cabinet Secretary had written to Clare about it, and she said, well, presumably the Prime Minister told him to write to her.

She had to clear her own memoirs, and apparently there's a little group in the Ministry of Defence who objected to them. She was quite open. I did ask her about the Cold War, and did she really think the Red Army had ever planned to come to Western Europe? She thought probably the West was afraid of communist ideas, which is what I've always thought. She was a typical civil servant really, talked about the balance of responsibility between security and civil liberties. I found it interesting to talk to her.

Anyway, we were taken to the Grand Hotel Krasnapolsky. Michael Buerk told one funny story, about signing books. He always asks, as I do, 'What name shall I put?' and a woman said, 'Emma Chizet.' So he wrote down, 'For Emma Chizet, with best wishes', and what she was actually saying was, 'How much is it?'

Sunday 7 March

Over the last few days Blair has been saying that international law should be changed in order to allow pre-emptive attacks. It is significant, because if he thinks the law needs to be changed, then presumably he agrees that the law at the moment prohibits it. So that suggests to me that the Attorney General had advised him the war was illegal, and he wants to change the law. Nobody's really picked that up yet, but I think it's important.

I'm getting switched off from politics. I can't go on doing at eighty what I'm doing now. I'm so tired.

Wednesday 10 March

Up at 4.30 and got a cab to Euston to catch the 6.55 to Manchester. The train was late.

I got a cab to my grandson William's accommodation in Manchester, had breakfast with him. He's so excited by political philosophy, he likes Plato, and Hobbes, and Marx, the theories are what interest him. He's also doing international relations, which he doesn't find very interesting, and comparative politics.

He took me up to a room, where about six or seven of his mates were gathered. They were so well disposed towards him. He's set up a group and is trying to record some music and send a really decent CD to some producers. So he's a happy lad.

Got the train back. There was a girl opposite me of about twenty-one or so, on the mobile phone all the time about her boyfriend, who's in prison. She heard me talking about an abscess in my jaw and a loose tooth, because I rang the dentist to see if he could see me, before I go to America. So we had a bit of a talk.

Saturday 13 March

Up at 5.30, and at eight o'clock Emma Mitchell, from Hutchinson, turned up with a driver, Adam, and we drove up to Cumbria. Stopped at the Welcome Break for tea. Motorway cafés are quite extraordinary – it is a predominantly working-class clientele that uses them. One man came up to me and took my tray. I said, 'What do you want?' He said, 'I want to shake your hand. I'm from Sheffield.' His wife was there and he said, 'I'm going up to see my seventeen-year-old play in a football match.' It was sweet.

Anyway, we got to the Lakeside Theatre, Keswick, by one o'clock. Kay

Dunbar, who organises the Dartington Literary Festival in Devon, also does this one. Lord Judd, the former MP Frank Judd, came up. He lives nearby, and he was going to introduce me. Talked to a few people, and then went into the Lakeside Theatre, which was packed with 400 people.

Frank introduced me, in a very generous way, and then I talked, followed by questions and answers, and that went on for about an hour. Emma and I walked down by Derwent Water, along the pier. It was chilly, but nice.

Sunday 14 March

The Spanish Government has had to admit that the bombing in Madrid was done by al-Qaeda and not by ETA, the Basque separatist movement. Of course this is polling day in Spain, and José María Aznar, the right-wing Prime Minister, had hoped he could blame it on ETA, which would strengthen him, but actually, now the voters know that it was al-Qaeda, of course the blame goes to Aznar for involving Spain in the war against Iraq. So it could have a tremendous effect.

Monday 15 March

Aznar was defeated in the Spanish elections. So it's a real warning to Blair. Also, Putin was re-elected in Russia; no surprise there.

I was picked up and taken to BBC White City to give a lecture on 'the art of persuasion' to 150 producers from various BBC factual programmes. The BBC is suffering from post-traumatic stress disorder after Hutton and the attack on the BBC. But it was quite an interesting discussion. I was asked who I wanted to be Chairman of the BBC. Would I apply to be Chairman? Would the BBC be handed over to Murdoch? The questions indicated their anxiety.

Then I came home and discovered that the new Spanish Prime Minister had called for the withdrawal of Spanish troops, unless the UN takes over, and that is tremendous.

Wednesday 17 March

A Dr Ray Greek, from Alabama, now working in California, came to see me to present the case against the use of animals for experimentation, for medical purposes on humans. His argument is that animals are not a valid model; the conditions are different. A lot of scientists say you've got a point, but he's up against the old scientific establishment and, to some extent, the pharmaceutical companies. He's a youngish man, married to a vet, and he said vets asked questions about how to treat animals based on what they know about human beings, and they tried it and it didn't work. He's an amusing, intelligent guy. He's been onto the BBC. I found him very agreeable, persuasive, and of course I agree with him. He's got lots of cats and dogs, so he obviously likes animals, but he said his argument is a medical one and a scientific one, and not one based on simply being an animal lover.

On the first anniversary of the attack on Iraq I was invited by my friends Joe McGowan and Sanjiv Shah to speak at a demonstration in New York City.

There were about 90,000 people marching round a part of the city that had been closed off, watched closely – but not interfered with in any way – by the police, with the Mayor of New York looking at us from behind police lines.

One of the organisers was the United for Peace and Justice Group, which has been responsible for many of these anti-war marches and demonstrations.

As the march set off, I came across a wonderful gathering of older women who called themselves 'The Raging Grannies'; they had peace badges all over their clothes and were shouting slogans like 'Money for homes and not for war', 'Money for health and not for war', 'Money for schools and not for war'. I went over and had a word with them and offered to join, but was told that Raging Grandfathers were not required.

The American peace movement gets very little coverage in the British media, but its success can be judged by the impact it had on the mid-term elections, when President Bush lost control of the Senate and the House of Representatives.

Among the many speakers was Representative Dennis Kucinich from Ohio, who declared himself for the democratic nomination for the presidency in 2008 and has been courageous in his presentation of the anti-war case.

Monday 22 March

The Israelis have assassinated Sheikh Ahmed Yassin, who's the co-founder and leader of Hamas. They sent a helicopter gunship to Gaza and killed him with a lot of other people, and Sharon took personal responsibility. It has been denounced everywhere. Even Jack Straw said it was wrong. All the Americans said was that they were troubled by it. Hamas have sworn mass revenge.

To Temple Church for Ralph's memorial. I got there early, and I sat outside with Peter Carter, who is an architect. He told me Temple Church had been built in 1140, and it was a Crusader church, and the rotunda was copied from a church in Bethlehem, I think he said. He's so knowledgeable about these things.

Anyway, I went into the church and found I'd been put next to Derry Irvine, who was Lord Chancellor until replaced by Lord Falconer. I can't say I really like him, but when I see him he's always very polite. He said he served under Ralph, as a junior.

I said, 'You must be glad to have a bit of time now.' Then I asked, 'What do you think about the war? How do you reconcile pre-emptive action with the UN Charter?'

He said, 'Well, freedom-fighters and terrorists are easy to confuse.' I just got the impression he was a bit uneasy about it. He didn't say more than that.

Afterwards I had a word with him and I said, 'I realise you can't say anything now, but at some stage, looking at the future, the legal problems of the combination of pre-emptive strikes with the UN Charter is something that needs to be thought about.'

He said, 'Yes, but not now.'

Anyway Lord Bingham, the Master of the Rolls, was sitting the other side of me, just across from the aisle, and Ann Gibson and the girls and Christopher and their spouses were there. All of my children except Hilary were there. I kept it secret to myself that Hilary was in Iraq, then Mary Wilson came up and said to me that she'd heard Hilary on the radio from Basra in the morning! His wife Sally had told me two security people went there two or three days ago to see everything was safe and secure, in advance of his visit.

Looking round, I thought how the Oxford Union, and senior civil servants and judges are all part of the mandarin Establishment class, who run everything. I was saying how nice everyone was to me, and Lissie commented, 'Well, it is all about class, you realise.' They are nice to me because I am part of their class. She is shrewd about that.

Wednesday 24 March

I caught the train to Wolverhampton for *Question Time*. I sat on my little stool at Wolverhampton station with a cup of tea, because I was hours early.

The other members of the team were Lord Thurso, the grandson of Sir Archibald Sinclair (the Liberal leader from 1935 to 1945); Barbara Follett, who with her husband Ken Follett worked closely with New Labour, but didn't like Mandelson, and got dropped by Blair (her first husband was killed before her very eyes in South Africa); John Redwood, the Tory MP, the great ideologue of the right; and Ned Temko, the American Editor of the *Jewish Chronicle*.

I had prepared very carefully, and it went well. I'm pleased with it. Then, as the programme ended, David Dimbleby was saying goodbye to the audience and I said, 'Can I say something, because this might be David's last programme if he becomes Chairman of the BBC; on behalf of all the panels and all the audiences, could I thank him.' There was a tremendous round of applause. I think he was pleased, because last time I intervened like that, during the fire-fighters' strike, I said the fire-fighters would settle for a 5 per cent increase on his salary and he was extremely angry.

Tuesday 30 March
I went to the dentist to have a tooth out and a new plate fitted. It cost £190, and I'm not sure whether I'm still a Health Service patient or not, but at any rate Ewan McLean is a really good dentist, and the new plate fits perfectly.

Wednesday 31 March
Tam Dalyell phoned me this morning. He said, 'I noticed that Hilary had only been to the green zone in Iraq', which of course is the highly protected government headquarters, and, 'perhaps you should have a word with him about it, and he should get out a bit.' So I spoke to Hilary, and Hilary said, 'No one can ever go there except to the green zone.' But, he said, 'As my DFID people volunteer to go, I felt I should' and of course he's quite right, but it's obviously a very limited view he gets.

Friday 2 April
Natasha Kaplinsky called round with a piece of cake attached to a balloon, and a birthday card, for tomorrow.

Monday 5 April
I had a phone call from the sculptor Ian Walters tonight. Bristol, after ten years, have finally bought his bust of me to put in the Council House. They're paying him £9,000. To be a Freeman of the City and to have a bust in Bristol is really something. Who would have thought fifty-four years ago, when I went there as a twenty-five-year-old, that that's how it would all end up? Still, all these busts are obituaries. I have to recognise that.

Wednesday 7 April
Hilary rang from Rwanda. He'd been there for the commemoration of the
Rwanda massacres, where 800,000 Tutsis were murdered by the Hutus.
Just a ghastly story.

Iraq is in a deeper and deeper crisis, because the Sunnis and the Shi'ites
are both rising now against the Americans, and other coalition forces are
pulling out. I don't know, it could be a catastrophe of a major kind. The
only comfort is it might cost Bush and Blair their jobs.

Friday 9 April
To Trafalgar Square, where a couple of thousand people were gathered for
a CND protest. Corin Redgrave was there, Bruce Kent, Jeremy Corbyn,
Ernst Rodker, who's been very interested in the Vanunu case, Julie
Christie.

The roof at home is being replaced, and Barbara Campbell helped
moved the ladder on the scaffolding so that it's a little bit harder to burgle
the house.

Sunday 11 April
Beautiful day! Latish lie-in. Went to the paper shop, and of course the news
over the whole of this weekend is entirely about Iraq, which has gone wrong
in a horrible way. There's even been a ceasefire between the militia and the
military in Fallujah, where 600 people have been killed by the Americans
as a revenge against the four Americans who were killed and mutilated.

Tuesday 13 April
I'm a bit depressed. I have to be honest. My dad used to get depressed, and
I didn't know why, but now I do understand. You know, you've had a very
active life, and been in the forefront of things, and then gradually you slip
into the background. The other factor is that you know you've got a limited
number of years to run, and what do you do with your life? I've got this
terrible conscience that I should work all the time, but actually I should be
seeing more of the grandchildren, doing useful things. Paul Robeson fell
into a deep, deep depression in his old age, and it worried me at the time.
I now understand.

There's an inquiry going on in Washington. The FBI is saying we gave
all these warnings, but we didn't have the resources, so Bush is losing
credibility on being the right person to defend American security, and
although Bush and Blair make all these aggressive speeches about thugs
and terrorists, actually they're losing control of Iraq.

More than a year after the war was declared over, it is the most difficult
war to control – namely, guerrilla warfare and suicide bombing. The
Americans want 10,000 more troops because the Iraqi army and police
they've been training are just not prepared to shoot their own people.

Wednesday 14 April

Sharon has gone to Washington, and his proposal that Israel should withdraw from Gaza, but retain the settlements in the West Bank, or most of them, has been endorsed wholeheartedly by Bush. So the Road Map has been torn up. Without Bush, Sharon couldn't do it. Sharon's under attack in Israel because some people don't want the Gaza settlements withdrawn. It won't end the violence.

Friday 16 April

Blair's gone to see Bush. He hasn't seen Senator Kerry, the Democratic candidate. He's just been endorsing everything Bush said, not only about Iraq, but also about the Sharon decision to bypass the Road Map. At the same time, a book by Bob Woodward has just come out, saying that Bush was so anxious not to endanger Blair's majority in Parliament that he said to Blair, 'You don't have to send troops if you don't want to.' But Blair still went ahead.

The truth is that America in Fallujah is engaged in massacres, in war crimes. When people look back on it, they'll see it so much more clearly, but it is a tragedy, and of course the Palestinians are absolutely up in arms, quite properly, about the betrayal of the Road Map. There must be a lot of uneasiness, even in the Cabinet.

Sunday 18 April

The rumours today, which obviously have been officially approved, is that Blair is going to capitulate and agree to hold a referendum on the European Union constitution. It's very important. It's done to outflank the Tories, but it'll blow up in his face.

Monday 19 April

I will have some difficult decisions to make. Blair's behaviour is absolutely outrageous! His plan is to upstage Howard, sign, ratify the constitution after a parliamentary debate, and then put it to the people after the next election. That's part of a deal he's done with Murdoch; there's no question about it, everybody admits that. So people, when they vote, will only be able to vote: do you want to come out of Europe? They won't be allowed to vote on the real question. It's an absolute fraud! I'm getting very angry, but I've got to think of Hilary, because not only do I not want to endanger Hilary in any way, but Caroline would reconstitute herself out of her ashes and strangle me if I did anything to endanger him. So that's a fact I have to take into account. But the thought that a prime minister who's destroyed democracy in the Party, ignored Parliament, ignored the Cabinet, didn't even get Cabinet consent to this European decision, and is ignoring the public, that he should be able to get away with stealing all the powers that belong to the people and to Parliament, it's a throwback to 1832. I feel terribly upset about it.

Wednesday 21 April
Alice Mahon told me that UKIP, the United Kingdom Independence Party, and the BNP have done a deal not to stand against each other in Halifax. That tells me all I need to know about UKIP.

Friday 23 April
Saffron Burrows arrived. I'd invited her for lunch; she was tall and glamorous as always. I had booked a table at Julie's in Portland Road, so we walked down and it was such a beautiful day, we sat at a table outside and Saffron had fish and chips and ice cream, and I had some mushroom risotto, and ice cream and coffee. I asked her all about her work. She's been making this film, *Troy*, which is being launched in May; she's going to Rome this weekend; she's got to go to Los Angeles for the premiere of *Troy*; then to New York; then to Cannes for *Troy*; then to New Zealand till the middle of August for a film she's making – I didn't quite understand it – a science-fiction thing, in which she plays the part of a policewoman. I asked her about her writing. People who write don't want to talk about it, and I understand that.

Tuesday 27 April
Fifty-two former ambassadors have written an open letter saying that the Iraq war is totally misconceived. Fifty-two ambassadors do represent a really sizeable body of opinion. The letter made banner headlines. When senior ambassadors say that a policy being pursued by the Government is doomed to failure, and denounce the way in which we do everything we're told by Bush, it is pretty devastating, because they can't be dismissed as the awkward squad, the troublemakers, anti-Semitic or anything. The most important thing in the letter was that they believed the war is doomed to failure. Whatever Blair says, you can't win the war.

Thursday 29 April
I dashed to the Four Seasons Hotel, for the 'Placemakers' Lunch. I was called in at the last minute because somebody who was to have talked about the Olympic bid for 2012 couldn't turn up. They were all in the property and construction industry. The Chairman, who was sitting next to me and introduced me, said, 'I see you were a pilot in the war.'
    'Yes.'
    He said, 'Oh well, I've got a plane and a helicopter.'
    'Oh really? Why did you get that?'
    'Well,' he said, 'my ex-wife did so many point-to-point meetings, I was fed up with driving round in a four-wheel jeep, so I got a helicopter.'
    They must have been as rich as Croesus! I gave my speech about the sources of power – you know, money and faith and technology, and so on – and there were one or two questions; they were very nice to me.

Friday 30 April
I got up early, and I went to Lissie's. When I got home I opened the front door, and I found the roof had fallen in on the stairs – great chunks of concrete and plaster, and if I had been on the stairs I might have been quite seriously hurt. I didn't know what to do, how to clear it all up.

Apparently, one of the guys working on the house was walking along the flat roof on the side of the house and just stepped right through. He might have fallen through. The wood's all rotten. So that's another thing to be done. But that will be a really big construction job.

Saturday 1 May
There were forty-six new peers announced today. The whole patronage system is corrupt. There's no other way of describing it.

Today, the *Daily Mirror* had pictures of Iraqi prisoners being forced to pose in sexual positions, and of somebody urinating over Iraqi prisoners – utterly disgusting! It was described as a 'public-relations disaster'.

Friday 7 May
Yesterday, Marks & Spencer opened a new food-only shop near me, in Notting Hill Gate. Got a nice range of stuff, but it's a very crowded shop, and the people at the tills have nowhere to sit. There was a huge long queue. I must say, I'll get a few nice things from there, and then I'll do my basic shopping up the road, where I believe there is going to be another supermarket at the end of July. That'll make my life a lot easier.

Sunday 9 May
I'm very depressed by the world situation. The utter brutality.

I watched this TV programme called *Children of Abraham*, and really, listening to Bush, that God had made America, and Americans are the chosen people, it is a religious war. He is a fundamentalist, and it's terrifying. Of course the Americans worship money. They don't worship democracy or values at all.

I have to keep my spirits up. It's difficult, because sometimes I feel I'm such a tiny sub-fractional part of this world. When I was a minister and an MP, I felt I played a part in getting control of it all, but now, I think perhaps nobody can get control of it.

I read the introduction and the chapter by my son-in-law Paul Gordon to his book *Between Psychotherapy and Philosophy*. It was a modest account of the role of therapists, but he analysed all the difficulties – do therapists behave badly, are they too judgemental? He's a thoughtful, decent guy, and I'm happy he's my son-in-law.

Monday 10 May
This afternoon I did something that gave me enormous pleasure. The

button had come off a very old pair of trousers, which I like. I had tried to put it on with an automatic buttoner device I bought years ago, but it didn't work, so I decided I would sew a button on. I found my old wartime sewing kit, had a hell of a job threading a needle, but I finally succeeded and I sewed the button on really firmly. I was just so pleased! I certainly haven't sewn a button on since I had Guillain-Barré illness in 1981. I doubt if I've sewn anything since I got married in 1949. But I got huge satisfaction out of that!

Thursday 13 May

I was picked up by Iranian Television and driven to their studios at Acton, and I did a forty-minute interview. The sound was so poor, I'm not sure I heard the questions correctly, but it was about Iraq, and about the torture, and about Bush and Blair, and so on. You get a huge audience in Iran, and you get a long enough time to answer properly.

There's a story I got via email that Sharon possibly intends to bomb the nuclear facilities in Iran, and has told Bush this, and it's understood that it would be acceptable, just as Israel did to Iraq in 1981. Of course that would set the whole place ablaze.

Bush is introducing sanctions against Syria. He's tightened the screw on Cuba. There's no evidence that he is in any way altering his position, and maybe he thinks if he's going to be beaten, this is the time to do a lot of things that he would like to have done in his second term. It's very dangerous.

Friday 14 May

The Editor of the *Daily Mirror*, Piers Morgan, is now on the rack because they say his photographs of the abuse of Iraqi prisoners were fake, but he sticks to the view that he believes them, unless it can be proved that they were false; and anyway, he says the story's true. It's ludicrous really, but the Government is seizing on Piers Morgan to divert attention from the war. But the war keeps coming back and coming back and coming back. You just cannot believe a word about the war.

Saturday 15 May

The papers this morning were all about Piers Morgan's dismissal. It is interesting that the four casualties of the war have not been the ministers responsible for the war, but Gavyn Davies (the Chairman of the BBC), Greg Dyke (Director General of the BBC), Andrew Gilligan (journalist for the BBC), who was absolutely right, and now Piers Morgan. It may be the media is now frightened about the way the Government treats them. I think it is quite right to be suspicious of the media, but in this particular case the media are right and the Government's wrong. They say Piers Morgan published hoax pictures, but Blair took us to war with false information about weapons of mass destruction. So it's an easy argument to make.

Tuesday 18 May
Sonia Gandhi, although she's the leader of the Congress Party and won the election, has decided she doesn't think it right to be Prime Minister of India. That is courageous and interesting, whether it is because as some people suggested, she thought she'd be assassinated, or because she didn't want to be the victim of racial hatred (she is Italian by birth), I don't know. The Congress Party is utterly despondent because she was very highly thought of. She's appointed a bearded, turbaned old Finance Minister, who introduced the so-called reforms (i.e., privatisation) in India, and this was I think her attempt to restore confidence in the Indian economy after there'd been this massive fall in the stock market following the election of the Congress Party.

Wednesday 19 May
I walked over to the Cabinet War Rooms, which I'd never visited before in my life, for a meeting of the British Academy of Audiology. The War Rooms are of course underground, just opposite St James's Park, and I must say it was absolutely riveting down there. Exhibits, and figures dressed in exactly the period of the time – marines standing in uniform with their First World War medals, a woman putting up a poster, a secretary at a typewriter. I wandered round, and just as I was going into the room where the meeting was, an air-raid siren sounded. It sent a cold chill down my spine. I haven't heard an air-raid siren for ages. We had photographs taken in front of some posters, including 'Never in the field of human conflict was so much owed by so many to so few'.

The British Academy of Audiology is made up of three groups who have come together, and they wanted me to make a speech. They were all very friendly, all audiologists, so I made a particular point of wearing my hearing aids.

On my way out, I met a man who said that someone had thrown some powder at the Prime Minister and hit him during PM's Questions. So I rushed into the House and heard that two men in the Gallery, who'd been guests of Llin Golding (who's now a peer), turned out to be from Fathers for Justice, and had thrown three little balloons, I suppose of harmless powder. One had hit Blair on the back, and others had landed near him, so it was a pretty accurate throw. The Speaker suspended the sitting, and everyone was laughing about it. The men were sitting in *front* of the protective shield that they've put up in the Gallery. Apparently Llin had made two tickets for Prime Minister's Questions available in an auction, to raise money for something, and the auction was won by Fathers for Justice.

The news on the television is awful tonight. The Israelis sent a helicopter gunship to attack a peaceful demonstration in Rafah at the southern end of the Gaza strip, killing a lot of children. It was so painful to watch.

Then also tonight the Americans accidentally bombed and killed people at a wedding in Iraq. Everything's crumbling. Then there was the symbolic bombing of Blair – I'm glad it wasn't an anti-war demonstrator who did it, I must admit.

Saturday 22 May

I went by car to the House of Commons for a Stop the War demonstration. As I left I had a word with the policeman. He said, 'Are you going to the demonstration?'

I said yes, so we had a bit of a talk, and he was totally opposed to the war.

Later a Palestinian said to me, 'Can you explain to me why the Labour Party has always been so pro-Israeli?'

So I said, 'Well, I'd been in favour of the establishment of the state of Israel, I must say, after the war.'

He said, 'I'm not blaming you. I'm just wondering why.'

I tried to explain, but it was a good question.

Tuesday 25 May

At 10.30 the Venezuelan Ambassador came to see me, Alfredo Toro Hardy, a man of fifty-four, a great intellectual. I had been asked to go to Venezuela this weekend to validate the names in the petition for a referendum for the recall of Hugo Chávez, but I couldn't go. At any rate, he gave me an extremely interesting book about the world called *The Age of Villages*, the small village versus the global village. Also he gave me an article he'd written called 'Is there a future for Latin America?' I must say, I found him charming. His study of globalisation was much like the analysis I did thirty-four years ago on the BBC *Horizon* programme, so just for fun I copied that onto a VHS and sent it to him.

Wednesday 26 May

Was driven back from a media interview by a sixty-year-old Ghanaian, a pastor of the Brotherhood of Cross and Star, which is a fundamentalist Christian group. He claimed that he had direct communication with God, who filled him with knowledge, and he was speaking in the authentic voice of God. Mohammed was Satan. The Jews had turned away from God, but he had given them Palestine. In a gentle way I tried to argue with him that other people take a different view.

Friday 28 May

Mrs Mac has decided to retire. It's really a big event. She's been with us for twenty-eight or twenty-nine years, knows all the family, is such a sweet woman, so I sent her a cheque to take her up to 1 August, and then we'll put her on a standing order and she will have the pension as long as she needs it. She's done a wonderful job looking after the house, and she was so supportive of Caroline, knows all the children and grandchildren.

Saturday 29 May

I got up at five, having set two alarms and having rung for an alarm call from British Telecom, for the trip to France with Lissie and the girls and Stephen's family. We met at Waterloo and caught the Eurostar to Lille.

In Lille, we walked with our baggage over the bridge to a different station and caught the high-speed train, the TGV, to Avignon, where two cars had been booked, and from there we went to stay with Stephen and Nita for three days. We had a meal down in Goudargues, which is the local village, by the canal.

It was just so strange – I haven't had a holiday of that kind for thirty, forty years, I think, where I had nothing whatever to do.

Sunday 30 May–Tuesday 1 June

I took off my watch, didn't look at it all day. It was a beautiful sunny day, and I explored. Even Melissa went swimming in the pool.

In the afternoon we walked down the hill and looked at the sights. Then came up, and we had lunch in the garden. There was a light rain. It was rather pleasantly cool. Played ping-pong, and later we watched *Love Actually* on a DVD.

Late in the evening we had a good old talk – Stephen, Melissa, Nita and Emily – just lots of old jokes and no politics at all. Emily likes being with grown-ups. So the tightrope walk of political differences was set aside. I just made them laugh as best I could. Went to bed about half-past two.

On the Monday we went down to Goudargues again, and we wandered round the church and some of the shops. I took my video camera and photographed a (for me) very sad thing, the statue of a French soldier, or *Poilu,* and under it the inscription: '*Pour les enfants de la commune, 1914–18*', for the children of the village who were killed. Oh . . . !

We came back and had dinner with Roger Lyons and Lance Price who were in the area. Lyons is the former General Secretary of the MSF (Manufacturing, Science and Finance Union), who is now President of the TUC; his wife Kitty is a Hungarian, who said she now had no enjoyment in life; Lance Price was a BBC correspondent who worked for the Labour Party for a time and then worked under Alastair Campbell at Number 10. Again we walked a tightrope, avoiding all reference to politics. Lance is absolutely 100 per cent supportive of Blair.

On Tuesday we went off to Bagnol, and then on to see the Pont du Gard, a 2,000-year-old aqueduct built by the Romans in order to provide water for Nîmes.

Wednesday 2 June

Talked to Gill Pharaoh, who rang me up a few months ago about a book she'd written called *An Ounce of Help*. She's been in the hospice movement and palliative care, and she wrote about dying at home, and everything you should do: do you tell the children? Do you carry on working? What happens when you die? What about the funeral? What about relationships afterwards? I've been encouraging her to publish it. She's a woman of sixty-four herself. I think her grandchildren live abroad. But at any rate, I wrote a marvellous foreword for her, and she rang today to say that a publisher has agreed to take it, although *An Ounce of Help* is not thought a suitable title, so it's going to be *Dying at Home: A Practical Guide*, which is exactly what it is. So she was terribly pleased.

Also I had a phone call from a man of eighty-six. I don't know who he was, but he was a lifelong socialist. He said his son was now a lecturer at Oxford. Then he told me that forty years ago he and his wife went to the local Catholic church, and there, crying on the altar, was a baby in a brown paper parcel. His wife picked it up and brought it home and they adopted him; the boy subsequently went to Oxford, did brilliantly. They did discover that the baby was by an Irish nurse who'd come to England, didn't want an abortion, didn't want to tell her parents, so she just left the baby in a church. I must say, life is full of fascinating stories.

I was picked up and taken to the Camberwell Methodist Church, for a Stop the War meeting. The SWP dominated, and there was an argument about whether one should vote Labour in an election, and an attack on George Galloway for allowing Muslims in his constituency to join his Respect Party when they sweat their own workers. The Workers' Power people said you should just write 'Withdraw from Iraq' on ballot papers. Really, the squabbles of the left are very boring.

Saturday 5 June

The *Morning Star* had an article by George Galloway, and in it he said, 'Britain is currently run by a blood-splattered, lying, crooked group of war criminals.' Now, first of all I think that's a totally ineffective way of getting your case across, but secondly, last November George pleaded with me to try to persuade the National Executive to let him stay in the Party. So if I'd succeeded, he would have been still a member of a party currently run by a 'blood-splattered, lying, crooked group of war criminals'. It put me off George Galloway in a fairly fundamental way. Anyway, that's enough of that!

The phone rang when I was up in the bedroom, just before I had my breakfast, and it was a woman. I said, 'Who is it?'

She said, 'The South African High Commissioner.'

'Oh yes?'

She said, 'The President of South Africa' – President Mbeki – 'wants to speak to Hilary.'

So I said, 'Well, I'm not sure where he is, but I'll try and get a message through.'

She gave me the President's number. So I rang Sal, Hilary's wife, and she said, 'He's in Leeds.' So I left a message, and he rang me and said he'd been onto the President's office, and he hopes to see Mbeki when he goes to Africa. Hilary's in demand!

Ibrahim Allawi came to see me. Ibrahim was born in 1942, came to London in 1950 as an architect student, got involved in the Movement for Colonial Freedom. He was in the Communist Party. He went back after the revolution, was sentenced to death, but escaped. Later, when Saddam came to power, he was sentenced to death again because he'd been to see the Kurds and that was thought illegal. I think he was sentenced to death three times.

He came to London in 1985 with his family, and his son has set up a computer company. He now runs the *Al Ghad*, a left newspaper in Baghdad, and spends about six months in Baghdad and six months in London. He was keen to encourage a global political movement along the lines of the old non-aligned movement, but more popular. Well, I haven't the organisation skill to help him, but I agree with him.

He thought that Ayad Allawi, his namesake, who is the new Prime Minister of Iraq, was so obviously a CIA/MI6 plant that he simply didn't count. Ahmed Chalabi, who was the choice of Donald Rumsfeld and the neo-conservatives, has now been discredited because he had links with the Iranians, and is apparently back in business because he strongly supports the Shi'ites and is working with Muqtada al-Sadr, this young Shi'ite mullah, in the mosque in Najaf. He thought there would be an intensification of the fighting after 30 June when the US hands sovereignty to Allawi because it would show what a puppet government it was. He thought the pressure was so great that the United States would have to close their twelve bases there. Well, I think that's a bit optimistic.

Allawi told me that Tariq Aziz was not in Saddam's inner circle, but what Saddam did was to arrest Tariq's son and torture him, with the intention that Tariq would go on his knees to Saddam and beg him to release his son. He used those tactics on everybody, to humiliate them so they were then utterly dependent on him.

I watched *Come Dancing*, and Natasha won. She was doing a foxtrot, I think. She was terribly good, and I must say, although I can't stand Bruce Forsyth, it is quite an amusing programme, and it makes ballroom dancing more interesting. So I sent her a little message.

Shopping in Notting Hill, I saw an old veteran with medals standing outside the Book Warehouse, so I asked him, 'Were you in D-Day?' He gave me a warm hand. 'No,' he said, 'I was in Burma, General Slim's

Forgotten Army.' I must say, the sight of this old man, who's eighty-four, overwhelmed me with tears. I thanked him for all he did.

Then there was a man coming up the street. He was obviously very tired, and he kept leaning against the wall and then sitting down. So I said, 'Are you all right?' I thought he might be having a heart attack. He said, 'No, it's my arthritis. I'm nearly sixty, and this arthritis is killing.' So I said, 'Would you like me to get a doctor?' He said, 'No, no, no, no.' Then he said, 'Are you Tony Benn?' I said, 'Yes.' He said, 'I ought to punch you in the face!' He was a real working-class Tory.

Somebody sent me an autograph book, because a ninety-two-year-old lady had written to ask if I would like it, and I wrote back, and so this friend of hers sent it to me. It is from 1925, and it had Labour Party autographs – of Susan Lawrence, Ramsay MacDonald, Tom Johnston, Sidney Webb, George Lansbury, Marian Philips, Margaret Bondfield, Bob Smiley, Jim Griffiths, Oswald Mosley and his wife Cynthia Mosley, Jessie Stephen, whom I knew, Ernest Thornton and Nye Bevan. So I put it in a big envelope and it'll go with my archives, but gosh, that really is something to have!

Bush went to see the Pope yesterday and got rebuked.

Tuesday 8 June
I was picked up and taken to Brixton to canvass in the mayoral elections. Ken Livingstone turned up, and for about an hour and a half I walked around – it might have been in Nigeria, really. I just had a brief word with Ken, but he's very busy, as any candidate is. At one stage a guy called Frank Maloney, he's the UKIP candidate for London, was passing. So I had a row with him. I said, 'Look, in Halifax, you're doing a deal with the British National Party.'

I felt a thing I quite often do feel, a cramp in the left of my chest. My chest hurt, but it wasn't the centre, which I believe is where you have heart attacks, it was just on the left side, and I found it difficult to breathe, so I thought I'd better get off before I collapsed. I got in the car and slowly drove home. I didn't get to bed till half-past midnight.

I'm beginning to think that my active life is coming to an end. I don't know how to describe it. I just haven't got the energy I had. But I'd rather die like this than with Alzheimer's.

Wednesday 9 June
At eight o'clock this morning a couple of people from BBC Bristol came to do an interview with me about conscientious objectors, and I had a great argument with them. They arrived with tons of gear, lights and cameras and tripods and boxes. All they wanted to ask me was about Vic Williams, a soldier who refused to fight in the first Gulf war – I said, 'No, this is about conscientious objection. How long do you want?'

Well, they wanted four minutes from me. So I said, 'I'll give you four minutes and I'll do it straight into the camera.'

'Oh, you can't. You've got to look to one side.'

I said, 'I won't, I'm sorry.' I'm obstinate on principle. 'I want to talk to the camera.'

'Well, we may not be able to use it.'

I said, 'I don't mind if you don't use it at all.' But I've got to the point where I'm just determined that if I'm asked to broadcast, I'll talk direct to people. So I did it.

The cameraman said, 'Of course, if the others don't talk to the camera and you've talked to the camera, you'll be so much more powerful.'

I said, 'Ah, you've got it!'

They were all quite friendly, and I was jolly with them, but I'm fed up with being an actor in somebody else's bloody play.

I got the Tube to the House of Commons because Hilary was due to make a statement on Sudan, and I went up to the Peers' Gallery of the Chamber. The attendant said, very politely, 'I'm afraid with security now, sir, only peers are allowed here.'

So I said, 'I am allowed to go in the Peers' Gallery.'

'Well,' he said, 'we'll ask the Speaker.'

So he picked up the phone, must have spoken to the doorkeeper at the back of the Speaker's chair, who must have spoken to Roger Daw, the Speaker's Secretary, who must have spoken to the Speaker in the chair, and the message came back that it was okay. Hilary didn't come up till half-past one, so I was there for nearly an hour, hearing Welsh questions, and Peter Hain, and Prescott answering for Blair, who's in America. Then Hilary made a brilliant statement! John Bercow responded very courteously. Everybody who put questions congratulated Hilary, because he'd only just flown in from the Sudan this morning and came straight to the House. One Tory got up and said, 'Has anyone thought of an aerial survey to find out where the refugees are?' So Hilary replied, 'That's a very good idea.'

It occurred to me, here was a supreme opportunity to get my House of Commons pass changed from 'Special Guest' status, which means nothing, to 'Freedom of the House'. So I wrote a letter to the Speaker, very carefully worded, and took my existing pass, photocopied it in colour, then removed the words 'Special Guest' and put in 'Freedom of the House' and 'Mr Speaker' underneath. A nice little job. I added a cover note to the Speaker's Secretary, but I want to be so sure that it will be dealt with quickly while the Speaker's memory is still fresh. I drove into the House at 8.42, took it to the Members' Post Office, and they said they guaranteed to get it through to him first thing tomorrow, because tomorrow is mayoral, council and European elections' polling day, and the House will be absolutely dead because all Members will be out in their constituencies. Anyway, that's wasted a bit of time, but it was fun.

Thursday 10 June

I had a phone call from the Speaker's Secretary, Roger Daw, to say he'd put to the Speaker my request that my pass should be amended to say 'Freedom of the House, Mr Speaker', and he's agreed, so I'm really pleased.

Friday 11 June

I left the television on all night with the sound down, and every time I woke up, I got the results. Labour has been really beaten into third place, the worst results for Labour for thirty years. Ken Livingstone won in London, quite heavily. Of course the BBC didn't give the results for UKIP or Respect. They just concentrate on the three top candidates. Ken's result was pleasing.

Saturday 12 June

Mrs Mac came for a little party we gave her for her birthday, with Barbara and Ruth. We bought her a scarf and a cake, some videos, a family picture and a bottle of whisky. We had a lovely talk for about a couple of hours. She wasn't as tearful as I thought she might be.

Sunday 13 June

The papers today are full of speculation, 'Will Blair be ousted?', but he won't; he's very strong.

Monday 14 June

I had a word with Ken Coates on the phone. He said something interesting. The idea that UKIP is only stealing support from the Conservatives is quite wrong. In the old coalfield areas UKIP got tremendous support, and that exactly confirmed what I thought, that it's a party appealing to the disillusioned working class. Ken's very shrewd.

My depression's lifting a bit. I have been very depressed and not feeling too well.

Tuesday 15 June

Tony Wardle arrived to interview me for *Viva* magazine. I think he said that fifty billion animals are fed and killed every year, and fifty billion animals of course eat food, and the rainforests are being torn down to find areas to grow grain to feed the animals, which is just crazy. It's the argument Hilary made when he converted me to vegetarianism.

I was very breathless in bed. Trying to lie on my face didn't work, so I lay the other way round, still very breathless. Turned on the television to divert me, and left it on all night with the sound down. But I was frightened. I didn't have a pain in my arm or my chest on this occasion. Anyway, I just felt that there was an amber light at the end of the road that could turn red.

Thursday 17 June

I worked at home in the morning. At the moment I'm getting an absolute flood of emails with obscene pictures. They're the same picture – I won't describe it. There's nothing whatever you can do about it.

I drove to the Commons and picked up my Freedom of the House pass from the Speaker's Secretary's office, and it's lovely! While I was coming away I saw Bill Cash, and of course we got on to Europe. That's all he ever talks about. He was very flattering; he said, 'You were the first to see that Europe was a democratic issue.'

I said, 'I did wonder whether you were going to join UKIP.'

'Oh, no, no, no, no,' he said. 'Just before he died, Enoch Powell called me, and he said, '"I made a mistake leaving the Tory Party. You did the right thing to stay in."'

The Fire Brigades Union today voted overwhelmingly at their Annual Conference to disaffiliate from the Labour Party. With the RMT out and the FBU out, there just is a possibility the Labour Party is going to disappear, because the Labour Party without the unions would be nothing.

The link between Saddam and 9/11 has been proved to be absolutely untrue. This new Commission on 9/11 has confirmed that, although Cheney and Bush still say they believe it. Also, they've exposed a total Defence muddle over 9/11, none of which will help Bush much.

Saturday 19 June

I watched *Come Dancing*, and Natasha and Brendan came top again. Oh, she was so good, I voted (several times) in support of her. Then I rang and said how fabulous she was, and then she rang back and said, 'Would you like to come to *Come Dancing* either next Saturday or the Saturday afterwards?' Well, I'll have to think carefully about whether it would be a sensible thing to do, but I would quite enjoy it, I must say.

When the ceiling fell in at home, a little paper bag fell out; it must have been there for nearly two hundred years! The bag said:

> Cheesemonger, Pork Man and Poulterer, Dealer in Game
> S. Phillips, 152 High Street, Notting Hill W.
> Families waited upon daily.

The bag is in very good condition.

Wednesday 23 June

There was major flooding at home all night. I'm not exaggerating when I say one full bathload of water came through into my bathroom, down to the kitchen, from the kitchen down to the bathroom in the basement. Some dripped into my office. I just thought, this is the end, you know; so

I rang the company who are supposed to be fixing my roof, and they turned up.

Sunday 27 June
The news from Iraq is horrific. I think an American marine has been captured and may be decapitated. The kidnapping and execution of people is just going on on a huge scale, and I don't know how we're going to cope. Saddam is going to be handed over to the new Iraqi Government, and no doubt he'll be executed. That is the world we live in . . . violence, violence, violence.

Monday 28 June
Paul Bremer, the US Governor, handed over to Ayad Allawi, who's been appointed Prime Minister of the new Iraq, the piece of paper called sovereignty and they swore an oath of allegiance.

To Hilary's office to have lunch with him at DFID. He's got a lovely office, just by Buckingham Palace. The Secretary of State's office is in panelled wood with a long conference table, much like the old Foreign Office rooms. His Private Office is terribly friendly. It's not like the old days when they spoke in hushed tones about the Secretary of State. It was, 'Hilary this' and 'Hilary that' and 'Oh yes, Hilary will have a word about that'. We had a bite down in the cafeteria. He had a salad, and I had a cheese sandwich and a banana.

I don't know whether Tim Henman has gone through to the next round in Wimbledon, because I switched it off, but the tension of these sporting events chews me up, to no good purpose, so I'd rather just know later what happened. It is about time somebody in Britain won the Wimbledon men's championship. I think the last time was about '36 when Fred Perry won it. Having done the commentary at Wimbledon in 1949 for the BBC Overseas North American Service, I feel I know a little bit about it.

Tuesday 6 July
I had a letter from Number 10 Downing Street from a Private Secretary. Blair refused the debate with me about Europe which I had proposed. I didn't think he would, but anyway, I tried.

Blair was being interviewed today by the Liaison Committee, and he said that he didn't think weapons of mass destruction would be found in Iraq, probably because Saddam had hidden them or had destroyed them, which is a wonderful argument. We arrested a man who hadn't committed a murder in case he had it in mind to commit a murder. Blair wouldn't apologise. He said, 'We got rid of Saddam and he was a danger.' So British foreign policy now is that if a man is a danger and you think he might have weapons, even if he doesn't, you're entitled to attack him.

Wednesday 7 July
I watched Prime Minister's Questions, and I must say, although I keep joking about it in my lectures, it is utterly revolting! Howard gets up, smirking, and produces a lot of figures. Instead of asking simple, factual questions without any polemics, he insists on sneering. Then Blair leaps up and says, this is what you did, this is what we've done. Then loyal backbenchers get up, exactly as I've described in all my lectures, and ask, 'Would the Prime Minister agree with me that the achievement of the Labour Government in my constituency has been outstanding?' No questions at all! It's awful.

Thursday 8 July
The house is becoming a slum, and to put it in order would cost so much money. It is absurd for an old man to be living in a five-floor house in effect using just four rooms – the bedroom, the bathroom, the kitchen and the office. So it will be a terrible agony, but I've got to begin thinking about a move and preparing the children for it.

Saturday 10 July
Royal County Hotel, for the 120th Durham Miners' Gala. I was given a lovely picture by somebody of Caroline and me in 1987 at the Gala. She looked so young. She was then sixty-one – didn't look at day older than forty.

We marched to the racecourse and the speakers were: Vera Baird, who's a northern Labour MP, and a lawyer; Steve Kemp; Bob Crow; Dave Prentice; and Tony Woodley. It is quite an expensive trip, but it's nice to be asked, and it certainly does inspire me every time I go. Arthur Scargill wasn't there. He hasn't been for years. Of course, Blair was asked and didn't come; since he's been Leader he has never come near the place.

Tuesday 13 July
To Number 10 for the Hansard Society's sixtieth anniversary, hosted by Cherie Blair. Her speech was all about democracy and how wonderful democracy was, and so on – it confirmed the idea that democracy is a sort of fobbing-off mechanism to keep people quiet. The idea that it's an instrument for major social change doesn't occur to anybody.

At any rate, that was it. In the course of her speech Cherie said that the three party leaders supported the Society and, 'Indeed, when it had been set up, it was supported by Winston Churchill, Clement Attlee and – and,' and she couldn't remember the name of the Liberal leader. So I called out, 'Archie Sinclair!' She said, 'Rely on Tony to know!' I went and kissed her hand, had a word with her. She said how wonderful Hilary was, and she couldn't have been sweeter – she always is. I said to her, 'You're going through all this media stuff – ignore it! I had my share of it, and it was horrible.' She gave me an understanding look.

David Butler was there, and Austin Mitchell, and so on. Iain Duncan Smith came up to me, and said he'd like to come and see me to discuss some project. I didn't quite understand what it was, but I said, well, come and have a talk. It would be quite interesting to meet him anyway.

As I walked down the stairs, I saw the photographs of twelve prime ministers whom I'd known myself, starting with Lloyd George and going right through to Tony Blair.

Wednesday 14 July

Steve gave me the Butler Report, which has been published today, the inquiry into the failure of intelligence briefing in the Iraq war. I had actually printed off a summary of it from the BBC webpage. In effect, the report blamed nobody. It just said intelligence had been defective, but there was no evidence that it had been changed. It didn't even enquire about Alastair Campbell's relations with John Scarlett, head of the Joint Intelligence Committee and later of MI6. It said Scarlett should continue in his appointment. But Butler did say that the Cabinet hadn't operated as a Cabinet. So it just spread a lot of doubt without dealing with the two questions: why did we go to war, and was it illegal? which are the only two questions that matter.

Thursday 15 July

Natasha rang and said she'd love to have lunch. I said, 'I've kept a month open for you' and she said, 'Only a month?', which was very cheeky. Anyway, next Wednesday is settled.

I have been approached for a long time by a guy called Nicholas Wood of the Stop the War Coalition about writing to the International Criminal Court. I was a bit reluctant to do it, partly because I didn't want to embarrass Hilary, partly because it's such a sensational thing to do. But I think now, in the light of Butler, it is possible to write to them and ask if they would be ready to give an advisory opinion on the legality of the war; not asking them to charge Blair with war crimes, but for an advisory opinion. If a lot of people signed that, I think that might possibly be a useful thing to do, pinpointing the real issue – not only why did we go to war, which the International Criminal Court couldn't decide (and anyway I know), but the legality of it.

Friday 16 July

Caught the 9.33 to Tiverton Parkway, where Ruth and I were met by Gary Cook, who is the shop steward from the Appledore Shipyard, now actually a director of the Appledore Employment Link, and Roy Harkness, a former trade-union official in the GMB Union (General, Municipal, and

Boilermakers). I was taken straight to the Royal George pub, where there was a meeting. There were quite a few of the boilermakers and welders and so on from the yard. There were two women from the Department of Employment, who would normally be expected just to organise unemployment benefit to the people at Appledore, where they haven't had an order for a year; but they actually threw themselves into helping the Appledore Shipyard to restart. What they have done is to set up a workers' cooperative, the first object of which is to keep in touch with all the skilled workers who were going and working in other yards. So I had a good talk to all of them, and then I was taken to the yard itself.

The order they were hoping for – and this is the tragedy of it – was a luxury yacht for a Lebanese multibillionaire, but they said well, it's work, and of course it is.

Anyway, when I got to the Appledore Shipyard, I saw the designers working at the computers, and I was taken to meet the Technical Director. I talked to them and he said how, when they went to Geoff Hoon, he said, 'I can't help you. Go and see Gordon Brown.' Hoon is a disaster as a minister. Then I saw the empty dock, and oh, I don't know, it was just very sad, but by God, those guys are really good!

Then to Tantons Hotel, where Rose Wiseman, the Bideford town librarian, had brought together the Bideford and Torridge readers' group, about fifty or sixty of them.

Ruth gave a party for me at her house in a cobbled lane in what they call 'East the Water' over the bridge from Bideford. Her parents and her twin sister; her neighbours Mrs Blight and Mrs Wilson, who is ninety-one and still walks up and down the hill every day; Jon and Bridget, who also live on the hill. Some of the lads from Appledore Shipyard – Dick Matthews and Gary Cook with his wife Heather. Sue Robinson, who is the Features Editor of the *North Devon Journal*, was there; Dr Peter Scott, a retired surgeon of seventy-three; and Ron, who worked on Ruth's house, and Kathy. Also some local politicians: Councillor Hugo Barton and his wife Ginny, who are Liberal Democrats, and Councillor William Isaac, an Independent. I was looking everywhere for a chair, so I sat on the stairs.

Monday 19 July
Tam Dalyell rang me about his obituary of Paul Foot, the journalist and SWP campaigner. I sent a note to Claire, his partner, and spoke to his son. It's a terrible tragedy. I sent him the words that appeared in *The Clarion* when William Morris died, saying 'We cannot help feeling for a while that nothing else matters.'

Tuesday 20 July
I heard there was a meeting organised locally to discuss Post Office closures, so I went along. There was a pompous, retired Tory councillor

who said, 'I want to introduce someone from Postwatch.' Now, Postwatch is a statutory body, as he explained, set up to look after the interests of consumers, nothing to do with PostCom, nothing to do with the Post Office, and he began blathering on. So one or two people asked questions, and then I got up and said, 'I'd like to thank the Council for organising the meeting, but I thought this meeting was to plan a campaign against the closures. That's certainly why I came.' I went on, 'I've lived here fifty-two years. I've had hundreds of thousands of letters delivered. I'm an old Postmaster General, it so happens, and this is a political act, to close post offices. After all, the Post Office is a public service and we should bring in the trade unions, bring in the pensioners and have a good campaign.' There was thunderous applause!

Wednesday 21 July

I picked up Natasha and drove her to the House of Commons. What was really nice was the number of people who came up to her about *Come Dancing* – all the staff, and all sorts of people. Anyway, we wandered round for a bit and then we had lunch, and then, oh, I took her up in the Gallery for a moment, just to hear a little bit of Geoff Hoon announcing defence cuts. Then, as she worked for Neil Kinnock in 1992, I took her to the Leader of the Opposition's office, which is now Michael Howard's office. There was nobody there, so we wandered in and she was absolutely thrilled. A couple of the doorkeepers remembered her. I think it gave her a boost.

Come Dancing was a triumph. She said eight million people voted for the final, which didn't surprise me. She told me everything about the show. It was sweet of her and, as I say, wandering around, everyone was very friendly.

Thursday 22 July

There was a completely fabricated picture of Natasha in her beautiful ballgown and me in evening dress in the *Daily Telegraph* gossip column, saying it was a platonic relationship. So I rang her up later in the day and said, 'I hope it didn't embarrass you in any way, but I have written a very angry letter to the Editor of the *Daily Telegraph*, saying how outrageous that he should suggest that it was a platonic friendship!' She laughed at that.

Friday 23 July

The news today is that Mandelson has been appointed by Blair as the new British Commissioner to the EU. It's a scandal. That's the only way of describing it. He's pushed to Brussels, deserting Hartlepool after being there for three years. Oh, it's just awful! But at the same time, at least he's out of the country.

Saturday 24 July
Gary Cook from Appledore rang to say that the luxury yacht they've
tendered for has been given to them, and it will be announced on Monday,
so that's great news. I'm thrilled.

Tuesday 27 July
I drove to Golders Green Crematorium for Paul Foot's funeral. There must
have been almost a thousand people there. It was absolutely packed, and
the best of the left were there. Michael Foot; Tariq Ali and his partner;
Geoffrey Goodman; Ian Aitken; Hilary Wainwright; Louise Christian;
Mike Mansfield; Bob Marshall-Andrews; Laurie Flynn; Jeremy Corbyn;
Victoria Brittain; Anna Ford; Jane Shallice; John Rees; Lindsey German;
Richard Ingrams; Mark Seddon; Arthur Scargill; Peter Jay; Alan
Rusbridger; Bruce Kent. Because of my hearing, even with hearing aids, I
couldn't hear the addresses that were given, but there was a lot of laughter,
so obviously it was a lot of fun, and they played Michael Flanders and
Donald Swann's 'I'm a Gnu'. I don't know why they played it, but it was
very funny. Paul was a remarkable guy. He inspired people, a brilliant
writer. I had letters expressing sympathy with me that he had died. I found
it very moving. Claire Fermont was there of course, and three sons by
different marriages. His coffin was carried up in a procession from Finchley
and afterwards everyone went off to a party, which I didn't go to, I was so
tired.

Thursday 29 July
The roofers are back at work today, and one of them said to me, 'Did you
meet Churchill?' So I said, 'Yes I did, why?' So he said, 'Well, I want to
write a film based on the speech he made: "We will fight them on the
beaches. We will fight them in the streets." When I write it, could you put
me in touch with the Churchill family?' So I said, 'Yes, I could do that.' It
just shows what brilliant talent there is in unexpected places.

Tuesday 3 August
The Americans have announced that they've captured an Afghan in
Pakistan, and on his computer were details of banks and international
financial institutions, which indicated there might be an attack. The thing
is being thought of as a hoax to boost Bush, after the Democratic
Convention; the information was four years old, and I'm just waiting for
Blair to say we have to take it seriously because there could be a terrorist
attack within forty-five minutes.

There's mass flooding in Britain – you know, cars half-covered and
people up to their thighs in water.

When I went shopping, I went into the new Marks & Spencer, and I
asked, 'Why haven't you got stools behind the cask desk?' Also, they told

me that it was very hot there, because of the plate-glass windows. So I said, 'Well, I'll ring Marks & Spencer.' So I came home and rang Marks & Spencer, spoke to the Customer Relations Officer, and she said she'd ring the shop and find out why they didn't have stools. I said, 'Will you also put my complaint to the top?', so she said she would, but of course that's what trade unions should do.

Saturday 7 August

I came home, and I went out and bought a DVD player. I installed it and it worked! I was absolutely staggered. I bought a few films: *My Fair Lady* and *Genevieve*.

Something funny is happening to me now; I'm beginning to see my life in completely different perspectives. It's very strange. I'm lonely actually. The truth is I'm very lonely.

Tuesday 10 August

Watched *Passport to Pimlico*, with Margaret Rutherford. I must say, it is a hilarious film.

Thursday 12 August

The Americans have decided to go in and destroy Najaf, where al-Sadr, the Shi'ite cleric, is protecting the holy city. If they do damage the mosque, or indeed occupy Najaf, it will create absolute waves of anger throughout the whole of Iran and the Middle East. The Americans are so stupid.

Saturday 14 August

Najaf is absolutely up in flames. The Americans have decided to obliterate al-Sadr's headquarters, and the language used about Islamic militants . . . well, the militants are the American troops, the insurgents are Americans.

I can't quite make out the strategy, except maybe Bush wants to draw the Iranians in, but the damage done throughout the whole Muslim world is on a scale you cannot imagine. But I say this every night.

Tuesday 31 August

Sal phoned to say that Hilary is in Iraq. He didn't want to worry the family, but he drove back from Stansgate, picked up some stuff at home, went straight to Heathrow and he'll be back on Thursday. If they kidnapped him, I'd try and persuade them to take me instead.

Wednesday 1 September

I walked to Notting Hill post office. The Post Office officials refused to receive our petition outside the post office, so we handed it over to Kay Dickson of Postwatch. I met a French nun, a very jolly woman. She must have been in her mid-seventies, and I asked her about married priests. I said, 'You know, the average age of Catholic priests in France is sixty-eight.' She said, 'Oh, I know.' And I said, 'Well, you'll have to have married priests', so she looked a bit puzzled. I said, 'And women priests.' 'Oh, you couldn't do that!' she said. 'You couldn't trust women not to gossip about what they heard in the confessional.'

I wrote a letter to Patricia Hewitt, expressing my disgust at what had happened with the Post Office.

Thursday 2 September
Hilary phoned. He saw Allawi, the new Prime Minister of the interim government. He also saw the American Ambassador, John Negroponte. Hilary's going to Leeds tomorrow, coming back on Saturday, going to Nigeria on Monday, coming back on Thursday, and then he's going to Washington and Addis Ababa.

Blunkett is introducing electronic tagging of sex offenders and prisoners, who'll be monitored by satellite and will be able to be identified within six feet of wherever they are, a sort of smart-bomb technique.

Friday 3 September
Watched a bit of *The Best Years of Our Lives* on DVD. I first saw that film with Fredric March and Myrna Loy and Teresa Wright and Dana Andrews in 1946, fifty-eight years ago, and it made a huge impression on me. The reason was it's the first time I'd ever got any sort of understanding about America. It's a powerful story. I think it was watching that that made me want to marry an American.

Sunday 5 September
I watched the end of *The Best Years of Our Lives*. Of course it was made two years before I met Caroline. I had my marriage and my life, and then Caroline died, and now I've had four years without her, and now I look back on the period before I met her. It's all very strange.

Tuesday 7 September
To the National Theatre with Ruth and Celia O'Connor for *Stuff Happens* by David Hare. They'd given me wonderful tickets in the stalls. Also, I picked up a loop system of earphones, which I've never used, but which are absolutely brilliant. It is a skilful, dramatic re-creation of all the key elements, from the election of Bush to the beginning of the war; Bush's part was played quite cleverly. It didn't look much like Bush, but conveyed the impression. Condoleezza Rice was brilliant, and so was Donald Rumsfeld – it might have been Donald Rumsfeld; and Colin Powell and Blix were featured. It was a very good play, and I stayed awake. I heard every word of it. It was the most powerful use of theatre for political education.

Wednesday 8 September

Campaign Group at 5.30. There was a discussion about impeachment, because this Plaid Cymru MP, Adam Price, has put down a motion to impeach Blair over the war. He looked up obsolete parliamentary techniques and found one that hasn't been used since Lord Palmerston in 1830, and discovered if you did table a motion for impeachment, it had to be debated. Whether the Tories will vote for it, I don't know, but they might. Labour MPs dare not, at risk of expulsion. I made a joke about it, and said I was coming to see the trial in Westminster Hall and see the execution in Whitehall Palace, but my own advice is not to do it. I think it's a mistake because, first of all, MPs would be voting for something they had already voted on, the war, so it would be overwhelmingly defeated, and that would allow Blair to say he's had a vote of confidence. If the same thing happened at Conference, if there was an attempt to get a leadership election, he'd win and that would be a vote of confidence in everything he'd done.

There was a long-awaited Cabinet reshuffle, by which I mean that Alan Milburn has returned to the Cabinet as Chancellor of the Duchy of Lancaster, and Alan Johnson, the former General Secretary of the Post Office Workers, is now at Work and Pensions, replacing Andrew Smith. This has reawakened all the stuff about Brown and Blair, and Brown and Milburn, and oh, it's so boring.

Friday 10 September

Clyde Chitty reminded me tonight that Alan Milburn used to be on the hard left. He had a bookshop up in the North-East called Days of Hope, which was inevitably nicknamed Haze of Dope, and now he's an arch-Blairite. I believe Blair has probably done a deal with him and said, 'Look, I am going to win the next election, and then I'll give up and then you can take over', and so Brown has not only been deprived of his responsibilities for running the election, but an alternative promise of the succession has been given.

Blair will have his six months as President of the Council of Ministers, and then I should think probably, less than two years from now, he'll go and there'll be a leadership election. So that's the moment when New Labour might finally die, 1994–2006, although I suppose you could say that New Labour began under Kinnock, 1983–2006, that's nearly twenty-five years, and that'll be the end of it, I think. So all the work has got to be in preparation for what happens afterwards.

Tuesday 14 September

I got the Tube to Bow Street Magistrates' Court to support Brian Haw, who is the peace campaigner camping in Parliament Square, and he was charged with having punched a policeman when they asked him to move during a security alert.

I had been on to the solicitors and I submitted a character statement. I couldn't hear anything, and I couldn't see anything. It was an elaborate hearing of procedural points.

In the end, they adjourned the case at quarter-past one, and I said, well, I think I'll have to go. A nice young solicitor said, 'I will ask the Prosecuting Counsel whether they'd agree to read out your statement, but the judge noticed you were in the Gallery, so that will help.' It may do a bit of good. The BBC was there outside, and also Reuters were there, so the publicity for peace, which is what he's about, is doing very well. I'm busy thinking of things for *Any Questions?* on Friday; it's a burdensome job looking through all the papers for a week.

Thursday 16 September

Four or five people supporting hunting broke into the House of Commons and disrupted it, got onto the floor of the Chamber, and now there's talk of armed police, and the Serjeant at Arms having to resign, and so on and so on. But once you allow something like that, which was after all a non-violent demonstration, as a pretext for putting a fence round the people you vote for, you're in trouble.

Friday 17 September

Dinner in London with Jonathan Dimbleby, Liz Forgan, and David Starkey and some of the BBC people. Then went on to do *Any Questions?* at Westminster School. We had a question, obviously, on hunting, where on the whole the audience was rather against it. Then there was Iraq, and there was tumultuous applause against the war; then education, where I was asked about Westminster School; and about whether Blair should resign. I managed to get in my joke about Batman and Bush. I said, 'Oh yes, the security situation is very serious. Batman got into Buckingham Palace, and in America, Bush got into the White House! We're in deep trouble!' Then I introduced Lord Button, the composite character of Lord Butler and Lord Hutton, and said, 'Whenever anything goes wrong, Lord Button is called out of retirement and proves the Government is not responsible.'

Chapter 4

How the Tories lost an election

Wednesday 22 September 2004

My article appeared in *The Guardian*, calling for Labour MPs to vote to withdraw British troops from Iraq. Seamus Milne had put my email address at the bottom, and I must have got between fifty and a hundred overwhelmingly supportive messages, a few abusive ones. They came from California, New York, Bangkok, Spain, Germany, as well as Britain. I haven't ever written an article giving my email address before. I was pleased – I worked hard at it.

The news today is that Ken Bigley has not been beheaded. There's an incredible controversy arisen: there has been a demand in Liverpool, his home town, for the release of all women prisoners – apparently there are only two – in jail in Baghdad, and the Iraqi minister said today that they were going to release them. Blair had said, 'Under no circumstances can we talk to terrorists.' Jack Straw said the same. The Americans said, 'We're not releasing them. They're held by us. They're high-value prisoners.' So it shows there's no independence in Iraq. Sovereign government doesn't matter a bit; the Americans run it all. Of course yesterday Bush made a speech at the UN, and Kofi Annan warned people about the illegality of the war. I think the thing is coming to a conclusion.

Thursday 23 September

To the TUC with brother Dave for the reception for Mikhail Gorbachev, who was giving a lecture on weapons of mass destruction: with him were Joseph Rotblat and Professor Robert Hinde of the Pugwash Committee. Brendan Barber presided.

We were taken for a cup of tea and, as Gorbachev arrived, Dave went forward and immediately began speaking to Gorbachev in Russian. Gorbachev was struck by this. Dave apparently said to him, 'I've read all your speeches on ideology', and Gorbachev said, 'Well, I'm not an ideologue, I'm a politician', so Dave did have a chance.

Then we went in to the reception, and I took some video of Gorbachev and Dave, side by side. I went up to Gorbachev myself afterwards and introduced myself and said, 'I was in Parliament for fifty years.'

He said, 'Oh, how boring that must have been!'

'No, not at all!' I said. 'I'm older than you, I'm eighty next year' – he's only seventy-three – 'and when I look back on the last century, I think the greatest tragedy was that relations between the West and the Soviet Union didn't take place as they might have done. I felt if we'd been more sympathetic, perestroika in some form would have come in the Twenties.'

He said, 'I agree with you.'

I said, 'We could have stopped Hitler.'

'Well,' he said, 'we got on well in the war, but after the war Churchill took a different view.'

'I'm thinking of before the war, if we'd had an Anglo-Soviet pact in 1938, we could have stopped the war from taking place at all.'

He said, 'I agree with you.'

I shook his hand, and he said, 'You have a very firm handshake.' I found him quite attractive. Then I slipped off.

Went on to the Imperial War Museum for the debate on the Iraq war, called 'Authors Take Sides'. In favour of the war were Duncan Fallowell, a writer, biographer and liberalist, who simply said it was a war against militant Islam. Then, supporting him, was Sir John Keegan, who lectured on military history at Sandhurst and is now at the *Daily Telegraph*; he said it was all about the threat from Islam. The columnist Melanie Phillips said it was all about the threat to our values from Islam. Their side just believed it was a religious war, and the arguments about weapons of mass destruction or human rights didn't particularly affect them.

On our side, Beryl Bainbridge and Harold Pinter made good speeches; I mentioned about the West's arming of Saddam. It was all right, wasn't sensational. At the reception afterwards a woman, I suppose in about her early fifties, told me she was just signing on to do an MA at the School of Oriental and African Studies. Then she said, 'I'm a duchess.' It turned out she was Jill, Duchess of Hamilton, now divorced from the Duke, and who's written a lot of books, so I looked her up afterwards. She's an intelligent woman and I talked to her for a bit.

Sunday 26 September, Labour Party Conference, Brighton
Jonathan was mugged by some youths of about fifteen when he went home from a pub at two o'clock this morning. They kicked him to the ground, stole £5 and a mobile phone, kicked him again and went off. It's happened to William, it's happened to Daniel, and it is just a part of the hazard of modern life, I must say.

To Brighton. The train broke down at East Croydon. I watched David Frost interviewing Tony Blair on television – Blair looks more and more and more like the Prince of Wales, very pained, and can't be specific about anything.

Then I went in to the Conference. They search you twice – outrageous!

Monday 27 September

I went to hear Gordon Brown's big speech. It was a passionate speech, radical, showing what a success his economic policy had been, and at the end, and this is what warmed my heart, he said, 'Hilary Benn and I are going to Washington to tell the IMF that they've got to do more to relieve Third World debt.' He got a standing ovation, and I stood up. I did it for two reasons: partly because of the kind reference he made to Hilary, but partly because I thought to myself a long, standing ovation for Gordon will undermine Blair tomorrow. I've got to the point with Blair and Brown that I have with Kerry and Bush: anyone but Bush, anyone but Blair.

Tuesday 28 September

I went over to the Conference, and I heard that the resolution to renationalise the railways had passed through quite substantially, with the unions voting in favour and 72 per cent of the constituency delegates voting against, which shows what's happened to the Party.

On my way in to the Conference, who did I see but Martin McGuinness? He gave me a huge hug. I said, 'How's it all going?' 'Oh, it's going fine, going fine. The two Prime Ministers [Blair and Ahern] tell us that Paisley may want to find a place in history.' Now, that was interesting.

I went in to the Conference, looked in at the bookshop, and who should be signing but Cherie Blair; her book is *The Goldfish Bowl*, about the spouses of Prime Ministers at Number 10. So I picked up the education book on Caroline by Clyde and Melissa, and wrote, 'For Cherie, with love'; she jumped up and gave me a kiss.

Then I got a cab back to my flat because I wanted to hear Blair.

It was a clever speech, confident, a touch of shyness about him, and all the things he'd done, all the things he would do. No reference to economic power or other people, none at all, just him, him, him – 'I decided this', 'I decided that'. Then he came to Iraq and said, 'I'm sorry the information I had was wrong, but I'll never apologise for toppling Saddam', as if he were an emperor. He's not an emperor at all! And then the final part of course, side by side with Bush, the long-term global war on terrorism. Then about Europe. I thought it was an awful speech, but he got a standing ovation, because the glue of an impending general election is coming.

Back at the conference centre, Michael Meacher told me the real story about Alan Milburn's resignation. Michael is absolutely obsessed about the leadership. Brown will be awful, Cook won't stand because he's going to do a deal with Brown – Cook as deputy leader – and so on. Was at the flat from two to five. I watched the Conference coverage on television. Bono, the pop star, is at the Conference. He paid a tribute to Hilary, and compared Blair and Brown to Lennon and McCartney.

Special Branch rang to say they needed to get on to Jeremy Corbyn, because there was a cleric in London who thought that Jeremy's strong line on the war might help to get out Ken Bigley, so I gave them his number.

To the Communication Workers' Union party. The General Secretary Billy Hayes was there, with his wife and two little children, a boy and a beautiful little girl called Melissa, who's two. She sat on my lap and I did all my grandfather tricks.

Gordon Brown was there. I went up and just said, 'Thanks for your kind reference to Hilary. He's greatly looking forward to coming up to Dunfermline to speak', because Hilary had told me he was going, and Brown gave a friendly smile.

One of the CWU guys came up and said, 'The union is going to propose that the post of Postmaster General be restored, and would you be available one day a week?' I said, 'Of course!' It's an amusing idea. PostCom has been established, with enormous power, but accountable to nobody.

Thursday 30 September
Heard Hilary, who opened the debate on 'Britain in the World', his first major speech as a Cabinet minister at a Labour Conference. I had to conceal my video camera, but I got it all.

He got a good reception, bless his old heart.

As soon as he had finished, I left. One delegate had actually been arrested by the police and his credentials taken away, because he sat during the standing ovation for Blair with a card saying 'Give peace a chance'. Somebody else was denied admission because he had a T-shirt that said 'I believe in peace', and he was told there were no political statements allowed in the Conference.

Somebody said to me this week that Blair keeps all the politics to himself, and ministers are technocrats.

Monday 4 October
I had a word with Jill Hamilton, who had come up to me at the Imperial War Museum, and has written a book called *God, Guns & Israel*, linking nonconformity with the establishment of the state. A very interesting book.

To the House of Commons, and then walked for fifteen or twenty minutes to the Royal Society of Arts for this lovely party for the book *Caroline Benn: Essays in Education and Democracy*. Clyde Chitty, who said this morning he might not be able to come, made a speech; Melissa made a wonderful speech. Caroline would have been so pleased, because she's such a modest person; she would have been thrilled to think that people had come to discuss comprehensive education rather than her.

Tuesday 5 October
At nine o'clock a car arrived to take me to the interview about war films. I had picked a few that I really liked, and so that was rather fun: *The Life and Death of Colonel Blimp, A Matter of Life and Death, All Quiet on the Western Front, The English Patient* and *The Bridge over the River Kwai.* They seemed quite happy. All they want is a few clips.

Thursday 7 October
I should have reported that yesterday the Iraq Survey Group came out showing there's absolutely no evidence whatever of weapons of mass destruction, but that Saddam had in mind that he might go back to them; and also there was the suggestion that he'd bribed the French and Russians with oil promises in the oil-for-food programme. Also there is a report that Tariq Aziz had defected, which I suspected somewhat. ITV News asked me to do an interview yesterday, and I said, 'Well, use the interview I did with Saddam last year.'

Friday 8 October
I thought I'd go and say goodbye to my grandson Michael, because he's leaving tonight for his world trip. Hilary's in Addis Ababa and won't be back in time to see Michael before he goes, a bit of an agony. I gave him several hugs, and all the dollars I'd found at home, about $250. He's got a huge backpack he's carrying, with all his bedding and his equipment and his camera and his films – he can hardly lift it! He's off to Delhi tonight. He's a lovely boy, twenty-three now. I must say, it reminded me of seeing my brother Mike off in January of 1944, the last time I ever saw him.

Sunday 10 October
Did the *Politics Show* with Jeremy Vine. He's a nice lad. He's thirty-nine years old and now a major player in the BBC. He began with Bigley and moved on to Iraq. I said we were systematically, deliberately and consistently misled; there were no weapons, Saddam had nothing to do with 9/11, Bush had decided to go to war, no preparations had been made, it was a catastrophe.

So then Jeremy Vine said, 'Well, given the fact that there'd be chaos if we left, why don't we stay?'

I said, 'That's exactly what the Russians said about Afghanistan, that they couldn't leave because there were terrorists there organised by Osama Bin Laden and funded by the Americans. The Americans armed Saddam. It's a catastrophe. We'll have to get out, and then the UN can come in later.'

His last point was, 'How do you explain the fact that Blair is more popular than Howard?'

I said, 'Well, the truth of the matter is that Howard isn't any good, and Blair is the most successful Conservative Prime Minister we've had, but I wouldn't read that to mean people support the war, because they don't.'

Blair has made a great speech about how Labour's next term has got to be even more New Labour. This is all the Milburn/Darling/Adonis influence, I suppose, all the right-wing people he has around him, as if somehow he was the source of all policy. He has no regard for anybody else at all. There's no sense of being a collective leader.

Tuesday 12 October

The Ilkley Constituency Labour Party had invited me for a meeting in the church hall. I haven't been to a local Party meeting for a long time. I didn't see anyone under about forty. It reminded me of the Chesterfield Party towards the end of my period as MP.

The first question was, 'Are you campaigning for the election of a Labour Government?', so I said yes.

'Can you think of anything good the Labour Government has done?'

I said, 'Yes. I think the attempt to get a settlement in Northern Ireland, and the minimum wage, and public expenditure on the public service, is excellent.'

They gave the impression that they thought it was only New Labour that got Labour elected in 1997. A man said we can't afford to renationalise the railways.

The decent progressive people, particularly the younger people, have left the Party. They were critical of me really, and the argument is that if you do anything to criticise the Government, you're opening the way for Michael Howard. Well, Howard hasn't got a cat in hell's chance of winning, but it reminded me that there is still an official, residual Labour Party who voted at the Conference against the renationalisation of the railways.

Thursday 14 October

When I woke up this morning, water had poured into the house overnight during a rainstorm. The bathroom next to my bedroom was absolutely swamped, I went down to the kitchen, and water was pouring down through the electric switches, onto the sink, onto the washing machine – it was a catastrophe. Last January, a roofing company came to look at it; in April, they started work; six months later and it's worse than it's ever been.

Saturday 16 October

I am getting more and more and more detached from the whole normal political scene and I think I have to be clear that as the months go by I'm further and further from ever having had any political responsibilities – it's, after all, twenty-five years since I was a Cabinet minister.

Sunday 17 October
To Trafalgar Square for the Stop the War peace demonstration. By the time I arrived the Square was absolutely full. I got there about a quarter to three, and when I left, at about five past five, there were still people pouring up Whitehall, at least 100,000, but typically the police said 20,000. Why they can't count, I don't know.

I saw Tommy Sheridan, whom I dearly love, and his wife Gail, who's pregnant, is expecting a baby on 17 June, which is his wedding anniversary and also mine. He had with him a family whose son was killed in Iraq, and the mother and sister and father were there.

I met Che Guevara's daughter. I saw Jeremy Corbyn there.

And who should I see but Sadoon al-Zubaydi, who had interpreted for me in 1990 when I came to see Saddam, and again in February last year, who was an ambassador in Indonesia in the meanwhile, and apparently he's out and free. He said that there were discussions going on about greater democracy in Iraq, which were broken up by the war.

He said Saddam is now seen as the great hero of the Arab world, and held Iraq together, but he said he was absolutely sure Saddam would be killed; the Americans would not try him.

So anyway, al-Zubaydi's a free man, and whether he's working for the Americans or not, I don't know, but it was a very interesting talk.

Tuesday 19 October
Had breakfast with Emma, and then we went and caught the train to Birmingham, and spent most of the day wandering round the windswept streets of Birmingham, visiting two Waterstone's bookshops and a Borders bookshop, and signing *Dare to be a Daniel*. People were very friendly, but there's something brash about Birmingham. I've felt it for years. It is really an American city. I think Birmingham was a small industrial town in the early nineteenth century: attracted immigrants from all over, developed a powerful industrial base of cars and machine tools, plus the old jewellery trade. There's something Thatcherite about it – brash and selfish. It's a New Labour town as well. It depressed me very much.

Wednesday 20 October
Had tea in the Members' Tea Room. Spoke to Alice Mahon who, along with a number of Members, is outraged that British troops are to be sent to relieve the Americans so that they can destroy Fallujah.

There was a message from Hilary on my answering machine, saying that he'd been walking across the park to meet Kofi Annan, and the first thing Kofi Annan said to him was, 'How's your Dad?', which was very nice.

Sunday 24 October

My old friend Pit Wuhrer, from *Woz* magazine in Switzerland, came to see me. When I first met him, he must have been in his early forties. He's a thoughtful guy.

He said that in Germany there are now officially five million unemployed, probably nearer six million, and Schröder is cutting benefits; there are now serious possibilities from the trade unions of strike action, and the German Government is passionate for privatisation. Five million unemployed in Germany did trigger my thoughts about Hitler in the 1930s.

Then we went on to talk about referenda; he thought in Switzerland they were a powerful democratic check. Governments can call for them if they want approval for a proposal or decision, or 100,000 people petitioning can get a referendum. I've often thought about referenda, but I've always argued that they took power away from Parliament. On the other hand, Parliament has no power, and supposing people had petitioned for a referendum on the European constitution, they'd have got it. So I'll think about that very carefully again.

I jumped in the car and went to see Hilary. He had a day at home. He's had a tremendously busy time: he's been in Washington; Addis Ababa; Dunfermline last night, speaking for Gordon Brown. Michael sent a long email a couple of days ago from India. He was ten days in the Himalayas where there were no Internet cafés. Hilary's going to see him next month when he's in Delhi, so that's nice.

Monday 25 October

Well, a fascinating day. I caught the 6.45 train to Bristol, and was met by a researcher for HTV. They are making a programme about Bristol and I was interviewed about the last hanging in Bristol, in December 1963, when Russell Pascoe was hanged for the murder of a farmer. I'd written an article in *The Guardian* about it at the time, which I took with me, so I was able to deal with capital punishment, and the campaigns for and against, and so on. They also asked me about the three-day week, in 1973–74, and how it was quite unnecessary.

While I was there, two of the technicians, Justin and Robert, both of whom I'd met before, told me that now that Carlton and Granada had merged and they own all the local ITV stations, there is in effect one ITV network, and they have decided to close down local programmes. There'll be about an hour a week available for local discussions. In addition to that, they said Disney wanted to buy Carlton Granada, so we could have a situation where British ITV was controlled by American ITV; of course Rupert Murdoch controls BSkyB, and he's an American. So what with BSkyB, *The Sun*, the *News of the World* and *The Times*, the media dominates our society on a massive scale. A very important point.

I was then driven to a church in Henbury, where there was a most moving ceremony at the grave of a young African slave who died in 1750, at the age of eighteen, owned by the Earl of Suffolk or something, and he had named the boy Scipio Africanus. There was this gravestone that mentioned Scipio Africanus, and on the gravestone was a little black face brought up in bas relief. Several people spoke and then I went on to the final event at the History Museum, where they've got a tremendous exhibition there of black slavery. Bristol has always been very embarrassed about black slavery, and if you mentioned it, it was thought to be a bit odd; but now they've recognised the fact that Bristol's wealth was created by the slave trade, and they showed these horrific pictures of the way the slaves in chains were treated in the slave ships, and how they were beaten and raped. It reminded me of Abu Ghraib prison and Guantanamo Bay. I've been up since five, seventeen hours, and I haven't even had an evening meal yet. But I've got to slow down a bit, I really have. I'm nearly killing myself.

Tuesday 26 October
Tomorrow, I think the European Commission comes up for approval by the European Parliament. The Parliament can't reject individuals, but it can refuse to endorse the Commission as a whole. Then I heard on the news that Blair had told the Labour MEPs they've got to support the Commission. They are just privates in General Blair's army. The principle of representation has died in the Labour Party, and it's a worrying thing.

Friday 29 October
ITV rang up because Johns Hopkins University in the United States estimates that 100,000 Iraqis may have been killed. They did a survey of a thousand families in thirty-three locations and checked it against death certificates. It is absolutely horrific! To my amazement, they did actually take it seriously on the BBC and ITV News, and I did a little interview, about fifteen seconds.

Saturday 30 October
Osama Bin Laden has made a broadcast, not in military garb, looking very relaxed, and analysing the reason for 9/11, saying that it was when he saw Israeli bombers destroying tower blocks in Beirut during the Israeli invasion of the Lebanon in '82 that he decided to take revenge, he decided on pre-emptive action. Of course it's caused a tremendous flurry in the American elections – who will it help, Bush or Kerry? – and people don't know quite how to respond. But the truth is this is the first reasoned case about the al-Qaeda movement to get the Americans out of the Middle East and particularly to establish the rights of the Palestinians. I must say, I'd love to put questions to Osama Bin Laden via Al Jazeera, but whether it can be done, I don't know.

When I came back, I opened my mail, and I must admit the most important item is a letter from the Parking Control Office in Kensington and Chelsea about the renewal of my parking permit. If I lost my permit, I'd be sunk. So I spent an hour pulling out all the evidence they require that I live here, and posted it off. That is the society we live in today.

There was a programme about the American Christian right, Billy Graham and Jerry Falwell and Pat Robertson, and how disappointed they were by Nixon, by Clinton and by Carter, and then in effect saying that George W. Bush was the greatest thing ever. It was actually a party political broadcast for Bush. I did get the flavour of it: the attack on lesbians, gays, birth control; and presenting it as a war between good and evil, with God on their side. I must say, in those circumstances, Bush did look a dangerous man. All of a sudden, that programme did bring home to me what Karl Marx meant about religion being the opium of the people, and very much the obverse side of the coin of Osama Bin Laden's broadcast.

Wednesday 3 November
When I woke up and finally got up at half-past seven, it was obvious that Kerry had lost. It drove me into a terrible depression, a deep depression. I wish desperately that Caroline had been here, because she's an Ohio woman and she'd have understood. We could have had a talk, and we could have had a hug. I really felt low.

We've got to recognise that Bush has got four more years. We've got to work like anything, because if the American economy goes into a recession because of the wild spending and tax cuts and war costs and deficit, then we could have a situation in Europe like the 1930s. America catches cold, Europe gets pneumonia, and that's when the extreme right begins coming out of the woodwork, and it's a frightening period.

Monday 8 November
The murderous attack on Fallujah is just beginning, and it is impossible not to be revolted, angered, and the media coverage is so bland – while these are Iraqis defending their own country!

I had a letter from a woman who is an astrologer, and she is interested in me because at the time of my birth there were few days in the year when Uranus and the Sun made a precise aspect to each other. There are only twenty-five days in any given year when this is possible, and she said other individuals with these two planets at a precise aspect include Guy Fawkes, Mao Tse-tung, Karl Marx, Salman Rushdie, Iain Duncan Smith, Vivienne Westwood, Sigmund Freud, Beryl Bainbridge, Alan Bennett, Mahatma Gandhi, Nikola Tesla, Screaming Lord Sutch and Germaine Greer.

Tuesday 9 November
Flew to Glasgow, the Theatre Royal, which holds 1,500 people; before the show I went off to BBC Radio Scotland and was interviewed by a very tall

man, in his sixties, I should imagine. I didn't know who he was, and I asked
him his religion. He said, 'Oh, I'm a Christian.' I said, 'Oh, Anglican?' And
it was the former Anglican Bishop of Edinburgh, Richard Holloway, whom
I'd often heard on the radio and greatly admired. I felt an absolute fool not
knowing, but I did say I admired him, and we had a lovely talk. He said
Christianity is a way of life – that's what it is, it's not a structure. He also
said something else: he said there have been gay bishops for hundreds of
years, but they never admitted it.

When I got home, I had received a letter from an R. S. Davis, who, to
cut a long story short, was a navigator in Lancasters, and he remembered
that on the night of 22 June he came in damaged, after bombing the
marshalling yards in Reims; he was due to land at Thorney Island, and he
was deferred because there was a Mosquito coming in without an air-speed
indicator, and he listened to the talk on the radio between what he called
Pilot A, who'd lost his air-speed indicator (which was my brother Mike),
and Pilot B, who'd been sent in to help him. So I rang him up, very late.
He's eighty-three now, Mike's age, and I had a lovely talk to him. He'd
looked up, you see, in his logbook, which he still had, his RAF logbook,
looked up exactly what happened, and exactly the date and exactly what
time. It was unbelievable that sixty years later I heard from a man who'd
heard my brother's voice for the last time. I mean, that is just astonishing!

Thursday 11 November
Yasser Arafat has died, the Palestinian leader, and his body was flown back
with full military honours from Paris to Cairo for the funeral, and then he'll
be buried in Ramallah, in a stone coffin that can later be moved to
Jerusalem, and that's very important. Of course Arafat was hated by
Sharon, and distrusted and disliked by Bush. The coverage of his death,
you know, made him out as a terrorist, whereas Sharon is a prime minister
– it's so disgusting!

Also, Mordechai Vanunu has now been rearrested.

Friday 12 November
Frank and Sue Ashworth worked away all day to mount the plaque for
Caroline onto the front wall of the house. It's really, really beautiful. Dark
red with white lettering. I wondered whether we'd have an unveiling
ceremony, but it means you've got to put up a little curtain, and it's not
worth it.

Blair went to see Bush and stayed in the White House, and there was a
press conference. Bush said that he thought there might be a Palestinian
state now, provided Palestine was democratic. Well, how can you be
democratic when you're occupied? It just turns my stomach. Blair smirks
and smiles, and is so pleased the President treats him in that way, but he's
just a tool.

Monday 15 November
Colin Powell, the American Secretary of State, has resigned, so maybe he'll say something now; obviously he's not wanted in the new Bush administration, and maybe Condoleezza Rice will take over.

Wednesday 17 November
Went to the Pugin Room, and there was Tony Banks with about four or five very glamorous women, who had been working with him on the hunting bill. It's a big success for him, because last night Blair voted to substitute regulation in place of a ban, and found himself with only sixteen Labour MPs in the Lobby, and overwhelmingly defeated by the Party. It's the first time he has been in a losing lobby since he was Prime Minister. Tony Banks said, 'Oh well, I went to see him, but he was talking about his conscience; he must do what's right, he must suffer', a sort of Christ obsession.

Thursday 18 November
To cut a long story short, the Commons voted to accept an eighteen-month delay on the hunting ban, which was what the Government desperately wanted, the minimum they wanted, to avoid hunting being an issue at the election; and when it went to the Lords, the Lords turned that down. So that forced the Government's hand, and then I had the great pleasure of seeing Michael Martin getting up and announcing that it would be passed by the Parliament Act. I mean, it couldn't be a more interesting end, and it's entirely the Prime Minister's fault. If he'd dealt with it seven years ago, it would all have been over by now, but he left it and left it and left it, and the only time he ever voted was not to ban hunting, but for an amendment that would regulate hunting. So it's all his fault, and it has enormously angered Labour MPs.

Tony Banks had a big success, and it was lovely to see him last night.

Friday 19 November
I went by Tube to Bow Street Magistrates' Court to give evidence for Brian Haw, who's been sitting in Parliament Square for 1,290 days opposite the Houses of Parliament, with all these posters about the war, using his loudhailer. In May this year the police saw a vehicle they thought might be a bomb, and so under the Terrorism Act they cleared the area, and Brian seems to have resisted an order to go, and he was charged with kicking a policeman. That's what the case is about.

Bruce Kent was there, and a Canon Warner from Windsor Castle. So he had a few character witnesses, and a lot of people from the peace movement there. Before I left for lunch, the Prosecuting Counsel came up to me and was very friendly. After lunch I went into the witness box and affirmed. I was asked to give my name and my occupation, and I said I was a

Member of Parliament for fifty years and a Privy Councillor, and that I had admired Brian Haw, who'd come to my attention when he started; and I said that he was a man of peace, that he'd inspired people, that he was seen internationally as someone who was bridging the gap between people of all faiths and all nations, and that I deeply respected him. Then at the end, when the Prosecuting Counsel said, 'Do you think he'd be aggressive?' I said, 'No, he's a tough man, but I dare say that when Jesus cleared the money-changers out of the Temple, there might have been a bit of a scuffle, but it isn't recorded in the Bible.' There was some laughter in court.

Monday 22 November
To the Kensington Law Centre, and several women told me that the Anti-Social Behaviour Orders, or ASBOs as they're known, were being used absolutely recklessly. Some children were told they could only go out in twos, and not in threes. One child was told that he couldn't use the word 'grass'. These orders are imposed; there's no proper hearing, there's no proper appeal; but if you disobey them, you can get up to five years in prison. I hadn't quite appreciated that, but I think this may be as gross an abuse of human liberty as the old stop-and-search law, only more so, because it could include a prison sentence.

Wednesday 24 November
To the Almeida Theatre to see *Earthly Paradise*, a play by Peter Whelan about the relationship between William Morris, Gabriel Rossetti and Janey Morris. I had a huge admiration for William Morris. He was portrayed as rather a bullying entrepreneur; and Rossetti I didn't care for, because he was a terribly screwed-up poet who was always on the verge of a nervous breakdown. Saffron Burrows played Morris's wife, Janey, who was having a romantic affair with Rossetti. Morris went away for months, leaving Janey with Rossetti. In the second act, Morris returned and virtually gave Janey to Rossetti. Saffron suddenly emerged, the first time I've ever seen her, with real passion, and what came out of it was different types of love. William Morris had had children by Janey and obviously loved her, but Rossetti had a romantic view, a completely detached romantic view of her, painted endless pictures of her. Then at the end Saffron, or Janey, said to William Morris: what about friendship and comradeship? So there you are, physical love, romantic love, friendship and comradeship; and it was very well done, and Saffron was extremely good.

Friday 26 November
I had a letter from a fascist today, with a death-threat in it, making a threat to Hilary as well. So I filed it, because it's so long since I had one. Even so, it's not very nice.

I attended a huge fundraising dinner of wealthy Palestinians. Before the speech they had an auction, selling pictures and tic-tacs, and the amount of money raised was incredible. One picture, that I wouldn't have paid £50 for, raised £7,000, and I should think between £50,000 and £70,000 was raised – wealthy Palestinians and Arabs and Muslims supporting Palestine. There was an extremely entertaining American Muslim comedian called Ahmed Ahmed, who made a lot of jokes about the difficulties of being a Muslim, and his relations with Jews, and so on. I thought it might have worried people, because he got near the mark on the Muslim faith, but they were all very relaxed, all wealthy. It wasn't a working-class movement supporting the Palestinians; it was wealthy Palestinians.

I have really changed my position strongly on the question of Israel. I now think it is behaving in such a disgraceful way that I really regret the support that I gave it at the beginning, and I regret the way in which this whole situation has developed. Sharon bears a heavy responsibility, and Blair is just weak.

Sunday 28 November
Apart from Blunkett's nanny, the Ukraine is the other story today. I'm getting more and more evidence now from the Internet, indeed from other sources, that American intervention in the Ukraine is similar to what they did in Yugoslavia. Indeed, it was put to me years ago that Yugoslavia was a trial run; they'd build up an opposition, pour masses of money in, tell the media that the elections are rigged, and in this way they force country after country to accept the disciplines of globalisation. Of course, when the government that they want has got elected, then market forces are applied and cuts in public services, and then repression to any opposition. So it's a bit like communism in reverse, when the Communist Party, allegedly, would have a revolution, seize power, and then it would join the socialist camp. Now, it's the much subtler financial, corporate and media pressure, ending up with the countries joining the capitalist camp.

The Americans would not allow an anti-American government to be elected in Britain – I mean an anti-capitalist government, a socialist government, to be elected in Britain. So how would you would ever make a change, unless you put on such pressure that the system falls and then people take over. The idea that a little debate in Parliament will change things is really an illusion. I'm not in favour of a bloody revolution, because we saw what happened with Stalin, but I'm not in favour of surrendering, step by step, the right of people to decide the policies that the elected government follows, because otherwise you might just as well hang the whole thing up. That is the issue that interests me very much, and Paul Foot's book, *The Vote: How It Was Won and How It Was Undermined*, is highly relevant to it.

Thursday 2 December
The phone rang and I was told that George Galloway had won his libel action against the *Daily Telegraph*. He'd got £150,000 in damages, and the legal charges were over a million. If George had lost, as he said outside the court, he would have been bankrupted and homeless and driven out of public life. It was a tremendous victory. I hope it warns the media off. They argue that it's in the public interest to print any old story, whether it's true or not, and the judge took a contrary view, so it's a significant judgement.

Saturday 4 December
Today I went and bought £100 worth of stamps, went to the bank, got some food, and I signed, stamped and posted well over 350 Christmas cards. I have a wonderful computerised system.

Monday 6 December
Natasha Kaplinsky arrived about 4.45 and we discussed, in a general way, the interview tonight at the Purcell Room.

She really works so hard. She did a dinner last night, didn't get home till ten o'clock. Got up at half-past three, did the news, then went and did a charity lunch, then came this afternoon with me, then she has to be up at 3.30 tomorrow morning; and she is beautiful and very friendly.

We drove off in two cars to the Purcell Rooms on the South Bank and were shown into the Green Room.

Natasha introduced me briefly. I read extracts from *Dare to be a Daniel*, which I had carefully selected, and then Natasha interviewed me for three-quarters of an hour, very sensitive, serious, and in a friendly way. She's a tremendous professional. Then it came to an end, and there was warm applause. I gave Natasha a big hug, I gave Emma a big hug, I gave Dave a hug, and he went home in a taxi, and then I signed books.

I really enjoyed it, and it was a big success, I have to say that; and that was because of the way in which Natasha handled it all. She said, 'Let's meet again and start a new scandal!' so I said that would be lovely. I gave her the book *The Art of Belly Dancing*, which I have been keeping for her, and she's going to send me the DVD of all the dances she did with Brendan, which led to her win *Strictly Come Dancing* last summer. I was aware yet again of how tremendously dependent I am on support – Melissa, Ruth, Emma, Saffron, Natasha and Barbara. I mean, considering I'm an old buffer, for all these young people to be so supportive is terribly encouraging and terribly sweet.

Tuesday 7 December
There was no hot water this morning, so I didn't have a bath.

Tuesday 14 December
Robert Wright, the Speaker's Chaplain, told a lovely story tonight at dinner in the Speaker's House for the outgoing Serjeant at Arms. A guy in Canada was attacked by a bear. He was a devout Christian, and just as he realised he had no hope, he said, 'Oh Lord, will you please make the bear a Christian?' So the bear approached him, and just as it was about to eat him, he said, 'Oh Lord, for what we are about to receive . . .', which I thought was quite an amusing grace.

Friday 17 December
The Law Lords this morning have come out against the detention of foreign nationals in Belmarsh prison without a charge or a trial. Nine Law Lords turned up for the appeal – they don't all have to turn up – and only one, Lord Walker, supported the Government. One Law Lord said that this type of legislation is more of a threat to Britain's civil liberties than terrorism, and another one said that laws like this remind you of Stalin's Russia. So it's created what's generally thought to be a constitutional crisis, but of course, since we don't have a Supreme Court, a constitutional authority over government, the Government now indicates they're just going to introduce a new law that legalises it. For the first time, you felt that fascism was coming in via New Labour. Hitler called his party the National Socialists, and Mussolini had been a socialist and ended up as a fascist. Frightening!

Monday 20 December
ID cards were debated in the House of Commons, but what was really interesting is that there are 412 Labour MPs, and with Tory support, at least front-bench support, they still only got 380 people voting for it, which implies that a lot of Labour MPs abstained and a few voted against – I think eighteen.

Tuesday 21 December
I went to the bank yesterday. They wouldn't let me cash a large sum of money for Christmas, unless I produced my passport. I said, 'How do you know I've got a passport?' 'Well, we can't take a risk . . .' I said, 'I have banked here for fifty-two years!' So then I produced my Freedom of the House card, and he said, 'Oh, Mr Tony Benn, oh yes, of course.' I suppose they have to be careful, but at the same time, a passport is a bit drastic.

Thursday 23 December
The Government has capitulated to the Countryside Alliance, who are going to court to argue that the Parliament Act was improperly used in the Hunting Act. Also, they are planning to go to the European Court of Human Rights in Strasbourg.

Blair's decided to have a conference in London about the peace process in the Middle East, but Sharon won't come, so it's going to be a conference to tell the Palestinians how to stop Palestinian terrorism, with a view to getting a state. It's an intolerable thing to do!

I think during the election next year I'm only going to go to constituencies where the MP is against the war, and also when I'm there just argue what I believe in, not as a candidate, but simply as somebody saying, 'Vote Labour *and* campaign for this', 'Vote Labour *and* campaign for that', and of course it will be easy to support my mates – Alan Simpson and Jeremy Corbyn and John McDonnell, and good MPs, of whom there are quite a few, in the Campaign Group.

Friday 24 December
I read this wonderful book by Richard Holloway about old age, how old people have to die, they have to give up, they do find they can't keep abreast, that things have changed, there is a desire to hang on to the old things and you've got to move on. I enjoyed meeting him, and I've heard him broadcast quite a few times.

Saturday 25 December
I was sweeping the steps outside when a nun came out from the convent next door and invited me in. It was about ten past twelve and I was expecting the family for Christmas lunch at one, so I popped in for a bit and had an orange juice. There were five nuns. They were of varying ages; one was immensely radical, booed Bush and said how well Cardinal Cormac Murphy-O'Connor had done. We talked about the ordination of women and the issue of married priests. They think there will have to be a new start with the Pope. I told them what Mother told me, that most men walk on the ground and kiss women, and the Pope walked over the women and kissed the ground. It was a bit risky, but they laughed. It boosted me no end.

Family arrived for Christmas lunch. Nita gave me Cherie Blair's book *The Goldfish Bowl*, and it was signed: 'To Tony, who's been an inspiration throughout my life, Cherie'. Nita said that when she signed it for me, Cherie added, 'Don't tell my husband!'

Monday 27 December
Yvonne Ridley arrived to do a television interview for the new Islamic satellite TV channel. Ridley was a *Sunday Express* reporter, went to Afghanistan, was captured by the Taliban and held there. They treated her very well, she converted to Islam, and she's now campaigning vigorously against American policy in Iraq and Palestine, and everywhere else. She stayed for two and a half hours.

Thursday 30 December
The tsunami disaster in the Indian Ocean is getting worse and worse, with deaths now thought to be well over 100,000.

Sunday 2 January 2005
I asked myself, in the light of what Melissa said yesterday, have I simply been running round for four years like a chicken with its neck wrung, saying the same things, without having really thought things out? Things have changed, and although I try to keep abreast of it, I do go on talking about the 1945 election and the Welfare State, and I'm a bit old hat. I've got to develop new thoughts, have a dream, but be realistic, try and understand the world and encourage people. At four o'clock Josh arrived, and we had two and a half hours, just as I did yesterday with Lissie. He's so generous with his time, full of advice. There was an interesting article about Hilary in the *Sunday Telegraph* today, a severe cartoon of him, saying he was a chip off the old wedge, but, in order to show how good he is, they have to say what a disaster I've been. If the *Sunday Telegraph* builds you up, that will impress Blair much more than anything else, I can tell you! So his future looks pretty bright.

Monday 3 January
Another bank holiday.
   I'm becoming very much a homebody at the moment. I don't know how long it will last, but at the moment I'm rather enjoying tidying up at home rather than dashing about making speeches.

Wednesday 5 January
Tony Byrne was in. He worked all day in the bathroom. He's a real hard worker. He does think that possibly a new bath and a new lavatory may be necessary because both of them leak.

Thursday 6 January
Tony Byrne is making amazing progress in the bathroom. The bath is cast-iron and to get it out of the house you'd have to saw it. He said, 'You'd never get a bath of that length again', so he might have it re-enamelled.
   Lissie rang me. She's had a long, five-hour talk, I think she said, to Fiona Millar, the partner of Alastair Campbell, who is passionately in favour of local schools and comprehensive schools.

Sunday 9 January
There's a book been written on behalf of Gordon Brown, a biography of Brown, explaining his bitter anger that Blair, having given him two assurances he'd stand down, hasn't done so; and of course, as a result of that, Blair went on the *Frost Programme* and said it wasn't true, and

Brown called in Andrew Marr and said it wasn't true, but it has left a wound.

Monday 10 January
I rang DFID, and Hilary's got back safely after his week-long mission to visit the victims of the tsunami disaster in the Indian Ocean.

Caroline used to say: 'At your age, you shouldn't take on more than one engagement in any one day.' Over the last few months I really killed myself, but I think that it is all changing, and it is a psychological problem – the feeling that you've got to be busy to justify yourself. But maybe, as you get older, that's not what you are supposed to do; you're supposed to think, and think of other people, and perhaps I'm not a very good grandfather at the moment.

Wednesday 12 January
Gerry Doherty, the new left-wing General Secretary of the TSSA, the Transport Salaried Staffs' Association, came to address the Campaign Group of MPs. I like him so much. He brought his Assistant General Secretary. He said, 'We're hoping to shift the union to the left, but I have to be pragmatic.' He said that the railway system is in a state of collapse, no railway building occurs now in Britain, and when you think we built the first railways, and built them all over the world, it is another example of de-industrialisation. He said the public subsidy is an absolute disgrace. I asked whether a European Union Directive made it impossible for us to renationalise the railways. 'Well,' he said, 'that may be so, but the French take no notice of it.' And I agree with that. He said that the railway operators own nothing; they just operate. They don't own the track, they don't own the station, they don't own the rolling stock, they don't own anything; and what we must do, among other things, he said, is to keep up the campaign for railway nationalisation, and restore the building of railway engines and railway rolling stock in Britain. I agree with that – it was wonderful.

Saturday 15 January
Alan Milburn was on at the Fabian Society Conference. I find the man absolutely impossible to watch, but he said New Labour has got to reform and reform and reform all the time, more New Labour; it will be very controversial, but it's got to be done. It's just a programme for the Tory Party, including privatisation of Housing Association houses. Milburn ought to join the Tory Party. He'd be a wonderful Leader for them, and this idea that New Labour has got anything whatsoever to do with the Labour Party, or the trade-union movement or the working-class movement, is a complete illusion, and it would be better if he was the Leader of the Tory Party. He'd be much better than Michael Howard, and then the Labour Party could perform its proper job.

Monday 17 January
Hilary went off to Afghanistan for two or three days. Seymour Hersh has written in *The New Yorker* that the Americans have planted agents in Iran identifying targets that might be hit by American forces, relating to Iran's potential nuclear establishments.

Tuesday 18 January
I read a wonderful article saying John Birt has now got a prominent and dominant position at Number 10, with his 'blue sky' thinking, setting up management consultants to look into everything, and he's going to wreck the New Labour Government the way he wrecked the BBC with outsourcing and everything.

Thursday 20 January
I went to Charing Cross Hotel by Tube to give a lecture on 'Effective political communication', which I really enjoyed, and was then picked up and taken to GMTV for a discussion with Mary Soames on the fortieth anniversary of Winston Churchill's death. I gave Mary a big kiss. She's always been very nice to me. She's a couple of years older than me, but of course she was brought up in a political family, just as I was.

She talked about what it was like to be at home, and how Winston didn't have a lot of money and he lived by writing. I said he was an old liberal imperialist, and I quoted what he said about Gandhi – she looked a bit doubtful about that. But I said he was a progressive politician domestically, and indeed would have been far to the left of Tony Blair: he'd introduced Labour Exchanges, which Brown is now privatising; he nationalised the Anglo-Persian Oil Company; and he took liberal views on prisons. Then afterwards we went back to the Green Room, and who should be there but David Owen, looking terribly remote and grey-haired and wise. I don't think he's ever quite made it somehow. He was Foreign Secretary when he was in his late thirties, I should think, and then joined the SDP (Social Democratic Party). I asked him about the Iraq war, 'Well, I was in favour of it,' he said, 'but I think some mistakes have been made.'

Mary Soames offered to drop me home because she lives down near me, so I said, 'Have you ever thought of writing your life?'

'Yes,' she said, 'I've decided to.'

So I said, 'Well, I've just done mine.' So when she dropped me home, I rushed into the house and gave her *Dare to be a Daniel*, and I think she will enjoy it. She said she'd send me a book written by Sir Jock Colville, which she said was very important, about her father.

Sunday 23 January
Talked to Tony Byrne, who is working on the house. He's so funny. He's

terribly dramatic and poetic. He said, 'I'm going to tell you something, and I swear on the life of my daughters,' and he put his hand on his heart, 'I don't like politicians, but your Tony Benn is the best of the fucking lot.' Then he said to me (because he has a set of house keys), 'Tony, I've got your keys, but I won't let anyone else have them. I'd never let anyone have them. If I go to the pub, I don't take the keys, in case somebody pinches them. Now Tony,' he said, 'if the Pope asked for your keys, I wouldn't give them to him!'

Monday 24 January
The One O'Clock News had an item that the representative for human rights or refugees in Europe had said it would be illegal to restrict asylum-seekers – Michael Howard has said that he would. Now, that will be an alarm bell across the whole of Britain, because if you can't elect a government that can make a law of that kind, then we are no longer a self-governing country, and I think that will register. Having said that, I'm against this proposal, but it will whip up the hard right and encourage the soft Liberals – who will say: thank God for Europe.

Wednesday 26 January
I had a phone call saying that David Bailey, the well-known society photographer, wanted to take a picture of Saffron Burrows with me, for *Vogue*. Well, I was a bit nervous because I'm not a society figure, and an old man with a beautiful young woman would just be a source of mockery, so I rang Saffron, and we thought we might have Stop the War leaflets or something in the picture. He won't do it anywhere but in his studio, because there are so many cameras there, but anyway I'm happy to do that. It will be in *Vogue*, of all things, in their election issue . . .

The Government has introduced detention without trial for people suspected of terrorist activities, or neo-terrorist activities; they've conceded to the Law Lords, who said that you can't hold people in prison, so they're going to tag them, imprison them in their homes, impose curfews, restrictions on what they can do. The reason I mention it, I was watching *The Sound of Music*, and the sight of these Austrians with their swastikas just frightened me.

Thirty-one marines were killed in an air crash in Iraq.

The referendum question was announced: are you in favour of Britain joining the new European constitution – a perfectly fair question.

Sunday 30 January
Hilary and Carrie turned up. We had a bit of a talk. He is of course a strong and committed supporter of the Government and of Government policy. He's much more self-confident now, quite rightly. Until five years ago I was the ex-minister and he was the young MP, but now he's the Cabinet

minister and I'm the old man, so it put me in my place. He's terribly sweet, awfully affectionate.

Monday 31 January
I was picked up by car, to take me to David Bailey's studio, where Saffron was waiting, and we were going to be photographed. I was a bit embarrassed by the whole thing. Saffron had collected all the Stop the War posters, which made quite a nice background, and then we sat and were interviewed by Lisa Armstrong, who is the Style Editor of *The Times*, but also writes for *Vogue*.

David Bailey is a funny man. He used to be married to Catherine Deneuve, a glamorous French actress. He was quite matey, said he liked me and he liked Enoch Powell and Mrs Thatcher, and so on, but he hated politicians and he'd never voted. He's an East Ender who came west. I found him quite agreeable.

The Iraqi elections are being hailed as a big triumph because there was a 60 per cent turnout, and I imagine this will be beneficial, but it depends what the new Parliament does. We won't know the full results for ten days. But obviously they can now present the terrorists as being against democracy, rather than against the American occupation, and it makes it more complicated. But the Americans have no intention whatever of withdrawing their twelve bases or of giving up control of the oil.

Thursday 3 February, Aberdeen
Richard Marsh from Tritech, a sub-sea technology firm, took me over to their conference. He's an ex-Concorde engineer from Bristol, so I had a lovely talk to him. I felt like Minister of Technology again – all these wonderful stands, wonderful technology – and I made a twenty-five-minute speech, which went down extremely well, I must say, talking about how actually the Government has no industrial policy and no energy policy, and they all agreed.

They were so enthusiastic, and they'd obviously asked me there in order to raise the profile of the Subsea Conference, and seeing all this little, entirely automated submarine equipment, which can go down and repair things under the sea, it's an extraordinary technology, developed enormously since I first heard of it. Then Richard Marsh took me to Dyce Airport and I caught the plane back, got to Heathrow, decided to get a cab because I was so tired.

It was the first time I had made what you might call a ministerial speech in the last twenty-five years, and I was afraid my ideas would be seen as left-wing and Old Labour, but not at all. I think British industry feels absolutely ignored by the Government. The Government doesn't have a policy. It just goes along with what big business wants. It is just a spokesperson for big business, in the way that the post-war Labour Government was a spokesperson for the Labour movement – that's the difference. It encouraged me in a new line of criticism. I was well paid for the speech and I worked hard for it.

Tuesday 8 February
Tony Byrne wasn't here today, and all of a sudden there was a power cut. Everything went out. So I thought, 'God, what am I going to do?' The computers didn't work, the phone didn't work, the kettle didn't work, so I went next door to the nuns to find out if they'd had a power cut, and they said no, they hadn't. So I came back, with a torch, looking for the main switch, and the lights came on again. Then about ten minutes later, after I'd made a cup of tea, predictably they went out again, but this time for a short period. The only long-term effect was that my printer doesn't work any more, so I'm really in a jam.

Martin Shaw, Bishop of Argyll, based in Oban, turned up with a BBC producer called the Reverend Stephen Shipley for an interview about Dietrich Bonhoeffer. I really liked them both. I did ask about Richard Holloway, former Bishop of Edinburgh: 'What is his theological position now?' Bishop Shaw said, 'Oh, he's now a humanist. He thinks there's no reality but life.' Bonhoeffer had talked about religionless Christianity, and he, Bishop Shaw, thought I was a humanist. So I said, 'Well, I'm a Christian agnostic, if you know what I mean. I believe in Jesus the prophet, and not Christ the king, and that helps me more, but I respect people and all their views.' I think they really enjoyed it.

Blair made a statement today talking about Iran being the source of terrorism. I do think it is very likely America will bomb Iran, and Blair will go along with it, but if Bush does it before the general election and Blair goes along with it, I think he'll pay a very heavy price.

Then Condoleezza Rice said that Iran would have to be warned.

Friday 11 February
Blair in Gateshead made an incredible speech, saying, 'I know that I'm not as popular as I used to be, but I have to speak my mind.' It was 'I', 'I', 'I', 'I' all the time! The dirty tricks they are using make the election look like gang warfare between two gangs: no holds barred, attacking each other personally, and issues really kept out, except for the most generalised, bland promises and pledges.

Tuesday 15 February
This Beirut bomb, which has caused terrible tragedy and killed the former Prime Minister of Lebanon, is thought by some people to have been done by the Israelis to create problems for Syria. You know, in the world we live in now, almost anything could be possible; the problem

about getting to my age is you realise how incredibly difficult it would be to solve problems.

Michael Howard has come out with health checks for immigrants – sounds sensible, but of course it's building up fear of ill health as a result of immigration. So then, within twenty-four hours, Blair says, 'Oh we're going to have health checks anyway.' So actually Howard doesn't need to be in office; he only has to suggest a policy and Blair adopts it. It's frightfully discouraging. The sort of hatred that's being built up, they'll pay a very heavy price for that.

Wednesday 16 February

Well, the Prime Minister has chipped in to the argument about whether Ken Livingstone should apologise to the *Evening Standard* journalist, who is Jewish and who had angered Ken, and Ken said, 'You're like a Nazi concentration camp guard', which was offensive. But then Ken has had to put up with a bombardment against him from the *Evening Standard*. Then, blow me down, today on television Blair said that Ken should apologise. Well, first of all, he shouldn't have involved himself, or should just have said: people get excited, and I'm sure Ken will deal with it in the way he thinks best. But he called for him to apologise. For heaven's sake, Blair's been party to a policy that's killed 100,000 Iraqis! Why doesn't he apologise for that? So Blair just can't keep his fingers out of anything.

Sunday 20 February

At 8.30 I went off by car to do the ITV News on the general election. Lance Price was also on, he worked in the BBC and then as number two to Alastair Campbell at Number 10. He said that Blair wanted to be knocked about now, to show how human he was, and if people kicked him, they'd get it out of their system, which is the masochistic theory of electoral preparation. People say, oh well, he can certainly take it, he's not on his high horse. It's nothing to do with listening or being influenced – just a device, which I described as psychotherapy. Price also said that he thought people weren't interested in politics, a typical media, political view.

He said to me beforehand he thought that Tony Blair would have to get rid of Gordon Brown after the election, put Milburn in the Treasury; Brown would be given one chance to be Foreign Secretary, but if he wouldn't take it, it would be the back benches. Also John Reid would get the Foreign Office or something. It was incredible. Milburn's a key figure.

Monday 21 February

Got up at 6.45 because I wanted to be the first man in the new supermarket in Notting Hill Gate. There was nobody hanging about, but I put myself in front of the door, and when the door was unlocked, I got in first. There were a lot of managers all clapping. I wandered round to see what they had, and there were one or two things I really have missed. They had these cup-a-soups, which I love. They also had ice cream. They had little pizzas. They had vegetarian burgers. So I felt really pleased, and I came home.

Tuesday 22 February
I left home at about eight o'clock, and drove to Feltham to give evidence at the hearing of the appeal by an Eritrean woman I have been helping, who came here in 1993 as an asylum-seeker after her husband had been killed in Eritrea and she'd lost contact with her family. She worked in my local supermarket and came to talk to me; she now works in the new Tesco.

The Immigration and Naturalization building is huge. I had to empty my pockets, and I was searched as if visiting an airport, and there were masses of Africans and Asians, mainly Africans, I thought. I went into the little room, where there was a cup of coffee, and I met a barrister, whom I didn't like very much. He said, 'Of course you realise you're going to lose this case, you realise that.' So I said, 'Why?' 'Well,' he said, 'the adjudicator has a reputation for turning everything down.' That depressed me a bit.

Anyway, we went into this room with the royal crest, and the adjudicator was sitting there and we all had to rise when he came in. He was a man of, I suppose, about fifty, with spectacles, looked rather severe, and a young woman representing the Home Office. Then our side, and the court usher.

Our barrister was asked questions such as, 'Is it an appeal against asylum?' He wasn't absolutely sure. The woman from the Home Office asked quite good questions. She wasn't nasty about it. Then I was called, and I said who I was; the adjudicator was perfectly fair and polite, and at the end he put to me, 'The criteria governing deportation, or governing asylum, have to be very special to justify anything different. What's special about this?'

So I said, 'Well, she came to see me, she was very distressed, she's a good Catholic, she's educated herself, she'd be a very good citizen, and I felt it was right.'

There were masses of hearing rooms, and you got an idea of the industry involved in dealing with immigration. It's a huge industry. There were a lot of barristers, and solicitors and people, in all these different rooms.

Later, the Eritrean woman rang me up to say she hadn't lost and she hadn't won, because the adjudicator had said that she would have to see whether she could get an Ethiopian passport. If she can, I think they'll send her out; if she can't, then she'll be allowed to stay. But I've done what I can – I did what I could for her.

Thursday 24 February
In the *Evening Standard* tonight the opinion polls showed only a 2 per cent gap between Blair and Howard.

The new terrorism laws being debated mean that Charles Clarke can put me under house arrest, without any judicial procedure whatsoever before he does it. He'd say, well, he had evidence; but how do we know? Magna Carta says that no one should be deprived of liberty without the judgement of their peers, and that's been sort of accidentally repealed. I think it may be that this government does have to be defeated, if the New Labour people are to go.

Friday 25 February
The Church of England– or rather the Anglican Communion worldwide – is on the brink of a split on gay bishops. Unbelievable! Still, there you are, that's organised religion for you.

Saturday 26 February
I rang Jill Jones, because her daughter died last week. She had multiple sclerosis and she died of an epileptic fit in the middle of the night. Jill is such a sweet woman, I knew her in Chesterfield. Her husband, Ray Jones, died in 1989. I just couldn't bring myself to write to her, a formal letter, it's so difficult; so I rang her up, had a long, long talk to her.

Then had a bite to eat, and I watched Jon Snow's programme *The New Ten Commandments*. It lasted for two hours, and it was full of gimmicky stuff: we all like a consumer society, we do commit adultery, and it was jazzy background, and all the things that make television intolerable to watch. But at the end, the new commandment that was voted on and polled, was 'Treat others as you'd expect to be treated yourself'. Well, that's 'Love thy neighbour as thyself' and it showed that the basic moral principle of the teachings of Moses and Jesus and Mohammed remain in the public mind as the most important thing.

Sunday 27 February
At half-past five my grandson Jonathan and two friends came for a talk. Jonathan had a list of things he wanted to talk about: hunting, Iraq and drugs. It was quite enjoyable, and they were nice. His friend Dominic said that my name was highly respected at Tory Central Office, which made me laugh!

Anyway, they ate all the crisps I'd bought them, and as they left, Jonathan ran off with the beer that hadn't been drunk!

Tuesday 1 March
Blair has said the whole international community is now committed to the Road Map. It's a load of absolute rubbish, because the Israelis are not proposing to abide by international law. They're going to stay in the West Bank, and have a Palestinian state that won't have the territory the UN has allocated to them. How these people can go on telling such lies, I'll never know!

Wednesday 2 March
Alan Johnson, the Secretary of State for Work and Pensions, had agreed to come to address the Campaign Group – to talk about pensions. He once led the CWU, and the Government is now sacrificing the Post Office to competition; but he dealt with all the questions, was very polite, and I was quite impressed. It reminded me of being a minister – you have to get down to the nitty gritty.

As the Lords had this great debate on the terrorism bill, I thought I'd look in. So I went into the Prince's Chamber, signed in and went to the steps of the throne, which were absolutely packed. I've never seen them so crowded with Privy Councillors (who are entitled to sit there). Next to me was John Morris, who was a Labour Attorney General; and David Steel, who was the first presiding officer of the Scottish Parliament. We had a friendly talk. He said, 'I'm so sorry I can't come to your party.' I don't know that I'd asked him!

In the Chamber there was Mrs Thatcher, Lord Lamont, Nigel Lawson, who's lost such a lot of weight that he looks like a scarecrow. Then on the Labour side, I think Doug Hoyle and Campbell-Savours, who came up and had a word with me.

It did remind me of what my dad said about the Lords, 'It is the Madame Tussauds of old parliamentary people.' The funniest part of the whole do was that, as I left, I got up from the steps to the throne and went through the Not Contents Lobby to go back to the Commons, and I couldn't get out the other end, and I realised a division was going on and I was locked in. I said, 'I'm supposed to be good at escaping from the House of Lords!' So one of the Lords badge messengers let me out.

Wednesday 9 March
I heard the first part of Tony Blair at Prime Minister's Questions, all about the terrorism bill, and the man is absolutely hysterical! 'I've had information from the security services and the police that I cannot disregard. The security of the nation must come first!' The truth is he's running not just against Michael Howard, but against Lord Irvine, the former Lord Chancellor, and the previous Metropolitan Police Commissioner.

Blair decides everything himself, and it's just personal to him; he always uses security as a justification.

Thursday 10 March
The Lords have reaffirmed the 'sunset clause' and the burden of proof in the bill. So tonight it's going back to the Commons. It's getting very hairy, and I think it may well be that Blair wants the bill to fail.

I read that one of the people held at Belmarsh prison has been released by a judge, saying he's been held far too long. If Blair thinks his terrorism stance will help him win the election, he may be wrong, though of course if there is a bomb attack, then the whole thing could look very different. But it's a miserable situation, really miserable!

Saturday 12 March
I was taken to the BBC to do News 24 on the terrorism bill. I'd thought about it very carefully. My points were: can you trust the Prime Minister, when he told us all this two years ago about Saddam having weapons of mass destruction? Is the Government trying to win the election on fear? If so, it is ridiculous, because you can't accuse the Tories of being soft on terrorism, without including in that Lord Irvine, the former Labour Lord Chancellor.

Sunday 13 March
On the way to Lissie's today, there was a hooting, and a car pulled up in front of me, and it was Natasha Kaplinsky and her new boyfriend, Justin. She gave me a big kiss, and he was introduced to me. I said, 'How long have you known her?' He said, 'Five weeks and four days.' So I said, 'That's quite long enough to appreciate her merits.' She said they were going off to have a late breakfast.

Monday 14 March
Ron Todd rang me to say he was dying of leukaemia and asked me if I'd speak at his funeral – very sweet of him. So I said, of course, but it may not be as bad as you think. But he said he'd told all his children, and they'd cried all afternoon. He's a lovely guy, Ron Todd.

Brian Haw was having his last stand, in Parliament Square today, because the Serious Organised Crime and Police Act, which the Government has introduced, will make it illegal to have demonstrations in Parliament Square. The trouble with the demonstrations there is that nobody can hear a word they're saying, because they shout into the loud-speaker. I went over there and was asked to speak, so I did, for a moment, as quietly and softly as I could.

Wednesday 16 March
I had a phone call from George Galloway's office asking if I would sign a petition for the release of Tariq Aziz, whom I know of course; Ben Bella, the former President of Algeria, Jean-Pierre Chevènement, the former French Minister of the Interior, Galloway, a couple of MPs and two peers had signed. So I signed – Tariq Aziz has been treated disgracefully.

Thursday 17 March
Rodney Bickerstaffe came to breakfast. He told me he hadn't been able to sleep all night. I asked, 'Why?'

He said, 'Well, in a broadcast I said I was a bit disappointed with the help given to pensioners.' And Ed Balls, who is Gordon Brown's adviser, rang him up and said, 'You want a Tory Government!' It so upset Rodney. He's too sensitive.

I rang Stephen, who is in Cincinnati on his way home, and he told me that Emily had won the top award for violin, the highest you can get until you're twenty-one.

Wednesday 23 March

I'm just going off to my birthday party, which is being held early because the election will have been called by 3 April and the House of Commons will be out of bounds.

People didn't turn up till almost seven o'clock, and I thought nobody's going to come, but they poured in! I don't know exactly who was there. Quite a number of them I hadn't expected. Ron Todd, who's dying of leukaemia, came with his daughter's husband, I think he said. Jack Jones couldn't come because he'd had a fall. There was a huge contingent of Ruth's family, and of course the really big thing at the party was the cake. Ruth had commissioned it from one of the House of Commons' chefs, with TB@80 in large letters, and in the middle of the @ was a picture of me with a cap on my head sticking out my tongue, taken in about 1930!

Who else was there? Bernadette Wilson, who's a sweetie, and Jen Laney. The nuns, from next door. The Reteys. Then Natasha arrived with Justin, gave me a million hugs, and then Saffron turned up, and gave me a million hugs. I just hugged everybody. My old girlfriends Jean Corston, Meg Crack, Ann Henderson, who'd come all the way down from Scotland. Jean Strutt was there of course, my oldest girlfriend, who I shared a pram with in the Twenties. Emma Mitchell was there, and she kept giving me hugs. Oh, it was such a party! Benjamin Zephaniah was there. The Speaker couldn't make it, nor could Ken Livingstone, but Simon Fletcher did, Ken's chief of staff who worked in my office as a student. Kenny Seth also used to work in my office as a schoolboy.

Stephen made a brilliant speech. Nobody can beat Stephen at that sort of thing. He's extremely funny. He stole most of the points I was going to make. I was a bit embarrassed while he was speaking, because I was standing on the platform next to him. I took my jacket off and lit my pipe, to avert people's gaze.

Alan Simpson was there, of course. I adore Alan. Peter and Jennifer Blaker, and David and Marilyn Butler, Charles Frater and Julia Frater. It was a lovely, lovely, lovely evening!

Friday 25 March

Had a very bad night. One of my dentures keeps falling out, and I've got toothache.

Saturday 26 March, Stansgate
In the evening we had a bonfire, and I gave a fake television 'interview' in front of it, describing it as the bonfire of the archives, because of the fact that the British Library and the Heritage Lottery Fund had turned my application down. I pretended that this was the burning of the archives, and I held up letters from Churchill, and Mandela, and Gandhi, which were all going to go up in flames. Great fun.

Wednesday 30 March
From the time I left Parliament to my eightieth birthday I've made 555 speeches in around 130 towns and cities. Did 1,089 broadcasts (683 radio and 416 television) to the UK and around fifty countries. I wrote 190 newspaper articles, three books. So it's not a bad record, but I'm now getting to the point where I just want to quieten down a bit.

Friday 1 April
I caught the Tube to Liverpool Street, and the train to Witham in Essex, and did BBC *Any Questions?*, with Nick Clarke. The big anxiety about the programme was that the Pope might die. We were told in advance that if the Pope dies before 7.15, they'll have the tributes up to eight and the programme will go ahead. If he dies after the programme, of course it's all right. If he dies during the programme, then what they will do is go straight to the news, and then come back to us to finish the programme for tomorrow. But although we heard when we arrived at the hall that he had died, that was the rumour, it wasn't officially announced, so we did the programme.

Saturday 2 April
The Pope has died. The BBC went into a complete tribute. The highlight was that the Pope had defeated communism. Very little was said about the Nazi occupation of Poland, just the defeat of communism, as if it were a personal victory. The fact that he'd opposed the Falklands War when he was in England, the fact that he opposed the Gulf War, that he opposed the Iraq War, were all just skated over. Indeed, the fact that he went to Cuba and said that capitalism was a brutal system was skated over. They did just mention the fact that he was against fighting Aids with condoms, he was against abortion, he was against homosexuality, he was against women priests, but all that was minimised.

So I felt it was just another attack on socialism in all its shapes and forms, and a restoration of religion and religious obedience to the centre of the political scene. I say this with some regret, because he was a good man. He was a committed guy and he worked very hard, but this idea of Papal infallibility sticks in my gullet, and also the idea that the duty of Christians is to take orders. One of the pictures on television showed him rebuking

Latin American priests for working with Marxists, so I thought it all very interesting.

Sunday 3 April
It is my eightieth birthday. The most important bit of the news today is that Joshua told us that he was giving up the Housing Corporation, taking voluntary redundancy, going to University College London as a student to take a BA degree in Information Management, which is a mixture of mathematics and computing. He's forty-five years old. Caroline would have been absolutely overjoyed by it. First of all, she always thought he would go back to education. Secondly, it's an entrenchment of the value of adult education. Thirdly, because he'll be so good at it; he'll become a lecturer, probably end up as a university lecturer on Information Management. What a lad!

The election announcement has been delayed, the royal wedding has been delayed, because the Archbishop of Canterbury and the Prime Minister want to go to Rome and therefore couldn't be there for the wedding. The whole thing is a complete farce really.

Friday 8 April
I was going to get on with work, but I watched the Pope's funeral on television. Every possible comment that could have been made has been made on the television since he died nearly a week ago, but the funeral did reveal a number of things. First of all, it showed the enormous power of religion in the world. Bush went over, Chirac, Schröder, representatives from Saudi Arabia, the Russian Orthodox Church – a tremendous gathering of people – Blair of course, Prince Charles, of all people, representing Britain. Mugabe was there; Prince Charles shook hands with Mugabe, possibly by mistake.

Also, the Pope himself: he was an actor really, a very skilful communicator. His attitude to birth control has led to thousands and thousands, millions perhaps, of people being born with Aids, to people who could have been protected if their fathers had used condoms. His attitude to women is outrageous. He's been given credit for having destroyed communism, but I think Gorbachev had much more to do with the transformation of the Soviet Union than the Pope. So the whole event was built up by the Establishment for exactly the purpose they wanted, and got that entrenched into the conventional wisdom.

But it was a moving ceremony, and people from Poland came in large numbers, and all the cardinals were there. Since the Pope appointed almost all the cardinals, it's very unlikely that a progressive cardinal will be appointed to succeed him.

Watched the news, and of course the Rover collapse is the big news, and predictably Blair and Brown are in Birmingham talking to the trade-union leaders. What I would like to know is how close have the links been between Rover and the Department of Industry over the years of difficulty? I don't think we have an industrial policy. I'm not saying it would be easy to deal with, but when you come to think of it, if a foreign enemy tried to bomb Rover, we'd bomb him back; but if somebody buys Rover and closes it, oh, that's market forces.

Saturday 9 April
It's very, very cold today, so I put on my woolly underwear.

The more I think about the Rover collapse, the more I think it's an absolute scandal. The Phoenix consortium bought Rover for £10, assuming all the debts. The directors absolutely ladled out money to themselves and allowed the company to go bust; probably hoped that the Government would bail them out anyway. So in Longbridge, one of the great motor-manufacturing plants in the world until forty years ago, there are just unfinished vehicles. It confirms everything that I have come to believe: that the Government has no industrial policy whatever, and Blair and Brown going there is just a gimmick.

Partly out of curiosity, having watched the Pope's funeral, and trying to understand the country I live in, I watched the wedding of Charles and Camilla. It was a civil wedding in the Guildhall in Windsor. You saw the guests arriving, the Prince of Wales and Camilla arriving, a few, rather straggly people outside, who'd been issued with Union Jacks, waving them in a desultory way. I'm not saying anyone wishes ill to the couple, but I wouldn't have said that there was any sense of excitement, not in any way comparable to the attitude of the Polish delegation in Rome yesterday to the death of the Pope.

Then a Rolls-Royce arrived, and they went back to St George's Chapel for the blessing. I really do feel we've been taken back to Edwardian Britain. Under Blair, we've gone back eighty, ninety years, all these toffs in their fancy clothes. No one's embarrassed about wealth any more, and the general public just stand there, with the police watching them, with flags, just waving. They're treated like idiots and imbeciles and servants and slaves.

The Queen was looking quite cheerful, because as a matter of fact Camilla is now the second woman in the country, because when the Queen dies, she will be Queen.

Tuesday 12 April
I went to the BBC headquarters in Wood Lane for a discussion with Lord Young of Graffham about the future of Rover.

He's seventy-three years old. He's a lawyer. He was Secretary of State for Employment and then for Trade and Industry under Thatcher. I was rather nervous of meeting him because I thought he'd be a tough Thatcherite, but actually he was very agreeable.

He told me that when he was Secretary of State for Trade and Industry he decided to take a huge meeting and address the whole department, and they said to him, 'That was a success. We haven't had such a meeting since Tony Benn was the Secretary of State!'

On Europe, he's a supporter of Business for Sterling, against the euro.

He was very concerned about anti-Semitism. I said, 'Well, you have to differentiate between anti-Semitism and critics of the policy of Sharon.'

He said, 'Yes, I know, but like de Gaulle in Algeria, you have to have a very strong man to bring about a peace settlement.'

I asked about Mrs Thatcher. He said, 'Well, she's had a few mini-strokes, she has days, even hours, on and off.'

I put it to him that Tony Blair had followed her policy. 'Oh yes, yes, ninety per cent of Thatcher's policy has been followed by Blair, but,' he said, 'trust has gone, because of the war, and you can never recover the trust.' He thought the election result might be quite narrow.

I put to him that I didn't think Labour had an industrial policy. He said, 'No, I don't think it has. I don't think Patricia Hewitt has any dealings with industrial people at all.' That is interesting, because it was exactly what I heard when I was up in Aberdeen.

Then he said he was a bit nervous of a recession. 'Privatisation is best for growth, but if the recession comes, I don't know what's going to happen.' I did say to him that I had a certain anxiety about the political consequences of recession, and he understood that.

He said when he was young, he thought religion was dead and socialism was the future, and now he sees that religion is alive and socialism is dead. Secondly, he said that the thing that converted him finally against the European Union was serving on the Council of Ministers; seeing the way that operated really frightened him, which is interesting, similar to my experience. He also said he thought that trying to close the lid on the many different interests in Europe, through this bureaucratic management, would lead to a nationalist explosion. It was quite interesting.

Thursday 14 April
To the Indian High Commission, to give a lecture on Dr Ambedkar, who was an Untouchable and became a lawyer, and the principal member of the commission that drew up the Indian constitution; he then became a Buddhist. I did speak ten years ago, in 1995, and when I looked at my speech then, I realised it was almost identical to the one I am making now, so I did wonder whether the time had come to move on.

Lindis Percy, one of the great campaigners against Menwith Hill, has had an Anti-Social Behaviour Order put upon her, preventing her from going to peace campaigns. So what began as a way of dealing with yobos is now being used politically. Also I read in the paper that Peter Tatchell, who went to the Prince of Wales and Camilla's wedding last week, had been stopped by the Prevention of Terrorism Act. So these new rules, which are allegedly to protect the country, either from foreign attack or from anti-social behaviour, are now in place and could be used by future governments against anybody. It really is terrifying.

Friday 15 April
Rover has finally collapsed. The Chinese have totally withdrawn, I think possibly in part because we've refused to lift the embargo on arms for China. But at any rate, it is also apparent that the four people from Phoenix, who bought it for £10, absolutely lined their pockets and did nothing really to put it in a good shape. If I were still the Secretary of State for Trade and Industry, I would have nationalised it, as I did with Leyland many years ago, but the Government would rather be seen dead than do that. The last British-owned motor company collapsing – that is New Labour for you.

Monday 18 April
At a quarter to eight this evening Jean Corston arrived. I gave her a meal, and we had a talk. Of course she's given up Parliament, and in the next few days the announcement of peerages will be made. I asked her – she doesn't know exactly – but I asked her who she thought would get one, and she said Chris Smith and perhaps Estelle Morris and perhaps George Foulkes; possibly Donald Anderson and Jack Cunningham. That is the way the system works. Former MPs are rewarded at the end of the Commons life. She, of course, was Chair of the Lords and Commons Joint Committee on Human Rights and Chairman of the PLP. She's had a lot of experience in the Labour movement.

There was a programme on Channel 4 called *Elections Unspun*, which I recorded because I was in it briefly. It was an explanation of politics entirely in terms of marketing skill. They had Sir Tim Bell, a marketing man who advised Mrs Thatcher. They presented the whole of the post-war period in terms of marketing. The only person who was vaguely on the left in the whole programme was me, and I had two little, not very meaningful clips. They interviewed Bob Worcester endlessly, Neil Kinnock, Roy Hattersley. John Major actually was much the best of the bunch. He said he had contempt for the whole thing. The idea that anyone else had played any part in who won or lost the election was completely obliterated. You got the impression of a highly skilled group of managers who were in, or out, according to their marketing skills.

Tuesday 19 April
I had a bit of a snooze. Then turned on the telly, and heard that Cardinal Ratzinger, a German, had been elected Pope, and is taking the name Benedict XVI. He was, for a while, in the Hitler Youth movement. He's the head of the Office of Doctrine, which is the ongoing version of the

Inquisition. He absolutely supports everything that the last Pope believed in. So I got absolutely gloomy. I thought to myself: Bush in America, Benedict XVI in the Catholic Church, Blair in Britain – it really did depress me! I spent most of the afternoon going through all my engagements for the election. At the end of the election I will have been to fourteen different constituencies, which isn't too bad.

Tuesday 26 April

Brian Sedgemore, my old PPS, who is standing down from Parliament, has announced he has joined the Liberal Democrats and said that he hopes Blair gets a bloody nose. It's typical of Brian! Always insults those he doesn't like! Actually he did make a good speech on the terrorism bill.

Just as I was going to bed, Stephen rang and said that Peter Hain had asked him to ask me if I would go to Blaenau Gwent, on Monday, to speak for Maggie Jones, who is the Labour candidate replacing Llew Smith. He had a majority of 19,500. So I said to Steve, 'I know, but it's going to be very difficult.'

Friday 29 April

I caught the train up to Leeds for Hilary, and we went to the Belle Isle Working Men's Club. There were about eighty people there. A beautiful club, rather like the Chesterfield Labour Club, only much, much bigger, and we talked to people. Then Hilary made a speech, followed by me, lots of photos. We went from there to Ingram Road Primary School, rather like Salusbury Primary School, with lots of immigrant kids there, and I think even a Refugee Advice Centre. The occasion was to launch a toy library; there was a young lad, who'd been given £6,000, and he bought toys and was going to make them available to children who wouldn't be able to afford them. It was a very imaginative idea.

Then we went on to a mosque. They'd been at prayers, because it was a Friday. Hilary spoke, about how you might think that voting doesn't matter, but it does; I took it up and linked it to my father and the Round Table conferences that ended the British Empire in India. People were very friendly, but by this time I was absolutely exhausted.

Saturday 30 April

I looked at my diary beyond the election, and I've got page after page after page with nothing on it whatever, and that's even more frightening than being overworked.

I had a message from *The Observer*, that Ron Todd has died. I feel so sad, because he told me the minimum length of his expectation of life was three months and the maximum six, and he died in less than a month. I was very fond of Ron.

Monday 2 May

Got up at 4.45 this morning. Had a bath and at 7.15 Stephen and Emily, and Nita's mother, Pratima, arrived and we set off for Wales. We stopped on the M4 for a cup of tea, then carried on. We went to Brynmawr: Peter Hain was there, who is the Secretary of State for Wales as well as Leader of the House of Commons, and Rhodri Morgan, who was the leader of the Labour group, the First Minister for Wales.

We went into a theatre, for the election meeting for Maggie Jones – about 150,200 people there. She was a UNISON (the public service union) candidate from an all-women shortlist, so a lot of the men didn't turn up, and Peter Law, who is the Labour Member of the Welsh Assembly for the same area, left the Labour Party and decided to stand against her. He had the support of the former Member, Llew Smith. So it was all rather tense.

I was resentful at being bullied to go, and I thought it was a bit bloody cheeky, because the Party takes no notice of my opinions. I'm marginalised and excluded – not that I care – but when they want to rally the Party, I'm the guy they call in. Anyway, I got there. Rhodri Morgan made a speech, and then had to dash off. I spoke for about twelve minutes, gave a rousing speech, but I didn't mention Maggie Jones by name unfortunately. But I did my stuff, and it was well received. It was about the constituency, Blaenau Gwent, and the former Members, Michael Foot and Nye Bevan, whom I knew.

While I was in Wales, Alan Simpson rang to say that Llew Smith had rung him, angry that I had spoken on behalf of Maggie Jones. So I said to Alan, 'Well, give him my number', but there was no message, so he obviously decided that it wasn't worth pursuing the matter.

I think, after the election, Blair is finished. He's absolutely busted. The whole Iraq war thing has damaged him irretrievably, and once we're back in power there will be a revolt. Blair's powers of patronage will be slipping away, the war will go on and be bloody and awful, the economy may not be in all that good shape, they're going to try and introduce nuclear power stations and extend our nuclear-weapons programme by replacing Trident with the latest American weapon.

Up in Sedgefield, Reg Keys, whose son was killed in Iraq, may make some impact. He is being supported by Martin Bell, Jon Lansman, Bob Clay, so he might make some sort of an impact. It won't unsettle Blair, but it could be a respectable vote.

But you've just got to stick to the Labour Party, awful as Blair is, and when Blair goes, you won't find a Blairite for love or money. They'll all disappear.

Tuesday 3 May

Apart from the fact that I don't want decent Labour MPs like John Cryer to lose their seats, I wouldn't be sorry at all if the Labour majority was slashed. The most interesting thing of all to me is that, at this critical moment, New Labour depends on Old Labour to help them. That's why I was bullied into going to Wales yesterday; that's why the Secretary of the Party rang me about telephone canvassing,

Wednesday 4 May
Eve of poll.

Well, I got up at a quarter to five, because I didn't want to miss the train to Leeds. *The Guardian* had a story: Benn swallows anti-war stance to support Blair. That was a result of talking to their Political Editor Patrick Wintour, and I was furious. Then I read the story and there was a picture of me there, and it said that, sheepishly, Labour headquarters had had to call on Tony Benn to save Tony Blair, and then reported all my views on the war and New Labour. So it wasn't too bad, and I laughed a bit.

At the Saxton Estate Community Centre there were a lot of real Labour people there round the table, mainly women, but there were two men, one a former miner. They were all so sweet. We had a good old laugh about the old times.

There was one woman who said, 'I'm really worried about immigration. Do you know, every immigrant is given a house, has it furnished for them, is given a black leather jacket and a mobile phone as soon as they arrive?'

Well, it's just incredible, it shows the power of the tabloids! So I said, well, I didn't quite agree with that.

It is the strangest election of my life. It's like three managing directors competing for the job of running Tesco. I thought it was totally boring and totally unprincipled. But maybe the Liberals will do well, maybe Howard will do better than he thinks . . . I wouldn't like tonight to predict anything.

Thursday 5 May
Polling day.

Up about six. Went and voted. I was the first to vote at the Kensington Temple. There was actually a composer, of about fifty-five, who'd got there ahead of me, but she let me vote first, so I was pleased.

In the evening I was taken to the ITV party, which was on a river pleasure boat – the *Silver Sturgeon*, moored at Waterloo Millennium Pier.

When I got there, the whole thing was a complete celebrity party! Mrs Thatcher was there; Mary Ann Sieghart, *The Times* journalist; Richard Wilson, who plays the part of Victor Meldrew, the grumpy old man; Miriam Karlin; Mike Mansfield; Yvette Vanson; Germaine Greer; Joan Collins; Jon Snow; Peter Hain, who said that at Blaenau Gwent the candidate, Maggie Jones, whom I'd gone to support, was likely to lose. Lauren Booth was there. Nicholas Parsons was there.

I went up to the London Eye and did a sort of three-minute interview, which was ludicrous – was Blair as famous as Thatcher? I was so fed up, I said, 'Get me a car home.'

Chapter 5

More time for politics

Friday 6 May 2005
Hilary left Leeds this morning, because he was told he had to be back for the reshuffle. He drove all the way down to London, then was told there wasn't going to be any change to his job, and now he's on the train back to Leeds for his surgery tomorrow. Hoon has been brought in, of all things, to be Leader of the House. Of course Blunkett came back as Minister for Work and Pensions. It's obviously been negotiated between Blair and Brown. Oh, David Miliband has been made Minister in the Deputy Prime Minister's office.

Saturday 7 May
David Trimble, who was defeated in Upper Bann yesterday in Northern Ireland, leaving only one Ulster Unionist in the House of Commons, has resigned as Leader. The Ulster Unionists, I think, are finished, and Paisley is very strong, but then Gerry Adams and Martin McGuinness are strong, and the two parties have got to get together. Whether Peter Hain as the new Northern Ireland Secretary will have the guts to force them together, I do not know. Blair will take an interest in it because he'd like to have one success under his belt before he goes.

Monday 9 May
Believe it or not, Blair has given a job to Shaun Woodward, the former Tory MP whom he parachuted into the Commons; and also to Andrew Adonis, the Education Adviser at Number 10, who was the Liberal Democrat parliamentary candidate for Westbury. He's apparently opposed to comprehensive schools, and he's been put there into Ruth Kelly's department, so Kelly is now a busted flush, because Andrew Adonis has been the real Education Secretary from the time he was appointed as an Adviser.

Tuesday 10 May

Well, *The Guardian* had the full list of the Government, and I looked through it and saw Chris Mullin had been dropped. He was the Minister for Africa in the Foreign Office.

I got the Tube to Dagenham East for Ron Todd's funeral. Got there early, so I had a cup of tea in Jack's Café, just at the end of his street. Then I went to his house, and his son, Peter, and daughters were there. His body was there in the front room, so I went and had a look at it, and he was beautifully laid out.

We were driven to the football ground, behind the hearse, and the police stopped all the traffic. There was a memorial meeting, with four or five hundred people. Rodney Bickerstaffe spoke, made a very amusing speech, which everybody enjoyed; and then I spoke; and then finally Tony Woodley. I was a bit overwhelmed and a bit emotional; I read that lovely poem, 'Do not stand at my grave and weep'.

After that, we had a car behind the hearse to the cemetery, and there was a Royal Marine contingent in their white helmets, because Ron was a Royal Marine commando in Hong Kong, doing national service after the war. The body was lowered in, and then, in remembrance of peace, they opened two little boxes and out flew two white doves.

It was a very moving Labour-movement occasion: trade unions, CND, and of course, obviously, the average age was quite advanced, but I was touched that Ron wanted me to speak.

There has been a Shadow Cabinet reshuffle bringing in younger people – like George Osborne and David Cameron, very young, in their thirties – so obviously the Tory Party is preparing for the succession.

I'm clear that under no circumstances must the Campaign Group be part of the demand for Blair's resignation, because it will frighten people off and it will deny the Campaign Group the possibility of recruitment of good people.

Wednesday 11 May

I went to the Tea Room and saw Chris Mullin.

He was very surprised to be sacked. Blair did ring him up and they discussed the election, and he said, 'I'm afraid I've got to let you go.' He's angry that he's been dropped, because he has been 100 per cent Blairite. It is rough on him, financially rough on him as well, but there you are. I said, 'You must write a book, go back to Select Committees', and so on, but still, he's wounded, and it's horrible being dropped.

Then I went to the Members' Post Office. I said, 'Just to thank you very much – I'm still getting letters as an MP, and it doesn't seem to matter whether you're elected or not.'

Thursday 12 May
The Guardian today reported that a US Senate Committee had linked
George Galloway with the oil-for-food-programme, implying that he had
received money from Saddam Hussein. George denied it, of course. There
was a reference to a man called Fawaz Zureikat, a Jordanian businessman
whom I had met when I went to Iraq two years ago to see Saddam Hussein.

I'm extremely glad that I paid my own fare to Iraq in January 2003, and
I paid my own hotel bill – I think the whole visit cost about 4,000 quid –
and I declined to receive any money for the programme that I made when
I was there. So I'm in the clear, and it would be very worrying if any finger
of suspicion stretched to me, but I don't think it will.

Saturday 14 May
On the way back from Natasha's engagement party, I caught the bus from
Oxford Circus. It was absolutely packed, and on board was a short cockney
guy, very short, who asked me, 'Are you an MP?'

I said, 'No, but I was.'

'Well,' he said, 'politics is all bollocks. The only thing that matters is the
Bible.'

So I said, 'Well, yes, I read the Bible as a child.'

'Yes, but only the Bible is worth having!'

So I said, 'I understand that, but I mean the Bible didn't give us the
National Health Service.'

'Ah, bollocks!' Then he said, 'Love your neighbour' and 'You know, *you*
are an evil bastard.'

So I said, 'I thought you were meant to love your neighbour?'

'Oh well, well . . . Who irons your shirts?'

So I said, 'They aren't ironed.'

'It looks ironed to me. I suppose you come from a wealthy family?'

'Well,' I said, 'my Dad was an MP.'

'I suppose you've got a lot of people to iron your shirts?'

'No, they just go in the washing machine and come out again.'

He got off. Of course this conversation was very loud on the crowded
bus, and people were laughing all around.

Tuesday 17 May
Heard George Galloway giving evidence to the Senate Committee, who
questioned him about the oil-for-food programme. He blasted them! It
made him a hero of the peace movement. It was a wonderful performance,
so I don't know what'll happen in the end.

Wednesday 18 May
The papers are full of Galloway's evidence yesterday, and I must say, he
scored an absolute triumph. It's being described as good theatre and all

that, but it was brilliant, and the peace movement will be so pleased in America.

In the course of the afternoon Ed Miliband sent me an email, containing his draft maiden speech, which he hopes to make on Monday. I made some points about it. Then at the very end, which I thought was extremely interesting, he said that he had come from an immigrant family, and he described how one of his uncles had died in Auschwitz. It was a hammer blow at Michael Howard, without being too crude, so I suggested he move that up to the front of the speech, and then at the end say that he had a brother David, who's an MP, and the House will be relieved to know there are no more Milibands, and he hoped he could be of some service. Whether he'll use my points or not, I don't know, but it was rather flattering that he asked me. I like Ed.

I did begin writing an article about Blair's modernisation, and how the biggest constitutional reform since he came to power was that he's reinvented the monarchy and is behaving like a monarch. When he goes, people will ask, 'When are you going to abdicate?'

Friday 20 May
The papers are full of the ban on hooded young people going into shopping centres, and Anti-Social Behaviour Orders, and uniforms to shame people doing their community service. It's: (a) gimmickry, but (b) desperately authoritarian.

Ruth and I went and met Celia O'Connor, who is in the Education Office of the House of Commons. All three of us went to visit the nuns who live next door to me, in the Society of the Holy Child Jesus. What amused me was that they said they're dropping the old clerical language. Each Order used to have a general in Rome, but now I think they're called Advisory Teams, and there used to be a provincial in England to go round and supervise the Orders, but they're now called Local Advisory Groups or Management Groups. So the language of bureaucracy has got into the Church as it has everywhere else. They showed us a charming chapel for prayer and contemplation in the basement of this lovely house.

Saturday 21 May
I got the Tube to the Embankment, where the Palestine Solidarity Committee was planning a march. Jeremy Corbyn turned up. Jeremy and Jenny Tonge and I went to Number 10 Downing Street and dropped a letter off to the Prime Minister, and then we rejoined the demonstration, which had passed by then and got up to Trafalgar Square. Paul Mackney and Billy Hayes were there. George Galloway was also there, and of course he got a tremendous response. So I said to him, 'Now George, you know why you won. It's because the Prime Minister has come out for Respect, and everybody thought it was their duty.'

'Oh,' he said, 'better than that, the Queen mentioned Respect in the Queen's Speech!'

So we had a bit of a laugh about that, and I paid a tribute to him in my speech, and to his courage in going to Washington.

Tuesday 24 May

Every day there's a ghastly story about Iraq. I don't report it always, but Iraq is going wrong, Afghanistan is going wrong, the question of Iran is still in the balance, Israel is still extending its settlements – I mean, the whole Middle East is in flames as a result of Blair and Bush.

The American Congress is beginning to take an interest in leaked documents that came out on 1 May showing that British civil servants or diplomats had sent a message to Blair in the summer of 2002 saying that Bush had decided to go to war with Iraq and all the intelligence advice was to be adjusted to fit in with that. Of course it passed without notice in London, or very little notice, but in America it's caused a huge storm.

Wednesday 25 May

Went to the Campaign Group at five o'clock. It was absolutely packed because Charles Clarke, the Home Secretary, had been invited along. I've known him for a long time, since he was a student. His father was my Permanent Secretary. He explained the ID bill in general terms: there weren't problems with civil liberties, or cost or technology. Then a whole range of people asked questions, but most of the questions were anxieties about the cost, because everyone will have to pay £93 for their card; about whether the cards were compulsory, and you had to carry them; about whether the technology was reliable. They were all sort of rather practical questions, and civil liberties didn't come in much.

I'm not an MP, and I've got no right really to ask questions, but I did. 'I've no objection to ID cards,' I said, 'I've brought six of them along that I've had for sixty years', and I put them on the table. Then I said, 'The real question is not ID cards, but what is on the card, because if you're really serious about using it for terrorism and crime, you'll have to link the crime dossier and the terrorism dossier with the cards, and will we know what's on the card, and will it be true?' I pointed out that the security services, when I was in Government, had said Jack Jones and Hugh Scanlon were security risks.

'The other thing is about who gets the information, because,' as Charles would know very well, 'under the arrangements we have with the Americans, in return for being allowed nuclear weapons, which they have, we have to share all our intelligence with them, so the dossier that's being built up on us would have to go to the Americans as well.'

All I could say is that Charles looked a bit uncomfortable; can't say more than that.

I went to have a meal on the Terrace; got my tray with a little salad and a quiche, and a bit of fruitcake and a banana. Then I went to the loo, and when I came back there was a woman MP standing by my table. She said, 'A bird picked up your cake and flew off with it!'

Thursday 26 May

The news all day has been absolutely dominated by the return of Liverpool, having won the UEFA Champions League final in Istanbul, defeating Milan. I turned on the telly when I was having my meal; half a million people, they say, turned out in Liverpool for the team bus. I might add, they don't say, 'The police estimate is a quarter of a million.' They only do that with left-wing meetings. But still, Liverpool is the European City of Culture, they're the European Champions and, having been hammered so hard, it's wonderful to see them doing well.

Sunday 29 May

France had rejected the European Union constitution, fifty-five to forty-five. It's really, really exciting! It's the first democratic response to the bureaucracy of the new Europe, and the scandal is that the German Parliament didn't allow the German people to have a referendum, so this is very important. It will put Blair in a difficulty – will there be a referendum? We don't know. The Dutch are going to vote on Wednesday, and then there are the Danes coming along. It brought out so clearly what the whole thing was about – whether you want a capitalist Europe working in a globalised economy on a free-market basis run by bureaucrats, or whether you want a democratic Europe. It's a very big issue with huge implications. I felt so cheerful, I can't tell you!

Wednesday 1 June

The Dutch, by 63 per cent to 37 per cent, rejected the European Union treaty, an absolutely devastating defeat, so great that even the Dutch Parliament can't reverse it, which I think they could if it was two-thirds. It has killed the treaty, and of course absolute panic everywhere! The European Commission is in a state of panic, Blair doesn't know what to do, doesn't want a referendum, but Chirac – in order to embarrass him – is saying we must all have our own vote on the matter. We'll see what happens, but it's an interesting development, I must say.

Thursday 2 June

I watched the Gorbachev programme on communism, which I followed with considerable interest. In effect, he said communism was a disaster; it took him a long time before he realised it, before he was President; and then he described how Russia went capitalist. I mean, you can understand why the old comrades in the Soviet Union hate the man. Of course, I don't know whether he really wrote the script, but he never mentioned the war of intervention, he never mentioned the support that the West gave to Hitler to destroy communism, so I thought it was inadequate. I saw him, in some ways, like the communists in the Labour Party who swung to Blair.

Friday 3 June

Got a cab to the Gielgud Theatre to see *Some Girls*, a play with David Schwimmer (who was in *Friends*, the American comedy series) and Saffron Burrows and three others, about a man who had had a lot of affairs in the past. He was about to marry a nurse, and he decided to invite his old girlfriends to come and see him. I thought it was a very interesting play. The man, played by David Schwimmer, emerged as a really dishonest guy who was trying to clear his conscience, and the women reacted in so many different ways. The first one just laughed at him. The second one wanted to seduce him all over again. The third one was a married woman whose husband was sitting out in the car, waiting all the time she was there, and then she also tried to get him to bed. The last one was Saffron Burrows, who was a doctor in Los Angeles, and obviously she was the one he should have married.

Went to Saffron's dressing room briefly, and came home in a taxi.

Tuesday 7 June

To Salisbury to talk to the officers and their wives at the First Battalion of the 52nd Cheshire Regiment.

I sat on my little stool at the station until a tall lieutenant-colonel arrived, dressed in combat outfit. We were driven to the Officers' Mess and I was introduced to all the officers. The average age was about twenty-six, twenty-seven, only a couple of years older than my grandson Michael. They come from the Liverpool area, of course. It was supposed to be officers and wives, but there were only about four or five women there. I talked about war, and the history of my life, and what war had done to my life, and then where power really rested.

One of the senior officers in the regiment, who was the brother-in-law of the Colonel, asked me for my view on nuclear weapons. I gave my view – and later when he came up to me I asked, 'What do you think about it?'

He said, 'I agree with you. I think they're absolutely no use whatever. Cost one point five billion a year, and the money would be much better spent either on better army equipment or on schools or hospitals.'

He also said he was strongly in favour of hunting, and was it a class struggle to get rid of hunting? He was a wonderful mixture of views.

One man said, 'Every society needs an elite, and you've got to keep people in their proper pecking order.'

Dinner was a mess dinner, with huge silver candelabra, holding about twenty candles, on every table, and although it was a lovely warm evening, all the curtains were drawn. There was a sergeant in charge of the mess, who was in a red uniform, and the soldiers who served the food were in fatigues.

Of course the army is very disciplined. They didn't laugh at my jokes, and they didn't groan at anything I said; they just took it, because I guess an eighty-year-old former Secretary of State overawed them a bit. Of course, it was absolutely rigidly divided into officers and others, and I tried to deal with that, said, 'We've got to discover the genius in people.'

I was asked about race and immigrants, and Englishness and English habits, so I tried to answer that.

There wasn't a lot of intellectual curiosity, I didn't think, but they took it. They've had Douglas Hurd and various MPs in the past.

At about a quarter-past eleven I was driven home in the staff car, with one of the young officers of twenty-six acting as a navigator, and a young guy, who was probably only about nineteen, driving. Apparently the average age of the soldiers in the regiment is about nineteen. They've served in Iraq, in Kosovo, in Bosnia; they've served, twice, in Ireland. I enjoyed the evening very much. I'm glad I went. They couldn't have been more friendly and kind, and I enjoyed it, but goodness me, the whole atmosphere is so different in a disciplined culture like that.

Thursday 9 June
Flew to Belfast, for *Let's Talk*, the Northern Ireland equivalent of *Any Questions?*

I met the other members of the panel: Rita Duffy, who is a feminist artist from Belfast, passionately keen on the arts, and very anti-political in that sense; a young Ulster Unionist councillor called Tyrone Power, who was an international rugby player for Ireland; he said he had taught Otis Ferry, who is the young man who broke into the House of Commons in a pro-hunt demonstration; and Billy Leonard, a man, I suppose, in his mid to late-forties, a Protestant who had served as a reserve policeman in the Royal Ulster Constabulary, been a member of the Orange Order and transferred to the SDLP, the Social Democratic Labour Party, and is now, of all things, a Sinn Fein councillor in Coleraine. He was an imaginative guy.

The questions were very good: was Bob Geldof just promoting Live 8 in order to improve his own reputation as an artist? I said I thought that was unfair, but the problem was a little more complicated than was made out, because actually the poverty in Africa had been partly caused by Europe. We sold them arms, they got into debt, and then we offered to relieve the debt if they'd sell off their public services. There was a lot of sympathy for Geldof, who is an Irishman of course.

One question was: will the IRA ever give up their arms? I did say that 'terrorists' all ended up having tea with the Queen, and I said Paisley and

Adams both distrust the British, and that might be the basis of their cooperation.

I was nervous, because Northern Ireland politics is like doing a ballet dance on a minefield.

Saturday 11 June

The world news is that Gordon Brown has announced, with the G8 Finance Ministers, a massive wipe-out of debt immediately. I'm somehow a bit sceptical about it, I don't know why . . . Where is the money coming from? Is it coming from other aid packages? And anyway the question is: why are the rich rich? I got some useful figures about the way that Africa, which is rich in diamonds and oil and copper, is being exploited by multinational companies, and they're the ones that bribe the political leaders to give them the contracts. So corruption is also a product of external influences. I don't think Bob Geldof is quite enough.

David Jason has been made a knight, a Harold Wilson-type glamour appointment.

Sunday 12 June

Read in the Sunday papers that whereas there were 700 people in 1997 with an income of over a million pounds a year, there are now 4,000, which is quite a big growth, and I think the number of homeless people has increased. These are just little insights into the nature of New Labour. I don't mean they make a lot of money, but their friends are all rich people, and they've no roots in the movement any more. I dare say that's not true of some of the best MPs, but certainly the guys at the top give the impression of just enjoying the good life.

Wednesday 15 June

I went down to the Campaign Group, where there was a really excellent presentation by three people from the London School of Economics about identity cards. Their approach was technical, whereas I think it's a civil-liberties issue, but they were pointing out that these systems have never been integrated before, that the computer problems are great, that biometric testing is inaccurate, that the thing is going to be overwhelmingly costly. What do you do anyway about people from Europe who are entitled to come here, and have no cards? How could it help with benefit fraud? What do you do with corporate crime, which would be totally exempt from any control, because they would just forge the cards? No country in the world has attempted anything on this scale. I did make the point, which I think they took, that there are a lot of people who think a simple identity card – you know, your picture, your address and your job – would be reasonable, but this is something quite different.

They also confirmed what I had suspected, that Charles Clarke, the

Home Secretary, seems to be absolutely opposed to it, and so it is certainly being imposed on Clarke, and it may well be that, with the Tories against it and the Liberals against it and enough Labour MPs with doubts, it might be defeated.

Saturday 18 June

After my wedding anniversary yesterday, and thinking about the future, I decided to throw away some old personal papers and tapes that I've kept. They were in a container saying, 'Please destroy when I die', but I thought there's no point in leaving them, so I destroyed them.

Wednesday 22 June

I had to go to the Iranian Embassy in Prince's Gate, to see the Ambassador, Seyed Mohammad Hossein Adeli, who is a banker and an economist. He is grey-haired, very courteous, and a young man was taking notes all the time.

I started by asking about the nuclear programme, and he told me that following years of isolation, the Iranian engineers had themselves discovered how to develop a fuel cycle, without help from the outside. They hadn't mentioned it to the International Atomic Energy Authority, who went there and were surprised at how far they'd got. They were now under pressure to admit inspectors, so they let inspectors in.

They were then faced with opposition from the United States, obviously, and from Europe, but he said that whereas the Americans are demanding the whole thing be wound up, the Europeans took a rather different view, and they reached an agreement last December called the Paris Agreement, in which the British Government assented, saying that they could do it; but of course they would not be able, under the Non-Proliferation Treaty, to develop nuclear weapons, which would require a much higher degree of enrichment.

Then Bush overturned that, and said the whole programme should stop. What the Ambassador indicated was that although Jack Straw himself had been quite good, Blair was moving towards Bush's position and wrecking the unity of the European position, which was more sympathetic and friendly. Apparently Jack Straw said a couple of days ago that he did accept that the EU had to recognise the Iranians' rights.

But of course Bush has totally abandoned the Non-Proliferation Treaty. The depleted uranium is a breach of the Non-Proliferation Treaty. The bunker-busting tactical nuclear weapons are a breach. The Star Wars with nuclear weapons in space are a breach. Also, the reversal of the 'no first use' policy is a breach – Geoff Hoon, when Defence Secretary, said, 'We reserve the right to be the first to use our nuclear weapons.' So the Western position is totally hypocritical, but of course the question is: will Bush, or even Israel, attack and strike? The possibility exists.

So I told the Ambassador the position that Blair was in, that he wouldn't be able to get public support if he supported the Americans. We had a useful discussion. He said, 'You must come to Iran', and so on, though I said, 'My only interest is to see this thing doesn't develop in a way that could threaten another conflict.'

He then said that, without the support of the Iranian Government, the Americans couldn't control Afghanistan, which was quite interesting.

When Blair was asked whether we would renew the Trident programme, he left it open, but made it clear we would have to have a deterrent, which is exactly the argument of course that every country that wants them, or has them, uses. If it applies to Britain, it applies to Iran, or applies to anybody. There's no logic in this. It's just power, power determines everything, and I think in a way if that was admitted, it would make political discourse a bit more credible.

Friday 24 June
Caught the train to Chelmsford, and actually walked to the cathedral, for the Chernobyl Children's Project. Twenty years ago Linda Walker and others decided to raise money for the children of Chernobyl affected by the explosion, and to bring them over. I think 3,000 children have been over. It's very touching and I was asked to give a lecture. The Bishop of Bradwell was there, with 500 people in the church. Apparently it raised £3,000. So that was really worth doing. After the Chernobyl Children's Project had been described, I spoke from the pulpit for twenty-five minutes and then answered questions.

On the train coming from Chelmsford to Liverpool Street there was nobody in the compartment, so I smoked my pipe.

I've got CND, and then I have got a bit of a break, and then Glastonbury.

Monday 27 June
A new anti-terrorism law has been introduced, under which there'll be a world database of people advocating or justifying terrorism, which in effect is ruling out all the anti-colonial struggles, many of which took a violent form. I don't know whether Palestinians trying to get back the territory that the United Nations says belongs to them would be terrorists. I don't know whether when Kuwait was attacked, and it retaliated against the Iraqis, they would have been terrorists. It is an absolute ludicrous and undemocratic rule, because it targets what people say, and that is a really dangerous development. But the Tories welcome this, and we're just losing our civil liberties hand over fist.

Tuesday 28 June
Debate on the second reading of the identity-card bill. David Davis, the

Shadow Home Secretary – he'll be the next Tory Leader – made a brilliant speech. So did Douglas Hogg and John Bercow – three Tory MPs. Mark Oaten, the Liberal Democrat, made a competent speech. Alan Simpson made a very good speech. I won't say I really wished I was back in the House of Commons, because I don't, but there was a whiff of grapeshot in the old warhorse's nostrils.

When the vote came, I thought it would be much closer, but the Government had nearly forty majority. I must say, I sat back and I thought, I cannot support New Labour. I couldn't leave the Labour Party, but I regard New Labour as an enemy of everything I believe in – it's a rotten government! It has reached the breaking point. It is strange how the libertarians of left and right meet round the back, and in a sense, liberty is what democracy is all about – civil liberties. So here I find myself far closer to David Davis, John Bercow and Douglas Hogg, Tory MPs, than I do to Tony McNulty and Blair and Charles Clarke.

Wednesday 29 June

I looked through who'd voted, and to my horror Chris Mullin voted for ID cards. Chris Mullin! And so did Ann Cryer, and so did Peter Kilfoyle. I just couldn't understand it!

Went to the University of Westminster, which used to be the Regent Street Polytechnic, founded by Quintin Hogg, Lord Hailsham's grandfather, to a meeting on ID cards, quite well attended. There were people in their thirties and forties largely. On the platform was Guy Taylor, in the chair; Shami Chakrabarti, who is in charge of Liberty, who did law, worked in the Home Office, and now it's universally thought that she has done a wonderful job as head of Liberty.

George Galloway turned up, and Lynne Featherstone, a Liberal Democrat, and Dominic Grieve, the Tory Shadow Attorney General. We all spoke. I was last, and I did make the point that libertarians meet round the back. I also made the point that ex-communists find it easy to support New Labour because the shift from Stalin to Blair is a minor one. I was open and frank about it all.

Saturday 2 July

I was very depressed this morning. I find it difficult to keep myself politically optimistic, and not to think I'm just a tiny little individual ant in the ant heap, and not really able to do much.

Watched the video that Melissa had lent me called *The Girl in the Café*. At the end I felt that it's part of this extraordinary popular takeover of a political issue, the Live 8 concert, which was in Hyde Park, and in eight other countries all over the world – Philadelphia, South Africa and all over the place. Having a pop concert alerting people doesn't solve the problem. It's an unreal world.

Blair has now put Iraq behind him, though bloodshed is going on on a massive scale, and is now able to appear as the pop star alongside Bob Geldof.

Tuesday 5 July

I walked over to 7 Millbank for the Sinn Fein party. I saw Martin McGuinness as I arrived, and he was hopeful about the IRA response.

Jeremy Corbyn was there, whom I dearly love. I saw Seumas Milne from *The Guardian*, who said, 'Life is terribly difficult in *The Guardian*', but I knew that. He said Polly Toynbee has now completely transferred her loyalty from Tony Blair to Gordon Brown.

I said to Martin, 'Ian Paisley is an old man. He must have some desire for a place in history.'

He said, well, last December, he was very ill, but Bertie Ahern and Tony Blair were sure he would come round to an agreement.

Thursday 7 July

At about half-past eight, quarter to nine, Charles Frater arrived to film me for a potential TV autobiography.

During filming the phone rang and Melissa said, 'Are you safe?' So I said, 'What do you mean?' She said, 'Well, turn on the telly.'

I did and saw there had been a number of explosions, in Underground trains and a bus, and many, many people killed and injured. We don't know exactly, although I think they said at the early stage there were only two killed.

I went on doing the interview with Charles, and we touched on the bombing, and the problem of giving an early response to the media.

By the evening the scale of the bombings had become obvious and I had been asked to do WBAI, the American public-service network; Air America, from Oklahoma, I think; Irish radio; *Newsnight* with Dame Pauline Neville-Jones, a professional diplomat, who was Chairman of the Joint Intelligence Committee in 1994, and with Dr Zaki Badawi, who's the former director of the Islamic Cultural Centre.

Friday 8 July

The number of dead increased all the time – I think casualties had probably gone up to a few hundred, and the number of dead had risen from two to twenty.

One little interesting sideline on today: the American authorities after the bombing banned all American troops in Britain – apparently there are 12,000 of them, I thought there were more – from visiting London. This caused such a lot of anger. Talk about solidarity with the British! We didn't ban people from going to New York after 9/11. But it was immediately reversed, so I think that was quite an interesting insight. One of the

American papers today describes London being so 'riddled' with Muslims that they think of it as Londonistan. That tells you something, too.

Wednesday 13 July
The news today is full of the fact that these bombers have all been identified as British-born Muslims. They all came together to King's Cross, and then killed fifty-two people and injured many others. Of course it's created a tremendous trauma. Some mosques have been attacked and windows broken, and so on and so on, which is the danger of it, but also it deepens the sense of crisis – why did they do it? They're being described as barbaric and cruel, which they were, but at the same time nobody ever takes any notice of the Iraqis we kill or the Afghans we kill. So it does show what a very deep problem this is, and a lot needs to be done about it. The Muslim leaders are trying to respond in the right way, denouncing the terrorism, but of course if you look at it from another point of view, not all Americans support Bush, and not all Christians support Blair, though he claims to be a Christian.

Train to Blackpool, and went to the Transport and General Workers' Union Biannual Delegate Conference.

After lunch, they suspended the debate that had been going on, so as to give the Frank Cousins Peace Award to me. Tony Woodley talked warmly about Ron Todd, who died in April, and then he paid a tribute to me, and I was called to speak. It is a great award: Fenner Brockway was the first person to get it; Willy Brandt, the former Chancellor of Germany, had it; the Northern Ireland peace people got it; Medical Aid for Palestine got it; John Hume from Northern Ireland got it.

Tony Woodley said: speak as long as you like. 'Well,' I said, 'I won't go beyond fifteen minutes', but I did seventeen. A very passionate speech. I went and was photographed with this beautiful silver medal with a white ribbon, then they took it away again because they hadn't had my name engraved on it.

On the train I read a book called *World Religions*, because I do think the time has come when we really have to devote a lot more time to a study of religion. I make a lot of references to the Christian roots of socialism, but this is rather different, about the impact of religion on the world.

The book went right back to early religions, primitive religions, animal sacrifices, human sacrifices, the role of Lao-tzu, Confucius, Zoroastrians, the Sikhs, the Buddhists. I knew nothing about any of it, and I did find it was a very scholarly book, published about twenty-three years ago. Religion is, first of all, about how to live your life – morality, faith, comfort and security. Then it's about the explanation of life, the myths, the personal god, life after death, the relationship with nature, sectarianism; then about the power of religion and control from the top, self-perpetuating hier-archies, the language, doctrine, dogma, division, the idea of sin, redemption and punishment. Then there is the link of religion to the state: to what extent is it compatible with democracy; does religion see democracy as good or bad; does democracy want to separate the state? Is it peaceful or warlike? Then there is the music and pictures and festivals, the culture of religion – birth, marriage, death, rituals, prayers, hymns, and so on. I'm really trying out a speech, but that's what I worked on today.

Saturday 16 July
I got a cab to the TUC for the Labour Representation Committee meeting. A couple of hundred people attended, John McDonnell chaired it. Michael Meacher spoke, very well. Jeremy Dear, from the National Union of Journalists, and Matt Wrack, the new General Secretary of the Fire Brigades Union, both spoke and there was a session with Katy Clark, the new MP, Paul Mackney from the National Association of Teachers in Further and Higher Education, and Mark Serwotka from the PCS.

In the afternoon session we had Senator Kox, the former General Secretary of the Dutch Socialist Party, Bob Wareing and myself. Later I had a chat to Senator Kox. He's fifty-two, a nice lad, knew all about me, which surprised me; he told me how his party had begun as a far-left party, had moved to be a democratic party. He was very intelligent.

Sunday 17 July
To the Tolpuddle Festival. I saw Nigel Costley, Billy Bragg, John Monks, who's now gone to Europe, Brendan Barber, and I did an interview for ITV and BBC television, about Tolpuddle. They both said, 'Oh well, it's all out of date now. What's the point? Trade unions are weak.'

There were about 6,000 people there, I think the biggest Tolpuddle there's been, lots and lots of banners.

I laid a wreath, then we had the march followed by speeches, including a Colombian woman, who made a most passionate speech saying, 'The Government have killed my husband, killed my mother, killed my brother and stolen my father's land, and we'll still carry on.' I'd worked out what I wanted to say, and I did listen earlier to what I said last year at Tolpuddle, in case I repeated myself.

Monday 18 July
Got up at 5.30, picked up at a quarter to seven and did a whole series of interviews: first, with Jim Naughtie of the *Today* programme and Lord Armstrong, about Ted Heath, who has died. Then I rushed from there and did an interview with Natasha Kaplinsky on BBC *Breakfast*.

The BBC had a fixed idea about Heath: Heath took us into Europe, his great achievement; Heath started the long-overdue confrontation with the miners, whom Thatcher dealt with later; and Heath sulked – that was the personal dimension – and refused to have any spin doctors. He was a man of eighty-nine, and to confine the assessment to his short period as a prime minister, on Europe, his fight with the miners, his moodiness and his failure to communicate, was such a denial of his life! I was the only one who mentioned the 1930s, when he went to Spain and supported the International Brigade, then more recently his attitude to the Iraq war, the Gulf War and the Yugoslav war. It just showed how a media impression of a man can compress him – I'm not saying it wasn't important, but it wasn't the real Ted Heath!

I went into the House of Lords to see my friend Jean Corston take her seat as Lady Corston of St George. Her two supporters were Alan Howarth, who had been the Secretary of the Parliamentary Labour Party, and Campbell-Savours, who was made a peer some while ago.

I had asked whether I could stand at the bar of the House, and they said no: only younger sons of peers and Members of Parliament. So I said, 'Well, I was the younger son of a peer!' so I won that, but then Black Rod moved me into Black Rod's box. The doorkeeper in the Lords said, 'Oh, this means trouble!'

Anyway, I sat in the Gallery with Dawn Primarolo, another Bristol MP, and saw Jean come in. She was all dressed up in her robes, and came in and they read the Letters Patent, and then she, in a clear voice, swore the Oath of Allegiance and there was a mild 'hear! hear!' while she shook hands with the Lord Chancellor, and that was it. Jean was the daughter of a trade unionist, got into Parliament in 1992, became Chairman of the Parliamentary Labour Party: she leaped from being a working-class girl down in Yeovil to being Baroness Corston. Peter Townsend, her husband, was there with her daughter, son-in-law and two little grandchildren.

Dawn Primarolo has been in the Treasury as long as Gordon Brown. When I think of the Dawn I knew in Bristol, twenty-five years ago, that's extraordinary. Anyway, she was very friendly.

Then I had a talk to Edward Miliband in the Pugin Room, and we had about an hour. He asked about constituency work, and I told him what was important. He asked about speaking in the House of Commons, and I said you didn't attack the other side, but you put your case forward, didn't intervene too often, got known to be a specialist in certain subjects. And I said he ought to go and see the Clerks.

'What do the Clerks do?'

I said, 'Well, my dad used to say they play with little toy soldiers. If you take an interest in them, they'll help you.' And I described many occasions when the Clerks have helped me.

I told him about the Librarian and the Serjeant at Arms and the Speaker's Secretary, and I said, 'Parliament is a complicated piece of machinery, and you need to know how it works in order to raise the issues you want as a backbencher.' I think he took the point.

Then he asked me about the Labour Party, and I said I didn't think it was a Labour Party. He said, what about the minimum wage, and tax credits – things that Hilary raises with me – and I said, 'I'm not saying it hasn't done good things, but it's a government that believes in market forces.'

Tuesday 19 July
I caught the Oxford Tube, which is a bus service that goes from Notting Hill Gate right through to the centre of Oxford. I've seen them going by every ten or fifteen minutes – lovely-looking buses. A bus came within five minutes. It was a comfortable journey, reclining seats. I went sound asleep, and when I woke up I was just heading into Oxford. It cost me £6 return – unbelievably cheap!

I met a group of young people aged between fifteen and eighteen, who come every year from America. I sat on a table and I talked for about twenty-five minutes about the war, how I'd met Caroline, about my debating tour in the States, my childhood, my hatred of war, how we avoided a permanent war, about the danger of religious war, about what empires were like, and so on. Anyway then there were questions, very good questions, and one of the organisers came up to me afterwards and said they had never, ever heard anything like that before.

I really liked them; they were so bright.

Thursday 21 July
My grandson William arrived, and we sat and talked. While we were talking, the phone rang and it was Lissie: 'Are you all right?'

I said, 'What do you mean?'

'Have you seen the telly?'

It was absolutely the same as two weeks ago today, so I turned on the TV and there'd been four bombs in London – not entirely clear at the beginning whether they went off, but detonators went off. Warren Street, Shepherd's Bush, the Oval and somewhere else were closed, and a little detonator went off in a bus. Since the bombs didn't go off, the people who did it are still in London, so the police will now try and crack down on them. They said later in the day that it was probably the same explosives that had been used in the bombs two weeks ago, so at least we know that.

Anyway, William stayed. We talked till about one. Then we went and had a meal in Pizza Express. We watched the news, and Tony Blair made an inconsequential comment. Ian Blair, the Commissioner of the Metropolitan Police, said, 'Stay where you are! Don't go out!' So I thought William would be stuck here, but at any rate he wanted to go home, so I drove him. By then the situation was easing, but these stations were still closed.

Friday 22 July

I took a cab to the Regent Street Mosque, which I'd never been to before – it's a huge structure, built in 1971 and expanded since – for a discussion, for Muslim TV (I think it's actually sometimes called the Islam Channel). Yvonne Ridley is on it. The people who took part in it were myself; Phil Rees, a BBC journalist; Makbool Javaid, who's a Muslim human-rights lawyer; Dr Azzam Tamimi, head of the Institute of Islamic Political Thought; and Mohammed Sheikh, founder and Chairman of the Conservative Muslim Forum. The question was about the bombing. What really interested me about it was that everybody was critical of the war in Iraq and linked it with the bombing.

The guy from the Conservative Muslim Forum, Dr Sheikh, had been in Uganda, driven out by Amin, had come to London, made a huge success, had an office in the City, all his children went to Oxford and Cambridge. He was a Conservative, but he did agree with me most of the time. Dr Azzam Tamimi was absolutely burning with anger at the war, and at the way the Muslim leaders who had met Blair had condemned the bombing, without saying anything about the war.

It took an hour to get home, the traffic was so awful, because today the police fired five shots and killed a man who was on a train. Whether he'd done anything wrong, I do not know, but it was a big event, and so the traffic around Stockwell, where this occurred, was congested.

Saturday 23 July

The big news at the moment is that there was a man shot yesterday by the police. He was seen rushing into a train and they followed him, knocked him to the floor and shot him five times in the head. He was a twenty-seven-year-old Brazilian boy. This is just part of this ghastly, ghastly mess of the war and the consequences and the terrorism, and I think this war against terrorism, it could last a hundred years, it could go on and on.

It's all triggered by this American domination, with the help of the British, in the Middle East. The Palestinian issue is the core of the problem, but Iraq and Iran and Syria . . . Blair is just totally insensitive! Apparently, when he was asked what he felt about the innocent people killed in Iraq, he said (and I looked it up on the Internet, but couldn't find it, but he said), 'I can justify that to my maker.' Well, that's exactly what the suicide bombers say: 'I can justify killing people to my maker.' So this has become a mad religious war, when it's really about politics.

In the summer of 2005 I went with my daughter Melissa and her children Hannah and Sarah on a family visit to Cincinnati – my wife Caroline's home city. It was to be the last occasion on which I saw Caroline's sister, Nance, who died the following year.

During our visit there was a special election (a by-election) going on in Hamilton

County, caused by the Republican congressman giving up his seat to take up a government appointment.

The Democratic candidate was Paul Hackett, who had served in Iraq and was passionately opposed to the war. I took the opportunity of visiting his headquarters and talking to some of his supporters, who were young and very keen.

Indeed, on polling day I was allowed to go into a polling station and was shown the 'Hollerith' voting system, in which electors use punch-cards to record their vote.

It was an absolutely solid Republican area, normally 70:30 in their favour. Talking to some old Republicans at a party, I was struck by their hostility to the war and to Bush himself. Indeed, one elderly woman said to me, 'It may seem absurd, but do you think this war could really be about oil?'

When the result was announced, the Republican percentage of the vote fell to 52 per cent compared to Paul Hackett's 48 per cent, representing a massive swing.

This gave me an early indication of what might happen in the subsequent mid-term elections the following year, when Bush indeed lost control of Congress.

Sunday 7 August

Looking back on the holiday, it was interesting to me. First of all, it's the first time I've had a proper holiday – i.e., taking no work, not thinking about work – for years and years and years, and I didn't have a conscience about it. Secondly, I realised that I was past it and an old man, and I'm not important any more. I said that to Lissie, and she said, 'Oh, I know, I know.' Also, I felt that being a good grandfather compensated for all my failures as a husband to Caroline, and I'm sure she'd have been pleased about that. Also, I realised what a small influence people have in the world, even in politics. So it was a useful, thoughtful thing, and Melissa was so like Caroline, it was just amazing! Everybody commented on it, and seeing her with the girls was lovely.

Wednesday 17 August

Train to Bristol Parkway, collected and taken to the Council House, where there was a packed meeting in support of Jerry Hicks, the Deputy Convener of the Test Division of Rolls-Royce, who was sacked by a new American management that's come in.

There's now a strike, and they've had support from all over the country, from all the Rolls-Royce plants, including Northern Ireland. They've had support from Derek Simpson, the General Secretary of Amicus, and from other unions.

Bob Crowe made a strong speech, and the mood was one of militancy, of a kind I haven't really seen since the 1970s. I spoke – not that there was much left for me to say. You just wonder whether the tide of opinion is really beginning to turn.

Friday 19 August

I was sitting reading the papers this morning and I noticed Mo Mowlam had asked for her life-support system to be switched off, and at 8.30 I had requests for interviews about her death.

Sunday 21 August

Stephen's fifty-fourth birthday. I gave him a ring, and he was just on his way to Waterloo to go back to France.

The big news at the moment, which has been going on for some days, is the role of Sir Ian Blair, the Commissioner of the Metropolitan Police, who, for the first twenty-four hours after the shooting of the Brazilian, said that he was a suicide bomber, and of course it was a mistake and they had people demanding his resignation, and so on. He seems quite a decent guy on the telly, but of course the Met is in a desperately difficult position, because they did kill an innocent man.

Monday 22 August

Well, the press this morning: first of all, the Iraqi constitution is being deferred and deferred, because the real question is: is it a federal system, under which the Kurds and the Sunnis and the Shi'ites have fair autonomy within such a system, or is it going to be, as the Shi'ite majority would like, an Islamic state with sharia law, in which case there will be trouble? The Americans are just so keen to get anything, that Bush appears even to have compromised on sharia law in order to justify an exit strategy for his troops, leaving his bases, of course, safely there.

Jonathan arrived about a quarter to eleven. He'd been delayed by a scare when somebody left a package on a train. He spent the whole day typing out envelopes, and then later typing some of the letters, so I managed to get thirty cards off. He's such a sweet lad.

The Israeli withdrawal from Gaza is being hailed as a great peace move, but there still isn't a Palestinian state, the Israelis are still in breach of their obligations to withdraw from the West Bank and to remove the wall, the Berlin Wall around the new territories. So I think this is just a gimmick to persuade the Americans that Sharon has made the ultimate sacrifice, and actually to put some of the Gaza settlers into the settlements in the West Bank, so it's a complete fraud!

Wednesday 24 August

Had a word with Dave. June is not at all well, it's very worrying indeed. Having been through it all with Caroline, you know, I know how June feels and how he feels, and I must be as supportive as I possibly can.

Tuesday 30 August

I'm still a bit depressed. I don't know why.

A hurricane has devastated the southern states in America – New Orleans completely evacuated, eighty or a hundred people killed, damage estimated at $26 million. The tragedy is that the people who suffered have suffered from nature rather than Iraq. It makes you realise that our true enemies are nature and not other human beings.

I sat down in the office. I cleared all my emails. I did ring the Shaw Theatre to find out how booking for my lecture was going, and 1,500 tickets have to be sold to fill it out, and forty have so far been sold, and of course the publicity was left too bloody late.

Wednesday 31 August
To Ealing Town Hall for a Stop the War meeting.

The first speaker was Andrew Murray, who is the Chairman of the Stop the War Coalition, and then there were two speakers from Gate Gourmet, who were sacked by megaphone at Heathrow some time ago and who have got a lot of solidarity. There were one or two critical questions. One man said, 'You can't leave Iraq unless the new Iraqi Government asks you to go.' Then an Afghan got up and said, 'I'm from Afghanistan. Whatever you say about the Taliban, they wiped out opium, and the Americans now depend on the opium barons to hold control.' Very shrewd points. It was totally multinational and multicultural. It was a short meeting and I got away within an hour and a half, which isn't bad.

Friday 2 September
Of course the really big news is the Katrina hurricane in New Orleans and the southern United States. It is an absolute disaster! They now think 2,000 people have died. What's come out of it? Most of the people weeping, who are homeless with nowhere to go, no food, no water, are black, it might be an African country; could have been one of these international-development films showing African poverty. Secondly, of course, it's about class, because the wealthy, who are white, did manage to escape, but the blacks got left behind. Then it's about war and peace, because it turns out that Bush cut the resources for rebuilding the levees – that is to say, the sea walls – in order to use the money on the war and for tax cuts for the rich; and the National Guard, which is a sort of Territorial Army in every American state, have been sent to Iraq, and so lootings occurred, and the police have been given instructions to shoot to kill.

Bush has been on holiday until a couple of days after the disaster, and then apparently went and played golf somewhere, then flew over the site today and gave interviews, and he was just so unimpressive. I think it's going to have a huge effect on his standing. So anyway, that is a very interesting reflection of the world in which we live. It's not just about superpowers and poor countries; it's about rich people and poor people in rich countries and poor countries, because of course in some poor countries there are a lot of very rich people. Anyway, that's my reflection on that.

Sunday 4 September
Went to Burston for the Burston School Strike celebration.

It's an amazing story. In 1914, Tom Higdon and his wife Ann, sometimes known as Kitty, who were Christian Socialists, had moved into the village and were teachers at the school. He was active in the Agricultural Workers' Union, and of course at that time, before the First World War, the place was completely run by the landowners and by the rector. In a local government election Tom Higdon stood against the rector and won, and the rector came bottom of the poll. So, to cut a long story short, they used this as an excuse to sack Tom Higdon, and sixty-six children, aged thirteen, marched round the village to support him, and they set up their own Strike School, which lasted from 1914 to 1939. Tom Higdon died in 1939 and his wife in '46. I think I first went in 1972, and I've been several times. It was a beautiful day! It usually is a beautiful day at Burston, and there were about a thousand people – lots of people I knew.

We went round the village and I wasn't absolutely sure I could do it, but blow me down, there was a horse and cart, all decorated with flowers, and so the Chairman of the meeting, Janet Young, who's a T&G General Executive Council member, and the Cuban Embassy political counsellor, and myself, and one of the women from Gate Gourmet who was there, climbed on to the horse and cart and we went round the village.

Monday 5 September
Over the last couple of days, I've been trying to collect and analyse all the emails that came in as a result of my *Guardian* article, 'Bush is the real threat'. I had 122 emails within five days. Eighty-two of them were supportive, twenty-three made comments or supplementary points, and seventeen were hostile, including my favourite one from an American marine, who said, 'If I had the opportunity to rip your throat out, I'd certainly do it.'

Wednesday 7 September
I spent most of the day working on my first lecture at the Shaw Theatre on war and peace. I went over it again, redid my notes, built them up, corrected them and added to them, and I was a bit anxious because I didn't think anyone was going to come.

I went round the theatre and then I went into the dressing room. Josh came and sat with me. Anyway I gave my talk, which lasted about thirty-five minutes, was all right, and then there was a break, and I sat in the dressing room during the break, because I didn't want to go out and sign books then. I went back for the question-and-answer session in the second half.

The audience tomorrow is going to be about the same as today, about 200. So it will be over at the end of this week, but I was very anxious about it, I must admit.

Thursday 8 September

I completed my application form to attend the Labour Party Conference, and it's like an application for an ID card. They want your passport number, your National Insurance number, your driving-licence number, your car registration number, even if you're not driving to Conference, they want to know your date of birth, they want to know your nationality, they want to know if you've ever had another residence, and they tell you that it will all be given to the police. They then ask for your photograph to be countersigned by someone who has also seen all the particulars. Really, it's terrifying.

Friday 9 September

Massive thunderstorms! I mean, really buckets of water came down. The rain poured through the ceiling above the kitchen and the living room.

Josh took me to the Shaw Theatre for the second lecture. I got back about half-past eleven, absolutely exhausted! These lectures are taking a lot out of me. I think it's partly the preparation, partly the slight anxiety and partly the pressure of listening and answering questions, but that's the last one. About 700 have attended the last three, which isn't too bad.

Sunday 11 September

I think the really big news today is that – it's on all the Internet sites – the new policy paper has been prepared for the Pentagon saying that the United States would be ready to use nuclear weapons in a first strike, a first pre-emptive strike, in order to protect the United States from possible attack by terrorists or anybody else. So the final remnants of the Non-Proliferation Treaty have been completely blown out of the water. I don't know whether Blair would answer questions on it. He'd probably say he wouldn't answer, because you don't answer questions on nuclear weapons. It is a very important development, and it just shows the state the world's in. Derek Simpson made a speech today saying that Blair should go within an hour. It may be, with the election over, the Conference will be a little bit more interesting,

Monday 12 September, TUC Conference, Brighton

At the Stop the War meeting, in the Quality Hotel, Andrew Murray was in the chair; Tony Woodley made a wonderful speech; an Iraqi trade unionist spoke. Then me. Very good response. I did say how lovely it was to come to a Labour-movement conference where you weren't searched for socialist literature on your way in.

England has won the Ashes, so that's good news, and I might add that at the Conference everybody was watching the cricket! Nobody was watching the television of the Conference. So it shows the real English nature is sport rather than politics, but still I went round and teased them, and they were all watching the telly. I said, 'It must be a fascinating debate!'

Wednesday 14 September
I caught the Tube to *The Guardian* party at St Pancras Chambers, which is part of the old Victorian building at St Pancras mainline station. I'd never been in it before.

The Guardian had called the party to celebrate the publication of what they call the Berliner edition, the small edition of *The Guardian*, moving from the broadsheet format. There was loud music, which meant that a deaf person couldn't hear anything. I found it intolerable!

I saw Jon Snow, who was talking about being in New Orleans and how shattering the devastation was.

I saw Michael White, *The Guardian*'s Political Editor, and raised the question of the noise with him, and said, 'Shall I suggest we pull the plugs?'

He said, 'I rather agree.'

'Well,' I said, 'you pull them and blame me!'

I had a word with Alan Rusbridger, the Editor, thanked him very much for inviting me and said Melissa was sorry she couldn't come.

Then an old man came up to me, Sir Claus Moser, who had been the Government's Chief Statistical Officer. He said, 'I'll never forget, when I came round to see ministers, you came out of your office and waited for me until my lift came up.' It shows that little gestures like that do matter.

I saw Heseltine. I saw Cherie talking to somebody, so as I went by I just waved, and she moved her head towards me, so I gave her a kiss.

There was no smoking, I might add. I should have mentioned that there were a lot of guys in blue jeans and black shirts that said 'The Guardian' on it. I said to them as I left, 'Are you Securicor?' 'Oh no, no. We're a private security company called Red Carpet.' They'd all dressed up in *Guardian* outfits. It must have cost the earth!

Hattersley was there; Peter Hennessy was there; Helena Kennedy; although I didn't speak to any of them.

The thing I remember about the whole evening was that I said I liked the new format. 'It's the same size as the *Morning Star*,' I said, and do you know, four or five journalists I spoke to didn't even realise the *Morning Star* was still published! I thought that told you so much about *The Guardian*. 'Surely it can't be?' they said. 'We thought it had stopped.'

One hundred and fifty people were killed and I think 500 hurt in

Baghdad today in a massive suicide-bomb attack on workers queuing up for work with a contracting company.

Friday 16 September
Charles Clarke has announced that glorifying, celebrating or supporting terrorism becomes a criminal offence, and people can be held for three months without trial. Some Algerians have been deported back to Algeria. One of them was tortured when he was last there, and there's little doubt they'll be tortured this time. It is an absolutely autocratic, authoritarian, very right-wing government, and Blair goes along with it.

Saturday 17 September
Hilary had just come back from the UN World Summit, and apparently he addressed the General Assembly. Bush first, and then a few others, and then Hilary, because of course for six months Britain is President of the European Community, so he represents Europe on International Development issues.

He told me how he met Howard and discussed the Ashes and one or two other things.

I also heard from someone else that, when Bush was sitting there, he was writing a note to Condoleezza Rice and a camera caught it, and it said, 'Condie, could we have a bathroom break?' So he even has to ask his Secretary of State whether he can go to the loo!

Sunday 18 September
In the paper today Lance Price, whom I met when I was in France last year, has published his diary. Although the Cabinet Office made cuts, the *Daily Mail* had the right to serialise it and they published the cuts that he was told to make, and so we now know a lot more about Lance Price's view. Spin doctors have absolutely no loyalty to the people for whom they work. So having spent half his time bitterly attacking the media and anybody else who criticised Blair, he now launches an even bigger attack on Blair, saying that Blair got a bit of a thrill from committing troops to war. He felt he'd come into his own as a leader. Blair did agree that he would make all decisions about Europe in conjunction with Murdoch, which confirms what I've just described. Price comes out of it very badly, Blair comes out of it very badly, and that type of scandalous diary, which has no substance and is written by people who have no political authority of any kind, tells you about politics today.

Tuesday 20 September
The news today, and there was a bit about it last night, is this absolutely sensational story of two SAS officers who were sent in to Basra, one dressed as a Muslim cleric, the other as a civilian, and they were arrested by the

Iraqi police and put in prison. This news reached the British Government, or the military in Basra, so they sent tanks and a helicopter, and one of the tanks drove straight into the prison wall, broke it open, 150 prisoners escaped, and the Iraqis then handed over these two British prisoners. This led to a huge riot outside the prison. The tanks were set on fire with petrol bombs, and the people inside escaped with their lives. The Government simply said they were glad to rescue people. They didn't say what they were doing. But it told you that the Iraqi police now hate the British, and they're supposed to have been set up by the British to deal with the insurgency. So it's just an example.

I went through my programme. I've got forty-two speeches to make between now and the end of the year.

Wednesday 21 September
I had a letter from the Labour Party Conference Office saying they'd received my cheque for £82 and my application form, but they couldn't send me the pass yet because my security clearance hadn't come through.

Thursday 22 September
Hilary rang up today and said the Party had suggested I might like to sit at the front platform when he makes his speech on development on the Wednesday morning. I thought about it. It was a sweet idea, and I'm proud to be there; and then I considered further and thought, I'll be with the Cabinet members, and Neil Kinnock, and of course the camera will focus on me. If he makes a reference to Blair and everybody else claps, would I have to clap? Then at the end, Cherie Blair will come and give me a kiss, and all these people will crowd round to congratulate me. And so I rang Hilary up this evening, and I said, 'I think it would be better, old son, if I watched it from the gallery.' I think it would not be a good idea. I don't want to be photographed not clapping when he mentions Blair. I don't want to be congratulated by the Cabinet. I think actually all the people I speak for on the left would also feel it was the wrong thing to do. It's a bit painful.

Saturday 24 September
Got the Tube to Westminster and an Australian boy of about fourteen or fifteen offered me his seat. I was really grateful.

I sat on my portable chair outside the House of Commons, talked to some of the police and then marched to Trafalgar Square. Tariq Ali said, 'Why do you stay in the Labour Party?' Lots of people ask that. I mean, the short answer is that my membership of the Labour Party is absolutely minuscule. I do nothing in connection with the Labour Party, except speak at meetings. I don't go to local Labour Party meetings. I speak at trade-union meetings. I do vote on polling day. But my link with the Labour Party is just about that, once every five years. The rest of the time I'm a completely free agent. I'm not persuaded that Respect or the Socialist Party or the Socialist Workers' Party or the Communist Party of Britain or the Communist Party of Great Britain or the Socialist Party of Great Britain or the Scottish Socialist Party really is a substitute, and we've got to try and build Labour up again.

Sunday 25 September, Labour Party Conference, Brighton
Half an hour's walk to the Conference to pick up my pass. When I got there, it was another two and a half hours standing in the street.

Blair made a speech about the war, in which he said he'd been surprised by the strength of the opposition, but he was 'not going to be influenced by urban intellectuals who were against the war'. Well, I suppose he's an urban figure, but nobody would call him an intellectual. It was just such a crude, vulgar speech! Everybody knows what's going on and why, and he still denies that the bombing in London had anything to do with the invasion of Iraq.

Just to sum up the day, I really did wonder whether it was worth coming any more to the Conference. Of course in terms of age, I'm thirty years older than anyone of importance in the Party now, and I just find it so offensive. I don't want to break with the Party, because I know them and like them, but it is only one fraction, one-thousandth of my life.

Monday 26 September
Gordon Brown made a leadership speech. He stood there and spoke about Labour values, and child poverty and world poverty, and ended up on moral values as a son of the manse, as if somehow values and morality would, of themselves, be enough to change the world. I found it quite extraordinary!

Blair was sitting there, and Gordon just pounded away. It was his first speech as the next Prime Minister, and he got a good response, but he's utterly committed to New Labour. No question about it, it was a New Labour speech through and through, all the modernisation would continue, and so on. He was talking at us, not in a way of trying to persuade us, but telling us what he had decided, and to that extent very like Blair.

The only reason we have all this security is because Blair is down here. If Blair didn't come and just broadcast on a big-screen television, it would save £4 million in security costs and his fare from London! He doesn't want to meet us, doesn't want to listen to us; he just wants to address us, and he could do it quite as well from London on the big screen. It's not that I'm hostile to the Labour Party, because the people you meet are quite decent people, but they're not interested in politics. Even the delegates aren't particularly interested in politics. Of course a lot of lobbyists turn up and there are lots of stands, so it is really a trade fair, and it is an opportunity for ministers to address the people they regard as the faithful.

I was a bit late for the joint Labour Action for Peace-CND meting in the Royal Albion Hotel. Michael Meacher opened with a scholarly speech about Trident, and then Alice Mahon spoke – I'm very fond of her – and her successor, Linda Riordan, who's the new MP for Halifax, whom they tried to keep out of the seat as hard as they could. Then there was a brilliant Iraqi novelist and poet, who gave the most vivid account of what was happening. I chatted afterwards to the peace activist Walter Wolfgang, who must be over eighty. I first met him at the Conference in 1973.

Tuesday 27 September

Emily is spending the week at Conference with Nita. She seems to be at all the private parties. It is a memorable opportunity for her.

I went and bought a cup of tea, and then watched Tony Blair's speech. It was an absolute tour de force as a Leader, telling us that change had to come, we had to work with the change, New Labour was the only answer; and what was interesting about it was that it had no relation to the audience. We were just a captive audience. He mentioned Iraq, but we were not allowed to debate Iraq, so he was telling us what he'd decided about Iraq, and linked it to terrorism and democracy, and so on.

It confirmed my view that Blair has made the Labour Party, the Labour movement, irrelevant. He's used it as the first stage of the rocket to get him in space, and has been circuiting the Earth for eight years, since 1997, and our role is just to look up and admire the satellite.

Anyway, when he finished, I was sitting in a chair. I took the chair back to the bookshop from which I'd borrowed it, and then I walked to the lavatory, and I was just going into the Gents when my memory went; and when I woke up, I found I was on the floor with a bang on the back of my head and a lot of people looking at me, and I said, 'Where am I?'

They said, 'You're in Brighton.'

So it all came back to me, and I sat up. I had collapsed, or fainted.

They said, 'Would you like to stand?'

I said, 'I don't think so.' I was afraid of standing. I thought it would happen again.

So I sat on the ground. Nick Raynsford was there, very helpful. I gave him Stephen's mobile number, and Hilary's adviser's mobile number.

By then an ambulance people had turned up, and so they carried me on a stretcher to the ambulance and did some tests. Then they said, 'We're going to transfer you to the hospital.'

By this time I was quite able to think clearly, and I was gradually recovering from the shock. I was taken to what I think is the Royal Sussex County Hospital, where Hilary went when he was a nineteen-year-old student, having a kidney damage repaired for six weeks before he was married, so I had been to the hospital before. It's on the hill overlooking the Pavilion and the Brighton Dome.

I went into Accident & Emergency, and there were a lot of nice people there, and then I was moved up to a cardiac ward, with a curtain partition. There were about, I think, eight people on the ward, maybe ten.

When I was in the ambulance, who should I see looking down but Stephen and Hilary, who'd both got the message at the same time and had come straight over. So they were very sweet, and stayed with me in the hospital for a while. Stephen said he'd come back later, and he did, very late indeed, long after visiting hours.

I managed to get a message through to Melissa and to Josh and to Dave, and to everybody who mattered. Apparently it was on the news, so that was how my day ended, quite unexpectedly. I talked to the doctors about what might be done about it.

Wednesday 28 September

I woke up, and a senior consultant came. Then another guy who was a consultant, who called himself The Electrician, and he drew it all out and he said, 'The connection between your natural pacemaker in the heart is broken to the left ventricle.' So, to cut a long story short, he said, 'I think you need a pacemaker.'

So I said, 'What does that involve?'

'Well,' he said, 'we slit the chest and slip under your collarbone something about the size of a credit card, or a bit thicker and a bit longer, and that's connected to your heart directly by a cable, which is also under the skin, and we sew you up. But,' he said, 'you mustn't drive now, because this might happen when you're driving. You have a duty to tell the Vehicle Licensing Office.' So I will do that. 'But,' he said, 'if you've got a pacemaker, there's no particular problem, so you'll be able to drive again, probably about a week afterwards.'

So it was all very optimistic. They asked me about my experience, had this happened before; and you know, when I look back over the last few months, I had been feeling quite exceptionally tired, in a way I've never felt tired before, and also a bit breathless, and a bit of discomfort in my chest. This problem is really of an irregular heartbeat, and apparently my blood pressure is a little high.

The Brighton *Argus* had a picture of me on a stretcher, looking on my last legs, with an oxygen mask; in *The Independent* there was a little story, and in the *Telegraph* a tiny picture.

Of course that was my day, and I was moved to another ward, on the tenth floor, the Albion Ward, which is absolutely luxurious, and I realised within a few moments that it must be the private wing; and I felt really worried about being put in the private wing, but they said, 'Oh, we use it for paying patients or NHS patients.'

So anyway, I've got this beautiful room, I've got a bathroom and I've got one of these things you put a card in, and for a £10 card you can use the phone and television.

I discovered there was a place where I could stand and smoke. It was actually just outside the entrance of the hospital. It was a bit chilly, so when I go down tomorrow I'm going to put on some warmer clothes and take my stool and sit there and have a puff, because I have missed my pipe.

Of course the big news today – forget all that – is that Hilary made his speech, and apparently a very good speech, a ten-minute speech, he got a warm reception.

Stephen was over in the morning, and Hilary popped in after his speech and said the Prime Minister had sent his best wishes, and so had John Reid and Charles Clarke. He gave me a whole list of people. I've been getting all sorts of flowers. Sanjiv Shah and Joe McGowan from America sent some flowers, even the Algerian Ambassador had sent flowers. It's all really rather friendly. I don't want to cancel the Cheltenham Festival, but I've just got to play it by ear.

This afternoon – this is still Wednesday – Ruth came down from London, bless her heart, and stayed for an hour or so. She's going to come back on Saturday and take me back to London, and will stay on Saturday and Sunday night, so that I won't be alone on my first two nights in the house, and I will wear my emergency button from now on.

Josh and Lissie are coming tomorrow. I spoke to Dave several times.

I believe the Conference passed a resolution against privatisation, which will be ignored. Gate Gourmet settled on the offer that was made, because I suppose they didn't have a choice.

I heard that Walter Wolfgang, who's eighty-two, shouted during Blair's speech and was violently thrown out of the Conference by the stewards. Really badly handled. But there you are, that is the new strong-armed Labour Party, and I heard a rumour – I don't know if it's true – that he was to be charged under the Terrorism Act for interrupting the Prime Minister.

Thursday 29 September
Walter Wolfgang was actually ejected for shouting 'Nonsense!' during Jack Straw's speech, and a young delegate, who is the chairman of a local party, sitting near him was ejected for protesting at the way that Walter was being treated, and he's become the hero of the Conference. There are pictures of him being ejected and he went, last night, to the meeting which I was to have spoken at, and of course was treated as the hero of the day, quite properly. Somehow, it confirmed what people think about the Labour Party.

I had a card from Tony Blair this morning, which arrived on the ward, in his own hand, a beautiful card with a picture of Downing Street: 'Dear Tony, I hope you are well, and that my comment to you in my speech wasn't a problem. Yours, Tony.' And yesterday I had flowers from Cherie

Blair, which I haven't done anything about yet, because you're not allowed to have flowers in the ward.

Friday 30 September

Just before nine I was taken down to the operating theatre. Masses of equipment, terribly complex computers and screens and all sorts of things, and I was put on a trolley, and Dr O'Noonan gave me a local anaesthetic and I was sedated, I think; and I lay there, and for a couple of hours they opened me up and put the pacemaker in, and then I was taken upstairs, and I had the rest of the day really rather quietly.

Saturday 1 October

Ruth arrived, quite early, and packed up, and I said goodbye to everybody. Josh had taken my heavy stuff back. Ruth put me in a taxi and we got to the station. Indeed, we left the hospital just after ten, and got home in a taxi from Victoria just before twelve – less than two hours.

Monday 3 October

I am beginning to appreciate that this is a new era. I am not only old, but I now have a complaint. Everyone has a complaint, and mine is a pacemaker and a heart condition of a kind. I've got to pull back from too many engagements.

Tuesday 4 October

The news tonight is about the Tory Conference, where all the leadership candidates are speaking. David Cameron, this thirty-eight-year-old former Etonian, who got elected in 2001, has put himself forward; he made a speech and got a standing ovation.

Then Ken Clarke got up, and he did his usual stuff: 'I'm a big beast, and I'll beat Gordon Brown', and so on, and he got a good cheer. But I must say, if I were a Tory, I wouldn't go for an old hat like Ken Clarke, who, having been defeated twice for the leadership, never took any interest in politics; he was only interested in the Prime Minister's job.

Wednesday 5 October

David Davis spoke at the Tory Conference today. You see, what's really interesting about the Conference is that none of these leaders have said anything about the environment, about democracy, about the war, about global warming, about pensions, about anything! They're just presenting themselves as being the best Leader to bring the Tories back to power, which of course is the way Blair carried it off.

Friday 7 October

A good night's sleep, feeling better.

The headlines today: 'Bush says that God told him to invade Iraq.' Apparently Bush said it to Mahmoud Abbas, the Palestinian leader. It hasn't been denied, as far as I know. It makes him out to be a mad, extremely fundamentalist Christian, who is a great threat to the world.

One interesting thing today about the Hatfield rail crash: there's no provision in British law for corporate manslaughter, which means that the individuals in charge of companies that ignore health and safety cannot be punished. Balfour Beatty, who absolutely failed to do proper maintenance, who ordered replacement rails that were never installed, were fined £10 million, and Network Rail, which is a public company, was fined £3.5 million, all of which will come out of the taxpayers' money. Then after Hatfield, Balfour Beatty got another contract for £130 million to continue track maintenance! So privatisation is being shown for what it is: a complete fraud. For the first time, they showed pictures of the Tory ministers at the time of privatisation, during the process of privatisation, and outsourcing and sub-contracting, and no clear management control of the railways. The argument about renationalisation we're winning, but Blair will take no notice of it.

Sunday 9 October–Monday 10 October, Cheltenham Festival
David Cameron has shot to the head as a potential Leader of the Tory Party.

Was picked up at nine o'clock to go to the Cheltenham Literary Festival, where Emma Mitchell was waiting, and my first session was with Geoffrey Robertson, QC on the subject of dissent. It was really a discussion on his book on John Cook, the lawyer who prosecuted the King in 1649 for crimes, and then was himself hanged, drawn and quartered, and disembowelled and his genitals thrown to dogs, after the Restoration. I've met Geoffrey Robertson before. He's an Australian, I believe. One of the things I differ with him about is that he thinks the law has an answer to every problem, whereas I think it's political. I think you've got to have the right law and the right constitution, but making it real means political pressure.

I had a bite to eat with Emma; I was so tired. I came up to my room, watched Rory Bremner. I was actually a bit frightened, because I was a bit breathless.

I woke at 4.30 in the morning, slept fitfully till eight, having lots of nightmares.

Walked to the Festival. Got lost on the way, asked for directions and a former GCHQ (Government Communications Headquarters) man took me part of the way, which was nice of him. I said, 'What do you do?'

He said, 'This is a company town.'

So I said, 'You mean you're at GCHQ?' and he nodded. I said, 'Well, information is the key to everything.'

'Yes, it is,' he said.

'Well, Iraq proves that.'

'Yes, but they should have learned from the past, when we controlled Iraq and the RAF bombed them into submission.'

So that told me a lot about him and GCHQ.

Anyway, I went to the tent, signed all my stock of books – masses of them – and I think they're doing very well.

Then I went to hear Tony Howard introduce his book on Cardinal Hume, the cardinal monk.

Then I went back to the Writers' Room there, where I met Lloyd George's great-grandson, and Professor David Reynolds, who made the programme *The Improbable Mr Attlee*. I told Lloyd George's great-grandson that I'd met his great-grandfather, and told him one or two stories about him.

In the afternoon I did a second session on freedom, with Tony Howard.

It was an interesting discussion, about Parliament and what had happened to it, and about apathy and democracy and presidential governments. It was packed, just as it was yesterday, 900 people. I found myself in more agreement with Howard, or rather he more in agreement with me, than I'd have expected.

Then I was driven home in a non-smoking car. Got home about 9.45.

Monday 10 October

Angela Merkel has become Chancellor of Germany; she's retained eight SPD ministers, including Fischer, the Foreign Minister, the Minister of Labour, and so on. I don't know what Schröder is going to do, but a black/red coalition is the end of choice in democracy in Germany – a product of proportional representation.

Tuesday 11 October

Tam Dalyell rang. He asked how I was, that was his main concern; but I discussed with him something of this story that a Scottish police officer has put in a report that the American intelligence people who visited the Lockerbie site planted an electrical circuit there, which gave the impression that it was a terrorist incident. The Scottish Criminal Cases Review Commission is quite likely to come out and acquit this guy who was charged with the Lockerbie murders, but, said Tam, 'The way they'll get round it is to send him to prison in Libya', and of course the Commission cannot make a judgement of somebody not in British custody. What Gaddafi will do, I don't know.

Wednesday 12 October

I went to the Campaign Group, which David Blunkett was addressing, about welfare reform. I felt I ought to go just to show I'm still alive – and people were very friendly. When we were asked to introduce ourselves, all the MPs went round the table and I said, 'Retired on benefit.' When Blunkett spoke, he said, 'Everybody gets old, except of course Tony Benn!'

I walked across at six o'clock to the Central Hall Westminster for a meeting, organised by Ken Livingstone, against the terrorism bill, which was published today. Ken was there, and all sorts of people whom I didn't know, people from the Muslim Association; the Bishop of Coventry, with whom I had a brief word.

The meeting started late; I was put on about ten past seven, and spoke for five minutes and fifteen seconds, and I must say it went down well. I had prepared carefully. I told the story of London, and said I was born in London, was proud of London, that many of the great fights for civil liberties had occurred in London.

Friday 14 October
The High Court has overturned the Home Secretary's decision to deport Zimbabweans back to Zimbabwe, where they claim their lives are at risk – a wonderful legal decision!

I found a very good article on the Internet, about the growth of the skilled workforce by one and a half billion people as a result of China and India developing. With a limited amount of capital, and a growing number of workers, of course wages will be depressed worldwide. It pointed out that in 2010, that's in five years' time, China will produce more graduate scientists and engineers than America. The world is changing so rapidly, but the imbalance between capital and labour does mean that there's going to be a lot of opposition if wages are driven down. I sent a copy of that to Hilary.

Saturday 15 October
At 10.45 Iranian Radio rang, and I did a twenty-five minute interview about Condoleezza Rice's visit round the world, and the hyping up by Bush and Blair of the pressure against Iran. This is something that could potentially lead to a military strike by Israel or America next summer. UN weapons inspector Scott Ritter believes it's likely next summer.

Sunday 16 October
One of the papers commented today, 'We are heading for the Dark Ages again.' There are all these economic anxieties. The average American employee has $350,000 as a share of the national debt, and 20 per cent of all expenditure in America is on borrowing. If the American economy were to have a hiccup because of the cost of the war, the cost of tax cuts, the cost of the hurricane, and so on, then the Chinese economy would be in difficulties, because China lives on its orders from America. If the dollar began falling, the Chinese would have to sell their dollar reserves and that

would pitch the United States into a 1929 situation. I worry about what's happening, and I look around the world and see all the ghastly events. My confidence that, if you vote for the right person and get the right policy, it will all come right is somewhat shaken.

Tuesday 18 October
I think I had the worst night ever for coughing. I coughed and coughed and coughed, and got up and coughed; and brought some lemon juice and honey and drank it, and coughed; and had cough medicine, and coughed. I felt simply lousy! I stayed in bed all morning, which is a thing I don't normally do.

At 5.30 the result of the Tory leadership first round was announced. Ken Clarke came bottom, and I'm not surprised, so he was knocked out. Liam Fox came a little bit above him, with forty-two, Davis came top, with sixty-two, and Cameron second, so it looked to me as if almost certainly all the Clarke votes will go to Cameron, and he will probably end up in the ballot with David Davis. The Tories are desperately looking for a completely new start, to get away from Thatcher.

When Blair goes, of course it will be a whole new era. Any doubts I had about the role of the old in contemporary politics were settled by Ken Clarke, aged sixty-five, who is seen as being too old to be a Leader. From their point of view, I think they're wise not to have chosen him. Maybe this guy Cameron, whom I've never even met – he was elected after I left Parliament, four years ago – will become Leader.

Wednesday 19 October
There's another email today from a Chinese economist, repeating the view that the American economy is in a ghastly mess. These are massive problems, and when I see the three Tory candidates – Cameron, Davis and Fox – talking on the telly in a cosy way, I just wonder whether any of them have turned their mind to these problems.

Saddam Hussein is on trial, and I saw him in the court room in Baghdad on television. It's funny, because of course I spent about five hours with that man, one way and the other, in 1990 and 2003. He's a lawyer, a clever guy, and he said, 'I'm the President of Iraq. This is an illegal court.' The judge, who looked very young and wasn't dressed up in the usual finery of a judge, seemed rather relaxed with him. They'll hang him, in public I should think, in a few weeks' time.

My doubts about war crimes, and tribunals, have deepened to the point where I don't agree with them. Truth and Reconciliation are far preferable. Have the trial if you like, bring it all out, give Saddam a chance to explain, to apologise if he wants to, but execution is brutal and is a big public act of revenge, and also it makes him a martyr.

STOP THE WAR CAMPAIGN

With David Gentleman
(*above left*); convener of the STW
Movement, Lindsey German
(*above right*); Respect MP George
Galloway (*left*); Mayor of
London, Ken Livingstone (*below*)

THEATRES OF PEACE
2003-07

In Trafalgar Square
(*above left*); two million
march from Hyde Park
(*above right*); the Left
Field at Glastonbury
(*left*); lecture tour
(*below*)

(*Left*) Against Blair's war in London;
(*below*) on the streets of New York

(*Above*) The Price of War: over half a million dead

(*Right*) The Doves of Peace: in honour of Vanunu

Family tree at Christmas (left to right): back row: Daniel, Jonathan, Roger, Nahal, Michael, William, Melissa, Emily, Caroline, Hilary, Ruth. Front row: Nita, Sally, Stephen, Nasrin, James, TB, Josh, Peter (PC), Paul. Sitting on floor: Hannah and Sarah

Family value:
Josh, Stephen
Hilary and Melissa

...at Tolpuddle

...in my office

...making a point

The plaque on our family house

BORN CINCINNATI USA 1926
CAROLINE
DeCAMP
BENN
AUTHOR TEACHER
AND SOCIALIST
LIVED AND
WORKED HERE
1952-2000
DIED LONDON 2000

No smoking, no flying!

Time out with David Davis (*left*)
and Rory Bremner

TB and friends: (*left*) Strictly Not Dancing
with Natasha Kaplinsky; (*middle left*)
my editor, Ruth Winstone; (*bottom left*)
sharing a joke with Saffron Burrows;
(*bottom right*) Jemma Redgrave and
Benjamin Zephaniah; (*below*) brother Dave
and his wife, June, looking thoughtful

Benn family at Stansgate, including David and June Benn, their son Piers (back row, standing fifth from right); their daughter Frances (seated next to TB); Frances's husband Michael Nestor (standing next to Melissa); and little Michael Nestor (sitting, right)

Thursday 20 October

A madman rang me at twenty-past two in the morning! He rang about four or five days ago, and then the following day left a message. This morning I was really bloody angry. If he does it again, I'm going to have to get the police to intervene.

Watched the television result of the last round of the Tory leadership contest. Cameron came top with ninety, David Davis had dropped from sixty-two to fifty-seven, and Fox dropped out with fifty-one. The Tory members in the country will have the final vote, and I think they'll certainly go for Cameron.

Kate Silverton, of BBC News 24, rang and asked me to the Foreign Press Association for a reception for the launch of a book by James Landale, the BBC's Chief Political Correspondent. As I had nothing to do I put on a smart suit, got a cab and met James and his parents and one or two Tory MPs. Then Kate turned up, and after a while we went to the House of Commons, to meet Abdel Bari Atwan, the Editor-in-Chief of *Al-Quds Al Arabi*, a Palestinian paper. Apparently he was on television with me the night in 1991 when the Americans bombed Baghdad and they tried to get me to leave the studio and I refused to go. They were just talking about how Baghdad was 'lit up like the Fourth of July', and I was so angry. I said, 'We're watching people being killed!' So then the producer came and said, 'Thank you for your contribution. Will you leave the studio?' I said, 'No, I won't!'

We got on well together. Bari Atwan said to me that he'd had a message from Saddam Hussein's lawyer, that Saddam had asked after me and George Galloway, which is something I don't know if I want to publicise much!

I came home, and I found a phone message from Hilary, from Islamabad where an earthquake has struck:

Hello, Dad. It's H. calling . . . Just to say that I got to Kashmir and back safely by helicopter.

. . . It's a real race against time to make sure that people have sufficient warmth and shelter to keep them through the harsh winter that's on its way; it will be here in just under a month.

Also saw President Musharraf and the Prime Minister. It's astonishing how people live, on the top of the hillside, little hamlets, individual houses clinging to the mountains. Stunningly beautiful, and awful devastation.

Anyway, just wanted to ring and let you know I'm safe and well, and I'm getting up very early tomorrow morning to fly back, and I'll be home sort of early afternoon. Anyway, I hope you're well. Take care.

I had an email from someone saying, 'I have to tell you that I travelled on the train with your father back from Bristol the other day, and he

coughed, didn't seem well at all. Please make sure you look after him.'
[Laughing] So there you are, you're getting medical attention on the
train from strangers!

Anyway, speak to you soon.

All the best. Bye!

A parrot has caught avian flu in quarantine in Britain.

Saturday 22 October

One of the most interesting news items was that Elizabeth Manningham-
Buller, the head of MI5, made it clear that evidence that had been obtained
by torture was acceptable (in court). That is to say, if people have been
tortured abroad, the evidence will be used at home in the UK. It's another
line that's been crossed.

There was a poll asking the public whether they would prefer David
Cameron or Gordon Brown to be Prime Minister, and the answer was
Cameron, by quite a substantial margin. When we come to the next
election, if the world economy is going down, which would hit Gordon
Brown's record at the Treasury, and if Blair leaves it so late that Brown
can't establish himself, it's quite likely that the media – and Murdoch in
particular – will decide it's time for a change and they will shift to Cameron.
That will be the final punishment imposed on the Labour Party by New
Labour and Blair.

Sunday 23 October

Bird flu has arrived via that parrot, and Patricia Hewitt, the Secretary for
Health, said that a pandemic was inevitable – it was a question of when,
and not if. The Chief Medical Officer had said 50,000 people would die in
Britain, at a minimum. So it could be it'll polish me off, in which case I'm
making a first advance warning of my own demise. I've got such a horrible
cold now that I've probably got one sort of flu, and so shall be vulnerable
to another.

Friday 28 October

The Iranian President has repeated what he said about Israel being wiped
off the face of the map. It's a horrific thing to say, although I think he
probably represents the majority view of the Iranians, but of course
Palestine has already been wiped off the face of the map because there is no
state in the world called Palestine. The Israelis and Americans contributed
to keeping it off the world map, apart from recognising the Palestinian
Authority, which has *no* authority. All the Arab states have got leaders who
are so gutless under American pressure. I just feel now the thing is on the
point of an explosion on a massive scale. Bush is so weak, that might
encourage him to bomb Iran and get support for that, but I think it's more

likely that Israel will bomb Iran, and Bush will then veto any criticism of Israel.

Sunday 30 October
Drafted replies to all my letters and emails, had lunch and a snooze, and then I watched *Dr Strangelove* on DVD, because I've got to discuss it next week in a TV programme. The first time I saw it was at the opening night, with Julie Andrews next to me. That would be about 1964. Although it is a comedy, it is terribly frightening, because it's so like today: the two mad American generals who think that communists are poisoning our body fluids, and so they launch a nuclear attack on Russia. Although there were funny bits in it, such as when the President of the United States phones the General Secretary of the Soviet Communist Party to explain there'd been a mistake – it is actually, for all that, a frightening film. Peter Sellers is brilliant. He plays the American President, he plays Dr Strangelove, the German scientist, and he also plays an RAF Group Captain.

Wednesday 2 November
David Blunkett has resigned after some conflict of financial interest. He went to the Foreign Press Association and gave an uncompromising press conference, saying he'd only made a minor mistake, but he felt he should go.

My mobile phone rang and it was the BBC, who asked: 'We understand your son has been appointed Minister for Work and Pensions to replace Blunkett. Is it true?' I didn't know whether it was, so I went to the House, to the Tea Room, arranged to see Hilary and we had a lovely hour's talk.

He didn't know whether he was going to be Minister for Work and Pensions, and indeed I was congratulated by a Labour MP who heard the rumour. In the event, it was given to John Hutton.

I heard at the Campaign Group that any demonstration outside a nuclear site would be covered by the terrorism bill, even if the gates of a site are locked. If you demonstrate outside the locked gates, you'd still be guilty. Terrifying!

Friday 4 November
David Shayler, the former MI5 officer, spoke at a Stop the War meeting in Hammersmith this evening. He was the first speaker, and he devoted himself entirely to trying to establish that 9/11 was a fraud – the buildings would never have collapsed, the Pentagon was penetrated probably by a bunker-busting bomb, not by an aeroplane. The trouble about the security services is that they live completely in a conspiratorial atmosphere. I don't know that it registers much with the public. Probably, in their heart of hearts, most people think the attack was genuine, but I don't rule anything out.

I saw Natasha Kaplinsky for the first time presenting the Six O'Clock News on her own, so it ups her in the world of news and current affairs.

Saturday 5 November

To St James's, Piccadilly, for the Musicians Against Nuclear Arms concert, organised by Joan Horrocks. It's a lovely church. I got there a little bit early, and sat outside and puffed my pipe. It is a great event, I must say. The conductor was Paul Watkins. There was a Rossini overture and then Mozart's Sinfonia Concertante, and then in the interval I spoke. Then there was a Baermann Adagio for Clarinet and Strings and Beethoven's Fourth Symphony. I don't know anything about music, but I did sit in the pew and watched the orchestra. Some ladies looked well into their seventies, and the youngest ones there may have been in their twenties. Joan Horrocks is a remarkable woman. I stayed afterwards and talked to one or two friends.

Sunday 6 November

I am gradually losing the Protestant work ethic. I felt so relaxed last night that I pulled out the VHS of the film *Notting Hill*, which I really like. I saw it first with Caroline in America in 1999, and I've seen it many times since. I took my tea up in a thermos, sat by the TV, turned the fire on and I watched it till 1 a.m. I went to bed before it was over, because I wanted to leave a bit for tonight. I spoke to Josh about it later, and I have no guilt at all about having a little bit of relaxation on a Sunday.

Read the Sunday papers – the Paris riots are quite significant, because they could happen in Britain and there was a touch of it in Birmingham the other day.

Monday 7 November

The French riots have now spread all over France, and it's obviously a really serious situation. Modernisation means cutting the Welfare State and adopting neo-conservative, liberal economic policies, and that hurts people, and many of them are of course low-paid immigrants. Modernising the poor out of existence just won't work, and it will be interesting to see whether the Establishment realises it in time and makes concessions or turns to repression.

From twelve to one Blair was addressing a press conference. I must say, the press are all that really matter to him. He knows all the journalists by name, and they can put any questions. It would be much better if, on Wednesdays in the House of Commons, anyone could ask the Prime Minister anything! The difference between the media and Parliament is so obvious.

Anyway, Blair was determined to have the ninety days' detention included in the terrorism legislation, said we had to obey the police – those who were against it were totally irresponsible. He was against a compromise. He's getting a bit manic now. After all, he did the same two and a half years ago about weapons of mass destruction – the security services had told him . . . we must consider the security of the nation. It is the police state being brought in through fear.

Tuesday 8 November
Walked to Westminster Abbey from the Tube for Ted Heath's memorial service. There were security barriers outside the Abbey, and just as I was about to go in, I remembered I had a pacemaker, so the policeman whisked me through. The whole British Establishment was there. I was sitting with a mass of Tory MPs and civil servants and military people, and I think some relatives in the front. David Cameron was in the very front row, Iain Duncan Smith was just behind me, and behind him was William Hague, sitting next to Ken Clarke. Coming in, I saw Merlyn Rees in a wheelchair. But otherwise I didn't see any other Labour MPs there, or any other Labour people, but I suppose Tony Blair must have been there. I'd hoped to see Major, but I didn't. I guess that Mrs Thatcher was there. The Queen didn't come, funnily enough; she was represented by the Duke of Kent. The Duke of Edinburgh was there, and the former Archbishop of Canterbury, George Carey, in his clerical garb, walking next to Cardinal Cormac Murphy-O'Connor, the Archbishop of Westminster. There was lovely music – that would have pleased Ted. I didn't hear very well I'm afraid, even with my hearing aid, because the acoustics weren't good.

I think probably I was one of the rarities there, but I'm glad I went, because I was fond of Ted, and he had integrity, which is more than you can say for the present occupant of Number 10.

Wednesday 9 November
This morning, reading the *Morning Star*, there was an article about Palestine and Israel, and I thought the time had come really to rethink my whole position on Israel. I went along with it, of course. My mum was always keen on a home for the Jews, and the Holocaust and all that, and so, with her influence, I supported it – not only supported it, but I went, was invited by the Israelis to come and give the Balfour Day Lecture, and I visited a kibbutz. It would be an admission of a mistake, but that isn't so important as getting it right.

I drove to the House of Commons and in the corridor, just outside the Library, I saw David Davis. He's coming up in the polls. I think his debate on television with David Cameron did him some good, and he's always been very friendly to me. I haven't spoken to him for ages, but he was conscious of that. I said I'd listened to the television debate, which I thought was extremely good, particularly their views on Europe.

Then he said, 'Now, this evening, we're voting against Labour fascism.' That was his view of the ninety days issue, so that was interesting!

I went up to the Tea Room afterwards and discovered that the Government had been defeated on the proposal for ninety days' detention without charge by 291 to 322; and subsequently, by a rather larger majority, the twenty-eight-day period was agreed. It later turned out that forty-nine Labour MPs had voted against the Government on this, and fifteen had abstained, so it was absolutely decisive. Heard Blair on the radio saying, 'I don't understand how Labour MPs could have voted against the ninety days', and of course it's true, he didn't understand. He doesn't understand anything – he doesn't listen to anybody!

I don't say it's the end for him, but it has done enormous damage, and with education and other things coming forward next year, the situation is much shakier for him. I think by next summer we shall see the end of Blair.

Thursday 10 November
Everyone is assuming that it must be the first nail in Blair's coffin, and Blair of course is totally overconfident, and says the Cabinet's united. Charles Clarke, who was overridden by Blair because he'd offered a compromise, which Blair rejected, said they were all united. It's completely phoney, but still. Blair just goes on as if, you know, a defeat in Parliament doesn't matter.

Friday 11 November
The *PM* programme, at the very end, broadcast short comments on what people thought during the two-minute silence. Mine was only twenty seconds, just saying Mike had been killed and quoting from one of his letters to me, sixty-one years after he died: 'We must never have children killed, as they are every night.' I think Dave will be pleased, and I know my mum and dad would.

Sunday 13 November
Went to the chapel of New College, Oxford, and met the Reverend Canon Jane Shaw, the Dean of Divinity. There was the service, evensong, and then I preached on peace. I was told no more than ten minutes, so I made it seven and a half.

There was no response at all to my sermon, which was quite reasonable – it was about the danger of war and religious war. It was all candlelit, so I couldn't really see the congregation, but apart from one man who came up and said how much he'd appreciated it, and a woman whose grandfather had been a Yorkshire miner, otherwise there was no comment at all. I don't know whether it was a bad sermon or not.

Afterwards we had dinner in the hall. I sat at the high table, in the hall where I used to sit when I was a student, sixty-three years ago.

Friday 18 November

At five o'clock Tina Brown, the wife of Harry Evans, came to see me for a book she's writing on the monarchy. I'd sent her an email saying I'm not prepared to discuss the royal family, but she did ask a little bit about Diana, and so on. We talked about Blair, and Bush, and Hilary Clinton's prospects for the presidency, and about Murdoch, whom she loathes, and David Cameron, who has strong neo-conservative advisers, she said. Murdoch would certainly support him, though she found him very shallow. She was interested in my views on the media. She said, 'You must come and have lunch with Harry and myself.' Harry is seventy-seven and she's fifty-three.

I began by saying, 'I see your dad made a film with my cousin.' (Her father was the producer George Hambley Brown.)

She said, 'Who's that?'

'Margaret Rutherford.'

'Oh, Margaret Rutherford used to come and see us often.' So that was a good start, and as I'd discovered her birthday by looking her up, as she left I said, 'Have a happy birthday on Monday' and she was quite touched I think by that. She wasn't aggressive, she wasn't tough, she wasn't too grand. She arrived in a limousine, of course. I quite enjoyed meeting her, I must say.

Monday 21 November

I was so cold in the evening that my hand was shaking with cold, and trying to drink my soup, the spoon was wobbling all over the place as if I had Parkinson's disease. So I put the electric blanket on, put on the fire in the bedroom, and I'm going up to bed now. Thinking a lot about Caroline, because it was five years ago tomorrow she died, and there's not a day, not an hour, goes by when I don't think of her. On Saturday Melissa and Fiona Millar are jointly giving the Caroline Benn Memorial Lecture.

Tuesday 22 November

I had a phone call from the Arabic television channel Al Jazeera, drawing my attention to a *Daily Mirror* story. Apparently, President Bush suggested to Blair last year that the US might bomb Al Jazeera's offices in Doha in the emirate of Qatar – and Blair apparently discouraged him. What's interesting about it is, first of all, it's likely to be true; secondly, this was in a document which was leaked by a civil servant to the researcher of a former Labour MP; the latter handed it back to the Government. We don't know exactly what's in it, but those two people are now being charged under the Official Secrets Act.

Lissie arrived, and then a few minutes afterwards Stephen. So I had got lunch for them, a light lunch, soup and sandwiches and strawberries. We just had a family talk, all about Mum. It was lovely!

Wednesday 23 November

I dressed up very smartly because I was going to appear before the Lords' Constitutional Committee about the royal prerogative powers. I was on a panel with Lord Lester, Clare Short, Neil Gerrard, who'd introduced a bill on war-making powers. We each were invited to speak, and then the rest of it was discussion. It was interesting. Lord Holme of Cheltenham, who's a Liberal Democrat, was in the chair. There were questions from Ted Rowlands, a former Labour MP for Merthyr Tydfil, who has now just been made a lord; from Lord Bledisloe and Lord Elton, two Tory peers, both of whose fathers or grandfathers had voted against me in the House of Lords on the question of renouncing my peerage in 1955; and from Lord Carter, who was previously Government Chief Whip. There were a few others there.

This whole winter-fuel crisis could be an absolute *coup de grâce* for Blair, because you know, he talks about security all the time. Well, security means many things: it means security against invasion, security of health, and all that, but it also means security of energy supplies. But of course everything's privatised: gas is privatised, electricity is privatised, power stations are privatised, nuclear is privatised, I think. So he's got no control of anything. Labour hasn't got an energy policy!

The BBC reported that the Attorney General is threatening prosecution against anybody who publishes the memorandum summarised in the *Daily Mirror* yesterday, that Bush wanted to bomb Al Jazeera, and the rumour is going round that the Government is frightened because Bush is hopping mad that his proposal to bomb Al Jazeera should have been leaked in Britain. I suppose all governments end in failure, and this one is certainly showing that it's not going to be left behind.

Saturday 26 November

To the Institute of Education for the fifth Caroline Benn Memorial Lecture. There were two speeches, one by Melissa, and one by Fiona Millar, who's the partner of Alastair Campbell. I took my little video camera, and I filmed the whole of Melissa and a little bit of Fiona. It came across terribly well.

Wednesday 30 November

My computer crashed today. It was humming and interfering with an interview, so I turned it off. When I switched it back on, it went berserk, the screen said it was in 'safe mode' and wouldn't do anything. I was suicidal – I can't tell you! I realised that the hard disk contained all my documents going back to 1997, when I bought it; I couldn't recover anything, couldn't print anything, couldn't work on my lecture to the British Library, which has got to be done for Monday. It was like a bereavement. I was just desperate. So I rang Josh. He thought the hard disk was virtually defunct.

Anyway, he came over and copied all the things from the hard disk onto floppies so that I would always be able to find them. He transferred them all onto my laptop so that I can find them there. He installed WordPerfect on my laptop. Then he changed the setting on my broken computer so that it goes straight to WordPerfect instead of going through Microsoft Word, and it all came right. I mean, the guy is an absolute genius. The most precious thing you can do for anybody is give them your time and your expertise. I was so touched.

Saturday 3 December
Caught the Central Line and the Piccadilly Line Tube to King's Cross, for a 'Hands off Venezuela' conference. Jeremy Corbyn was there; he is such a brilliant man, he's known Latin America for thirty years. I had worked quite hard on my speech, because I've never made a speech on Latin America before. I dug out the American policy towards Latin America, way back from the Monroe Doctrine, through the Manifest Destiny, the Big Stick Policy, the Cold War, and now the Project for the New American Century, and then I did a comparison of different types of socialism: in the Soviet Union, where dictatorship of the proletariat failed because it didn't have consent; in China, where capitalism is being introduced under the Chinese Communist Party leadership; and then in Cuba, which fought and won. Then how social democracy sold out completely to market forces, and how Venezuela was actually carrying through a revolution by consent.

When I read about the achievements of Venezuela, I did think how close it was to what we were trying to do, even twenty years ago, in the Labour Party – cooperatives, state control of industry, and so on. So it gave me a bit of a boost, and that was my theme: that we owed a lot to them.

There was a woman there from the Posadists, the most weird group of people.

Tuesday 6 December
After lunch Walter Wolfgang arrived with Mentorn TV, who are giving him a half-hour programme, after he shouted 'Nonsense!' at the Labour Party Conference and was interrogated by the police under Section 44 of the Terrorism Act. We talked about democracy in the Labour Party, about terrorism legislation, about civil liberties, about CND. He's an old friend of mine. I've known him for years. I was so pleased to see him given a chance, and he's really enjoying it.

David Cameron's election as Leader of the Conservatives is the end of an era, because the Murdoch press will transfer its allegiance from New Labour to Cameron, and Gordon Brown had to present, in his economic forecast yesterday, a rather gloomy picture of the economy, with increased taxation on oil companies. I think it's not impossible that when Blair finally goes, they will be looking for a new younger leader to rival Cameron.

When Walter had gone, Nicholas Wood arrived. Nicholas is, I should think, in his late sixties, early seventies. He's an architect. He worked in Iraq, loves Iraq, and he has worked like a beaver preparing a request to Kofi Annan, with a copy to the Attorney General, for an inquiry into twenty-one breaches of international law committed by the coalition forces in Iraq. He did all the work, he looked up all the names, he wrote to all the people, and he's got about sixty names, I think, so far. Harold Pinter, Bruce Kent, Andreas Whittam Smith have signed it.

Wednesday 7 December
Melissa rang and said that Sarah wanted my comments on the origin of the universe. So I spoke to her on the phone, said we didn't really know where we were before we were born, or where we'd go, but we were part of the universe and we had to respect all the animals in the universe. She said, 'That's fine, Dan-Dan.' I said that the alternative view, which her other grandmother, Wilma Gordon, believed, was 'that God made everything'. I said I didn't want to disagree with that, but if God made the universe, who made God? She said, 'I thought of that myself.' She is a clever little girl!

I put stamps on my domestic Christmas cards, and removed Jim Callaghan and Ted Heath from the list. Mrs Thatcher is ill today.

Today was the first exchange between Cameron and Blair. Cameron began by saying he promised to support the Prime Minister in his education policy, a clever thing to do, because it infuriated the Labour backbenchers. Then another question on climate change. Then, when Hilary Armstrong, our Chief Whip, heckled him, Cameron said, 'She's behaving like a child.'

Friday 9 December
I had a word with Dave. June is in hospital. She's got terrible back pain. I am very worried about her. Dave's on his own, and he's her carer; he finds it hard.

Saturday 10 December
Just after eight I got the train to St James's Park and walked to the Royal Horticultural Hall for the huge International Peace Conference, called by the Stop the War Coalition of which I'm President. There were 1,400 people there; it was brilliantly organised.

I was asked to deliver the welcoming address, which I recorded and managed to video. I saw Phyllis Bennis, a distinguished American academic and writer, whom I had met ages ago. Tariq Ali spoke; I had a quick word with him. Craig Murray was there, and I just had a quick word with him, didn't really have a proper talk. Talked to Cindy Sheehan, the woman whose son, Casey, was killed in Iraq, and she has camped outside President Bush's ranch in Texas – a tall, tough woman, very impressive.

She made a wonderful speech. Saw Billy Hayes and his little boy, who's seven. Saw Bruce Kent. Had a word with Jeremy Corbyn. Jane Shallice was there, of course, and Lindsey German and John Rees and Andrew Murray.

I had had an email from a woman called Joyce Chumbley, President of the Florida Tom Paine Society, so she came and had a word.

Then a man called Frank Maunder, who'd written to me saying he wanted to set up his own political party. He's a single parent with a five-year-old child, living on benefit. So I had a word with him. I must say, I discouraged him a bit from setting up a party.

I was absolutely whacked! Had a meal, and am going to bed – it's quarter to ten now, and it'll be some time after ten. I'm absolutely pooped out, but it was a really good day. I must say that the Stop the War Campaign, with its international dimension, is quite unprecedented in my experience. I have nothing to do with the organisational side, but they seem to think it worthwhile leaving me as the President of honour, because that's all I really am.

Wednesday 14 December

To Church House for the Communication Workers' Union Christmas party. The General Secretary Billy Hayes had asked me, and I said to him when I saw him a week or two ago that I was bringing my Editor, who has a great crush on him.

Tom Sawyer, former General Secretary of the Labour Party, turned up and was very friendly. Tony Clarke, who used to be an extremely right-wing member of the National Executive Committee, with whom I had terrible rows, came up for a chat.

I went on to the *Guardian* party and who should appear but Lissie, with Fiona Millar and Alastair Campbell. I've always found Campbell friendly. He's absolutely loyal to Blair, personally loyal to Blair. He's a tremendous communicator, and he's thoughtful. He said he hated the *Daily Mail* – well, I knew that; I do too. He hated Clare Short, he hated Mo Mowlam, and he said he had a love/hate relationship with Mandelson. So I talked to him a little bit about diaries. He writes his diary in longhand.

He said he was very worried about China. So I said, 'Well, this is not going to be the American century, it's going to be the Asian century.'

'Yes, I know,' he said, 'but what will happen?'

'I think the truth is you just have to learn to live with China, as you learned to live with the United States, and I've no doubt they will behave just like the United States.' I said, 'Introducing capitalism under the Central Committee of the Communist Party in Beijing is not so different from introducing capitalism in Britain in the nineteenth century, when you couldn't really put a postcard between the views of the Liberals and the Conservatives.'

The press is now full of speculation: 'Will Kennedy be replaced as Leader of the Liberal Party?' We've had Blair and Brown, then we had Davis and Cameron, and now we've got Kennedy and somebody else. It's a complete switch-off for me.

Friday 16 December
Blair is in a last-minute attempt to solve the European Union budgetary crisis. He wants to retain the rebate that Mrs Thatcher had won, and they don't see why we should have it, when the Eastern European countries need money for development. The French won't make any move on the huge subsidies that their farmers get under the Common Agricultural Policy. So Blair, who is currently President of the Council, has either got to give up five or six billion pounds a year, or if he doesn't, his presidency will end with no solution to the budget and he'll be hated in Europe. So he's in a bit of a jam, but if he gives away five billion pounds, I think it will cause an angry reaction at home. But as usual Blair looks so confident, and smirks and smiles his way through.

Saturday 17 December
Blair did a deal over the EU budget, which involved giving up one billion pounds a year – over the seven-year budget, that's seven billion pounds. He said he had to do it in order to keep the EU together.

Sunday 18 December
Gordon Brown is absolutely furious. Over the next seven years, he has seven billion pounds less to spend, which will have to come out of other expenditure. That on top of the war. Apparently Blair didn't even consult him.

Went to see Dave and June in Blackheath. June is out of hospital, but very poorly. One leg is completely unusable, so she's confined to bed; she can't stand up. It is really a big strain for him, and awful for her, though I don't quite know what it is. She has sciatica, and of course she had cancer, but that's in remission, and she's got Bell's palsy, which is a condition of the face. But she was very cheerful.

Monday 19 December
My attention was drawn to an article in yesterday's *Observer* in which David Cameron had said, 'One of the books that got me interested in politics was Tony Benn's *Arguments for Democracy*, which is just a great book. Lots of it I disagree with, but I loved reading it.'

Also, in November, Peter Preston was reviewing a book about Osama Bin Laden in *The Observer* and said that the British politician who most reminded him of Bin Laden was Tony Benn (though he did say our policies have nothing in common).

So to be compared to Osama Bin Laden, and be credited with the influence that brought Cameron into politics, is a strange start to the day!

Tuesday 20 December
This morning, two of the nuns from the Church of the Holy Child Jesus convent next door came in, and brought a huge box of chocolates and a calendar.

Wednesday 21 December
In the afternoon the front doorbell rang, and it was Kate Silverton, who came with a card and said, 'I can't stop because I've got a marine officer in the car, he was the one who trained us as foreign correspondents' – sort of toughened them up at the SAS headquarters in Hereford. She told me she'd got a job with *Panorama*, so I was very pleased.

Saffron arrived at 7.45, and I had laid on a little bit of salmon and salad and mince pies and tea, and we sat and had a couple of hours' talk. She's got a short film in Austria to make, another one in Berlin. She's been in America twice in the last three or four weeks. She now wants to devote January to writing in Thaxted, where she has a house.

One email I had, which I liked very much, said, 'Dear Tony, I'm very glad to hear that you've had a peacemaker installed', and that I must say is a nice way of putting it.

Thursday 22 December
At two o'clock a Sister from next door came to see me. She's plump and jolly, thirty-seven. She taught biology and is now over here learning about school management, in order to go back and take over control, I think as the head teacher or administrator of a private Catholic school in Africa. She was fascinated by the work that Caroline had done. She brought Caroline's book for me to sign.

I'm always very delicate and careful with Catholic nuns, particularly ones from Africa, but she was so progressive, it wasn't true! 'Of course women should be ordained,' she said. 'You know, if the priest doesn't come on a Sunday, we just give wine to each other', which did make me laugh! She said it's just about power, men want power in the Church. We discussed gay men becoming priests and the Pope's line which was very restrictive: you can't go to a seminary if you're gay, or have been for more than five years.

We had a talk about theology and religion, and her view is similar to mine. There are the mysteries about the Virgin birth and the physical ascension, but really what mattered was how you lived your life, and that religion is part of culture. She said there are a lot of Muslims in Nigeria of course, and there has been conflict between Christians and Muslims, but it's a cultural cover for a political struggle. I must say, I'm deeply grateful to my mum for introducing me to theology, because now, in this period in time, it is just so important, and if you are confident in dealing with it, it helps.

Anyway, then I came back to my Christmas cards, of which I've had hundreds and hundreds, many from people I don't know.

Sunday 8 January 2006

I heard this evening that Tony Banks has died. He'd had this ghastly stroke last Thursday, in Florida. It is just incredibly sad. So I went through all the references to him in the diary – his is an extraordinary story really, when I look back on it. At least the diary helps to jog your memory.

I first met him at the Conference when I was Chairman in 1972. Then he was very much involved in the Public Sector Working Group. He was then a researcher at the AUEW. He came to a meal at home, this was about '73, and we decided to call ourselves the 25 Club, because we were going to nationalise the top twenty-five corporations. We discussed industrial democracy, and he said the AUEW was against having workers on the board.

Then, later, he moved to BECTU, the Broadcasting Union. He was a member of the LCC, the GLC, and he was the last Chairman of the GLC. He was Chairman of the Rank and File Mobilising Committee.

He was a great organiser for my deputy leadership. When I was ill in 1981 he came to see me in hospital. In 1982 he argued that I should stand against Foot for the leadership of the Party. Then in 1983 he was elected to Parliament.

He invited me to go to Feliks Topolski's studio in July '83 – and Topolski did a drawing of me.

Then of course, the big thing was, when I was defeated in 1983 in Bristol, he offered to give up his seat to me. I mean, it wouldn't have worked, but an incredibly generous thing to offer.

He supported the miners and campaigned at Wapping against Murdoch. In 1985 he said that Kinnock's men had warned him to keep clear of Tony Benn – not that he ever did! He accused me once of sulking. He said, 'You're not active enough.' That was in '86.

Then at the party in 1990 to celebrate my fortieth anniversary in the House of Commons he played a leading part and gave me a Gladstone Plate.

He pressed me to stand for the Speakership. When he took the oath as an MP, he kept his fingers crossed.

He was a passionate supporter of Chelsea and became the Sports Minister in 1997. He made a suggestion that there ought to be a United Kingdom football team instead of England, Wales and Scotland, and there was outrage about that. So he made a statement in the House saying, 'Madam Speaker, I just would like to say that I made that statement under circumstances which I feel sure you will understand, and I fear that my transformation from a saloon-bar genius to a statesman may take some time to bring about', and they hooted with laughter.

He was, of course, passionately keen on animal rights and badger protection, opposed to hunting and worked immensely hard to get the Hunting Act passed. Later he became Chairman of the Works of Art Committee in the House of Commons. Actually, I think he was the one who arranged for my bust to be bought by the House of Commons, when he was Chairman of the Committee. His political views wobbled at the end: in 2005 he was made a peer, Lord Stratford. He wanted to be known as Lord Banks of the Thames, but that was vetoed! He was a very popular figure – no question about it. I'm very sad that he's gone, very depressed. He's only sixty-two or -three.

Monday 9 January
I had a letter from the United Nations, from the Under-Secretary for Legal Affairs on behalf of Kofi Annan, acknowledging my letter, saying he didn't have the power to investigate war crimes because he was answerable to the UN, but there were various organisations that might be involved and he was going, in view of the seriousness of the charges, to refer it to the President of the Commission on Human Rights.

Wednesday 11 January
There's no doubt whatever that this is a slow build-up, not to an invasion of Iran, but to the bombing of Iran. I just think it's incredible that that could be contemplated. I mean, at the very moment when Blair is doing this, saying this, he is himself arguing for an upgrading of our Trident nuclear missile. When he complains about nuclear power for Iran, he is arguing for nuclear power in Britain. I mean, language is so important in politics.

Thursday 12 January
Tried to contact Sally Banks, and finally, through Chelsea Football Club, I found out that she was returning today. Apparently her sister went over to America and was with her, and she was coming back today. Tony's body is coming back tomorrow. Sally didn't want to go into her house alone. I'll probably ring her tomorrow.

Friday 13 January
Lindsey German and Nicholas Wood came to see me about the next stage in the campaign on the war-crimes question, about how we could advance the cause of the letter. There's been no coverage in the press, although Kofi Annan has replied. We went on to discuss the whole question really of whether we were demanding a war-crimes tribunal. My view is that you shouldn't do that. I think it's a complete waste of effort trying to put Blair and Bush on trial: (a) it won't happen; (b) it's so negative; (c) it's all about

personalities. To my surprise, quite a number of Labour MPs would not sign the letter to Kofi Annan, including Bob Marshall-Andrews, so it's still a bit of a struggle.

I was just coming to the end of the diary when Sally Banks, Tony Banks's widow, rang. She was on the phone for forty-three minutes. She's a very strong woman. She told me all about the circumstances of Tony's death. They were staying with Brian Davies, the founder of IFAW (International Fund for Animal Welfare) in Florida, whom they know well. Tony was having a meal and planning to do an animal-welfare meeting in the locality, and suddenly he had a stroke. Oh, she was so sweet! I mean, she must have had a million people to ring. She asked me to invite Ruth Winstone and Patricia Moberly to the funeral. I was really touched. They both knew Tony very well.

Saturday 14 January

The media coverage of *Big Brother* shows George Galloway dressed as a cat, accepting a saucer of milk from a woman, an actress called Rula Lenska. The thing is so humiliating!

The political news today is that Gordon Brown has decided to try and launch a day of Britishness, where we would all fly the Union Jack in our back gardens to emphasise our Britishness, and to seize back patriotism from the far right.

Tuesday 17 January

Got up at seven and read the papers, and came downstairs. As soon as I got downstairs, I was so tired I went to sleep for two hours. I'm having to come to terms with the fact that I'm eighty now, and I have not got the energy I had. It isn't that I want to do more, I just don't think I could.

Thursday 19 January

Melissa, who has had severe flu, bless her heart, rang me this morning and said she'd decided to attend the meeting in the House of Commons to launch the pamphlet that she and Fiona Millar have written, although she's not well.

So I picked her up at 4.15. We got to the House of Commons, went to Room 14, which is the biggest committee room in the House, and the room was absolutely crammed.

Neil Kinnock was in the chair, and he was the old Neil Kinnock, the education spokesman, and he really came out clearly against the Government proposals to hand over selection to independent schools.

Then Fiona Millar spoke. That was very good. Her partner, Alastair Campbell, was sitting in the audience.

Then Lissie spoke, and she did terribly well! I had my little video out, and I picked up twenty-eight minutes of it.

Then we had Estelle Morris, who was very good, and Angela Eagle, and then Steve Sinnott, the General Secretary of the National Union of Journalists.

I did get up and make one point. 'In fifty-six years in this place, I've never seen such a crowded meeting, and what occurred to me was that the Government line is about choice, except when it comes to choice of policy, and choice for local-education authorities who want to organise education in their area, and choice for students who want to go to a school where there's a full range of knowledge.' Neil introduced me as an old veteran and was glad my pacemaker was working, so that was quite friendly.

Fred Jarvis, the former General Secretary of the NUT (National Union of Teachers), was very friendly. I went up to Alastair Campbell afterwards, and I said, 'Last night I watched *A Very British Coup*, and I saw you listed as one of the researchers on it.' 'Oh yes, I was,' he said. That was interesting.

Friday 20 January
I had a note from a publisher saying would I like to do an illustrated book? And so my Editor had the idea that I might do a book of stories for children, beginning with the 'Daddy Shop', which I had invented when the children were young to expunge my guilt about being so busy, and then the Tubby stories. Tubby lived in the plughole in the bath, and so we invented Tubby's relations – Mohammed Tubi, Tubby Junior, Comrade Mikhail Tubbski, and all that. We had such a lot of fun.

Saturday 21 January
To Tony Banks's funeral at the City of London Crematorium. It was a beautiful day, beautiful cemetery. We'd been told it was a small family funeral, but it was packed – Sally of course, Sally's mum, Tony's mum and sister, Chris Mullin, Jeremy Corbyn, Diane Abbott, Alun Michael, Tessa Jowell, Margaret Beckett, John Prescott, Tony Lloyd, Alastair Campbell.

Tony's body was brought into the chapel in a wicker coffin. The music was lovely. It was actually very interesting – all the aspects of Tony's life were covered. Don Brind conducted the service, although it wasn't a Christian service, but a celebration of Tony's life. Margaret Beckett was very emotional: she spoke first, talked about his political work and said he had offered his seat to me. Brian Davies, the founder of IFAW, with whom Tony and Sally were staying when he died, talked about Tony's commitment to animal welfare and described the circumstances of his death. Philip Mould talked about him as an art collector and member of the Commons Works of Art Committee. David Mellor, former Tory MP of course, was active with Tony at Chelsea Football Club and he gave a perfectly good and amusing speech.

I learned a lot about Tony; the thing about him was that he loved life. He loved the trade-union life, he loved political life, he loved the life of animals, he loved the life of art, he loved the life of sport, and there was a completion about it all. There were lovely photographs of him on the programme illustrating all these loves.

At West Ham Town Hall afterwards I just sat, I was so tired, but I did have a word with Alastair Campbell. I said, 'To see you twice in two days is a bonus!' We talked about his diaries, and he said that the day he left Number 10 he was offered millions for his diaries. He said he wouldn't touch the *Daily Mail* with a bargepole, and he was hostile to me for serialising mine with them. I didn't say, 'Well, what about Tony Blair in the pocket of Rupert Murdoch?' I thought it would not be appropriate. He said his diaries had a lot of abuse in them. Whenever Clare Short's name was mentioned there was an expletive. I said, 'Well, you can leave it out, and just publish a factual account of what you saw.' 'Oh no, I can't leave it out,' he said. Then he said, 'I now realise I can't publish them until Gordon Brown has gone. Even then it will reveal that I told a lie, because I was always telling people that Gordon and Tony got on wonderfully well.'

Monday 23 January

I was phoned up and told that Hilary has won the award of Politician of the Year, which *The House Magazine* and Channel 4 run jointly, and the ceremony will be on 1 February. I was asked, 'Would you give him the award?'

Of course I was absolutely thrilled! I said, 'Who did he beat?'

'Well, the other people on the shortlist were David Cameron, Gordon Brown and Michael Howard.'

It's absolutely secret and I mustn't tell anybody. Hilary doesn't know yet.

Wednesday 25 January

I tackled my household chores, I did the laundry, the washing up. Put all the black sacks outside.

Galloway won his appeal against the *Daily Telegraph*. If they had won, he would have been bankrupted and out of Parliament, so that was really good news. Also, he was booted out of *Big Brother*, which is probably the best thing that ever happened to him. Everybody's making fun of him for dressing up as a cat and supping milk from an actress's hand and looking ridiculous, but when you come to think of it, he hasn't lied to Parliament, he hasn't sent soldiers to their death, he hasn't authorised the rendition of people through British airports to be tortured. So I rang up his office and congratulated them on his victory in the courts.

Thursday 26 January

Hamas won the election in Palestine, overwhelmingly, with seventy-four seats, forty-three for al-Fatah. So that is a decisive moment, and somehow, although they are fundamentalist and linked to terrorism, it's probably the best chance of peace with Palestine, although immediately the Israeli

Government said they wouldn't deal with the new Palestinian Government if Hamas is in it, and Bush said he wouldn't have any dealings with Palestine because of the Hamas victory. So much for democracy! Bush allows you to have a democratic election so long as you elect somebody he likes. The Liberal Democrat leadership election is getting a bit messy.

Saturday 28 January
The Council of Europe has passed a resolution condemning Nazism and communism. Of course it's not just condemning the ideas, but putting them in the same category that offends me. They're not going to condemn imperialism, which would involve Britain and France and all the other European imperialists; they're not going to condemn the Armenian massacres, because Turkey is trying to get into the European Union and of course Turkey denies the existence of them. But denial of the Holocaust may now become a criminal offence in Europe. You must be free to give your opinion! If I were to say I didn't believe that Jesus lived, is that going to become an offence? So civil liberty is going to be a much, much bigger issue than even I realised. It's not just the legislation and all the rest of it, it's the attempt to clamp down on unacceptable opinions that I object to.

Tuesday 31 January
I was taken to ITV for a discussion with Bob Stewart, whom I have met before, the Colonel who was the British UN Commander in Bosnia. He and I really agreed about withdrawing troops from Iraq. I talked to him afterwards, and he said such interesting things. He said he was stationed in Germany a few years ago – he's only fifty himself, I think – and the American officers were all taking cannabis, and he asked to be moved. He said they had no respect whatsoever for the people they commanded. He was against nuclear weapons. A very nice guy.

I heard that the 100th soldier had been killed in Iraq, and at five the Stop the War Coalition was going to read the 100 names in Parliament Square, so I'm going to join them. Then I'll go on to Kofi Annan's lecture tonight.

Caught the Tube to Westminster, and went to Parliament Square; about 150 people turned up for the vigil. They'd got hold of little crosses, the ones they use on Armistice Day, and planted 100 of them in the square. George Galloway turned up, and a lot of my old mates. Some media were there, but not the BBC – the BBC does not cover opposition to the war. That's what the Hutton Report and the Butler Report have done.

The names were read out – not only the names of the British soldiers killed, but 100 Iraqis, including professors of neurology and education, and so on. It was done in a dignified way. I had had a word with the police; the event is of course illegal under the current legislation, but I said, 'Play it light', and they did, and it wasn't made wildly political.

Peter Tatchell was present. Peter of course fought Bermondsey in a by-election in about 1983 against the Liberal Simon Hughes. The Liberals ran a violently homophobic campaign, and on the Liberal literature it said, 'The straight choice – Simon Hughes.' Now, of course, we know Simon Hughes is gay. Peter Tatchell was asked about this and he said, 'Oh, I forgive him', so I said to Peter, 'That was a very good thing for you to say.' He said, 'Well, the left has to live by its own principles.' The truth is Peter Tatchell is becoming a national treasure – after twenty-three years, partly because of his campaign on gay rights, partly because of his campaign against Mugabe, partly because he's taken up Green issues. But he's very much the same old Peter Tatchell – shy, but immensely determined.

Then I walked over to the Central Hall Westminster for the Kofi Annan lecture. Everyone had been told to be there by 4.30. I got there at six o'clock. They let me in at once, and put me in the second row. Then Kofi Annan and Jack Straw came in, and Lord Hannay. Jack Straw made a Jack Straw-type speech, and then Kofi Annan talked about our hopes, and what the UN should be and what we've got to do. Such a modest guy.

Afterwards, as he was going by, I said, 'I'm Hilary Benn's dad!' Oh, he was so warm. I said, 'Your big job begins when you leave the UN, when you're free to go round the world talking about what you believe in, without that bloody man Bolton there' – John Bolton, of course, is the American Ambassador at the UN. He gave a big laugh!

Wednesday 1 February
Had tea with Hilary in the Tea Room at about four o'clock, and had this agony of not being able to tell him what was going to happen this evening. I did say, 'Oh, I was invited tonight, so I'll be there.'

To Channel 4 for the awards ceremonies, Jon Snow presiding. David Butler turned up, because his book was one of the political books of the year. John Bercow, the Tory MP, who does such wonderful imitations of Hilary and me, was there; Michael Howard was at the same table; Dorothy Byrne, Head of News and Current Affairs at Channel 4. It was the whole media-Westminster establishment. There were quite a number of awards, and the last one was 'Politicians' Politician', and there was a little film of clips of Hilary, Michael Howard, David Cameron and Gordon Brown. Then Jon Snow said, 'And to present the award, Tony Benn!'

So I came onto the platform. I opened the envelope, and I said, 'And the winner is Hilary Benn!' And there was tremendous applause! I had thought carefully about what I was going to do.

'I want to say something about Hilary. He's only fifty-two, but in 1958, when he was four, my dad – who was elected to Parliament on Tuesday of next week 100 years ago – took him there, and he saw Churchill, and he said afterwards that Churchill's legs were so short, they couldn't reach the floor.' And then I said, 'Harold Wilson, the Prime Minister, came to Bristol in 1964, when Hilary was ten, and he had a meal and Hilary was there, and he called him Harold throughout the whole meeting, which was very sensible. He saw Clem Attlee, campaigned in all the elections, was in the Ealing trade-union movement, went to be an MP in Leeds. He said he was a Benn, but not a Bennite, which is exactly my position.' All this went down well. Then I said, 'I don't give him advice, unless he asks me to, but there is one fault. Whenever he speaks, he waves his hands about! I've told him so many times, "Keep your hands down!"' Then I said, 'With your permission, I'm going to give him a hug!'

So he got on the platform and I gave him a huge hug, and then he made a speech, saying, 'You naughty man!' Afterwards everybody came up to congratulate him, a tremendous response. I talked to a few people, and then I drove him home. Poor lad, he thought he'd be back at half-past nine, and it was actually eleven o'clock and he has a speech to do tomorrow . . .

Thursday 2 February

Got a cab to King's Cross and caught the train to Cambridge, for the Cambridge Union. The last time I did a debate there, I think, was on 2 November 1956 when the students threw lavatory paper and tomatoes and ruined it. This debate tonight is 'That this House believes that military action is counter-productive in the fight against terrorism'. George Galloway was one of the speakers; he has completely risen above *Celebrity Big Brother*, and he was well received.

I got a taxi back five minutes before the last train, I put my bag on the train and stood on the platform to have a puff of my pipe. All of a sudden the doors closed and the train pulled out of the station. I felt such a bloody fool. So I went out, picked up a cab and paid £170 to get from Cambridge to London, got home at about ten past twelve. Fortunately a kind lawyer on the train had spotted me, saw my bag, saw an address tag on it with my details, left a message on my answering machine and then rang me on my mobile, and said he'd keep the bag overnight and deliver it tomorrow.

Friday 3 February

I am afraid that yesterday convinced me, not that I need to be convinced, that I am a total addict to my pipe.

The lawyer, bless his heart, called Richard Parks, sent my bag over by courier this morning. I spoke to him on the phone and thanked him. I found out the address of his chambers and sent him a copy of *Dare to Be a Daniel*.

Saturday 4 February

There are demonstrations by Muslims all over Europe attacking a cartoon that appeared in the Danish papers depicting Mohammed with a bomb on his head instead of a turban. *The Times* rang me yesterday for my view on the matter, and I said, 'Well, it's a matter of not insulting people. You can't legislate for it. You have to respect people', which is fair enough.

Sunday 5 February
Kate Silverton came and had a cup of tea from 10.00 to 11.30, fresh off her breakfast programme. She's still learning Arabic, wants to be a foreign correspondent. She's a very intelligent woman. Her interest in the military is certainly very strong.

Thursday 9 February
At 10.30 Meirion Jones from BBC *Newsnight* came to talk to me about discoveries he'd made through Freedom of Information requests, which suggested that Michael Michaels – a civil servant whom I well remember when he was in the Ministry of Technology, in charge of nuclear matters – had done a nuclear deal to supply Israel with plutonium in 1966, without telling me. I do remember Michael Michaels, and I noted in my published diary I didn't trust him very much. He is now dead. But it really shook me to think that things of that kind were going on, and according to this guy, Meirion, the Foreign Office was advising against it and the Ministry of Defence had doubts about it, but it was the Atomic Energy Authority and the Ministry of Technology – that is, Michael Michaels – who were promoting it and going ahead with it.

Friday 10 February
The Liberals won Dunfermline in Scotland where Gordon Brown lives, a 14 per cent swing I think, and a Labour majority of over 11,000 was toppled, so that's a big event on the eve of the Labour Party Spring Conference.

Saturday 11 February
I heard that Alastair Campbell is now advising Gordon Brown, and that explains why he said to me he couldn't publish his diary yet.

Sunday 12 February
Gordon Brown has now emerged as the great alternative Prime Minister, announcing the need for a longer period of detention and stricter action against terrorism, and he's being prepared for the takeover. Whether that means Blair is going soon, I don't know, but it is interesting, the way it's being presented as a succession – a bit like Anthony Eden and Churchill. Eden took over from Churchill just after the election – no, just before the election in 1955 – and less than two years later, he was out.

Tuesday 14 February
I was very depressed indeed this morning, sitting in the bedroom reading

the papers, at the possibility of ID cards going through. The more I think about it, it isn't the ID card, it's the database of information, and now, although they say the ID cards will be voluntary, anyone who applies for a driving licence or a passport will automatically be registered on the database and given an ID card. I was thinking of the uses to which it could be put. I mean, the information on the ID card may not be true. It might include the fact you'd failed the Eleven Plus, that you had lost twenty points on your licence, that you were seen at a demonstration against the war, information from bugging your phone, which goes on all the time, from opening your letters. They could use it for blackmail. They could use it against MPs, because if it was thought an MP might vote against the Government, they could ring up and say, 'You wouldn't want it known that you'd been going out with rent boys' or whatever. It might not be true. It absolutely terrified me! I felt so powerless in the face of it. Of course, in addition to that, the Americans have got a plan for taking control of the whole Internet.

Friday 17 February

For nearly a couple of hours there was a meeting at my house about the UK breaches of the Geneva Conventions. Lindsey German came; and Professor Richard Dawkins, who is a well-known atheist who's just made a series on religion; Craig Murray, who was the sacked British Ambassador, in Uzbekistan; James Thring from the Ministry of Peace. For some, like Nicholas Wood, their main desire is to have a war-crimes tribunal of Blair and Bush. My argument is that our purpose now is persuasion, to broaden our appeal, to get more coverage. It was useful, but I was landed with the job of organising the next meeting, and I do need a secretary or some help for that, so I don't know what I'm going to be able to do.

Saturday 18 February, Edinburgh

Train to Edinburgh and then changed for Linlithgow, where there was a plaque saying, 'Opened by Tam Dalyell, MP'.

Went to the Binns, which is a fabulous palace of a place, built by a butter merchant at the beginning of the seventeenth century. Tam and Kathleen were both there. There are twenty-nine peacocks wandering around the grounds. My bedroom was the same one I had before, with these incredible decorations hanging from the ceiling, made of egg white or something; I don't know how it's done. There was a circular stone stair to climb up, terribly difficult.

Tam drove us to the Whitburn Miners' Welfare, for the Burns supper, and there were 200 people there, including his son and daughter. The haggis was piped in, and there were tons of songs and speeches. I spoke for seventeen minutes, which may have been too long, on the immortal memory of Robert Burns – but mainly about Tam, which is what they really wanted.

We finally left the Whitburn Miners' Welfare about a quarter to one, got back and I went to bed after half-past one. I was so exhausted, I just took off my suit and got into bed in my underwear. It was a memorable day, and Tam is an interesting guy. Kathleen is also an interesting woman. She's the daughter of the Scottish socialist John Wheatley and the great-niece of the earlier Wheatley who set up council housing under the Labour Government in the 1920s. She said she wished she'd known Caroline better.

Tuesday 21 February

I got a cab to the Serpentine Gallery to see the Welfare exhibition by two Nordic artists, because I am giving a lecture on 'Utopia and the Welfare State' tomorrow night. It was very effective. You walk in and there's a wheelchair, and then you go along a corridor and there's a cashpoint machine, and a model of a baby in a carrycot on the floor. Then you turn a corner and go into a room, where a ticket machine dispenses those little tickets that you collect when you're queuing up, and there are four empty chairs and a machine that simply flashes 0000 all the time. Then you go round another corner and there's a hospital corridor with two beds, with a model of a woman in one bed and the other one is empty. Round another corner there's an empty room with four Securicor guards sitting there. It is about bureaucracy really, and the heartlessness and brutality of it. It's very powerful – completely silent.

Wednesday 22 February

I worked in the afternoon on my lecture to the Royal Geographical Society, 'Utopia and the Welfare State'. I did something I have never done before in a lecture. I had sent them slides of our trade-union banners, including the one with my portrait on, and they projected them on to a wall and rotated them around, very effectively. Then I had arranged that they would play the song 'We are the women of the working class' by a group called Flaming Nerve. I must say, as they played it, tears rolled down my cheeks. I couldn't control them. I have not been able to listen to that for twenty years – it makes me cry. Here were lots of young people and artists; apparently 50 per cent of the 800 people there were art students.

Thursday 2 March

At eight o'clock Rodney Bickerstaffe arrived and we had a talk for an hour and a half, and discussed his work. He's a decent guy, is Rodney. Apparently he's given an hour interview to the BBC for my obituary, of which only a couple of minutes will be used.

He showed me his new BlackBerry hand-held computer, and a Sony

Cyber-shot camera – I think they might turn out to be my new toys for my eighty-first birthday. I'll have to think about it.

Friday 3 March

I got a cab, got to St Pancras about an hour and ten minutes before my 7.25 train for Betty Heathfield's funeral in Chesterfield. It was icy cold, and I had a cup of tea and sat there shivering. The train was delayed. They said the heating didn't work. I was absolutely terrified I was going to be late, but they moved us to another train and I got to Chesterfield just before ten.

Margaret and Tom Vallins drove me up to the crematorium and, to my delight, there was a huge crowd of people there! Dave Hopper had brought one or two people from the Durham Miners. Arthur Scargill was there. Anne Scargill was there. (They're now divorced.) Vic Allen, who wrote the book *Militancy of British Miners*, was there. Tom and Avis Murphy; John Burrows, who was a miners' official, now leader of the much-depleted Labour group on the council; Colin Hampton, from the Unemployed Workers' Centre, who said he was now getting together with all the charities to try and set up a network of 'Make Poverty History in Britain'. Linda Skinner was there and a couple of Dennis's brothers. Betty's children were there.

Mel Finch and a friend sang 'Women of the Working Class' – the second time I'd heard it in two weeks. I find it hard to bear the emotional strain of that.

I was told I had to be brief, so I said, 'Comrades' and described what an inspiration Betty had been. I talked about her work in the miners' strike of 1984–5, the brutality of the strike and the lunacy of the Government's policy; I reminded them of the time Jimmy Nolan, the Liverpool docker, had come to the Chesterfield Labour Club (because the 'Women Against Pit Closures' had inspired the 'Women of the Waterfront') and had said, 'What is the difference between a terrorist and a Liverpool woman?' And we were all shaking in our shoes, and he said, 'You can negotiate with terrorists.' It went down all right.

I spoke to Anne later, she was quite tender about Arthur as a great trade-union leader, but she said he never understood the difference between being a union leader and a political leader; he just expected to give orders, and that was impossible.

Monday 13 March

I had a good sleep, got up about eight to the news that Ian Blair, the Commissioner of the Metropolitan Police, had apparently tape-recorded a talk he'd had on the phone with the Attorney General, and the conversation they were having was about whether it was permissible to use phone-tap evidence in court. I could hardly keep myself from laughing out loud!

Since the Prime Minister said he may bug Members of Parliament, because nobody can be exempt, why should the Attorney General be exempt?

Tuesday 14 March

I got a response from the Attorney General's office apologising for their lack of response to my letter, and saying that the Attorney General would reply by 7 April, which is twelve weeks after he got my original letter. If it's later than that, he said they'll explain why.

Just had time to eat in about five minutes, paid my congestion charge and then drove to Parliament Square for the reading out of the twenty-eight charges of war crimes, which we've sent, under my signature, to Kofi Annan. There was Mike Kustow, Jane Shallice's partner; Lindsey German; Ken Loach, the film director; Martin Bell; Jeremy Corbyn; Bruce Kent; and Craig Murray.

I had a word with Craig about the control of people's memoirs, and he said that the Foreign Office is trying to prevent him from writing his book. The line that the Foreign Office is taking is that every bit of information that you get as a result of being a Foreign Office official is copyright. Even if you hear something, it is official and you can't report it. This is absolutely typical of this government. They want to know everything about us, but they don't want us to know anything about them.

It wouldn't surprise me if they returned to the eighteenth century and banned Hansard!

Thursday 16 March

The big news is these enormous loans to the Labour Party before the general election that were never declared, not even reported to the Treasurer of the Labour Party, Jack Dromey, who is Harriet Harman's husband. Nobody knows how many there were, who the lenders were, what the money was used for, whether they've been repaid, whether there was interest, who paid the interest, and indeed how many of the people who lent the money got honours.

Other news today, the Prince of Wales has won a case against the *Daily Mail*, who published his diary of his trip to Hong Kong when the handover occurred, saying that the Chinese leaders were like a lot of waxwork models, which wasn't very tactful. But he can't go on pretending he's the heir to the throne and above politics, and at the same time engage in current politics.

Saturday 18 March

The weather was icy cold today. I got up early. I put on a double set of clothing. I had a small cup of tea, because I was afraid I'd want to wee at the demonstration.

The artist David Gentleman had covered Parliament Square with posters, each one of which had 100 blobs of red paint, representing 100,000 deaths. It was so powerful.

I saw the march off, and I stood with Joe and Sanjiv, my doctor friends who were making a video. My woolly boots were very uncomfortable, and we went in and had a sandwich in a pub just at the bottom of Parliament Street and then walked up to Trafalgar Square. We just wandered around and everyone was friendly, except one man, a Scotsman, who shouted at me, 'Why do you never attack Islamic violence?'

I said, 'Well, I do. I say stealth bombers and suicide bombers are the same.'

He said, 'It's not the same! You're dodging it! There's no democracy in Britain. I shouted and they took me away and they were trying to stop me.'

I said, 'Well, you're trying to wreck a meeting. What's your position?'

He said, 'I'm a born-again Christian.'

So I said, 'Oh, you follow George Bush.'

He said, 'I don't. I follow my Lord Jesus!'

It was interesting – I'd never come across a Scottish fundamentalist before, and how you cope with that I ought to think about.

Tuesday 21 March

I did an interview with BBC Wales on the Labour loans and the peerages, and I said it was corrupt. I'm getting stronger about it, because I feel absolutely outraged about it.

What Blair is doing is privatising the Labour Party. He wants to get rid of the trade unions. After all, seven million trade unionists give seven million pounds, and ten people contributed nearly fourteen million pounds and some end up in the Lords. My dad left the Liberal Party because Lloyd George was so corrupt in his use of patronage.

Thursday 23 March

Up just after six. I bought all the papers, preparing all day for *Question Time*, going through the budget, and loans and peerages, and the war, and everything I could imagine.

I was put on because Number 10 pulled out Harriet Harman, who was supposed to be on, presumably because her husband, Jack Dromey, is Treasurer of the Labour Party. Number 10 put an alternative up, but Mentorn stuck to their right to choose. I should think the Party must have been furious. All the predictable questions came up. I can't say it was brilliant, but it was okay.

Saturday 25 March

I got up at six, had my breakfast, and then the phone rang and it was Dave. He said that June, his wife, died this morning at 1.30. I saw her last week and she was all right to talk to, but she was totally immobile and he had carers in. A couple of days ago her situation deteriorated and there was a complete collapse of her haemoglobin count. So he tried to get her into an NHS hospital yesterday, but there weren't any beds, so he paid for her to go in an ambulance to the private hospital. She arrived at six o'clock last night and died at 1.30 this morning. Having been through all that with Caroline, I know exactly how he felt. His daughter, Frances, and Michael, her husband and little baby Michael are with him, and Piers is there, so he's now making the funeral arrangements.

Wednesday 29 March

I sat in the Central Lobby of the Commons waiting for Saffron, and talking to people. Lots of people came up. We went and had tea in the Strangers' Dining Room. They were so friendly there! They said, 'We don't often see you. You must come more often!' Saffron had her hair flowing back and no make-up. She's a Fellow of the Royal Society of Arts.

Alan Simpson came up and had a long talk. He liked her very much, not just for her beauty, but for her intelligence and commitment to the left. Then we passed Chris Mullin and David Triesman in the Pugin Room, and I waved at them.

I forgot to mention, I got my new Freedom pass. Oh, what a to-do! I had to fill in a form, have photographs taken, and so on; but anyway, I've got it for the next two years. So when it expires I'll be eighty-three, which is a year older than, at the age of sixteen, I forecast that I would die. So this might see me through.

Saturday 1 April

To All Saints Church, Blackheath, for June's funeral.

Father Nicholas Cranfield took the service, and Father William Chatterton, who is actually a senior Manager of Social Services who took holy orders, gave a very nice homily and speech.

Dave gave a good eulogy, beautifully structured and read. Then we all went off to the crematorium at Lewisham for a little, short service, with some Schubert piano music, and then we stood for a while, among the flowers. Back to Frances's house for a while, which was absolutely crowded with friends and family.

Dave rang later. He told me that he couldn't get June into hospital two weeks ago when her hacmoglobin level dropped to the point where it was dangerous, so he put her in a private hospital. When he arrived he was told, before they could receive her, he had to put down a deposit of £3,000. I think they took it off his Visa card or something. June was there for eight hours, and she died, so the cost of those eight hours was £1,440, without even including the doctors. That is private medicine for you.

Tuesday 4 April
Just as I came in, the phone rang and it was Stephen. Daniel, who is on a skiing holiday, has had a serious kidney injury and is being airlifted to a hospital in Grenoble, where he is alone. It sounds very serious, so Stephen and Nita have decided to fly there tomorrow.

Thursday 6 April
Stephen rang from Grenoble to say that Daniel was a bit better, but may have to stay there longer.

Monday 10 April
The French Government has capitulated to those people who were opposed to the new labour law that would give under-twenty-fives no security of employment. It's a tremendously critical popular demonstration! I must say, I wish the British trade unions and public were as active as the French.

At 10.15 I was invited to go on *Newsnight* to discuss the twenty-three new peers announced today.

They included Ian Paisley's wife; David Trimble; Bill Morris from the Transport and General Workers' Union – that's absolutely predictable; and Maggie Jones, who was defeated in Blaenau Gwent last May in the general election, when I went there and spoke for her – she's been compensated by being put in the Lords. It's an utterly disreputable process! The argument was put that the Lords were necessary to protect people from a government who were oppressing civil liberties. I must say, I did blow my top a bit. So on that happy note I came home.

Friday 21 April
I got a cab down to the Israeli Embassy, just off Kensington High Street, and met these cyclists who'd cycled from Faslane, the British nuclear base, all the way down to London in support of Mordechai Vanunu. Ernst Rodker was there, so I stayed for a bit and then they asked me to speak, so I read a statement by Vanunu, which was very moving. Others spoke, then we released thirty doves – rather lovely, to hold a white dove in my hand and release it. It flew straight off, knew exactly where to fly back to.

Monday 24 April
The lights fused. I couldn't fix them before I had to go by Tube to Euston Square, to the Bloomsbury Theatre for the Paul Robeson evening with Sir Willard White, a famous bass baritone. It was full of lefties. Willard White had dignity and strength and a beautiful voice, and he sang almost all the songs I knew. Afterwards I was introduced to him, because there was a little drinks party for him. He's not a leftie himself. He's an actor. He was brilliant at it, but it was an act.

Tuesday 25 April
I went to the Speaker's party for Ian Paisley's eightieth birthday. It was nice of Paisley to put me on the list. I got there before anybody else, and we all held back till the Speaker arrived. I had a word with him and said how fit he was and how was his heart, because he'd had some surgery.

I thanked Ian so much for putting me on the list, and I said, 'I've never said anything political to you before, Ian, but I think the hand of history is on your shoulder.' And I put my hand on his shoulder and said, 'You have it within your power to bring permanent peace to Northern Ireland.' He gave me a rather friendly look, and I did wonder whether he was mellowing.

Betty Boothroyd, the former Speaker, was there. I spoke to her and to Tom King, who'd been a Minister for Northern Ireland; to Peter Tapsell, the Tory MP, who said that the Central Bank in Europe had been thought up by Hitler; to Angus Sinclair, the Speaker's Secretary; to David Steel, who might be considered as the first Speaker of an elected House of Lords – how they'd deal with that, I don't know. I talked to Nicholas Winterton and a number of Ulster Unionists.

They were all friendly, but of course they all know my view – I'm 100 per cent for a united Ireland and for Sinn Fein. When I think about the event, it was a real parliamentary event, all very cosy. Paisley could, like Mandela and Desmond Tutu, be the instrument for reconciliation in Northern Ireland. I'll probably get into trouble from Sinn Fein for having gone to his party, but I'm not sorry.

Wednesday 26 April
Patricia Hewitt was booed and heckled at the Royal College of Nursing Annual Conference – normally the Royal College of Nursing is very respectable.

Friday 28 April
I did six hours of filming with David Parker from Bristol for the launch of a major new museum in Bristol. They had a twenty-two-year-old researcher called Jonathan and a shy thirteen-year-old called Tamsin who is doing work experience. At the end she interviewed me herself with some very good questions! What was interesting was that my granddaughter Hannah came, without her mum, and she sat and listened and took phone messages and made tea. She followed it all, got to know Tamsin. Incredibly grown up for thirteen.

At 10.40 I'm doing a half-hour interview on Radio Iran about the decision to report Iran to the Security Council for non-compliance with the IAEA request to abandon the enrichment of uranium. I'm not quite as up to date as I should be, but I think I know it. I am going to say quite plainly that Iran is entitled to have nuclear power. There is nothing in the Non-

Proliferation Treaty that says it can't. If they bomb them, it will be an act of aggression, a terrorist attack, and yet the whipping up of hostility in America is on such a scale that some people think Bush wants an attack to boost his popularity. It could be catastrophic for America, and it really would be Armageddon for the Middle East.

Tuesday 2 May
Professor Ted Honderich, who is a Canadian and now a Visiting Professor of Philosophy at Bath University, came to do an interview that is being shown on Channel Five, based on his book on morality, terrorism, Iraq and Palestine. He put a lot of difficult questions, and I tried to answer them as best I could. He's actually a distinguished philosophy professor. But when a philosophy professor turns his mind to all these problems, it's so theoretical: 'What happens if democracy comes to the wrong conclusion?' and 'Are people really able to distinguish between right and wrong?' To be cross-examined almost for a university final exam was good for me, and I enjoyed it.

Friday 5 May
I woke up at five o'clock. Labour had lost 250 council seats in the local elections. I think it went up to 274.

There's a huge reshuffle that's been trickling in all day. Charles Clarke has been sacked. John Prescott has lost all his ministerial responsibilities. John Reid has gone to the Home Office. Jack Straw has been moved to Leader of the House. It's rather like Macmillan's Night of the Long Knives. Blair's last reshuffle. He will never recover his confidence after this, because of the number of angry people, including Charles Clarke.

Sunday 7 May
MPs have sent a letter to Blair saying, 'Set a date.'
· Straw was obviously sacked by Bush, who objected to the fact that he'd said it was nuts to invade Iran and it would be 'inconceivable' to do so.

I was picked up at half-past eight and driven to the BBC in White City. Anthony Howard and I had this little discussion on the news, beginning with Beckett's appointment as Foreign Secretary. They showed little clips of her at various stages, having been a figure of the left. I had looked her up on the CD-ROM of my *Diaries*, and noted that I asked her to become my research assistant in September 1973: she turned it down because she wanted to continue to work for the Labour Party at Transport House. She supported me in the deputy leadership. I supported her in the leadership. It was put to us that she was on the 'hard left'. I said, 'Well, Tony Blair wrote to me when he became Leader, and he said my speech for Cherie [when she stood as a Labour candidate in Thanet] was the finest statement of socialism he'd ever heard. And,' I said, 'he was going round in '83, supporting withdrawal from the Common Market, and unilateral nuclear disarmament . . .'

We moved on to the whole Blair situation. So I said, 'Well, just as Cameron says, "Vote blue and go green", we say, "Vote red and go blue".' I was really quite funny and very relaxed, because I think ridicule is the best way of dealing with Blair now.

I rang a friend, who thought the reason Straw was sacked was because he was too independent, not just on Iraq; apparently he was much more independent than we realised, on Iran; absolutely opposed to the war; he had also been talking in Cabinet in an open way, and Blair was not prepared to have it. Blair wouldn't have any independence at all: you were one of us; for us or against us. So that threw an interesting light on it all.

Monday 8 May
Watched Blair's press conference in which he, predictably, said he was going to carry on and brushed aside all criticism. He said only people who hated New Labour wanted him to go. So there is no need to have a Parliamentary Party meeting – Labour MPs will have seen that!

Tuesday 9 May
I walked over to Number 10 Downing Street for the presentation of this letter to Blair: a cover letter to 1,800 signatures from American physicists, headed by five Nobel Laureates, warning of the danger of a nuclear attack on Iran. This was a letter drawing the Prime Minister's attention to the warning. The organiser of the Campaign against Sanctions and Military Intervention in Iran is Professor Abbas Edalat, who is the founder of the society, and who teaches somewhere in London.

General Sir Hugh Beech, who was Deputy Commander-in-Chief of Land Forces, a distinguished gentleman, very tall, neatly dressed, with an umbrella, was there. He said we'd met when I was campaigning on land mines. For a retired army general to come out against an attack on Iran, I thought was interesting.

Anyway we went, a few of us, to Downing Street; the usual business – we banged on the door, Abbas handed in the letter. He thought we might be invited in, but they don't do that. Outside there were a lot of journalists, permanently camped opposite Number 10, so Abbas and I went and made a statement.

Tea with Alan and Pascale Simpson and his little baby girl, three months old. The main interest in my talk to Alan was to hear what happened at the Party meeting yesterday.

He confirmed that at Party meetings people are barracked if they say unpopular things. David Winnick and Gerald Kaufman both made speeches attacking critics, but quite a number of people said to Blair, 'Look, the problem stems from you and Gordon Brown. Your supporters keep briefing each other. You've got to work it out between yourselves.' A number of people had been very critical. One MP said, 'The Party has just disappeared. There are no local parties. There's nothing to campaign with. It's all top-down and instructed from Party headquarters; all the experienced regional organisers have gone, and there are people on short-term contracts.' The nature of the crisis in the Party must be becoming apparent to people.

Thursday 11 May
I had an email from the General Secretary of the Labour Party saying, 'Have you ever thought of joining the Labour Party?' So I sent a reply saying, 'I joined the Labour Party on my seventeenth birthday in 1942, and I have been a member for sixty-four years. Tony Benn.' I don't suppose he will see it, or have it brought to his attention.

Monday 15 May
By Tube to Tower Hill to walk over to City Hall, Ken Livingstone's HQ. For the first time ever in my life, I crossed Tower Bridge on foot.

Hugo Chávez, the President of Venezuela, was about an hour and a half late. He'd been with the TUC this morning. Apparently yesterday he spoke at a public meting for four hours! I think the meeting must have been four hours, but he did speak at great length.

We were on the top floor, a beautiful view of London, where all the tables were laid out. Of course, he's come to England as a guest of Ken Livingstone. He's not seeing the Queen, and he's not seeing Blair. Blair made a horrible attack on him recently.

I sat on a table next to the Chief Executive, the top administrative boss at the GLC. On the other side of me was the Venezuelan Minister for Trade. The whole left was there in force. Simon Fletcher, of course – he used to be a Teabag – i.e. a member of The Eminent Association of Benn Archive Graduates, all of whom used to work in my office; Will McMahon; Tariq Ali; Jeremy Corbyn; Richard Gott; Diane Abbott.

Then Ken came over, he's done terribly well as Mayor of London. It's an extraordinary story really, quite extraordinary. He's very imaginative, is old Ken. Anyway, he came over and then he took me over to meet Chávez.

The Ambassador and an interpreter explained who I was. 'Oh,' he said, 'Tony Benn – I know very well!' and he gave me a bear hug, and we had a wonderful talk. I said to him, 'You know, we have got to carry this battle beyond this. Your vision and programme have given us hope,' which is true, 'but we've got to look beyond this, at how we can deal with the World Trade Organisation, the IMF, and so on, which set the framework within which governments have to work – that and the American Empire.' I said,

'I was born in an empire and played some part in helping to dismantle it, so I know exactly what the problems are.'

Lots of photographs taken, then I went back to my table and Chávez made a speech. He referred to our talk, 'Tony Benn reminded me that he was born in an empire' – he went out of his way to be friendly.

In his speech he said, 'Of course England is the centre of socialism, because all the early socialists and Marxists worked here, and we see in England the first challenge to neo-conservative capitalism, and we need socialism.' He said he was a dedicated Christian. He'd been to see the Pope. He'd just come back from Vienna. He's building links with Europe, which are of tremendous importance to him and also to us. So I was very impressed by him . . . thoughtful, scholarly; did go on a bit too long, but then who am I to complain about that?! But excellent answers, excellent comments, and terribly friendly.

When the lunch ended, Tristan Garel-Jones, a former Tory minister and now a Tory peer, offered me a lift back to the Commons with Bianca Jagger. There's a meeting this afternoon that Chávez is going to address later in the Banqueting Hall, which I can't go to. We talked in the car.

I was dropped off at the Commons and I went to the Churchill Room, and there was this packed meeting and Chávez was speaking again. A good speech, very thoughtful, and then questions were asked. I repeated the question about does he think it's possible that we could get some democratic control of these institutions, so that the world's resources would be controlled by the people, and he said he thought it would be very difficult, and so on. He couldn't have been friendlier.

Then afterwards we had another photograph with him, and I talked to Jeremy Corbyn, who knows Venezuela well, and the Campaign Group crowded round.

Tuesday 16 May
The President of Iran has written a letter to Bush, so I rang up *The Guardian* and said, 'Why don't you publish it?' And they said they would.

I was driven to BBC Radio London by a Polish driver, he said he had been here six years and didn't like living in England; he found it too fast and wanted to go to Mexico. I was driven back by another Pole, who was thirty-two. He didn't like England because there were so many blacks. I said, 'Well, I heard that before the war – of course then there were too many Jews.'

'Yes,' he said, 'and that is another problem – the Jews are everywhere!'

I said, 'A number of the black people I meet say they don't like all these immigrants from Eastern Europe' – that rather surprised him.

Saturday 20 May
MI5 files have now been disclosed and they reveal that in 1946, sixty years

ago, the Stern Gang, the Israeli terrorist group or Jewish terrorist group, wanted to assassinate Ernie Bevin, the former Foreign Secretary, on the grounds that he was anti-Semitic. So I did a little bit of research on that, and I looked up the bombing of the King David Hotel, and so on.

Wednesday 24 May
I had a letter in Italian today from Fausto Bertinotti, the leader of the reformed Communist Party in Italy, who, with the new coalition under Prodi, has been elected President of the Chamber of Deputies. I read it out to Dave, my brother Dave, who's a wonderful linguist, and this is roughly what it said:

Dear Tony,
    Your words have given me new strength in facing the highly delicate duties that I have from a constitutional point of view. I continue to think of you as a dear friend and comrade. You are a political man whose ideas are there to give encouragement to the entire European left.

It was a very nice letter.
John Reid, appearing before a Select Committee yesterday, attacked the Home Office as totally dysfunctional. The interesting thing about John Reid is this: by his attack on the Home Office, he rubbished Jack Straw, he rubbished David Blunkett and he rubbished Charles Clarke, his three predecessors, so he will not have made many friends there. Of course, Jack Straw is the only one still in the Cabinet.
I caught the Tube to the House of Commons and I went to see Brian Haw in Parliament Square. There was a huge crowd of supporters, quite a few police, because yesterday the police bundled up most of his material and put it into a skip. There was another demonstration at the other corner of the square, in favour of legalising cannabis for medical purposes, and I had a talk to them. Brian said he was going to sue the police for stealing his property. But he has got to think it all out, and actually the police have given him permission to continue in Parliament Square. He was told he can have three metres for placards. He's under terrible stress.

Thursday 25 May
At ten o'clock Tony Lee, who is the producer of this Channel 4 series *Tony Benn Interviewing the Interviewers*, arrived with his research assistant, a nice girl called Eve Lucas, to discuss how I would tackle the interviews.
I watched Jon Snow on Channel 4 News, talking about pensions, and what was interesting about it was that he interviewed somebody from a pension fund, and an academic, and somebody who was in the City, but he never thought of interviewing anybody from the National Pensioners'

Convention, and they follow these things closely. Even though I think Jon's a wonderful guy, I wanted to ask him (and indeed all of the interviewers): why did you choose them, and not have somebody who was on a pension?

Friday 26 May
Tonight, Blair made a speech in which he said we want to have progressive pre-emption, allowing any country to go into any other country, in effect, if it is thought that human rights are being denied. So on that basis, Venezuela could invade Cuba, or Cuba could invade Guantanamo Bay, in order to deal with what's going on. It is the old imperialism come back large.

I had, from Mentorn, the television production company, a list of twenty-five health questions before I could sign a contract – everything from heart attack to diabetes to prostate. So I wrote and said I was not prepared to answer them, that I was in good health and could certainly perform the programme, although I couldn't guarantee that I wouldn't be knocked down by a bus, stabbed in the street or be recalled to the air force (because I am still an RAF pilot, on the reserve list). For all I know, they could sell the details to somebody else, so I'm just not doing it.

I'd better watch Jeremy Paxman on *Newsnight*, because I've got to watch it for these interviews I'm doing. I want to discuss things with them in a genuinely inquisitive way, and not raise issues that will put them on the defensive, although you can do it in a delicate way.

Saturday 27 May
To the Coronet Cinema to see *The Da Vinci Code*.

Now, this is a film based on the book by a guy called Dan Brown, it's sold about forty million copies. I tried to read it, but after about ten pages I couldn't deal with all the complications. This book suggests, in effect, that Mary Magdalene was Jesus's lover, and that she became pregnant before the crucifixion and now has a descendant living in France. In it, there are some wonderful characters.

It gave me a new perspective on Jesus. I have concluded before that what matters about him is his teaching, not the fact that he ascended into heaven, that he sits at the right hand of God as Christ the King, and all that. That has no interest to me.

But the idea that he actually had a child, and that there is a line from Jesus to today, is of course devastating as a story, because it completely undermines everything that's said about Jesus by the churches. I found it interesting just to think about it. It could be true. I must look up what happened at the First Council of Nicea, because it was there that the divinity of Jesus, I think, was first decided, and that was hundreds of years after the crucifixion. The Catholics are absolutely denouncing the idea. There was a monsignor in Rome saying the whole thing was absolutely ridiculous, a conspiracy theory, but there's nothing very odd about the possibility that Jesus, at the age of thirty-three, fell in love with Mary Magdalene.

Monday 29 May
I worked all morning finalising my list of questions for the Channel 4 programme, *Tony Benn Interviewing the Interviewers*. I amended it an endless number of times.

Tuesday 30 May
I was picked up and taken to Channel 4 for the first of the interviews, with Jon Snow. He kept me waiting a bit because he was interviewing Madeleine Albright, but at least he did allow me into his studio and gave me forty-five minutes. I tried to make it friendly, but he was very sensitive about it.

I said, 'Why don't you invite trade unions?'

'Well, they don't matter any more. In the old days trade unions mattered, but they don't any more!'

Jon's the son of a bishop.

I asked, 'Have you ever been convinced by anybody, or persuaded by anybody, you've listened to?'

'Yes,' he said, 'every time I go to Number 10, I think the Prime Minister is right.'

So that showed him in a rather different light, and although, as I say, I was friendly, I wasn't in any way critical. I said, 'To whom are you accountable?'

Then I asked his advice to anyone who wanted to get a case across, and he said, 'Listen. Listen.' When I said that people he interviewed wanted to say something: 'Oh, they're not there to say something. They're there to answer my questions!' So there was a certain contradiction – I think I can bring that out by decent editing.

Friday 2 June
Up at six, and went to the BBC for the John Humphrys interview for Channel 4. Humphrys was very good. I asked all the same questions as I did of Jon Snow.

Saturday 3 June
To Hungerford School for the Labour Against the War Conference. Alan Simpson was in the chair – I do dearly love him. They're great people, they asked about Afghanistan, Iran, about the Labour Party and New Labour, about the US war economy, about the Internet as the new media. A little boy of eleven and a half who comes to all these meetings was there; he's so sweet and he keeps saying, 'We mustn't blame ordinary Americans.' They're decent people, but my God, the average age was about fifty-five, I

would think, and that is the problem we have. New Labour has just destroyed its own grass roots.

Sunday 4 June

Up at six and listened to the early bulletins.

At seven o'clock I was taken to BBC Radio 4, Broadcasting House at White City, to do the papers with Saffron Burrows and Dominic Lawson, who wasn't there, but did it on the phone. Paddy O'Connell was in the chair. I must say, it was great fun. Saffron was extremely good and very jolly and friendly, and we had about fifteen minutes one way and the other, and I got across a lot of the points I wanted. It has an audience of two million people.

Monday 5 June

I was picked up about 8.50 in the morning and driven to the University Women's Club in Audley Square for the interview with Nick Robinson, the BBC's Chief Political Correspondent.

He had thought carefully about it. He'd given a lecture on interviewing up at the Edinburgh Festival and was clear about it all, and his answers were good. When it comes to editing, I'd be quite happy to leave my questions out actually and just let them speak for themselves.

Then I came home briefly, and I was picked up at 1.30 and taken to White City for the Jeremy Paxman interview. He kept me waiting for about forty minutes. He was a bit nervous. He took off his tie and was terribly friendly, and expected me to hit him on the head, and I didn't. I think it was worth doing that way. He'd thought about it well; he was quite sensible.

My three-month forward diary where I keep my engagements, three months in advance, the end of it is already in early September, 5 September, and boy – it sort of frightens you that winter's on its way; and by the time you get to September, the diary will stretch to after Christmas. I find the cold weather terribly difficult to cope with. Also, I'm a bit shaky on my pins, and I'm always afraid I'll go down to the Underground and I'll keel over and fall before a train, so I'm very careful. My legs are very wobbly.

Tuesday 6 June

Eve Lucas turned up with the transcripts of the interviews, I had a candid talk to her and explained my anxieties about them trying to take the programme over from me, because I do want to be consulted about the rough-cut and about the video clips they want to add to it. I think she understood, so she'll be a good go-between. I like her very much.

To Brighton, for the Stop the War meeting at the Public and Commercial Services union conference. As well as Mark Serwotka of the PCS and Lindsey German, there was an Iraqi writer.

That raid on a house by 250 police, where a young Muslim lad was shot, has turned out to be a complete fraud. There was nothing there at all. It did make me wonder one thing: whether perhaps someone from al-Qaeda rings up the police and tells them this site has got a bomb, and then innocent people are arrested and shot, and the hostility of the Muslim community for the police grows. It's a bit conspiratorial, but it makes you wonder.

Wednesday 7 June

Every year, for the last four years, the RMT union has had a Cuba night at its headquarters in Clapham. I went along and it was packed with all my old mates. Ann Henderson was there, which was nice. She'd come down from Edinburgh. The Cuban Ambassador was there. Ken Gill, Matt Wrack, Brendan Barber, Jennie Walsh, who used to come to my office and now has a little three-year-old girl, who just loved the Cuban music and danced and danced and wandered about. We danced together around the floor. It was lovely!

Tony Donaghey, the President of the RMT, is a guard at St Pancras, whom I've met on the train many times going up to Chesterfield. He spoke and introduced me, and I spoke about Cuba, with great feeling and passion. Then (I had been told in advance), when I finished, Bob Crow made a little speech and gave me an honorary membership card.

Came home and I began watching *The Sound of Music*, but it was so boring that I changed to *Dr Strangelove*, which is brilliant and terribly contemporary, because now it's not the commies they're after, but the terrorists – but exactly the same mechanisms come into play.

Saturday 10 June

Caught the Tube to the Friends' Meeting House for the Stop the War Annual Conference. There were about 600 people there. Lindsey German, John Rees, Andrew Murray are really the mainspring of the Stop the War Coalition; they and Jane Shallice were there.

As President of the Stop the War Coalition, I was asked to speak first. It wasn't a wonderful speech, but it set the scene. Then I wandered round and talked to people. There were some really good speeches made. The left are still seen as the mindless militants, but they're tremendously intellectual, and it was interesting just to listen to what they had to say.

I have been researching the ending of the slave trade, for a lecture in Bath Abbey, and I went onto Google, and there was all this information about William Wilberforce and these very wealthy Conservatives, Christian Evangelicals, who believed in the proper order of society, but thought it was wrong to have slavery and were opposed to blood sports and other things. I would never have known of it otherwise.

One of the things that's interesting me is to look at the repressive legislation introduced by Pitt just after the French Revolution, and realise that it's exactly what's happening now. Habeas corpus was suspended for a year, the Combination Acts made it illegal for anybody to meet, to organise for political reform. There was an exact parallel. It did all get repealed later, but somehow things are moving faster and quicker and are more dangerous now, and I just wonder whether we are slithering into a situation where we give up all our rights.

Monday 12 June

I wrote short manuscript letters to Jon Snow, John Humphrys, Nick Robinson and Jeremy Paxman, just saying: 'Thank you very much for sparing the time to see me for the interview about your work. I appreciate what you've said and hope that when the programme, now edited, comes out, you will feel it does full justice to you.'

Tuesday 13 June

The news today is interesting. The two young brothers, one of whom was shot by the police in the Forest Gate raid, when they were allegedly looking for a deadly chemical weapon, gave a press conference; what they said was so credible – they had been shot, beaten up, dragged down the stairs by the police and were absolutely innocent.

I spent the morning working on an aide-memoire for the BBC about the coverage of the Iraq war and the way in which the Stop the War Coalition was treated, for a meeting today with Helen Boaden at the BBC. When I got there I went to the wrong door, and there was a rather gruff-looking, thirty-five-year-old doorkeeper. Then he saw me and said, 'Oh, Mr Benn! My grandmother was a constituent of yours in Bristol, and you helped her with a housing case. I'll take you over!'

Helen Boaden, Director of BBC News, turned up and we walked up to her office. Mark Byford, the Deputy Director General, was supposed to be there, but he had another engagement. I didn't want to make a fuss about it or a complaint, but the note was quite clear. Anyway, she gave me a big hug when I arrived, and it was all over in about fifteen minutes, and then she gave me another big hug as I left.

I also sent a copy of my aide-memoire to Mark Byford, and to Michael Grade, who's the Chairman of the BBC, so I think it will have registered.

Wednesday 14 June

Got the Underground to Paddington and caught the train to Bath. Was met by Edward Mason, who is the Prebendary of Bath Abbey. We walked through the streets, and people stopped me and wished me luck and everything. It's a nice, warm feeling in Bath.

There were four or five hundred people in the Abbey for my Wilberforce lecture, 'Faith, Hope and Freedom'. I'd done a lot of research and I spoke for about half an hour.

Then there were lots of questions, some funny ones. One man got up and said, 'When do you think the Second Coming is coming?' And I said, 'Well, it doesn't help me to believe that, but if it helps you, you go ahead.' Being in a church, there wasn't quite the sort of atmosphere of a public meeting, they were a bit more restrained; but at the end I got applause, much to my surprise, because Bath is a Liberal town, not exactly my area.

Then they walked me back to the station and I caught the 9.52, got home about a quarter to twelve.

When I got home I had a call to say that somebody has unearthed a letter that Tony Blair wrote in 1982 to Michael Foot: 'In one sense, he's quite right in saying the right wing of the Party is politically bankrupt' – this is Blair about me – going on to urge Foot to expel the Militant Tendency. Towards the end of the letter he wrote to Foot that he should 'Indicate firmly that you believe the Party needs radical, socialist policies, that the scale of the problems we face as a nation in 1982 means a different approach than to previous years. The job of reconstruction, particularly against a background that includes new technology and a USA in the grip of the same economic madness Mrs Thatcher visits upon us, is mammoth.' Oh-ho, it was very funny!

So I looked up in my diary 28 April 1983, when Tony and Cherie picked me up, the first time I'd ever met him, and drove to Margate. Cherie was the candidate in the '83 general election for Thanet West and I spoke from the platform for her. Then I also found that on 2 August 1994, I wrote to Tony and said I hadn't voted for him as Leader, and he wrote a nice personal letter saying how much he'd enjoyed Caroline's book on Keir Hardie, and referring to the fact that I spoke for Cherie. I remember him saying, 'I've always regarded your speech for Cherie as the finest statement of socialism I've ever heard.' Much later on, I found the tape of my speech in 1983, copied it, and sent it to him and said, 'As you were so kind to ask, I thought you'd like to hear it.' Of course it was the speech on the 1983 election manifesto – to leave the Common Market, adopt unilateral nuclear disarmament, extend public ownership!

Monday 19 June
I worked all morning on this idea of doing *Sentimental Journey* for the BBC, and with the help of a map and a measuring tape I discovered that 90 per cent of my political life has been spent within half a mile of Big Ben. They want me to do it with a guy called Arthur Smith, who apparently is a very amusing man.

In the evening I rang Malcolm Kendall-Smith's mother in New Zealand. She works at a university, and her son, a Flight-Lieutenant, has recently been sentenced to eight months in prison for refusing to go to Iraq. I got her number from the Stop the War Coalition, and I rang her at a quarter-past eleven our time. I told her that I'd been a pilot, and my brother was a pilot and was killed, and my father was a pilot, so I think she was glad to have a bit of contact. Her husband is not very well; indeed, I got the impression he was seriously ill. Malcolm should be out in about another couple of months, and I've no doubt as soon as he comes out he'll go back to New Zealand to see his father.

Wednesday 21 June
According to the news, Thames Water, who lose 800 million litres of water a day, paid vast profits to their shareholders, and failed the targets laid by the regulator. The regulator is allowing Thames Water to make these profits whilst absolutely failing to meet their requirements to mend the leaks – not only that, but increasing the prices by 21 per cent in a year. God, the case for socialism is coming back, and I think people are beginning to tumble to it.

Thursday 22 June
I was asked to do a live broadcast about the refurbishing of Trident, with Lord Gilbert, a former Labour Defence minister who *sounds* like an old-fashioned Tory imperialist! He talked about the white men and the yellow men and he said, 'I don't see why the brown men shouldn't have nuclear weapons.' He favoured India and Pakistan having them. Then he said, 'The President of Iran, whose name doesn't fall off my tongue, is a real danger.'

The Trident story is big today, because Gordon Brown went out of his way to say he favoured it. It'll cost between twenty and twenty-five billion quid, but he's keen to prove to the Americans how reliable he is. Of course it has led to a lot of Labour MPs saying they will never vote for him as Leader.

Friday 23 June
I caught the Underground to the Embankment and walked to Trafalgar Square for a huge demonstration in the Square for World Widows, sponsored by Richard Branson, in which Cherie Blair was involved. Objectors were standing up holding posters saying, 'Cherie – how many widows did your husband make today?' rather like 'Hey, hey, LBJ – how many kids did you kill today?' I don't terribly like it.

I thought it was going to be cold, so I put on my woolly underwear, but actually it was boiling hot in the sun. I took a little cushion, and I sat on the steps of St Martin's for a couple of hours.

Blair made a speech today in Bristol saying we must tilt the criminal-justice system in favour of the victims, which of course is popular with the *News of the World* and *The Sun*, but what about the women and the children he's killed in Iraq? What about those victims?

Saturday 24 June
Watched *South Pacific*. It took me back to the America of sixty years ago, because it was 1947 when I went to America first. Then, America was so friendly, so confident, so happy, the sort of Roosevelt-Truman era was there, the right hadn't surfaced at all, and everyone was so friendly. Seeing these soldiers on the South Pacific islands singing 'There is nothing like a dame', you know, you warm to them, and then realise that if you were seeing American soldiers now in tin hats, you'd think, 'Oh God, who have they invaded now?' I found it quite an emotional experience.

Monday 26 June
I typed a letter to David Cameron about his proposal for a Bill of Rights, saying that he might remember I sent him my Crown Prerogatives (Parliamentary Control) Bill, and that I had, ten years ago, introduced a Charter of Rights into another bill, which I enclosed; and I asked if he or one of his Shadow Cabinet colleagues would have a public debate with me, perhaps with a High Court judge in the chair.

Tuesday 27 June
Tony Blair had written an article in *The Guardian* in which he called for an open and clear debate 'on where we are . . . in order to identify the future of progressive politics'.

So, emboldened by my letter to David Cameron yesterday, I wrote to Blair, welcoming his article and asking if he would agree to debate with me. I said in the letter, 'David Cameron has agreed to debate the Human Rights Bill.'

Charles Clarke's attack on Blair has further eroded support for him. He hinted that Gordon Brown should take over if Blair couldn't 'recover his sense of direction'.

Wednesday 28 June
Four hours' sleep. Up at 5.30. Got a cab to the House of Commons for *Sentimental Journey*. I had sent them a map of where I was born and lived and worked, with little blobs on it, and all within a quarter of a mile of Big Ben.

I got to the House of Commons, and Dilly Barlow, the producer, was there, with Arthur Smith. We went into the House of Commons and did a bit of interviewing there, and then to Number 10 Downing Street, where they let me in, and I stood in the street and talked about the first time I'd been at Number 10, about being a Cabinet minister and all that.

Then we went and had a cup of tea in Parliament Street.

Then I did a commentary on my birth and my childhood in the house on Millbank, now Millbank Tower. On the eleventh floor we met the Local Government Ombudsman, who now occupies it. Finally I got a cab to

Trafalgar Square, and sat and had another cup of tea, and talked about the meetings I'd done in Trafalgar Square. Got home at half-past twelve absolutely exhausted! Tried to have a snooze, but the phone rang continuously.

Later I got a cab to St James's, Piccadilly, for this benefit concert for Malcolm Kendall-Smith; Mark Steel gave a brilliant talk. He was followed by Sami Ramadani, the Iraqi writer, and Vivienne Westwood, the designer, who kept saying in the middle, 'I've forgotten what I'm going to say', and everybody clapped. She finished up by demanding the immediate withdrawal of British troops from Vietnam, and nobody batted an eyelid.

The presenter and political activist Mark Thomas was there, but I missed his speech. Janet Suzman, I think, was there, and there were pianists. It was a wonderful evening.

Thursday 29 June
Came back and had lunch. Then, it was a lovely day, so I took the deckchair into the garden and I had about half an hour's snooze.

Friday 30 June
In the Bromley by-election, Eric Forth's old constituency, Labour came fourth, below the United Kingdom Independence Party.

Saturday 1 July
I watched the World Cup Quarter Final. It began at four, and by the time of the penalty shootouts it was ten to seven. As history will record, England lost to Portugal. The Portuguese seemed to have the ball most of the time. Then, in the second half, Rooney was given a red card, Beckham injured his knee and came off, and there was no substitute sent in, so for the rest of the game only ten players against the Portuguese eleven, and they did extremely well. Nobody scored, so they went to extra time. Nobody scored, and then they went to the penalty shootout, and then we just lost. I mean, Portugal scored three and we only scored one. So that was the end. English fans were terribly depressed, and I was a bit depressed actually.

Sunday 2 July
All the news is football, football, football; five soldiers have been killed in Afghanistan in the last few days, but football has just obliterated everything.

Tube to Tower Hill to do this 'History Matters' event at the Tower of London, organised by the National Trust. It is an attempt to make history seem more important to young people. David Starkey was there; he said that Melissa had been one of the brightest pupils he'd ever taught; Boris Johnson, the Tory, was there, with his hair all over the place; and Tristram Hunt.

We stood in the open air in the boiling sun. I spoke after Starkey. I don't know what they expected me to say, but I said history matters because we've just been commemorating the 20,000 people who died in the Somme – why did they die? The leaders of the three countries were the grandchildren of Queen Victoria. Why was there war? Then after, the war, Russia went communist and Germany went fascist, and there was another war – why, why? In Afghanistan, we've lost soldiers – why? We went and invaded Afghanistan in the nineteenth century, captured Kabul and were driven out with a loss of 14,000 people – why? 'We're by the Tower of London, and the Tower represents where the rich and powerful have always been, with everybody else outside.' I said, 'Henry VIII married Anne Boleyn in the Tower of London, and then had her executed – so much for the British tradition of human rights.'

It wasn't what they expected. David Starkey, when he answered me, said, 'That was the most dogmatic statement of history I've ever heard', so I got rebuked.

But I didn't like the atmosphere of it. It wasn't me. It wasn't my view of history. But still, I said I'd do it, and I did.

On the way back I passed two of those large yellow vehicles which can go on the road and on the River, owned by London Duck Tours. I've always been fascinated by them. There were two of them parked up, so I talked to the driver of one and he said, 'You should have a word with Tony Merrick. He was one of the Pentonville Five.' So I went over, and there was Tony Merrick working on one of the Ducks. He's seventy-one. This lad, who'd been a stevedore, got this job, is very knowledgeable about London history. So I took a leaflet about it, and it'd be fun to have a trip with the grandchildren one day.

Tuesday 4 July
I went to the Fabian Society party, which I haven't been to for years. Harriet Harman spoke, and she said, 'We're talking a lot about Labour renewal, but the first way to get Labour renewal is to renew the attacks on the Tory Party and remind people of what happened under Thatcher.' I thought it was such a bloody negative thing to say, and anyway, what Thatcher did is exactly what we did.

Wednesday 5 July
To the Campaign Group. John McDonnell wants to stand for the leadership of the Labour Party. Well, I think that's a good idea. He's done a wonderful job in setting the Labour Representation Committee up. He's doing meetings all over the country. He's speaking at the Durham Miners' Gala on Saturday.

I had noticed that the plaques I'd put up outside the Admission Order Office in the Commons had got so dirty no one could read them, so I took with me some Brasso and cloths and rubber gloves, and I polished them.

Unfortunately, I made a mark on the paint work around it. While I was there, the Serjeant at Arms, General Peter Peterkin, went by and he said, 'I think it's terrible that you should have to do this. I'm going to have them unscrewed and cleaned up properly, and then laminated so that they'll always be clean.'

Thursday 6 July
I went to get the car to go to *The Guardian* party and the bloody battery was flat again. It's about the third time it's happened and I've really got to do something about it.

Alan Rusbridger, the Editor, had asked me, so I went up and had a word with him, thanked him.

Then Lynn Barber came to talk to me. She'd interviewed me some time ago, I thought for the *Daily Mail*, but she was friendly, she remembered the interview. I said, 'I expect you cut me up a bit.' She now works for *The Observer*, and I said, 'I'm afraid I don't read *The Observer* now because of the war.'

Then I was talking to somebody and David Lammy came up. He's a minister now. I said, 'I remember your maiden speech', and he said, 'Yes, you mentioned it in your *Diaries*, and that's the thing my parents are most proud of.' So that's a funny thing. I do remember his speech, it was very good.

I saw Will Hutton. Now, Will is a real sort of SDP type, but he's quite nice. He was talking to a couple of businessmen about capitalism and stakeholders. He began arguing with me about socialism. I said, 'Well, the public are to the left of a Labour Government, and I don't feel isolated at all.' He said, 'What about the power of capital? Surely capital is constructive?' I said, 'It transfers or it exercises power by wealth and not by citizenship.' He couldn't quite cope with that – it was fun.

It was a nice party, an open-air party just by the British Library. When I wandered round, I hardly recognised anybody, and I thought why the hell have I come, but lots of people came up, and I've mentioned some of them.

Friday 7 July
Packing for Durham. I got on the train and there was a man sitting opposite me and I fell to talking to him. He said he'd been in military intelligence for twenty-two years. He was stationed in Northern Ireland and he said, 'We bugged absolutely everybody. We bugged telephone calls from north and south. Nobody knows what went on. We had informers in safe houses', and so on. It just confirms everything you suspected. Then he went on to say that he was absolutely opposed to nuclear weapons – he thought it was a complete waste of time.

When we got to York, I was yearning for a smoke. The door was open, so I leaned out to puff my pipe, and there were ten young men between about twenty and twenty-eight, I should think.

One of them said, 'Are you Tony Benn?'

I said yes, so they all gathered round, and they began singing, 'Tony Benn, Tony Benn, Tony Benn, Tony Benn, Tony Benn, Tony Benn.' They were smoking, and I was smoking. Then they got on the train, and then they sang it in the train – 'Tony Benn, Tony Benn, Tony Benn' – and of course it went right up and down two carriages! I was embarrassed, but also very flattered.

Anyway, I got a cab to the Royal County Hotel, Room 255, one of the fancy rooms. Sat next to Janet and Tony Woodley, the General Secretary of the Transport and General Workers' Union, at the dinner.

Tony is always so terribly friendly to me, and Janet, his wife, was the secretary to the Finance Director in the company where he worked. Of course, she couldn't marry a trade-union leader when she worked for a Finance Director, so anyway, she changed her job. I sat next to Derek Simpson, General Secretary of Amicus. I don't know him well, but he said he had been a member of the Communist Party. He said, 'I am a simple Sheffield boy,' but he's very shrewd. He said, 'It must be Gordon Brown for Leader, because if anybody from the left stands, it will drive Gordon to the right. If people stand against Gordon from the right, it will drive him to the left.'

He was suspicious of Michael Meacher, because there was a letter that appeared in *The Guardian* this morning, signed apparently by Derek and others, which they were apparently bounced into. They'd been at a conference and agreed to something, but they hadn't agreed to the letter.

Saturday 8 July

Up at seven o'clock. Was on the balcony by 8.45 and there for nearly five hours. I saw all the banners go by.

David Miliband came up to me. He was there; he's a Member in the North-East. He said, 'What do you think of nuclear power?'

I said, 'I'm absolutely against it. I was once in favour of it. I'm absolutely against it.'

But he said, 'Oh, these environmental arguments . . .'

I said, 'There are hundreds of years of coal under our territory.'

'Oh, you can't do coal, can't do coal.'

He just wasn't interested. There was no sense of engagement.

Then my banner came by. I said to him, 'Now, look at the slogan on that. It says "Socialism through Evolution". You couldn't be more moderate than that.'

The Gala is like recharging your battery. You feel, on the balcony, you're looking at the whole of humanity. The words they have on the banners –

'Peace in our time' and 'Lions shall lie down with the lamb' – are wonderful.

It is the Labour movement, and I'm very proud that they asked me. I wouldn't mind speaking one year, but I think I'm beyond that now.

Tuesday 11 July

There is a move in the Government to change the unfair extradition laws, under which the Americans can call on us to extradite businessmen here to America, or anybody here, without a court hearing; whereas the Americans have failed to ratify it, so it isn't reciprocal, and the Americans won't extradite people from America to us. Although three bankers may be guilty of serious fraud, the idea that anyone in Britain can be picked up by the United States Government without any preliminary hearing, and then be tried and jailed in America, is outrageous!

Wednesday 12 July

I had a phone call from Tony Lee, the producer of the 30-minute programme, saying Channel 4 liked it so much that they've decided to make it a one-hour special, which is really good news.

Today Israel has invaded the Lebanon, on the grounds that Hezbollah, the so-called terrorists, have captured two Israeli soldiers. I mean, Israel can do what it likes, and the media coverage is disgraceful. So I went to a meeting called by Third World Solidarity.

The main speaker was Manuel Hassassian, the Palestinian 'Ambassador' in London. He made a clear, powerful speech, describing how Israel had behaved, the aggression, the double-standards, the lying, the failure of Britain and America to tell the truth, the suffering of the Palestinian people.

Also today, there were arrests in connection with the sale of peerages. I wonder whether this could be the thing that brings Blair down, but I'm not sure. It will depend upon the police or the CPS.

Thursday 13 July

I'd had a phone call yesterday, from a woman who left a message saying, 'Mr Benn, there's a real crisis.' I thought she might be in trouble, so I rang her up. I said, 'What's the problem.'

'Well,' she said, 'it's about the pigeons in Trafalgar Square. Ken Livingstone has banned people from feeding them, and now the steps of the National Gallery, which were originally where they could be fed, that's banned as well; and those pigeons, they're homing pigeons, they don't go anywhere else for food, they're dying in their hundreds – something must be done!'

So I said, 'Well, Tony Banks was very keen on saving the pigeons.'

'Yes, I know,' she said, 'but he's dead. Will you take on his work?'

So I said, 'I sympathise with you and I'll do what I can, but I'm not sure how much I can do.' Extraordinary!

Of course, today was Tony Banks's memorial meeting in the House of Lords.

Sunday 16 July

I walked back to the Tolpuddle Festival site. Very, very hot. Masses of banners. I just sat and talked to many old friends. Meg Crack was there, with her husband or partner. Anne Scargill was there. Shami Chakrabarti, who's the Director of Liberty, was there. Billy Bragg – I had a brief word with him.

Peter Hain was one of the speakers, and I did have a quick word with him about Northern Ireland. Shami made a good speech. I took up the theme of John McDonnell's candidature for the leadership. 'We must be absolutely clear what we want.' I said, 'We want an end to privatisation, trade-union rights fully restored, end of means testing for pensioners, end of student loans, local authorities should be free to do what they like.'

Tuesday 18 July

At about half-past two, my brother-in-law Graydon phoned from America to say Nance died this morning – Caroline's sister. I was absolutely shattered. I burst into tears.

She had breakfast this morning, at six o'clock, a few hours ago, fine, and then the nurse came in an hour later and she was dead. I really was thoroughly upset.

I rang all my children – Stephen and Hilary and Melissa and Josh. Hilary I got through to, via his office, in Sierra Leone. Then I rang as many as I could of Nancy's children.

I gathered the funeral might be this Friday, and I'm just not feeling very well at the moment. I mean, I could go and come back again the same day . . . but Stephen wants to go.

Wednesday 19 July

I heard this morning, Stephen and Hilary have both decided to go to Nancy's funeral, which is very sweet of them, and both of them think under no circumstances should I go, which relieves the pressure on me.

Lissie rang, and she told me that the first publisher who had read her novel had said it was wonderful!

It's got to the point now where Blair's made a statement that Israel should have another week to finish the bombing and deal with Hezbollah. When you also take on board the fact that, in an exchange between Bush and Blair, which was picked up on the microphone, Blair offered to go to the Middle East before Condoleezza Rice, to do the preliminary work for her, I mean he's a disaster. We don't have a foreign policy.

On Saturday I am due to speak at the Labour Representation Committee, and I'm going to say, 'We are today refounding the Labour Party. We're not founding a section of the Labour Party. We're not founding a new party. We are refounding the Labour Party on the basis that it is there to represent people, and what people want now is . . .' and I'll list the policies, and then say, 'And this is now the centre ground of politics.'

We won't be the hard left of the Labour Party; we will be the mainstream of what is needed, in a nation that is not represented.

Saturday 22 July

Well, today was Nancy's funeral in Cincinnati.

I got a cab to the TUC for the Labour Representation Committee conference, the third conference they've had.

I had a brief word with Matt Wrack, who is the General Secretary of the Fire Brigades Union. I sat next to him on the platform. I said I desperately wished they could rejoin the Labour Party to save us. I saw Bob Crow afterwards, as I was coming home, and said the same to him.

Tuesday 25 July

I went to the Commons by Tube and picked up the report of the Public Administration Committee on memoirs, the committee to which I had given evidence. They did reproduce, in the written evidence, which gave me great pleasure, the brief memorandum I submitted, plus the full text of the Cabinet minutes of 18 March 1975, and my diary for the same Cabinet meeting, which I used to show that an independent account cannot do any damage.

The report itself was terribly disappointing. I mean, there's something ineffectual about the Public Administration Committee – they get caught up in making minor changes for contractual arrangements with ministers, and how civil servants and advisers 'need to be responsible'.

Wednesday 26 July

I'm being picked up for my fourth broadcast today – *The Moral Maze*, on the morality of immigration, with Melanie Phillips and Claire Fox (I can't stand either of them), Clifford Longley and Michael Portillo. When I've appeared before, there was such a ghastly punch-up with David Starkey, I vowed I'd never do it again. I'm just going to try and keep calm and put across the point as best I can.

The other witnesses were: Frank Field, Keith Best, who had been a Tory MP for a few years and is now at the Immigration Advisory Service, and somebody from Civitas, which is linked to the Institute for Economic Affairs. I was brought in first, and I was just very candid. 'I look at it from a personal point of view. My mother was a Scot, my wife was an American, all the way through, my granddaughter is at primary school with seventy-seven nationalities. My father helped bring Jewish refugees here. We shifted ten million slaves from Africa. Capital can move, so why can't labour? I remember Mosley, and the hatred he built up.'

'You haven't answered the question.'

I said, 'I have answered the question. What I believe is happening is that people are building up power for themselves by whipping up hatred against others.'

'Are you suggesting those that are worried about immigration are racists?'

I said, 'Not at all, but I think the people who whip up the feeling are doing it deliberately.' I kept coming back to that, and it threw them.

Frank Field was in after me, and he was talking about the danger of too much immigration.

Portillo said, 'Constituents raise it with MPs.'

I said, 'I know they do. When I went to Nottinghamshire years ago, I was told about the immigrants, and I said, "Who do you mean?" and it was Scottish miners who were coming down.' I told them a story about a guy in Leeds who believed every asylum-seeker is given a car, a mobile phone, a black leather jacket and a home, and they don't even speak English. I said, 'What are you going to do?' 'I'm going to Portugal,' he said. I said, 'Do you speak Portuguese?' and he nearly hit me.

I just tried to keep my head above water.

Thursday 27 July
The House of Lords Select Committee on the constitution report came out today, and recommended that the House of Commons, or Parliament, should determine when Britain declares war. It was a tremendous victory. That provision was in my own Crown Prerogatives Bill of about 1993, I think. My evidence to the committee was published. So it's just another of the little acorns that I've planted in my life, which have grown into oak trees.

It's now so obvious Lebanon is an American war, in which Israel agreed to be the spearhead, and that's why the Americans won't dream of agreeing to a ceasefire. When Bush was asked, he said, 'Well, Israel has the right to defend itself.' He didn't say that about Iraq. He didn't say that about Afghanistan. There's no logic in it at all, and I think public opinion is now two to one against what the Israelis are doing, so Blair looks pathetic and irrelevant. He's not even a member of the coalition of the willing.

Friday 28 July
I caught the 148 bus to Westminster, got there very early, about quarter-past four. Sat just by the statue of Field Marshal Lord Montgomery, where there was a wall I could sit on that was in the shade. We went, with a

nine-year-old girl, with a Lebanese flag, to Number 10 Downing Street and presented a letter, and a lot of journalists came; nobody from the BBC – the BBC make it a principle not to cover that. They were standing there filming as we came in and out.

Saturday 29 July

Up early, and at 9.30 *Sentimental Journey* with Arthur Smith was broadcast on Radio 4. It was lovely! I laughed and cried.

Blair did an interview on TV, and is justifying the refusal to support a ceasefire, or even just a seventy-two-hour pause in the attacks, because Israel is determined not to allow Hezbollah to re-arm. The truth is that Israel has failed, in ten days of the most violent bombing, to make any impact on Hezbollah, who are now seen as great heroes in the Arab world.

Tuesday 1 August

Josh and Naz picked me up about quarter to six, to see a film called *Who Killed the Electric Car?*, which was the story of how electric cars came onto the market in California and were very popular, and how General Motors finally crushed them. How the oil companies and the American Government are all against the electric car.

On Saturday, in Parliament Square, I'm going to say what we want is Israel out of the occupied territory, Israel out of the Lebanon, Israel out of the Golan Heights, Britain out of Afghanistan, Britain out of Iraq, Blair out of Downing Street! I just feel that's got to be said.

Wednesday 2 August

I listened to the BBC's *The Moral Maze* and it was very muddled and unsatisfactory.

Friday 4 August

Heard that Tommy Sheridan had won his libel action for £200,000 against the *News of the World* for suggesting he went to a swingers' club and had an affair with various women. It's a tremendous achievement. He represented himself, he sacked his lawyers and did very well. The *News of the World* is really in a jam.

I also heard that Ian Walters, the sculptor, had died; he did my bust, and Harold Wilson, Nelson Mandela, Frank Cousins, Eric Heffer . . . a brilliant artist, very committed.

Saturday 5 August

Walked over to Parliament Square, joined about 100,000 people in all protesting against the Israeli attack on Lebanon. It was a wonderful demonstration. Bianca Jagger was there; Craig Murray, the former British Ambassador to Uzbekistan; Barry Camfield from the Transport and

General Workers' Union; Billy Hayes from the Communication Workers' Union; John McDonnell.

Sunday 6 August
I drove to Tavistock Square for the Hiroshima Day commemoration. There was a guy called Sheikh Dr Muhammad Yusuf, who is an imam and is actually the Research Fellow of the Interfaith Alliance. He made a wonderful speech, in which he said that God didn't differentiate between people of different colour, people of different race, people of different religion, people of different sex or sexual orientation. So afterwards I went and congratulated him on that, and he said, 'Well, I've always been a supporter of yours.'

I said, 'Do you get into trouble for what you say?'

'Yes, I do,' he said.

Thursday 10 August
Bush was on the air talking about Islamic fascism, which is a terribly dangerous phrase to use, because it links terrorism with a religion, just as if we talked about Zionist fascists or of Bush as a Christian fascist. You just whip up religious hatred.

Thursday 17 August
The Independent has a big splash, because John Prescott went to see some MPs about the Middle East, and Harry Cohen reported that he'd said Bush was crap and he was a cowboy with a Stetson hat. Of course Prescott said he was misreported, but it's very funny – has no political relevance, except it might mean that Bush asks Blair to replace him.

Sunday 20 August
I had a reply from Blair to my letter suggesting a debate on the future of progressive politics. He said it'd all be debated within the Party, and then added a note about Cameron, saying he hoped the question of the Human Rights Act would come out, and then a personal scribbled note at the bottom, 'Sounds like an interesting debate'. So that chapter is closed. Cameron's not followed up, so I think he's pulled out of that.

Tuesday 22 August
A car picked me up and took me to *The Guardian* for a one-and-a-half-hour interview with Nick Stadlen, QC, on the prospects for socialism and the failure of the left. He'd got all the *Diaries* and other books marked up, he'd put little tabs in, and he did the most remarkable introduction, lasting about ten minutes, and then he put all these questions: 'Why had the left failed?', 'Why is there no left?', 'Why don't you set up a new party?', 'How can you be in the Labour Party?'

Thursday 31 August
Well, Blair's back from his holiday and now says you can identify difficult children before birth, and you've got to intervene in a family to put it right. I mean, the man is an absolute control freak. He won't be there to see if any of it worked, and his Social Exclusion Unit has folded now. It's all gimmick, gimmick, gimmick, gimmick, gimmick.

Friday 1 September
The political news today is a huge row about whether Blair should go, and the Conference will be stormy, and Blair says he won't. I think we are seeing the end of him, but it's unpleasant for the Party. The real issue anyway is not whether he goes, but what the policy is.

Saturday 2 September
I watched the end of *The Way to the Stars*, which I began last night. I burst into tears when Rosamund John read that little poem from Michael Redgrave: 'Do not despair for Johnny-head-in-air. He sleeps as sound as Johnny underground . . . Keep your tears for him in after years . . . and see his children fed.' I was stationed as a RAF cadet at Pershore, when a thousand bomber raids were taking place, and one of our jobs was to clear the kit out of the barracks of the people who were killed and never came back from the bombing trip. I thought of Mike, and I thought of the war.

I have got to go to Coventry this evening, so I thought, let's look up and see what happened in Coventry during the war; on 15 November 1940, 500 German bombers attacked Coventry for ten hours, there were 1,000 casualties, 500 of them dead, 4,330 houses destroyed, the cathedral, two churches and two hospitals destroyed. Seeing that, and having watched *The Way to the Stars* – that's why I'm against war. If you haven't experienced it, you can go on sending troops to die and all the rest of it.

John Rees drove us and we got to Coventry in about an hour and three-quarters, to the Methodist Central Hall. There were about 500 people there – lots of old friends who'd met me and known me at different periods. One of them I think was Tom the Pict, who'd fought the great campaign against the toll ferry up to some island in Scotland; there was somebody from the Military Families Against the War; there was a Muslim woman; there was a trade unionist; there was John Rees; and myself.

Sunday 3 September
I have a pretty busy week ahead. I've got Camden tomorrow, and then I've got a couple of receptions on Tuesday, and then on Thursday I've got to go up to Manchester. I must get back that night, because Friday I'm in Croydon, and Saturday I'm in Scotland, and then the following Monday I'm at the TUC at Brighton, and then on the Tuesday I've got another Stop

the War. I've got twenty-four meetings this month. I must be absolutely out of my mind.

Tuesday 5 September

To the Marx Memorial Library and had a talk to John Callow, who is the librarian. He's in his thirties, I guess, a sensitive, thoughtful man, who has given up any political affiliation now, although he was in the Communist Party. Then he took me into the room where Lenin worked for a year – 1902–3 – and I must say, it was really quite exciting to be in the room, possibly sitting on the very chair he sat on.

I went on to *The Guardian*. I must have walked for about an hour and a half today. David Fairhall, who used to be the Defence Correspondent with *The Guardian*, invited me to come, because he's published a book about Greenham Common, called *Common Ground*. I saw Helen John, one of the founders of the Greenham Common women, she'd been in and out of prison endlessly; Sarah Hipperson, who's a little bit younger than me, came up to me; Joan Ruddock was there; Helena Kennedy, very warm, and said how wonderful Lissie was. Had a talk to Richard Gott, who's a great expert on Latin America.

According to the *Daily Mirror* today, Blair has planned a spring farewell tour, doing *Songs of Praise*, radio and TV things, going round the country. It's totally unreal. I think he is now within a few days of having to announce. I think he's bound to say at the Conference, 'This is my last Conference.' But it's so boring! The only one who's ever done anything right about it is John McDonnell. He said he would stand, and he published a political programme.

Thursday 7 September

Well, the press is full of a flaming row between Blair and Brown, and we heard that Blair was going to make a statement today, and Brown was also going to make a statement. So, to cut a long story short, in the course of the afternoon Blair said that this would be his last Labour Conference, he didn't give a date for going; and Brown said, 'It's for the Prime Minister to decide.'

I got the Tube to Euston, and as usual I caught an earlier train than the one I had planned to Manchester. To the Mechanics' Institute, where there was a great gathering of people to launch John McDonnell's leadership campaign. Lord Monkswell was there; Jeremy Dear, the General Secretary of the National Union of Journalists; Alice Mahon, the former MP for Halifax.

Saturday 9 September

Got to Heathrow at 6.15, and got a British Midland flight to Edinburgh. I was met by Ian MacIntosh and two other people, and I was driven to the Miners' Welfare Club in Cowie. It's a tiny village, and I'd been asked to go by this Irish councillor, Gerard O'Brien, who rang me up and promised to pay all my expenses – insisted I travel first-class, and so on. We marched to the Memorial to the Cowie miners who had died, a beautiful memorial put up in the village. There were all the miners' villages represented. There were all the families, old women, old men, kids who of course were born long after the Miners' Strike. There was a pipe band.

The Memorial was beautiful – black marble and an inscription, and a great ceremony took place there. MSP Dennis Canavan was there; Annie McGuire, who's the local MP and is also a minister in the Government; George Reid, who is a Scottish Nationalist Member of the House of Commons and the Presiding Officer of the Scottish Parliament. Then there was the Deputy Provost of Cowie. It was a great crowd of people, and a couple of old miners in wheelchairs, who laid wreaths.

Then we marched back to the Cowie Miners' Welfare Club, I think it's called. It was just like the Chesterfield Labour Club: all the tables laid out, and a little top table. We sat there and I had a long talk to Dennis Canavan.

There were speeches and I was presented with a beautiful miner's lamp, and a beautiful walking stick with a carved handle, which I think had been melted and turned, and with the Freedom of Cowie, a scroll in a little silver box to put on the mantelpiece. I found it very moving. It wasn't a big municipal or civic event. It was just local people gathered together to remember their dead and injured, and the spirit of the trade-union movement there was very strong.

Monday 11 September
I got the train to Brighton and walked down from the station, down West Street, to the front. Picked up my Conference pass, and what's so lovely at a TUC Conference, there's no security – I just wandered in, produced my identity card and they gave me a pass. I went into the TUC debate on trade-union rights. There was a brilliant speech made by a young woman who is now President of the National Union of Students.

Then I went up on the balcony and had a puff.

Monday 18 September
Saffron Burrows came to lunch. I'd laid on some asparagus soup, smoked salmon and salad, and strawberries, and we had a lovely lunch and then a talk.

She said she'd drive me to Victoria, and when we passed through the park she said, 'Would you like an ice cream?' I said, 'Well, I love ice cream', so we stopped and I bought a cone and ice cream with a chocolate bar stuck in it. Then she said, 'Would you like a cup of tea?' so I paid the parking meter and we went and had tea in the Kensington Gardens Tennis Club. Then she dropped me off at Victoria for the Liberal Democrats' conference.

On the train I saw Charles Kennedy, the former Liberal Leader, and had a chat to him. I said, 'You'll get a very warm welcome in Brighton', which I'm sure he will do.

As I passed the Grand Hotel, I thought that it was thirty-five years ago that I stayed there in my year as Chairman of the Labour Party. Thirty-five years ago!

Anyway, I went to the Brighton Metropole, and there was a fringe meeting organised by DAGGER, a campaign group for single transferable votes in multi-member constituencies, and they asked me to talk about democracy. I made a good speech and there were a lot of questions. At the end I got a standing ovation – at a Liberal Democrat conference!

Tuesday 19 September
I had a meal and went by Tube to St Pancras, and caught the 3.25 to Sheffield. It was a lovely day, a sunny autumn afternoon, and all the green fields, and the trees, and the cattle – the real England, which made me feel very emotional. I passed Chesterfield. It's a bereavement still to have lost my connection with Chesterfield. I realised that I went there twenty-three years ago, and twenty-three years is the difference between 1917, when the First World War was going on, and 1940, when the Blitz was starting in London. I mean, it's a long, long period.

Met by Maxine Bowler, a very nice woman who's in the Socialist Workers' Party. Anyway, there were eight to nine hundred people at the Stop the War meeting, including Mike and Lesley Matthews, from Chesterfield, old friends, and Peter Heathfield, former General Secretary of the NUM, whom I haven't seen for years. I gave him a bit of a hug.

Thursday 21 September
I went by Tube to Victoria, and then to Brighton, to the Institute of Development Studies. There was Professor Haddad, who's the Director, and Raphael Kaplinsky, who's been there thirty years, and his wife. There were lots of people brought up at dinner. I didn't know who they all were, but at any rate a distinguished group, because this was a three-day conference, and the peak of it is this evening apparently. Natasha, who is Raphael's daughter, had been asked to interview me, so I especially wore the lovely jumper she'd given me for my birthday. It was very enjoyable, excellent questions.

Friday 22 September
At 8.12 I caught the Peace Train, which was chartered by the Stop the War Coalition, to Manchester. I felt like a teenager! There were tons of people on board, mainly older people, I must say. As it was a chartered train, I lit my pipe and nobody minded. I sat opposite Bianca Jagger, and next to Craig Murray and Jane Shallice. We had a meeting in one of the

carriages, where I spoke. Everyone came up. People brought tea, so friendly.

Then, when we got to the station, Bianca and I caught a cab to the Britannia Hotel, Room 425. She asked if she could leave her bag in my room. Nicola, the woman who's sent me a postcard almost every day for ages, was there. She's a photographer, and she came up and took a picture. At least I now know who she is. The march lasted two hours, all the way round the Conference Centre in Manchester. The police kept slowing us down. Then, about halfway through, in order to remember the people who have died in the war, we were asked to lie down. Somebody put their bag under my head, and I was almost asleep – it was lovely!

Then went back to the square. Malcolm Kendall-Smith, the New Zealand doctor who was imprisoned for refusing to go to Iraq, was there, and I had a word with him.

Sunday 24 September, Labour Party Conference, Manchester
The media coverage at the moment is incredible. It's all about Brown, Brown, Brown and Blair, and possibly Alan Johnson.

Monday 25 September
I went in to hear Gordon Brown's speech. It was his leadership bid, and he paid a huge tribute to Tony Blair, and Tony was sitting there nodding and smiling. Then Brown explained that he was the son of the manse, that justice was what it was all about . . . it was a sermon. No mention of the trade unions at all, no mention of socialism at all; if we are responsible and work together and are British, capitalism will be okay, so long as Labour is in power. It was an extraordinary speech and he got a standing ovation. I took advantage of it to get up and slip out.

I can't complain. Everyone's been so nice to me, I love the Labour Party, but the Conference is absolutely irrelevant. It's a trade fair with a few ministerial speeches, and when ministers aren't speaking, the media are interviewing ministers, who haven't spoken, about what they're going to say. The Conference is less and less important, and the security is massive! Because I have a pacemaker, I don't have to go through the security barrier; they just search me.

Tuesday 26 September
Of course the big banner headline is that, during Gordon Brown's speech yesterday, Cherie Blair was supposed to have said, 'That's a lie' when Gordon said how much he enjoyed working with Tony. That's obliterated, or greatly damaged, Gordon Brown's speech.

Then I watched Tony Blair making his last speech at the Conference – a very skilled, professional performance. He made a joke about Cherie, by saying, 'Obviously my wife won't run off with the man next door.' But he sounded like a Victorian Prime Minister at the height of the British Empire; had absolutely no history in it at all. He hectored us and bullied us, and 'Change', change, change', 'Got to change!', 'You've got to change!', making us feel totally inadequate. No mention of the United Nations. Anyway, he got a seven-and-a-half-minute standing ovation.

Wednesday 27 September
While I was having tea with Stephen, just outside the Conference Centre, the mobile phone rang and it was Saffron Burrows. She said, 'Oh, I had dinner with Bill Clinton last night.' It does make me laugh! I said, 'Did you give my good wishes?' 'Oh, of course I did,' she said. Clinton had given this big lecture at the Albert Hall, for which the charge for tickets was £300, and he's paying off his debts or something, I don't know. Of course he's addressing the Conference today.

While I was having tea I saw Tony Blair's Sedgefield constituency agent. I'd seen him on television, a guy with a moustache, and I went over and had a word with him. I said, 'Joe Slater, your predecessor MP, was my Assistant Postmaster General forty years ago.'

'Oh yes, I remember Joe!'

I said, 'In '83, when I lost my seat in Bristol, you invited me to Sedgefield to be considered as your candidate.' I think he knew that, and we had a friendly joke – I asked if there was going to be a by-election. I said, 'And if you're still looking for a candidate, I'm available!'

Then I went in to hear Bill Clinton's speech. Now, Bill is the cleverest speaker I've ever heard. He doesn't issue a press release; he's thoughtful, he looks as if he's thinking it out, he looks round. He paid a warm tribute to Tony Blair and to the Labour Party. His speech had a historical background. Last time he spoke, he made a reference to some Pope who had got it wrong in the Crusades. This time, he quoted Machiavelli, who said, 'When there's a change, people who would lose by the change know about the change and fight it. Those who would gain by it don't know what they'd gain.' He encouraged us, he praised Tony, he endorsed Gordon, though not specifically, and he got a huge ovation. He's just a very attractive character, but by God, his policy is bombing the Sudan, bombing Belgrade; I mean he is a total Blairite, and so my enthusiasm for his style should not be mistaken as being support for his policy.

Yesterday, in the Conference, the Government was defeated on a resolution condemning the privatisation of the NHS. They won't take any notice of it. Apparently Tony Woodley, who did a broadcast, made some sharp comments about Gordon Brown. So things are not totally settled. I have said to myself, and said at fringe meetings, 'Don't worry. It's all coming right,' but I can't really pretend, as far as the Party is concerned, it is coming right at all.

I did far too many fringe meetings, but I was sensible this year. I just made a point of having a couple of hours' sleep every afternoon. I have to be careful of my health, but I got terribly tired. I did masses of walking, sometimes two hours' walking a day to and from the Conference. I did walk slowly. I didn't eat anything like enough. I just lived on sandwiches and bananas and tea.

Sunday 1 October
The Tory Conference began today. David Cameron made a speech about the need for the Conservative Party to move to the centre right – no policies. Cameron is moving into Blair's territory and leaving the Thatcherites out in the cold, whereas Blair moved into Thatcher's territory and left the left out in the cold. I don't see any difference, politically, between them. It's an extraordinary situation. I don't ever remember a situation like this. They used to talk about Butskellism, the link between Butler and Gaitskell and all that, but this is quite unique. The political element is absolutely disappearing. The idea of political choice is disappearing entirely from the agenda.

I think people see that, and they don't bother to vote. It may be that, with billionaires in China, and the widening gap between the countryside and the towns, Americanism is just the politics of a satisfied, powerful minority who are able to con everybody else to go along with it. It's a depressing thought.

Monday 2 October
The Tory Conference has begun, a row about tax cuts – not a substantial matter, but . . . I mean, talk about the one-party state!

Saturday 7 October
I got to Reading, I hung about for about forty minutes and then I jumped on a train for Cheltenham, and Emma Mitchell from Hutchinson was there, and we drove to Moreton-in-Marsh where, sixty-five years ago, I was stationed for a weekend as an Air Training Cadet.

We went to a hotel, to a gathering of about ninety-five people, almost all of them retired, City people, bankers, diplomats, academics, the old Tory Party. I was slightly nervous, but I gave a speech, about war, and about religion, and about democracy, and then questions and answers, and I got thunderous applause. You could have knocked me down with a feather!

Then we went to a debate on the media – are they better or worse than they were thirty years ago – chaired by Jim Naughtie, with Clare Short, Libby Purves, Jeremy Paxman and Nick Clarke, who wrote this brilliant book about Alistair Cooke. Nick's had his left leg completely removed. There wasn't even a stump. Paxman was a bit awkward about being asked questions, and has just written a book on royalty.

I did the best I could, but the journalists were so bloody defensive! What I wanted to discuss was how we could use the talent of the world, through the media, to solve the problems of the world. I think I made my case quite well.

Then on to a discussion with Nick Clarke in the chair, about Simon Jenkins's book on Thatcherism. On the cover he's got Mrs Thatcher, and then behind her Major, and behind him Blair, and behind him Gordon Brown. He told me what Tina Brown had told me – that Cameron was a neo-conservative, but he might be very clever, all touchy-feely.

Monday 9 October
Well, I was asked by Pat Mason, who's a Labour councillor in Kensington for Golborne Ward, whether I'd go up and help him in his campaign to save an old people's home, which is being closed by Kensington Borough Council. It's called the Edenholme Home. It's been there for thirty years. There are forty-seven people, the oldest nearly 100, many of them with dementia, and it's being closed because the council wants to sell the land, which is very valuable in this area, and scatter the people to homes in different parts of London.

Pat met me and we went in and met some of the residents. There was one guy who was really quite coherent. He'd been a plumber, had had three strokes. There was the granddaughter of someone there, and she was incensed, so angry about it.

I felt as if I were still an MP, and sat down and chatted to some of them. ITN appeared, and they took films and interviewed people. I made a little statement myself.

Then a man came from Kensington Borough Council and said, 'You've all got to leave.' So I said, 'Why?' He said, 'Well, I've been told you've got to leave.' So I said, 'We're not going to leave. This is their home, and I've been invited to come into their home.' He was an obstinate bureaucrat.

When I got home I had seventeen messages on my answering machine to deal with, tons of emails, a mass of letters.

Tuesday 10 October
Gordon Brown has come out in favour of Jack Straw about Muslim women not wearing the veil, which is absolutely ridiculous, but it fits in with his idea that we're all British and must have the Union Jack in our front garden.

Wednesday 11 October
David Blunkett's diaries were published in *The Guardian*, and they dealt with the war and the Cabinet discussions, saying that Gordon Brown had had to be driven to accept the war, because if he didn't Blair would sack him; which may be helpful to Brown, I don't know. But also it's the first indication of any disagreement in the Cabinet about the war.

An American medical team have estimated 650,000 Iraqis have been killed since the invasion in 2003. Of course the American Government denies it, but these are American doctors and a medical team who went round and talked to people and came to that conclusion. So it all builds up and builds up to the final end of any public support for the war.

Thursday 12 October
I watched the first of *The Blunkett Tapes* on Channel 4. His published diaries have been serialised in the *Mail* and *The Guardian*. It's strange watching them. He has dictated a tape since 1997, and they were reproduced, although an actor played the part, because they weren't very audible apparently.

The programme did include a bit about David's childhood, the death of his father, who fell into a vat of boiling oil and water and didn't die for six days – it must have been awful. David, being born blind, was sent to a special school when he was about six. It must have been a shattering experience. It's amazing that he's come through, got his university degree, listening to tapes and using Braille – incredibly courageous. But the young David I knew in Sheffield of course was very radical, a sort of Christ-like figure, with his guide dog, which used to growl when people applauded him, in case the applause meant they were going to attack him.

It's part of the history of New Labour, but watching it made me realise the whole of that whole New Labour business is over now. It's crumbling.

Headlines on all the news bulletins: General Sir Richard Dannatt, who is the Chief of the General Staff, has given an interview to the *Daily Mail* saying, in effect, that the war was poorly planned, that it was totally idealistic to think you could set up a liberal democracy in Iraq, and that the presence of British troops there were exacerbating the situation rather than helping, and we should get out soon. Now, of course never before has a Chief of the General Staff made such a political comment, and it transforms the whole situation, because Blair dare not sack him, and what he's said no doubt reflects the view of the army and a lot of other people.

Sunday 15 October
Well, I had a late lie-in this morning. Very depressed, though I don't know why. I just wasted the entire morning, did nothing useful.

Drove to the Royal Society of Arts for the wedding of Simon Fletcher and Gaby Kagan. Simon, who's thirty-eight, worked in my basement office twenty years ago, one of the 'Teabags' along with Ed Miliband and others. Simon is now of course Chief of Staff to Ken Livingstone.

Ken was there, and also some of Ken's mates: Redmond O'Neill; John Ross; Joy Johnston, who was a spin doctor sometime at Number 10 and quit; the MP, Dawn Butler; *The Guardian* journalist called Charlotte Raven.

There was a lovely ceremony in the vault, in the basement of the Royal Society. Built before the American Revolution and before the French Revolution. The Royal Society of Arts is 'to encourage the growth of manufacture, arts and commerce', sort of early capitalist aspirations.

I could hardly hear anything. We went to a sit-down dinner, and most of the guests ate vegetarian food, and then there were speeches, first of all, by Gaby's sister, and then by Simon, and then by Ken Livingstone. It was all very amusing.

Tuesday 17 October
Just before lunch I watched Tony Blair wriggling at a press conference, trying to explain cuts in the NHS and why he agreed with General Sir Richard Dannatt, who had said something absolutely the opposite to him. He's making a fool of himself really.

Friday 20 October
I found in my mail this morning a handwritten letter from an opera singer who'd stopped and spoken to me on 4 October about my book *Dare to be a Daniel*. She said she'd now finished the book and would love to have a talk about it. She signed her letter Charmaine Ahmed. She's actually a Bangladeshi, I think lived in England – perhaps she was born in England. Her husband is Australian. She speaks French and German and Italian.

She did a doctorate in music at a German university, a very bright, tough woman. I liked her. Her husband is an investment banker in the City and lives nearby. So I rang her up and she came over and we had an interesting talk, and then she went off.

Clare Short, who has said she wanted a hung Parliament, has been hauled over the coals, quite properly, by the Chief Whip, because if you want a hung Parliament, what you're actually saying is that you want enough Labour MPs to be defeated to destroy the Labour majority. So she's responded to that by saying she is resigning the Labour Whip and is sitting as an Independent in the House of Commons. I have no time for her, I must admit. She said she'd resign for the war and didn't, and then resigned just in time to avoid being sacked. It'll create a bit of a stir, destabilise the Party a bit, and she'll get some support.

Saturday 21 October

At about 8.15 I went to Saffron Burrows's birthday party. Salman Rushdie was there. I had a word with him and said we'd last met – and he remembered it – at a function with Hilary Wainwright, and Caroline had won in a raffle a signed copy of *The Satanic Verses*, just before he was forced to go into hiding.

The only other item is that I had a letter a few days ago sent to all Privy Councillors, saying that on the death of the sovereign the Accession Council meets within twenty-four hours to proclaim the new sovereign. (I knew that anyway.) I have never attended a session of the Council. My dad attended the one called on the death of George V in 1936, and after the abdication of Edward VIII, when they proclaimed George VI, and he also lived to see the Accession Council when George VI died and Elizabeth became Queen in '52. But the strange thing to me is, why did they send it now? They said they wanted to check all my addresses, so I sent them the answer. Of course Hilary will also be able to go. The thought just crossed my mind, could the Queen be contemplating abdication?

Tuesday 24 October

Up at 5.30. Taken by car to the BBC to do the *Today* programme on whether the House of Commons should have a debate on the war. I was up against Clive Soley, former Chairman of the Parliamentary Labour Party and now a peer. His argument was that the Commons doesn't need to debate the war because it's debated in the media. So I said, 'Well, that is the strongest case for not voting. Why bother to vote for an MP, because he will be on the *Today* programme? Write to the *Daily Mail*.' He was livid with that.

Monday 30 October

The papers are dominated by the climate-change report that suggests an absolute catastrophic global disaster. The only query I have in the back of my mind is what the meteorologist Piers Corbyn says, that the climate has often changed, the temperature was higher a thousand years ago than it is today, when there were no manmade CO_2 emissions. My interest in Piers is not only that he is a very successful weather forecaster, but he has a theory of his own, that it's all due to sunspots: and (a) I always have an interest in people who stand against the conventional wisdom, as he does; (b) I think if we are going to tackle climate change in the way that is suggested, it would be so destructive of capitalism they won't let it happen; and (c) if global warming is coming anyway, perhaps we should put all our effort into trying to cope with the consequences and not pretend you can stop it. But that's all by the by.

Tuesday 31 October

I went to hear Margaret Beckett for the last three-quarters of her speech on Iraq. She read every word of it, and from the Peers' Gallery where I was sitting you could see how many pages were left. It was the worst speech I've ever heard anyone make, utterly repetitive, utterly unyielding – the war was right, this is not the time to change, and so on and so on. So I listened to that, and I felt not only disappointed with Parliament, but utterly ashamed of New Labour and where it had led. I think it's coming so near the end.

I went out, as I promised I would do, to the demonstration in Parliament Square, which must have been authorised by the police. There were two or three hundred people there, with banners, and Brian Haw was there. I did a little bit on the loudspeaker, and then I was interviewed by the Press Association, by Iranian Press Television, by the Muslim Channel, by Al Jazeera, and then taken over to College Green to do an interview with James Landale, the BBC political correspondent. I was so bloody cold by then I said, 'The least you could do is to send me home in a taxi', so he said all right.

The Government won by a majority of twenty-five, so one can honestly say, any thirteen Labour MPs could have brought the Prime Minister down, because if they had voted against, the Prime Minister would have had to resign – no question about it. Thirteen Labour MPs kept him going. I'd be interested to know who voted and whether Blair himself bothered to vote, because he should have opened the debate – it's his policy, but he left it to Margaret Beckett! I wouldn't want to be there now. I actually wouldn't want to be there. I don't think there'd be any point in being there. I'm doing much more good going round to meetings, I think.

Saturday 4 November

To the London School of Economics to the Palestine Solidarity Committee meeting with Manuel Hassassian, who's the Palestinian delegate to London, in effect the Palestinian Ambassador. He made a passionate speech, and all of a sudden, very clearly, one could see the role of an ambassador is not to have a chit-chat with diplomats in the Foreign Office, but to go and argue their case, and he did it very well.

Sunday 5 November
Sky TV rang to say that Saddam Hussein had been sentenced to death, to be hanged, and would I go on, and I said no. I wanted to think about it.

Wednesday 8 November
Woke up to hear that the Democrats had won the House of Representatives and the Senate; at the moment I dictate this, which is a quarter to four in the afternoon, the Senate is still in the balance, but it's a massive rebuff for Bush, and hence for Blair, and it will change the whole future. It means Iran is safe, I think, which is a great thing. So I'm celebrating quietly in the bedroom.

To the Royal Institute of Chartered Surveyors, where there was a tremendously impressive list of academics of one kind and another. Dr Whitty, who is the head of the Institute of Education; Margaret Tulloch; Mike Baker, who was in the chair, he's a BBC education correspondent; Stephen Ball, Professor in the Sociology of Education; then Melissa; Simon Burgess, Director of the Centre for Market and Public Organisations; Les Lawrence, who is a Tory councillor, I think, in Birmingham; and Sir Cyril Taylor.

Lissie spoke first. She sent me her speech last night, and I made a few suggestions. She's always so good! You know, she has common sense, and said, 'I believe in comprehensive education, I went to a comprehensive school, my kids are in comprehensive schools, and selection is disruptive.' It was very interesting. I thought she made a wonderful speech, well received.

All the others who followed were corralled into the central argument about choice, and none of them attacked Melissa and they all sounded terribly consensual, even if they didn't really agree with her. What I did feel, after listening particularly to Melissa and everybody else, was that the days of selection at eleven, the Eleven Plus, is really dead now. What they're now interested in is protecting selection in a more subtle way.

Thursday 9 November
The Democrats have won the Senate as well as the House of Representatives. It is a staggering overturn! Rumsfeld has been sacked from the Defense Department, and Bush is now talking about a new tack in Iraq, and they've taken up James Baker's proposal for talks with Iran and Syria. So the whole thing has changed, and everything the peace movement ever said has turned out to be correct – it's just fantastic!

I watched Channel 4 News from Washington with Jon Snow, and it was unbelievable! There was a guy – I've forgotten his name now, he'd been a former Assistant Secretary of State – who said, 'I blame Tony Blair for not being tougher with Bush!' Just so ludicrous, fantastic!

Friday 10 November

A car picked me up at 9.30 and took me to see the Iranian Ambassador. He's been here three months, said he had wanted to meet me, so I had a friendly talk, about the role of an ambassador and the new situation after the American elections. I said to him, 'As you may know, I had hoped that I might do an interview with President Ahmadinejad,' the President of Iran, and I got a very positive response. He said, 'Well, do you think any media channels would be interested?' and I said, 'Yes, I'm sure they would.' So at any rate he said he'd put it to Tehran, and I said I would enquire with Channel 4.

Sunday 12 November

Nick Griffin of the BNP has been acquitted of incitement to racial hatred because all he did was attack Muslims. Now it appears that Lord Falconer wants the law changed so that you can't attack a religion – well, that would be an infringement of free speech.

Tuesday 14 November

Up at seven. Caught the Tube to St Thomas's for my pacemaker examination. The pacemaker is in use 96 per cent of the time, so obviously I need it, and also they printed out five or six occasions in the last year when I had a fibrillation, some failure in my upper ventricle. The printout showed what date they occurred, when they began and when they ended, and the duration. It was absolutely fascinating. Came home on the 148 bus.

A strange thing happened to me today, and it's still with me twelve hours later. A strange sense of calm came over me. I didn't feel at all agitated. I felt calm. I don't know why it was. I think I've been reading Buddha, and Buddha's idea of happiness is when you rid yourself of all desire. Well, I've rid myself of all political ambition, but I thought perhaps if I just didn't want anything for myself at all, that would help. Whether it was that, or the pacemaker and the realisation of my mortality and how I might go, and I've got to prepare for it, I don't know, but I feel totally calm and relaxed.

Thursday 16 November

I had time for about half an hour's snooze, as I'm not feeling at all well, and I drove up to Lissie's. She and the girls and I went to Queen's Park Community School to give the prizes. We got there early, and the Head, Mike Hulme, was there, and the Chairman of the governors was there, and some of the other governors. We talked a bit, and then went in to the assembly. There were prizes for some people, including Hannah, who got a prize for French, and everybody else got a certificate. So the children were hooting and cheering, because it's obviously very popular. I thought I would talk about peace, so that's what I did. It was a bit emotional, but I feel very emotional about it. It was like addressing the General Assembly of the UN – there were so many different nationalities there.

Friday 17 November
In the afternoon Sir Christopher Meyer, who is the Chairman of the Press Complaints Commission and was Ambassador in Washington, and was bitterly criticised for writing a book about his experiences there, turned up with a film crew, making a programme for BBC4. The interview was about the 1945 election, the American loan, and so on. Christopher, who was born in 1949, you know, wasn't aware of the period. He was interested, but he had the idea that we'd gone into 1945 in an idealistic way, building the new Jerusalem. It wasn't that. It was just that we had a bloody awful war and we wanted a better society and we wanted to plan for it. I think he took it on board. He asked me about individuals whom I knew, like Stafford Cripps and Ernie Bevin and Nye Bevan.

Saturday 18 November
Time for a quick lunch, and then I got a cab to the Brixton Recreation Centre, just by Brixton Market. This was a meeting on adult education, because there'd been major cuts made by the Government in adult education, affecting foreign students learning English, and moving to what they call contestability, to private ownership, private colleges, and it's an absolute disgrace. I spoke, and then came home on the Tube.

Blair, apparently while being interviewed by David Frost, said yes when asked, 'Isn't it a disaster in Iraq?' He said yes, and then later had to clarify himself – he would still have gone in, but things have gone disastrously wrong. The man is just impossible.

Monday 20 November
I had to renew my passport. It'll cost £101, but I can do it if I go to the Passport Office at 7.45 in the morning on Wednesday next week. Mind you, having said that, no news at all on the proposed Iran visit, and I'm getting a bit depressed about that.

Tuesday 21 November
To the Hutchinson party to meet Caroline Gascoigne, who's just been appointed Publishing Director of Hutchinson. Tony Whittome was there, of course, and Emma Mitchell, and there were some authors there. Robert Harris, he's always very friendly; Ruth Rendell, the great crime writer, was there; and one or two other authors whom I didn't recognise or didn't

know. That's the disadvantage of: (a) being totally ignorant of the literati; and (b) being deaf.

Went on to the Al Jazeera party at 1 Knightsbridge. This was the launch of their English-language service. David Frost was speaking when we arrived, because he's been taken on to do a programme called *Frost over the World*.

Sue Phillips, the London Bureau Chief of Al Jazeera, took me over to meet Wadah Khanfar, who is the Director General of the Al Jazeera English service, or the network, and also to meet the owner of Al Jazeera.

Wednesday 22 November
Lissie and I went to Marks & Spencer, bought some sandwiches and strawberries.

Then who should knock at the door but Chris Mullin and Sally Banks, who'd gone for a walk in Holland Park and thought: I wonder if Tony is in? So we all had tea. It was lovely, just lovely. I don't think Chris has been here for ages, and Sally, I don't suppose she has either, and the fact Lissie was here was lovely.

Thursday 23 November
At 11.30 the BBC came, with Michael Portillo, my local MP. Portillo has always seemed cool, friendly but cool. The interview was perfectly fair. He asked why I supported rearmament in 1951 and so on, was I putting a gloss on history? I said, 'No, I was wrong.' He said that he liked my *Diaries* very much; what amazed him was how enthusiastic I was. He said, 'You'd say, for example, you went to a trade-union meeting – it was really wonderful', and he was a bit puzzled by that. He was perfectly courteous, and I said to the producer at the end, 'When Michael is retired, if you're looking for somebody to do some of these programmes, I'm always available!'

Friday 24 November
Up at 5.30. Got a cab to King's Cross and caught the 7.45 to Cambridge. Went to Churchill College for an all-day conference on Open Government, organised by Professor Mary Jacobus and Allen Packwood from the Churchill Archives Centre.

The first item was a discussion with Lord Wilson, Richard Wilson that was, who was in the Department of Energy with me, and who subsequently became Secretary of the Cabinet. He was Cabinet Secretary for the first five years of the Blair government. I had looked him up on the CD-ROM of my *Diaries* and found sixteen references to him. I didn't show them to him, but I was critical of him at the time because he was dealing with the nuclear question.

He did say two things that interested me very much, afterwards when we had a word: he said, 'Labour MPs are a total failure. They don't hold the

Government to account in any way.' Also, when I said to him that I understand the Cabinet now is very brief, just long enough simply for the Prime Minister to announce the decisions he's made: 'Oh no! It's worse than that!' he said. 'The Cabinet is now simply a briefing for Cabinet ministers about the line to take.' He was very contemptuous indeed. He couldn't have been nicer.

Also there was Hans Blix, the former weapons inspector in Iraq, whom I think I may have met before; he was absolutely charming. When I made my speech about the UN and how I'm passionately committed to it, he was very warm and generous.

Also, Sir Jeremy Greenstock, who was British Ambassador to the UN and then became Special Representative in Iraq under Paul Bremer, after we 'won the war'. He supported what Blair had done. He said Blair had not told a lie (I had said he had). Blair believed that weapons could be there; and as for Bush, he also believed weapons could be there, and also Wall Street was worried about the uncertainty, and that made it necessary to go to war. Also the weather was getting very hot. Well, if you go into a country because you have a suspicion there might be a threat, and Wall Street wants you to and the weather is getting too hot to delay, it's not exactly a good reason for war. Greenstock was utterly loyal. He's written a book. They don't want him to publish it, and so he's withdrawn it.

He did tell me one funny story, that many years ago, when I had gone over to the US on one of my visits, the Ambassador was Sir Peter Ramsbotham (I vaguely remember him). He said, 'We decided to play a hoax on him at Christmas, so we concocted a telegram from the Prime Minister,' I suppose that would be Wilson, 'to Ramsbotham asking him to go and see Henry Kissinger, then Secretary of State, and tell him that Tony Benn has been appointed Foreign Secretary.' It took Ramsbotham in completely, and I imagine must have worried him desperately! It was extremely funny. Greenstock was quite friendly.

Also there was Oliver Miles, who had been our Ambassador in Libya, who had collected fifty-two signatures of retired diplomats for a letter to Blair condemning the war, a courageous and imaginative thing to do.

Bridget Kendall was also there, and Patrick Cockburn. I enjoyed it very much; it was an excellent conference. Mary Jacobus asked me if I'd sum up at the end, so I made a little speech. Blix was very grateful.

By I was then so bloody tired I couldn't stay for the reception, so I caught a train and got home by about 9.30.

Saturday 25 November
I drove to the Institute of Education in Bedford Way for the conference against academies, quite a big one. Clyde Chitty was there, and Melissa was there. Somebody asked me, 'Is Melissa Benn a relative of yours? I suppose

she's your granddaughter.' So from now on, I'm going to call her my granddaughter Melissa.

Then to London South Bank University for a conference organised by Robert Taylor on the history of the Parliamentary Labour Party; Ken Morgan, Lord Morgan, was there. Harry Barnes, of all people, former Member for North-East Derbyshire; and Barry Johnson from Chesterfield – I was amazed! I developed, as I had this morning, the idea of a new concept of organisation called PUMPS: Politically Unaccountable Management of Public Services. I thought it up to explain Ofsted, and PostCom, and Ofcom, and the Bank of England. It's an interesting idea, I must say; I'm going to develop it further, because political power has been taken away from the Government now. Governments have very little power because the world is dominated by non-elected authorities.

Looking back over the last six days: I have made six speeches; done two television broadcasts, one to Iran about nuclear power, and one to France about the established Church of England; and two radio broadcasts, two BBC broadcasts.

Sunday 26 November
The newspapers are full of the murder of this former KGB man, Alexander Litvinenko, who was murdered in London using radioactivity. It's all rather strange to me. First of all, nobody knows who did it, but before he died, he said, 'It's those bastards! They can kill me, but they can't kill everybody!', which pointed straight at Putin. He worked with Boris Berezovsky, the Russian multi-millionaire who escaped to Britain. There's something funny about him. The finger is just pointed endlessly at Putin. He may or may not be responsible, but then the Americans have an assassination policy, so do the Israelis, so the thing seems to be whipped up for a slightly different reason, whether to take attention off the war or to build up a new Cold War with Russia, I don't know.

Monday 27 November
Up at six.

To Central Hall Westminster to talk to 2,000 A-level economics students. Economics students are absolutely ghastly! They just sit there. I began by saying: your generation have an important decision to make, and don't believe what you're told – including what I tell you – think it out for yourself; I took the case for market forces, and talked about customers and how the power in the world is shifting. Absolutely no response and all the questions that came were very critical: 'Surely consumerism is changing inequality in capitalism?' and all sorts of questions. Every question got a round of applause. Some of them might remember it later, I don't know.

Tuesday 28 November
Up at 5.45 because I had to go to the Passport Office and be there by about 7.30 to get my passport issued in a single day. A huge queue of people had formed outside.

It was very efficient. The passport says I am still an MP – they must have copied that from some information not provided by me. But also, there was a biometric chip in it. So in effect I now have an ID card, and of course I don't know what's on the chip. It says if there's any false information on the passport, you must report it immediately, but I don't know what's on the passport, because I don't know what's on the chip. I'm going to write to the Foreign Secretary and say, 'Can you please give me a printout of all the information? Does it include educational qualifications? Does it include any biography? Does it include any medical information? Does it include any security information? Any political information?' I'd like to see that.

Thursday 30 November
At half-past eleven Lindsey German and John Rees from the Stop the War Movement came, and we went over to have a lunch at Pizza Express. What we discussed really was the next stage of the Stop the War Movement, and the need to bring all the issues together. I suggested it might be a national convention, a People's Assembly, a coalition of issues, which would back up John McDonnell's campaign without being in any way linked to the Labour Party. It couldn't be a Respect meeting, or I wouldn't be able to take part. It would just be an opportunity to bring together hospital closures, student fees, with the cost of the war, and all the things that people are concerned about, bringing in the pensioners, and so on.

One other thing happened today which I should note. I had an email from a woman about her son, who joined the RAF after school – he's nineteen – and was sent to Iraq. When he was there he decided to leave the RAF, but the time to give notice of his desire to leave had expired, and they won't let him go. He's been downgraded from weapons duty because he's been depressed. He's been bullied and harassed. He used to be outgoing and happy. Now they have upgraded him back to weapons duty and they're thinking of sending him to Afghanistan. She says he's told the doctor that he would drop his gun and run, if faced with a threat. 'He says he would not protect his colleagues, he would try and save his own life; it is very sad, because he's not a coward or a traitor. He's a young kid, scared to death, and depressed and with no self-esteem left.' She said, 'What can I do?' So I sent her an email back saying: get on to your Member of Parliament at once, and ask for a question to the Minister of Defence. But it's just one of those human stories that don't get mentioned much in the press. I had a nice email back thanking me for my response.

Friday 1 December

I caught the Tube to the CND office at 162 Holloway Road, for a meeting of Vice-Presidents of CND.

In the chair was Air Commodore Alastair Mackie, CBE, DFC and Bar.

He joined the Air Force in 1940, and left it in 1968. At the beginning he was a bomber pilot, with hydrogen bombs on board, and it converted him against nuclear weapons. He was a very charming man, about my age.

There was an interesting collection of people there. Bruce Kent, the former Chairman of CND; Walter Wolfgang, now on the National Executive of the Labour Party; Joan Horrocks, who runs the Musicians Against Nuclear Arms; and Kate Hudson, who is the current Chairman of CND. We just went round the table and made a report.

Saturday 2 December

To Islington for the CND Conference. The average age was late fifties probably, and almost half of them were women, dedicated and committed people.

I saw Alice Mahon before it began, and she told me an astonishing story. She said she has macular degeneration of one eye, and she's been refused treatment on the grounds that each treatment would be too expensive. It is a complete transformation from the original idea of the NHS, although to begin with, people got more than they expected, and now they expect so much and can't get it. It highlighted the issue of the day, which was Trident.

Kate Hudson was in the chair, and she reported that the Government White Paper would be coming out, and it was thought they might suggest a reduction in the number of nuclear warheads and rebuild or upgrade Trident. The Liberals were in favour of cutting the number of missiles and deferring the issue, but there will be a vote in the Commons later. It was argued that we needed a free vote, that the consultation must be real, and on Monday there's a presentation of an alternative White Paper issued by CND to Number 10 at noon.

Anyway, they've been canvassing the embassies of non-aligned countries to get support.

Then, to my surprise and without telling me, the Chair said, 'Well, as this is Tony Benn's first visit as a vice president, we welcome him.' So I got up and said I was very grateful for the invitation; I had resigned from the front bench over nuclear weapons in 1958; I said the argument was simple: we don't need it; it didn't protect America from 9/11 or allow them to win the war; we can't afford it – it's taking money off all the things we need; and we don't have it, because Bush is the only man who can switch on the system that would allow the British Tridents to be targeted, and what that does mean, in effect, is that it ties us completely to American foreign policy.

Then, soon after that, I slipped off because there was nothing I could really do.

Tuesday 5 December

The Iraq Study Group is going to report tomorrow. Robert Gates, who was a member of the group, is the new US Defense Secretary, replacing Rumsfeld, and he gave evidence to the Senate in which he said that we hadn't won the war in Iraq. He didn't actually say we'd lost it, but we hadn't won it. There were a lot of senators there: John McCain wants more troops; Edward Kennedy wants to withdraw at once; Hillary Clinton was just being cautious. So it is absolutely clear that the war is lost and they know it. Blair's announced new hospital cuts. They're going to close a lot of Accident & Emergency services because some treatment is so important it's got to be done in a bigger centre, so people will travel twenty and forty miles for better treatment.

Tuesday 12 December

World news. Blair has come out with a new plan under which trade unions would be limited in the amount they could give to the Labour Party, because he wants to break the link with the unions and bring state funding in, and it has led to massive opposition in the Parliamentary Labour Party, so I think he'll be beaten on that. He's running out of friends at this stage.

Wednesday 13 December

I tried to get on with the Christmas cards, but I'm just in a state of total confusion. I wondered whether I'd send them this year.

Thursday 14 December

News today is fantastic. Tony Blair, the *Prime Minister*, has been interviewed by the police on the cash-for-honours question, but he wasn't cautioned and he wasn't arrested. As only the Prime Minister can give honours, it must all end up with him, but I doubt whether the police will do much about it.

Another thing that made me suspicious of the police is that the Attorney General announced today that they were not proceeding with the fraud inquiry into the nature of possible bribes paid by British Aerospace for billions of pounds worth of aircraft sold to Saudi Arabia. It was quite obvious the Saudi Arabians said, well, if you do that, we'll cancel the order. So on grounds of realpolitik, they dropped the inquiry. I remember when I was Minister of Technology and Secretary of State for Industry, we all knew that if you wanted a big contract in an Arab country you bribed a prince. Of course it was done! Market forces at a top level. But it is just too hot to handle.

Friday 15 December

The cash-for-honours is continuing to develop, but the real question is: where did the money go when it was lent? It didn't go to the Labour Party account; it went to somebody else – now, who was that? Who signed the cheques? If they lent the money to that account, how did the money get from that account into the Labour Party account? I don't think this story has really begun to get properly developed yet.

Some real criticism is building up about the cancellation of the Saudi arms case.

Put one way, it is about market forces, only in Saudi Arabia market forces include a bribe to a prince. The Lockheed Airbus was sold by Lockheed to Italy by bribing. Bribery is at the heart of it all! They haven't got the courage to admit that, though it has totally undermined Britain's case about dysfunctional governments in Africa where corruption is rife, as in Nigeria, when we're doing it ourselves.

Tuesday 19 December

Chatham House, the Royal Institute of International Affairs, has blamed Blair for an error, a major error of judgement, in going along with Bush at the time of the Iraq war. So the Stop the War Coalition is now reflected in Chatham House – it's so interesting! You would never have guessed it from the way the media treated us – anti-American, left-wing and all that – and now everybody takes that view.

Saturday 23 December

The United Nations Security Council unanimously passed a resolution imposing sanctions on Iran. I must say, why the Russians and the Chinese went along with it, I do not know, but I suppose the Americans have put the screws on people. When you think: Israel has got nuclear weapons, Britain wants a new generation of nuclear weapons, and all Iran is doing is enriching uranium for nuclear power, I mean it's incredible.

Tuesday 26 December

Saddam Hussein's appeal against the death sentence has been turned down by the appeal court, so I've no doubt that he will be executed, they say in the next thirty days, and so that's the end of that era. It's the first time in my life I've ever known anyone who's about to be executed, but so many people have been killed in the war. It's a horrific end to the story, and it may cause more trouble.

Saturday 30 December

Came home, and I discovered when I got home that actually while I was in the CNN studio, at about three o'clock, Saddam was hanged. Pictures have been appearing on the screen of him standing there with a rope round his neck and his body – very, very gruesome.

Monday 1 January 2007

I woke up in the middle of the night, the moon was almost full, and the whole river was silver with the light. Today, although it had been a bit windy, it was a perfect day, absolutely lovely!

Got home from Stansgate and wrote to Bob Marshall-Andrews, making the point that we need to examine into whose account did the loans to the Labour Party go, who owes the money back and, if it was given as a gift, did they declare the gift?

Wednesday 3 January

Mary Fletcher rang, she's had a fall and she's been on a walking frame. I got to know her when I was training as a pilot in Rhodesia and she was a nurse. Put quite simply, I had a crush on her. We corresponded over the years, and five years ago she came to see me. It was just rather fun to talk to her again. Josh told me that she's the mother of Duncan Fletcher, the England cricket coach.

I watched Sir Christopher Meyer, the former Ambassador in Washington, in his programme, talking about the repayment of the American loan, from 1946 until the final repayment at the end of last year. I appeared in the programme two or three times. He drove round, for some reason, in a Rolls-Royce, and you saw endless pictures of it – the gleaming front of it, or Meyer sitting in it.

He interviewed distinguished Americans in Washington, including Deputy Chief of Staff Karl Rove. Meyer reported how, after the war, many people in America didn't want to support a socialist government, and anyway they felt that they had carried the brunt of the war in the Pacific, and they didn't feel a moral obligation to support Britain. He described the tremendous pressure on the Attlee Government, how in the end the Americans agreed to a loan, but also, as a part of that, insisted of course on convertibility in 1947, which we couldn't do and we had to ask for a deferment.

The fact is that there was a tremendous pressure for reform in Britain, and the Americans, in the end, agreed because the Cold War was coming up, and they saw Attlee as a supporter of America against communism.

Tuesday 9 January

My bloody printer doesn't work! I rang Josh. He fiddled with it remotely and of course it worked. He's planning to do his dissertation on the subject of 'Is e-voting a threat to the democratic process?' He says it's all a moral question – it's not just about the technology, it's a moral question.

Wednesday 10 January

Watched Blair doing Prime Minister's Questions today. The number of times he says, 'Let me make one thing absolutely clear . . .' – he sometimes says that twice in an answer. Then 'The important thing is . . .', then a mass of statistics about what we did. He's impressive in the sense that he dazzles the Labour MPs and keeps the Tories on the defensive.

Thursday 11 January

I had a phone call, I couldn't hear who it was at first, and it turned out to be Marion Thorpe, Jeremy's wife, and she said: would I come and have a drink with him tonight? So I thought, well, it's irresistible really. The last time I saw Jeremy was at Ted Heath's eightieth birthday party. He's very frail, he's got Parkinson's disease.

So I caught the bus to his massive house off Bayswater Road; it would make the American Ambassador feel that his place was shabby. He's got a housekeeper, he's got servants, a woman looking after him – I could see these great dining rooms, and reception rooms, and studies, and the walls were covered in cartoons. It was rather sad really. Jeremy himself was sitting there, struggling. I could hardly hear anything he said, he's very ill with Parkinson's.

But at any rate I did discover, listening to him, that he wanted to ask me my view of the Middle East. So I told him what I thought, and he said what we really need is a conference, indeed a series of conferences, of all the major participants – Iran, Syria, Afghanistan, Iraq, Jordan and Saudi Arabia, and so on – and what did I think? Well, I had actually put forward a similar proposal to this some time ago.

I said, 'The best thing to do would be to get some of the people who've retired from high office, like President Carter, President Gorbachev, Nelson Mandela, Kofi Annan, to promote such a conference.'

He insisted on me coming upstairs to his study, which was covered in cartoons and pictures of himself with Kissinger, Mandela, Nixon, and so on.

I left after about three-quarters of an hour, but I'm glad I went. While I was there Dave rang and said, 'Where are you?' I said, 'I'm with Jeremy Thorpe,' so I handed Jeremy the phone, but it was difficult for him to say anything intelligible to Dave.

Bush has announced 21,000 more troops are to go to Iraq to clear up Baghdad. He said the Iraqi Government is living on borrowed time.

Friday 12 January

Tony Blair made a major speech today saying, in effect, we've got to be prepared for war – no good Britain opting for soft power, peacekeeping forces; we've got to be prepared for war. No mention of the United Nations at all, and it was really as if the British Empire had been re-created and he was Churchill or Gladstone or Disraeli.

Saturday 13 January
I had to go and pick up my car. I'm beginning to wonder whether I can justify owning a car; apart from the cost of the car, you've got the road tax, the insurance, the MOT test, the congestion charge, the petrol, the repairs, parking meters. It would be cheaper to go by public transport all the time when I can, and by cab or hire car when necessary.

To my amazement, Peter Preston, of *The Guardian*, wrote an article headed 'Tony Benn is absolutely right!' – that there must be an election for the Labour leadership. Last time he made a reference to me was when he compared me to Osama Bin Laden, said I was the British politician most like Osama Bin Laden.

Sunday 14 January
I went to lunch with the nuns next door. I'd bought a little history of Notting Hill, and a Notting Hill Gate mug, for Sister Antoinette, who's been here for a year and is going back to Nigeria on Thursday.

There were eleven nuns there, and me. They were absolutely wonderful! I did show off a bit, but I think that's maybe what they wanted. There was the German nun; the Swiss nun; the Irish nun, Sister Hilary; a large, jolly one, who remembered when I came in and switched off their water with a spanner when they had a leak; and another nun from Yorkshire, who did the cooking; next to me was a youngish nun, who was a primary school teacher; and then me. I took my video camera, and I wandered round the table and filmed the little speech made by Sister Antoinette.

Thursday 18 January
Violent gales all over London and all over Britain last night – a man was killed at Waterloo when his car was hit by a tree.

To the Palestine Solidarity Committee patrons' meeting. I have recently been made a patron; Bruce Kent was there; Caryl Churchill, Victoria Brittain, John Austin, Jeremy Corbyn were there.

I asked whether it was possible to get President Jimmy Carter to go over to the Palestinian territories, and they said, well, he wouldn't go unless it was well organised. The Cardinal Archbishop of Westminster has been, and so has Rowan Williams, to Bethlehem, but they just talk about the Christian need to love each other, without saying anything radical about the political situation. A Palestinian woman who was there said that in her view it wasn't possible now to have a Palestinian state, and it would have to be a single state, which would be the end of Zionism, but not the end of Jews living in Palestine. I think that is very interesting.

Friday 19 January
I was driven by an Afghan driver, a man aged thirty-six, the other day and

I asked him about the war and he said, 'I'm a hundred per cent in favour of it!' That surprised me, so I said, 'Why?'

'Well,' he said, 'because Pakistan is always afraid of a powerful Afghanistan, and so Pakistan is now encouraging destabilisation in Afghanistan, and the NATO forces are going to crush it.'

So I said, 'Well, lots of people have tried to conquer Afghanistan in the past.'

'I know,' he said, 'but this time it's all about Pakistan!'

Monday 22 January

There is a rumour that Jonathan Powell, who is *the* most powerful man at Number 10, may be interviewed again by the police. Also, *The Guardian* this morning said if any of the people at Number 10 were arrested and charged, they thought Blair would have to go early.

Tuesday 23 January

Up early and caught the Tube to Paddington, and then the Heathrow Express. It's the first time I've ever had a ticketless ticket – an email with a code number. I just went to a sort of cashpoint, typed in the number and out came a boarding card.

I went over to Dublin for the meeting of the Trinity College Historical Society. There were about a hundred people, absolutely packed into a relatively small room, and I'd prepared my lecture with care, and then there were a lot of questions. Only one woman asked a question – there were very few women there, it was a sort of anglicised version of the Irish Establishment; they might all have been at Oxford – and you realise the influence of Britain on the Republic is enormous, because it was controlled by London for so long.

Dublin is a booming city. I hadn't been there for many years. It's doing so well out of the European Union. I hadn't eaten all day, so I ordered an egg sandwich before I went to bed and had about four bananas. That was all I had all day.

Wednesday 24 January

Blair was under attack for not coming to the debate on Iraq, a scandalous thing not to turn up! He said he chose to go and talk to the CBI, instead of Parliament – gutless, and contemptuous of Parliament.

At PMQs he was asked a difficult question about cash-for-peerages – would he resign if one of his officials was charged? – and he didn't answer that. He's got a certain cleverness about him with questions.

Saturday 27 January

As the inner Circle Line was not running, I got a taxi to Euston and caught the train to Manchester. Got there, waited to be picked up to be taken to

Rochdale and no one turned up, so I rang them and they said, it's tomorrow! So I went back on the train to London, a very slow train, and I've wasted the whole bloody day! I thought to myself, you know, there are only 365 days in the year; if I have three more years, that's 1,000 days, and I've wasted one of 1,000 days. I was really angry!

Sunday 28 January
I went to Manchester yet again! Was picked up by a couple of people and driven to Rochdale for the Ramadan meeting in the Town Hall. The local MP, a Liberal Democrat from Rochdale, was there, who had beaten Lorna Fitzsimons in the last election because of her support for the war. There were various other people there, including an Orthodox Jew, and I asked him about Zionism. He said, 'Well, Zionism has nothing to do with Judaism, and God never intended that there should be an occupation of Palestine by force.' He favoured a single state, where Jews and Palestinians lived in peace, which is the view that Martin Buber put to me when I saw him in Jerusalem many, many years ago.

Anyway, there were about 400 people there. I spoke, then I was dropped back at the station and came home.

Monday 29 January
I went to see a film at the Gate Cinema called *Venus*, with Peter O'Toole, and Les Phillips and Richard Griffiths. It's a huge cinema, and there were about ten people there, mainly my age. It was disgusting, that's the only way of putting it.

There were these three old actors, who meet in the pub; one of them has a niece, who comes to help Peter O'Toole, who, I would like to say, fell in love with her, but actually he lusted after her. It's a complicated story, but it just put me off old age completely!

Tuesday 30 January
To Room 21b, on the second floor of the House of Commons, for John McDonnell's leadership campaign meeting. They went through the list of possible nominations, and they have at the moment seventeen firm nominations, and twenty possibilities, but that's not a good start, although they remain optimistic. One of the problems of course is that Michael Meacher is going round putting pressure on people to support him.

Saturday 3 February
I got the Tube to King's Cross and caught the seven o'clock train to Newcastle. It was a beautiful day! No wind, white frost on the ground, a pale moon in the left window as I was going up, and on the right the bright-red sun as it rose. The moon gave you a silhouette of the

trees without leaves, and the water was absolutely still. It was beautiful!

Was met by Sophie Hughes, the daughter of my cousin's adopted son. I'd never heard of her until her father wrote and said that she was up in Newcastle. She's the curator of an exhibition by a painter called Gerald Laing, about the Iraq war. Sophie is very tall and friendly.

We went to the Globe Theatre, and they were showing my interview with Saddam Hussein, and films made in Iraq by Iraqi film-makers about conditions there, and Laing's paintings.

Later I got a cab to the Sage theatre across the river in Gateshead. Before I went in, two ladies – in their sixties, I should think – had written to say they wanted to meet me, so I took them into my dressing room and we had a bit of a talk. They couldn't have been nicer.

Then we went in to the show with Roy Bailey, and it was lovely! I get very moved by reading the peace extracts. All the cassettes were sold.

On the train back I read this book by Nick Cohen, *What's Left?* – one of these guys who's swung from the left to the right, like Melanie Phillips and John Reid, and so on. The book is just a denunciation of a whole range of people, from the Stop the War Coalition to Noam Chomsky . . . anyone you can mention. There wasn't a positive idea in it. I'm doing a discussion with him and Adam Boulton tomorrow, so I think I shall be very patient about it and say I was disappointed that I didn't see anything constructive in it. He denounces everyone you can think of – George Galloway, Tariq Ali, Chomsky, anyone who opposed any of the recent wars.

Sunday 4 February
I did this discussion with Adam Boulton and Nick Cohen for Sky TV. I said to Cohen, 'I don't think we've met before.'

'Oh yes,' he said, 'I've interviewed you.'

Anyway, he wanted to be aggressive and I just laughed. I was serious, made some serious points, but when he said socialism was gone, I said, 'You've abolished it unilaterally. What about Chávez in Venezuela?'

'Ah!' he said, 'well, he goes and supports the mullahs.'

He sounds to me like a right-winger pretending to be on the left!

Tuesday 6 February
I recently had a letter from Uganda, from a girl called Sandra, who wrote pleading for me to help pay her school fees. I've had a few letters like that, but I thought, well, I'll send her a cheque for £100. So today I had a letter thanking me and asking for more money. I can't enter into that; I feel guilty about it, but then I fear she'll write and say she has a friend . . .

Wednesday 7 February
I was taken to the BBC at 4 Millbank for an interview about Jack Straw's

proposal for a 50/50 appointed/elected Lords. I did a little research on Lloyd George and the creation of baronetcies, and I took a notice I had made saying: 'Peerages for Sale. Apply here with cheque.' I didn't say that it was happening now, but I said that was the old system.

Of course the BBC didn't use my interview, because there have been letter bombs all day, and the news has been entirely dominated by them, apparently sent by angry motorists.

Thursday 8 February
I rang Sylvia Dunstall today. She was ninety-eight yesterday, my oldest and last remaining true cousin.

Sunday 11 February
Michael Moore arrived to talk about his film *Sicko*, which is about the need for a National Health Service in the United States. I'd met him before and he told me, in the course of the morning, that he had seen me doing *Question Time*, talking about the impact of debt on young people, which makes them subservient to their employers.

Anyway, he arrived with a crew of about ten people, one of whom was a producer called Giovanni Ulleri. I'm not kidding, we did about a two-hour interview, I should think. He filmed outside the house, he filmed the plaque to Caroline, he filmed in the house, and then after the interview was over he went round just looking at everything. I really liked the guy.

So many things were interesting: his father was a trade-union official, working for the automobile workers at General Motors in Detroit, and was involved in some great sit-in there; Michael himself never went to college – he was modest about his achievements. He arrived wearing the baseball cap that he wears all the time.

He asked about Karl Marx. I told him about Cuba, that Cuba had better health provision than the United States; he didn't know that. I said the Cubans have a higher literacy standard than the United States, and he didn't know that. He was very friendly, and talked and talked and talked.

We went out in the street again and we talked. People stopped him in the street.

Thursday 15 February
Had a slow start, and then at nine o'clock Gill Pharaoh collected me and drove me down to St Christopher's Hospice by the Crystal Palace.

Gill Pharaoh had sent me her book about the care of the dying, and I wrote a foreword for it, she gave it a new title called *Care for the Dying at Home* (which is rather boring). She was a bit reluctant to come to the hospice, because she thought they were all rather religious there, but actually the seminar they had on death today was wide-ranging.

It began with Anthony Grayling, who is a philosopher, and he really made the case for euthanasia. The Muslim speaker didn't turn up, so I was asked to speak second. I'd worked very hard on my speech, and there were a lot of jokes in it and it went down well. I touched on euthanasia, and then there were questions and discussion.

It sort of quietened me down about dying. One of the reasons I accepted was that I want to think it all out, and then meeting all these people whose speciality is looking after you when you're dying in a hospice, it was inspiring.

Friday 16 February
News all about the shooting in south London, and about Bernard Matthews's turkeys.

Yesterday, I think, the court ruled that the consultation that the Government launched on nuclear power was seriously flawed. Blair was immediately on the telly saying it wouldn't make any difference to the policy; he's absolutely unaffected by democratic decision-making. I mean, the idea that he might ever be outvoted on anything is almost treasonable in his mind. It doesn't matter, he's only got a few weeks left, but my God, what a wonderful thing it will be when you see him leave Number 10 for the last time!

Saturday 17 February
To the CND anti-Trident meeting at the TUC. There were about fifty people there, and it was the usual brigade.

I think every organisation tends to get old and die. That's even true of the Labour Party. It's got to renew itself by taking up new issues and attracting new people, and that will always be seen as a bit of a challenge by the people who've stuck to the old groups, rather like the chapel folk who go to chapel every week.

I thought, why not give yourself a bit of a rest? So I went upstairs and I put on *Love Actually*, which I've seen an endless number of times, but it's so romantic and so cheerful, apart from Alan Rickman deserting Emma Thompson, which I don't like at all. The whole thing is such fun, it's a film for the 'Free Hugs' Movement.

Sunday 18 February
I came down to my office about quarter-past eleven, and there was a phone message from Alan Simpson on my mobile. He rang to say he has decided not to stand again for Parliament; he's standing down, because he thinks all progress will come from social movements. So I rang him immediately. I said, 'If you've announced it, nothing I can do to dissuade you, but don't forget Members of Parliament are the buckle that links the demonstrations to Downing Street, and the streets to the statute book, and you're needed.' But still, he's made that decision. I was absolutely shattered.

Monday 19 February
The inner Circle Line was broken, so I got a cab to the Venezuelan Embassy for a meeting with the Ambassador Alfredo Toro Hardy and the Venezuelan Foreign Minister, Nicholas Maduro, the Minister of Foreign Affairs and an interpreter. She'd come over with President Chávez last year and remembered it, and said how the President had enjoyed it.

Maduro began by describing the revolution in Venezuela. He said it was of enormous international importance, and that they wanted to carry the case forward because there had to be a new start for socialism, and they wanted to have a big conference in Caracas to discuss the alternatives.

He said Africa is in a terrible mess, and it's very difficult to solve, the impact of colonialism was so bad, and so on.

I said, 'Remember this: the immediate situation is the United States is a declining empire. I lived in one myself, and wounded tigers are very dangerous, and so we have to consider the present situation.'

Maduro said, 'If America attacks Iran, Venezuela will stop supplying oil to the United States' – an important statement.

I said, 'Well, you supply about one-third of American oil.'

'Yes,' he said.

I said, 'Can I quote you?'

And he said, 'Well, you can say this yourself', so obviously it's a hint they're dropping.

Finally, I said we've got to try and make the United Nations into a democratic world government like Parliament, because globalisation means internationalism, and that's what it's all about, and we need a discussion with Chávez as a world leader, and just to talk to people across frontiers.

Maduro said, 'I very much hope you can come to Caracas.'

So it was very friendly, an hour's discussion, and flattering.

Tuesday 20 February
I drove to the House of Commons, and walked over to Central Hall for a campaign against post-office closures, organised by Billy Hayes of the CWU. There were people from the Townswomen's Guild; Age Concern; local community groups; and, of all people, the Countryside Alliance. Susan Kramer, who's a Liberal MP, and Kate Hoey, Labour MP, said a word. Alan Duncan, the Tory, got up and said he remembered as a student coming to Central Hall Westminster and hearing a Labour MP speak, and, 'There,' he said, pointing, 'he still is!', which was very nice.

Afterwards I had an hour and a half to spare, I thought I'd go and see Alan Simpson because he's made this statement about leaving Parliament. I thought as I'd been critical of his decision, he'd be a bit upset, but he's very happy. He said that his wife, Pascale, thought it was a good idea, and he's utterly fed up with the House of Commons. He's been there since

1992, so he'll get a bit of a pension. He's fifty-eight, and he'll go into pressure groups, just as I've done. So it was very friendly, and we had a lovely talk.

I had another email from the producer of Michael Moore's film *Sicko*, saying they wanted an extract of a film of anything I'd said in the House of Commons and a photograph of me. So I photocopied a photograph of me as an RAF pilot.

Thursday 22 February
Meacher's announced today he's going to stand for the leadership. Whether either he or John McDonnell will get forty-four nominations is uncertain. The main thing is there's got to be a debate about the future.

Tuesday 27 February
At ten o'clock a musician called Colin McIntyre came to see me. He's thirty-four, he's married to an American girl, whose mother is from New York and father is Palestinian. The Mull Historical Society was the name of his group, and he'd brought me three albums that he'd produced. He's been in the Top 40 two or three times, and I did wonder afterwards, because I looked him up on the website, whether I should have heard of him, but I hadn't. He wanted me to contribute to a song, reading something, and he recorded that. We had a long talk, I liked him.

Thursday 1 March
To the Savoy, and Saffron Burrows met me there – filming all morning. She'd asked me to be photographed for a book about friendship by a photographer she's known for some time, Andy Gotts. So we went to the Pinafore Suite and we talked; at one stage, she put her arms round me and gave me a big hug; he took lots of photographs.

I walked over to the House of Commons, for a meeting about a restoration of trade-union rights. All the top trade-union leaders were there. I referred to the fact that my dad, as a young MP a hundred years ago, had voted for the 1906 Trades Disputes Act, which gave unions the right to strike, and we've never got full rights back since Thatcher's massive anti-trades-union legislation removed them.

Then I walked over to 4 Millbank and did this extraordinary programme for BBC World television, with a Professor Jagdish Bhagwati, who is on the Council on Foreign Relations in America and advises the World Trade Organisation; and the President of the Adam Smith Institute, Dr Madsen Pirie, who is passionately in favour of privatisation. An Indian woman Zeinab Badawi chaired it.

I worked out that I was going to say that Adam Smith had said the rich are the pensioners of the poor, and I agreed with him that the rich live off the backs of the poor, which annoyed the guy from the Adam Smith

Institute. I said that capitalism was a philosophy underpinning an empire, it worshipped money and it was prepared to use force to get what it wanted.

Monday 5 March
I went to Pimlico School, where I'd been asked to talk to some students. When I got there, I met the headmistress and discovered the school is on special measures, Ofsted had said it was a failing school and it had tremendous problems of morale. The architecture is awful, because it was too hot in the summer and cold in the winter, and I think there was a discipline problem, judging from the number of kids who were jumping all over the place. But they asked some very good questions: about faith schools; about public school; about debt. They were worried about all the debt that they would have to take on in order to go to university. Jack Straw, of course, used to be the Chairman of the governors, and his son, William Straw, was at the school. This failing school business, it thoroughly disorients me.

Wednesday 7 March
The Campaign Group was cancelled because the votes on the alternative ways of dealing with the House of Lords were on tonight. At the end the House of Commons voted, by the biggest majority of all, for a 100 per cent elected House of Lords and for the total removal of the hereditaries. It's a sensational victory! It's against what Blair wants, what Straw wants, and they'll try and fiddle the decision, but that was the decision.

Saturday 10 March
I went over to the Royal Academy at quarter-past ten for this 'Power in the City' day organised by an American.

Then I sat and listened to a lecture by Jean-Louis Cohen, a Frenchman who also teaches in America. He was talking about revolutions and city planning, and showed lots of graphs, delivered in a monotone, and I found it hard to keep awake. There's no vitality in academic life.

I'd prepared carefully, on how buildings represent the old power and the streets represent the new power, and how I had moved between the two. I showed extracts from three videos: first of all, the Post Office Tower, which, unlike churches which worship God and the banks which worship money, worshipped communication between us; and then I showed a bit of the peace demonstration of 2003, with Jesse Jackson; and then I played a couple of verses from 'Women of the Working Class'; and went on to the last scene of the film of *Brassed Off*, where the Grimley Colliery Brass Band wins the award, and then Pete Postlethwaite, who's the band's conductor who's been in hospital, gets out of bed and comes all the way to the Albert Hall, makes a speech denouncing the treatment of the miners, says he wouldn't receive the award. I just stood there, I'm afraid, weeping!

Monday 12 March

I caught the bus to Waterloo, no. 148, and caught the 5.05 to Winchester and was met by the Bishop of Southampton. He looked very young – mid-fifties, I should think.

I asked him about the church, and he said, 'Well, I'm all for women bishops and all that, but on homosexuality I'm a member of the Scripture Union.'

Then he drove me to Winchester Courts, where I was going to give this lecture on slavery. The Bishop of Winchester came – a man, I should think, in his late-sixties, who is in the House of Lords of course. There were about two or three hundred people in this long room. It was difficult – I was in the middle, and you had to turn from left to right. They videoed the whole thing.

They were all Christians. I should think the average age was probably fifties, with one or two young people and maybe one or two older.

I talked about slavery and Wilberforce and related it to the present situation, globalisation and democracy. It was a speech I have delivered before. There were a lot of thoughtful questions.

I felt as if I might have been meeting the members of the diocese of my dear brother Mike, who would undoubtedly have become a bishop. I'm eighty-two so he'd have been eighty-five, nearly eighty-six now. I find dedicated Christians without much political commitment rather too tame, but still, you have to respect them – they were decent people. What I had prepared went down well.

Tuesday 13 March

I had a bit of fun with English pronunciation today. I sat down and wrote a short story setting out all the pronunciations of 'ugh':

Going thro*ugh* the Boro*ugh* of Slo*ugh*, I bo*ugh*t eno*ugh* do*ugh*nuts to give me a co*ugh*, which made me la*ugh*.

That's eight different pronunciations. It was rather fun.

There was a wonderful Greenpeace demonstration on a crane right by the Houses of Parliament. Some activists climbed up it last night or early this morning and hung a huge banner, which said 'Tony ♥ WMD'. I talked to the police and they said, 'Well, if we climbed up there, there might have been an accident either to us or to them, so we just left it.' But with the Trident debate tomorrow, it was very amusing.

Wednesday 14 March

Today was the Trident vote. At the end of the day the Government had huge majorities against deferment and in favour of Trident, but ninety-five Labour MPs, I think, rebelled and some abstained. Among the people who voted for deferment were Charles Clarke, the former Home Secretary, so it's now become a much more serious argument.

Friday 16 March
I worked all morning on my evidence for the Charity Commission on behalf of Europeans for Medical Progress Trust of which I am patron. The Trust challenges animal testing on the grounds of patient safety and is being investigated by the Charity Commission because the Research Defence Society, which promotes animal-testing, has complained about the Trust.

At twelve, Dr Kathy Archibald, their Director, picked me up and took me to their lawyers for a couple of hours. Dr Margaret Clotworthy was there – their science consultant – and an American from Detroit, James Eliason, who is chief scientist for Asterand, the world's leading human tissue company.

We walked across to the Charity Commission building and went up to the fourth floor, to a committee room where there were three women and a man, and the presentation began. Kathy made her points, then James Eliason, and Margaret Clotworthy, who showed videos. Then I came in and discreetly recorded my evidence. I had prepared an aide-memoire of what I wanted to say: my interest in it was because when Caroline was pregnant with Hilary, it was recommended that she took thalidomide. I said I had no legal or medical experience, but I argued that campaigning and controversy were an essential part of progress.

There were a lot of questions. I was quite argumentative, because the Charity Commission were trying to suggest that there was a difference between education and campaigning. I said to them: 'Are you saying that a bishop can think Christian thoughts, but if he makes a sermon, that puts him into a campaigning position? and 'Are you saying that charities have to be balanced in their approach – and does that mean that Oxfam or War on Want has to make the case for poverty before it can make the case against it?'

I dare say it worked out all right in the end. The Commission may make suggestions to help Europeans for Medical Progress Trust, which the EMP will accept, and it will retain charitable status. But it really was a discussion about how many angels dance on the head of a pin.

Sunday 18 March
I wasted a bit of the morning, but I did a few things, and then I was picked up at half-past eleven by a nice driver – we both smoked – and he took me to the ITV studios in Gray's Inn Road, for *The Sunday Edition* with Andrew Rawnsley. They had a little extract from this film, *Amazing Grace*.

I'd done quite a bit of work on slavery, because I felt that in the previous speeches I'd made, I'd paid too little attention to the question of what other countries did about slavery. I discovered, for example (which I should have known), that in 1780 the northern colonies in America abolished slavery; in 1794 the French abolished it at the time of the French Revolution; Haiti liberated itself entirely – the slaves led a revolt; and therefore the role of Wilberforce was a more limited one.

Later I sat down and watched *The Great Global Warming Swindle*: distinguished scientists saying there's nothing in global warming that has anything to do with man's activities, with flying, or anything else. Some distinguished people taking part. It was one of those moments when you realise you have to think again.

I don't want to find myself up against the environmentalists. On the other hand, you can still make many of the same arguments: 'Yes, there is global warming. It's nothing to do with what we're doing, but there is global warming. The world's oil will run out in twenty years. We've got to save oil. We've got to stop the things we do. We've got to help Africa to develop', and so on, and see a way through it in a way that makes sense. But I felt I really needed to sit and have a discussion with people with my political sympathies, examining what that really meant, without alienating all those lovely young people who join the Greens.

Monday 19 March

I went and had a talk to Dennis Kucinich, who is a leading Congressman from Cleveland, Ohio, an announced Democratic presidential candidate. He's sixty. He had his wife with him, a very young woman, Elizabeth, who it turned out was from Essex. I thought that really is funny: I'm an Essex boy who married a girl from Ohio; and he's an Ohio man who married a girl from Essex.

He described his plans, which were explicit and radical and progressive, and he said the Democrats in Congress were absolutely gutless – they would vote the money right the way through for the war to continue until the presidential election, which doesn't surprise me because they're just like the Parliamentary Labour Party.

He said Britain has a key role, because if Britain were to pull out, then the Americans would get really worried.

I said, 'Well, I think that's absolutely right, and I'm glad you're not working with the Democratic group in Congress, because your job is to give people leadership from the outside.'

Tuesday 20 March

I walked over to the Central Hall and went over to the Platform Room at the back, and it was absolutely packed with people from Democrats Abroad, many of whom came up and had a word with me in a friendly way.

Then we had the People's Assembly. I chaired the first session. There were about a thousand people there, I guess. Dennis Kucinich was the first speaker, and I welcomed him, and then pointed out to him that this was the room where the first meeting of the United Nations General Assembly took place.

Then there were a lot of other speakers; to chair a meeting for two hours and keep awake was extremely hard, and also I had to do all the preparatory work on who they were and give an introduction to each one.

I had a nice talk to Lynne Featherstone, the Liberal Democrat spokesman on international development, whom I've never really spoken to before. She's the opposite number to Hilary, and made a friendly reference to him, of course.

The third session began with Michael Meacher, who made an environmental speech – he always does that. Then next was Craig Murray; and then myself.

My speech wasn't really what they wanted to know, because people had been calling for mass disobedience, revolutionary talk, because it's a Stop the War/Respect audience, but I was saying that we were in the information business. I was quite pleased with it, but it wasn't sensational and certainly wasn't in any way designed to whip them up.

It was a broadly based event, and apart from the end, where revolutionary action was demanded and mass disobedience to bring the Government to a halt, it was measured and successful, I thought.

Saturday 24 March
As soon as I got off the bus at Notting Hill Gate, my bladder knew we were approaching home, and although it had behaved quite well on the Tube, the nearer it got to home, the more it began to cause me anxiety. When I put the key in the door, the bladder gets the message it's almost over, and so as I opened the door I rushed to the back corridor. I kept talking to my bladder, very seriously, saying, 'We're nowhere near the lavatory', but it knew more than I did. I got there and just managed to relieve myself. But it is funny, I think it has a satellite navigation system.

Sunday 25 March
Fifteen sailors have been arrested in a rubber dinghy; the Iranians claim it had moved into Iranian waters in the controversial area in the Shatt al-Arab, which is divided between Iraq and Iran and God knows where. Of course the British claim the right to be in Iraqi waters, but it could be a big incident. No one will know the truth. We say the sailors were in British waters, and the Iranians say they were in Iranian waters, and how can you prove it, although maybe satellite identification will help one side or the other. But in a situation like this, it's just . . . propaganda.

Saturday 31 March
Rory Bremner played Hilary and me in his show; it was set in Hilary's office in Whitehall. Hilary was taking a view in favour of the war and I was

arguing with him, and then in the end he kept saying, 'Oh, shut up, Dad, shut up, Dad.' Then, in the second half of the programme, Hilary was developing his argument and he said, 'What do you think of that, Dad?' and he looked over to me and I was sound asleep. It's the first time Hilary has ever been on *The Rory Bremner Show*, and although I was made to look a bit aged and decrepit, it was quite funny.

Wednesday 4 April
One o'clock I watched the news, and they showed a press conference given by Ahmadinejad, the President of Iran; it had a huge media attendance, as you can imagine, because of the British sailors. He took the opportunity to speak at enormous length about the way that Britain and America had toppled Mohammad Mossadeq, who had nationalised Persian oil in 1951, and how the British and the Americans had put the Shah on the throne, how they had supported Saddam in the war against Iran. At the end he said, 'And I'll release the sailors as a gift to the British people, and I hope Mr Blair won't prosecute them' – put them on trial! It was a great PR success for him. There were pictures of Blair, looking extremely embarrassed, outside Number 10 Downing Street, with Margaret Beckett next to him, flushed and saying nothing, and John Bolton accusing Britain of being weak. So Blair isn't in good odour with Washington now, which is amusing.

Thursday 5 April
I had a phone call that knocked me sideways. I said, 'Who's that?' and he said, 'It's Kofi Annan.' He said, 'I'm in Edinburgh, and I just rang to wish you a happy birthday, and your son, Hilary, has just made a very good speech.'

Monday 9 April, Stansgate
Lissie drove me home. All the way home she gave me, in the nicest possible way, a lecture. She said, 'Dad, you are a bit provocative.' She pointed out the pressures facing each of my children, including her. I felt so ashamed of myself. Later I rang Hilary and Sally and Stephen at Stansgate and apologised for being difficult, and they all said, 'Oh, don't worry, Dad.'

Tuesday 10 April
Lissie turned up, from about 12.40 till nearly three, and we had a lovely talk, going over everything that had happened at Stansgate, and she was very candid. She's so thoughtful; she did defend me from members of the family who were roughing me up a bit.

Sunday 6 May
In the evening I went to the May Day celebrations, at the Pakistani Centre

up in Willesden Green. There were about 150 people there. I sat on the platform and I didn't really know who they were, which is so difficult; and then most of the meeting was conducted in Urdu, so I sat and clapped when other people clapped, and looked wise.

There was one beautiful poem, read by the author Mahmood Jamal, who's a film-maker and makes programmes for Channel 4:

You want to speak of war; I want to speak of peace.
You say punish; I say forgive.
You speak of God's wrath; I speak of his mercy.
Your Koran is a weapon; my Koran is a gift.
You speak of the Muslim brotherhood; I speak of the brotherhood of
    man.
You like to warn others; I like to welcome them.
You like to speak of hell; I like to speak of heaven.
You talk of lamentation; I talk of celebration.
You worship the law; I worship the divine.
You want silence; I want music.
You want death; I want life.
You speak of power; I speak of love.
You search out evil; I warm to the good.
You dream of the sword; I sing of the rose petal.
You say the world is the desert; I say the world is a garden.
You prefer the plain; I prefer the adorned.
You want to destroy; I want to build.
You want to go back; I want to move forward.
You are busy denying; I am busy affirming.
Yet there might be one thing on which we see eye to eye: you want
    justice; so do I.

Monday 7 May

I rang Kofi Annan and spoke to his wife at the hotel, and he rang me back, and I've agreed to meet him tomorrow at ten o'clock at the Dorchester, before he goes to meet Hilary and on to his lecture on slavery.

I then prepared a little paper on the case for a group of Elders of the UN, Elders of the UN Tribe, the really distinguished people – like Carter, and Gorbachev, and Mandela, and Kofi Annan, and others – who've held high office and have now retired and are free. I'm going to hand it to him tomorrow, just as an idea.

Tuesday 8 May

Caught the 148 bus to the Dorchester.

The two doorkeepers greeted me like old House of Commons people – they couldn't have been nicer.

I sat and smoked my pipe, and then a smart young man from the Foreign Office Protocol Department, who's looking after Kofi, came to greet me, and I went up to his apartment, a beautiful, luxurious apartment. Kofi came in, with his wife, a Swedish lawyer who is now a painter – a woman, I suppose, of about sixty probably.

I asked him about his plans, and he said he was keen to develop human rights in Africa. He said he and Mandela and Carter were getting together, with Richard Branson, for some charitable work in Africa. He said he very much wanted to get the non-governmental organisations involved; that climate change was a huge issue, and would produce a mass of refugees that would have to be dealt with.

He also told me that Jimmy Carter and Mandela and he had offered to go to see Saddam, but he'd concluded that, if Saddam had not made any concessions, the Americans would have used that and advanced the war, which was quite a shrewd point. I think I had vaguely known that, but of course Mandela did send me a letter of support when I went to see Saddam in 1990.

I made my point about the Elders of the Tribe – that we ought to build up a troop of people who've held high office and had retired, and were still interested, but had no ambition.

We talked about religion. He said he was an Anglican, and his wife (Nane) said she was a Lutheran. We talked about the danger of religious extremism, and I made my joke about why is it that when the world is full of men who hate each other, when two men love each other, the Church splits; and he laughed.

We had a good old laugh – it was lovely! It couldn't have been nicer, and we had a photograph with him.

Wednesday 9 May
My mobile phone rang and it was Richard Branson of Virgin. He said, 'I saw Kofi Annan, and I've been working on a project called the Elders', which is very similar to my idea for the Elders of the Tribe – but he'd thought of it before me. He said, 'We've got a conference in Africa at a game reserve in a couple of weeks. Kofi can't come, and we wondered whether you'd come?'

I said, 'Well, do send me the details.' I gave him my email address, but I don't see how I could possibly go to Africa, but still, it was nice of him to ring me.

Thursday 10 May
Well, a momentous day, because this was the day Blair announced he was going to resign.

My dad would have been 130 today, if he'd lived.

One thing I must mention first from yesterday. I went to a BBC party, where I met two officers, or senior civil servants, from the Ministry of Defence. We talked about nuclear weapons and I said, 'Well, of course we can't use them ourselves.'

They said, 'Oh, we can, we can! The satellite navigation system uses the stars.'

I said, 'What would happen if the Americans decided to cut it off?'

'Well, our equipment would last for about eighteen months and then we would be in difficulties.'

So I was partly right in what I've been saying, but apparently it's only the technology that Bush could withdraw. He couldn't prevent us targeting. I didn't know that.

I was driven to BBC Television headquarters in Wood Lane, and who should I see there but Neil Kinnock. I reminded him that when he was first elected, he was seen as a bit left-wing, and he had asked me to come down to south Wales and I reassured people in his constituency! He said his grandson is going to Salusbury Primary School, where Melissa's children are.

Then I was dropped home and went up to Melissa's for a cup of tea. She told me that Sarah, her ten-year-old, had said, 'Mum, have you heard of Jekyll and Hyde?' So Melissa said, 'Yes.' Sarah said, 'Well, when I'm at school, I'm Dr Jekyll, and when I'm at home, I'm Mr Hyde!'

Came home and watched Blair live on television as he gave a press conference at the Labour Club in Sedgefield. It was an amazing speech. '*I* did this', '*I* did that', '*I* did the other', '*I* decided', '*I* did the right thing', '*I* did what I believed was right'. No reference whatever to anybody else! Didn't pay tribute to Gordon Brown; didn't mention any other minister, or anything to do with the Labour Party, anything to do with the Cabinet. It was a monarchical address, the abdication of King Tony.

Thursday 5 July Postscript

The progressive centralisation of power in the hands of the previous Prime Minister, who took all the decisions himself, ignoring the Cabinet, Parliament, Party and the public, was possible because of the patronage, deriving from the Royal Prerogative, that he exercised and abused.

The most vivid example of this was the decision to go along with Bush and invade Iraq in 2003, a decision that had been agreed in secret, while we were told that it was all subject to Iraq disarming, at a time when Iraq had no weapons of mass destruction.

As a result of this war, many hundreds of thousands of innocent people have died and many of our own service personnel have been killed or injured.

The Cabinet was denied access to the full legal advice sent to the Prime Minister, and in any case the question of weapons of mass destruction was never used by President Bush as his reason for a regime change. To this extent, it can properly be said that the Prime Minister subordinated British democracy to the diktats of an American president.

A second major factor affecting the powers of British governments in recent years has been the transfer of decisions once made by them to the EU, NATO, the IMF, the WTO (World Trade Organisation), and the World Bank and the multinational corporations whom we do not elect and cannot remove.

Believing, as I do, that all progressive change comes from below, Parliament has to be seen as the buckle that links the demands in the streets to the laws in the statute book, the demonstrations to Downing Street, and that requires a much more powerful House of Commons, which is seen as a representative of the popular will and not as an instrument of management used to control the public.

The fact that the *new* Prime Minister presented his ideas as an agenda for wide discussion – and not as if it were an announcement in the Queen's Speech, to be imposed by a new constitutional Czar, complete with league tables to chronicle his progress – comes as a massive relief and imposes a heavy responsibility on everyone to contribute their own opinions during this formative period.

Some of the decisions that will have to be faced are controversial, and rightly so, including the so-called 'West Lothian Question', which will not go away, because it reopens the devolution debate by highlighting the fact that England has been denied the benefits now enjoyed by Scotland and Wales.

We must also deal with the absurdity of a house of Parliament based solely on appointment in the House of Lords; this can only be resolved by a fully elected chamber in line with the recent vote in the Commons, whose decisions we are now told must be respected.

There is also the issue of the new European Treaty, which reproduces the old constitution that was defeated in the French and Dutch referendums, and which some want to slip through without a public vote – which would be an outrage, since MPs have no moral right to give away powers they do not own, but only borrow from their constituents in an election; and these powers must be returned in full to the electors, to lend again to those whom they choose in subsequent elections.

In putting these, and other points, forward now, it is like a breath of fresh air to know that the new Prime Minister himself will consider them on merit, as will ministers and MPs; and that they will not be dismissed out of hand as a typical Old Labour assault on a modernisation strategy that is to be imposed from the top, as we have seen so often since 1997.

But for most people who do not plan a political life, what matters is to campaign for the issues to which they are committed, in the hope that if public support can be won, ministers and MPs will respond. That is how I have spent the last six years – campaigning for peace and pensioners, students, trade unionists, civil liberties and more generally for human rights, democracy and internationalism.

It has been like a six-year election campaign, without being a candidate, and because you are not asking anyone to vote for you, they are often prepared to listen and respond positively.

When my dad was my age, in 1958, just before he died, I took my two eldest boys to Parliament to be with their grandfather. In a broadcast describing his political and family life for the BBC, my dad ended with these words, 'So you will understand that I live in a blaze of autumn sunshine.'

I, too, am enjoying that autumn sunshine now with my grandchildren, and though I may never publish another volume of diaries, if I ever did, I think the best possible title would be just that: 'A Blaze of Autumn Sunshine'.

Index